IN FACT

IN FACT

AN OPTIMIST'S GUIDE TO IRELAND AT

100

MARK HENRY

GILL BOOKS

Gill Books
Hume Avenue
Park West
Dublin 12
www.gillbooks.ie

Gill Books is an imprint of M.H. Gill and Co.
© Mark Henry 2021

9780717190386

Designed by www.grahamthew.com
Charts designed by Heather Griffin
Edited by Djinn von Noorden
Proofread by Ruairí Ó Brógáin
Indexed by Adam Pozner

For permission to reproduce photographs, the author and publisher gratefully
acknowledge the following: ©Alamy: 98, 176, 248, 274, 366; ©Buyenlarge/Getty
Images: 294; ©Flickr: 8, 10; ©Irish Photo Archive/Lensmen Collection: 58, 395;
©iStock/Getty Premium: 116; ©Ronan Henry: 76 (photograph of the young author
and his mother); ©RTÉ via Brand New Retro: 220; ©Shutterstock: 342, 408;
©Wikimedia Commons: 34, 378; ©Wiltshire Photographic Collection/National
Library of Ireland: 443.

The author and publisher have made every effort to trace all copyright holders, but if
any have been inadvertently overlooked we would be pleased to make the necessary
arrangement at the first opportunity.

Printed by L&C Printing Group, Poland
This book is typeset in 11 pt Piazzolla.
*The paper used in this book comes from the wood pulp of managed forests. For every tree
felled, at least one tree is planted, thereby renewing natural resources.*

A CIP catalogue record for this book is available
from the British Library.
5 4 3 2 1

To my father, Ronan, because he asked first.
To my mother, Brenda, who passed her love of books on to me.
To my wife, Ann, for her constant encouragement throughout.
And to my children, Fionn, Gráinne and Susan, in the forlorn hope
that it might compel them to read it one day.

Contents

Introduction 1

1 Living Longer 11

2 Living Healthier 35

3 Eating Better 59

4 Living Easier 77

5 Learning More 99

6 Earning More 117

7 Opening to the World 177

8 Cultivating Culture and Sports 221

9 Strengthening Society 249

10 Better Lives for Women 275

11 Better Lives for Children 295

12 Increasingly Environmentally Conscious 317

13 Helping the World 343

14 A Happier People 367

15 How We Achieved This 379

16 Why It's Hard to Believe 395

17 Room to Improve 409

18 Continuing Our Progress 443

Acknowledgements 451

Endnotes 452

Index 471

Introduction

IRELAND IS ONE of the very best nations in which to live on planet Earth. It is a remarkable place.

The United Nations identifies our quality of life as the second highest in the world.[1] Over the past thirty years we have risen above twenty other countries, with only Norway ranked ahead of us today.

I have spent the past two decades telling people overseas what a great place Ireland is. I have promoted tourism to our country from around the globe. Whether it was addressing gatherings in the British Houses of Parliament, lunches for German tour operators, Saint Patrick's Day events in the United States or sales missions to cities in China, the story of Ireland's progress has captivated audiences wherever the job has taken me. Now I want to tell our story to you at home.

You will be surprised at how far we have come.

Ireland has achieved remarkable economic growth and social progress since its foundation as the self-governed 'Irish Free State' on 6 December 1922. In just one hundred years it has risen from being one of Europe's most poverty-stricken places to truly take its place amongst the nations of the world. We Irish live longer than ever before, have never been healthier, and have never been better educated. There have never been more of us at work, yesterday's luxuries are now commonplace and our society is more tolerant and safer than ever. The lives of women and children have improved vastly, and we are amongst the happiest people on the planet. Covid-19 hit us hard and set back some of our progress, but we came together to fight it so much better than many other countries.

Yet people's impressions of countries change at a glacial pace. The research undertaken of Ireland's image amongst Americans, Britons, French people and Germans shows little change over the decades. We are, first and foremost, perceived as a country of rolling green hills and wild coastal landscapes. Secondarily, we are considered a friendly and engaging people. And after that a few will mention our music and dance (that's U2 and Riverdance) or our drink (Guinness and whiskey).

How different is that from the image in the poetry of W.B. Yeats or the paintings of Paul Henry? You could reasonably call it outdated. The only significant change I have observed over the past two decades has been in perceptions of our food: twenty years ago, people expected our food offering to be limited to corned beef and cabbage (or fish and chips!) and to taste pretty terrible. Now they don't expect it to be that bad. Which is progress.

But we can't blame others for not having a good understanding of contemporary Ireland. They don't live here. I believe that most of us who do so also fail to appreciate the degree of change that has happened to our own country in our own lifetimes. I will not ignore where there has been change for the worse or where problems remain to be addressed. But, standing back and taking a longer-term view, practically all of it has been for the better. Our own image of Ireland needs updating too.

Now, everyone thinks their country is important. One study showed that, on average, British folk believe that their country has contributed a whopping 55 per cent of the total history of the world. And that is not the highest score: Russians believe that they have contributed 61 per cent of the world's history. Americans are relatively modest, only believing that they account for 30 per cent. Needless to say, the numbers add up to more history than there has been since humankind started walking upright.[2] Had Ireland been included in the study, we would have certainly overestimated our global impact too.

I am not going to tell you that Ireland has transformed the world. If anything, I will be telling you that the world has transformed Ireland. But

I am going to tell you that life in Ireland has unquestionably transformed for the better over the past century and that our success is important. Important to those of us who live here, of course. But also important to those elsewhere who can learn from studying Ireland's success and how we have achieved it.

Remarkable Achievements

We are a small nation, just shy of five million people. However, we are a people transformed. The world has changed in so many ways over the past century, of course, but Ireland has come further and faster than others. Most of that transformation occurred only over the past fifty years – in a single lifetime – and our success was far from guaranteed.

I arrived in New York the day after the US presidential election that brought Donald Trump to power in 2016. Much of the city – home to Hillary Clinton's Senate seat – appeared to be in shock. I wandered irresistibly along to Trump Towers, where makeshift barriers had been thrown up and police swarmed around trying to manage the flow of global media reporters, 'Not my President' protestors and curious onlookers. I will never forget the young man beside me – on his mobile phone to a friend or lover – in tears at the prospect of a loss of freedom and reduced tolerance for gay people under the new administration.

I walked a short distance around the corner for a meeting and introduced myself at reception. As I made small talk about the election result, the receptionist declared she was wearing black in mourning for America's future. 'How easy is it to emigrate to Ireland?' she asked in all sincerity. Gone are the days when it was one-way traffic from Ireland to America. The people flow now goes the other way too. And why wouldn't it? The quality of life in Ireland is now higher than that in America.

Our lives have changed. Twenty thousand fewer people die in Ireland each year than they did a century ago despite our population increasing by half in the meantime. Deaths from tuberculosis, measles, scarlet fever, whooping cough and diphtheria have been entirely eliminated. The proportion of children who die in their first year of life has declined by 95 per cent. We live an incredible 25 years longer, on average, than those who were alive when the State won its independence.

Our work has changed. Ireland was an agricultural economy in the 1920s – more people were employed in the agriculture sector than in industry and services combined. Today agriculture accounts for less than 5 per cent of the jobs we do, yet the amount of food we produce has never been greater. Our spending power has grown seven-fold in the past fifty years – from half the amount of a typical German to precisely the same.

Our society has changed. There was a significant rise in emigration after independence in the 1920s: 40 per cent of those aged between 15 and 34 left in just one decade. It happened again in the 1950s when half of that same age group left our shores. Nowadays, Ireland is a place people want to immigrate to. The proportion of our population born outside of Ireland now stands at 18 per cent – nearly one in five of us.

Women's lives have been transformed. In the early 1970s six out of ten women were occupied in home duties and fewer than three out of ten were at work. Now most are working and only two out of ten say they are primarily involved in home duties.

Children's lives have been transformed. The number of children entering primary school has remained relatively constant over the past century but the number entering second- and third-level has radically changed. The proportion of us who have completed higher education has increased ten-fold in the last 50 years.

All this change has improved our physical and mental well-being. The Irish now consistently rate themselves amongst the happiest peoples on the planet.

How We Did It

It took newly independent Ireland a few decades to put down its roots before the country began to grow and flourish. I have analysed hundreds of trends for this book and interviewed nearly fifty experts. It is evident from all the data that I have examined and all the people that I have spoken to that there are four factors that ultimately enabled our success as a nation.

They are **stability**, **community**, **education** and **openness**:

The four factors that have enabled Ireland's success

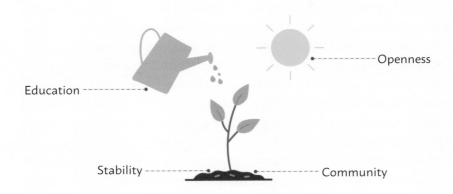

Education

Openness

Stability

Community

Ireland has been blessed with **stability**. Our island geography helped to ensure that we survived World War II with our democracy intact and without the appalling social and economic disruption that was rained on countries in continental Europe. The impact of the Northern Ireland troubles in the 1970s and 80s, furthermore, was far less pronounced in the Republic of Ireland.

Relatively consistent centrist governments, with few swings to the hard left or hard right, ensured a continuity of policy and investment programmes over a sufficiently long time to ensure their success. This was bolstered by a social partnership approach that resulted in shared investment priorities across civic society and the building of 'institutional capital'.

Civic partnership and a lack of extreme politics engenders trust throughout society. As we are a small nation with a strong sense of **community**, trust in each other tends to be higher than in other places. That is an essential foundation for the building of the social capital that is needed to underpin sustained progress. Societies cannot grow on financial capital alone; they also require so-called 'social capital' – that is, positive relationships between different groups in society whose shared values and common understanding enable cooperation – to encourage people to live and work together for their mutual benefit. Ireland has it in abundance.

Onto the fertile soil of stability and community, successive governments have ensured that the seeds that have been sown there have been well nourished through investment in **education** to develop our 'human capital'. A continued commitment to open access to education and to increasing the proportion of students progressing to the next level has paid strong dividends. High education levels have both attracted foreign investors and stimulated local business development. They have enabled our citizens to attain world-leading skills and knowledge that, in turn, provide our professions and our private and public sectors with outstanding capability.

Given such strong nurturing, our people need only turn to the light to reach for the sky, and there is hardly a nation on Earth more **open** to the warmth of external influence than ours. Ireland has been rated as the most globalised country in the world. We have shown ourselves to be open to new ideas, to new technology, to social diversity and to immigration. The trail of Irish emigrants throughout the twentieth century left a path open for new ideas to find their way home.

Our accrual of institutional, social and human capital allowed us to compete strongly on the global stage for the financial capital necessary to help our people flourish. This has empowered individuals to lead social change and to deliver progress for us all, with outstanding results.

Why Don't We Believe It?
Yet we are slow to acknowledge our success. Rarely does a radio programme or TV documentary dwell on the progress we have made. Despite our incredible achievements, it is the progress we have *not* made, or the road bumps on the way, that get the airtime.

The fact that no mother died giving birth this month is not news. The fact that no one died doing their job this week is not news. Reductions in annual road deaths get a mention once a year, when the figures are compiled, but that is an insufficient counterbalance to the 150 tragic news stories about the individual deaths that have taken place over the preceding twelve months. No wonder 66 per cent of us believe that driving behaviour on our roads is getting worse despite the fact that road deaths have dropped for many decades and are near a 70-year low.[3]

Human beings have an inbuilt bias to pay more attention to the negative things that happen around us – leading us to believe that things are generally getting worse rather than the reality that they are generally getting better. The sad and traumatic news story will win our attention and outrage to a much greater extent than the positive news story will, thereby justifying news outlets focusing more on what is going wrong than on what is going right.

Progress takes time – often several decades – and that is a big challenge for our prehistoric brains to comprehend. The average lifespan of early humans was around thirty years. We were not built to easily attend to slow-occurring change in our environment. In fact, we are programmed with inbuilt nostalgia to believe that our past was rosier than our present. Extrapolating from that personal bias can lead us to declinism: an expectation that the future is tending towards decline.

Furthermore, if you are told often enough that things are getting worse then you will begin to believe it. Even if your own experience is different, and even if you know that the facts don't reconcile with what you are being told, if a media commentator or a politician tells you that we are in a 'crisis' and things are going downhill fast then a part of you will believe a bit of it. It's the power of fake news and opposition politics. You can't help yourself believing there's fire if someone tells you there's smoke. And if lots of people are telling you there's lots of smoke then it seems like the whole world is burning down – when it's not.

We have to understand and overcome our inbuilt biases to fully appreciate the progress we have made. From time to time commentators call us out as a nation of begrudgers. Are we less inclined to credit the improvements delivered by our fellow citizens? Do we live in a country inherently biased against acknowledging the progress that we have made? If you believe we do, then I hope to persuade you to reject this perspective by laying out the facts of Ireland's journey as an independent country.

A Celebration of Achievement

This book is a celebration of where we have got to and of what we have achieved. It is just as much a book about Ireland today as it is a book about the history of how we got here. There have been many, many accomplishments over the past century, but I have selected just one hundred of them. Together, they will tell you an incredible story.

Acknowledging our progress is not the same as saying that the job is done. There are many areas in which we need to make a lot more progress to be anywhere close to a leading nation. I will highlight our less impressive track record in limiting our carbon emissions, preventing loss of wildlife, providing housing and addressing homelessness, and fighting obesity, amongst others. In each of these areas there are individuals, voluntary organisations, companies and state institutions fighting for positive change and working to make a difference to the benefit of all. It is important that they have our support and succeed in driving forward the next wave of improvements.

We should also recognise that continued progress is not certain. The Covid crisis surely taught us that lesson well. We must protect the four factors that have delivered our success: stability, community, education and openness. Forces that seek to undermine them must be resisted, whether that is political extremism, the sidelining of local communities, a reduction in investment in education, or a desire to pull back from our increasingly globalised world.

The pace of change can be unnerving. We enter our second century at a time when the technology change and globalisation of recent decades is accelerating even further, and unprecedented environmental change is underway. Ireland's next one hundred years will be marked by even greater uncertainty about the future.

Nevertheless, the story of Ireland's first century has demonstrated that we have more to gain by embracing change than by ignoring it. By identifying what has worked so well to get us here, and by continuing to nurture the factors that have underpinned our success, I believe we can give the next generation the best possible chance of leading the finest life liveable on planet Earth.

Living Longer

WHO BELIEVES IN MIRACLES? WELL, SCIENTIFIC AND MEDICAL MIRACLES AT ANY RATE? WE HAVE EXPERIENCED ONE IN IRELAND IN THE COURSE OF A SINGLE GENERATION: THE GREAT BIG MIRACLE OF HUMAN PROGRESS. WE ARE WINNING THE BATTLE AGAINST AN EARLY DEATH.

WOMEN ARE SURVIVING childbirth, children are living through their early years and adults are avoiding fatal accidents like never before. We therefore live much longer than our ancestors. That, alongside the occasional baby boom and the elimination of emigration, has contributed to record population growth.

 ## The Population of Independent Ireland Has Never Been Higher

There was no growth at all in the population of independent Ireland for its first fifty years. From 1921 until 1971 there were no more than 3 million people living here. An historic low was reached in 1961 when we recorded only 2.8 million residents. Then an explosion happened

The population of Ireland, 1926–2020

SOURCE: CENTRAL STATISTICS OFFICE

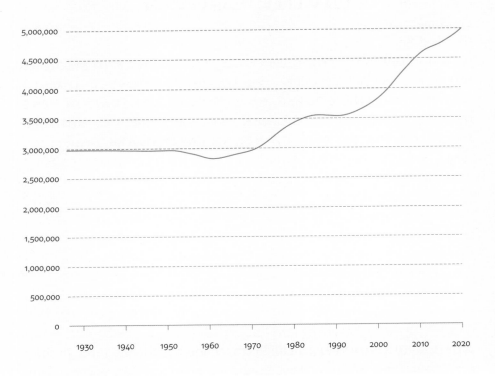

Over the following four decades, up to the turn of the millennium, we added one million additional souls. In just the past two decades, we have added a further million. I expect that more than five million of us will be here to celebrate the 100th anniversary of Ireland's independence in December 2022 – a record high.

The last time the population of the 26 counties that constitute the Republic of Ireland exceeded that number was 170 years ago in the immediate aftermath of the potato famine that was responsible for the death and departure of so many people. Before that occurred, the figure peaked at 6.5 million people.

So what happened in the past 50 years to reverse so many decades of stagnation and decline?

Population change is easy to calculate. It is the number of births minus the number of deaths (the so-called 'natural increase'), plus the number of people immigrating into the country minus the number that emigrated (labelled 'net migration').

Independent Ireland has always had a positive natural increase. Yet for fifty years our population did not grow. The sole reason was emigration.

The outflow predated the birth of the State but continued unabated until the start of the 1970s. We had a net inflow of migrants for the first time then as we joined the European Union (at the time called the European Economic Community or EEC) and the country benefited from increasing international trade. They were mainly Irish people returning from working overseas to avail of new job opportunities at home. Despite a return to emigration during the recession years of the 1980s and early noughties, we have had a nearly unbroken run of net immigration since the start of the 90s with an increasing number of migrants from other EU countries helping our population reach new heights.

The natural increase in the population exhibited some notable ebbs and flows too. There were approximately 60,000 children born every year in Ireland from the 1920s right up to the 1960s. A baby boom occurred in the 1970s and early 80s with an additional 10,000 children born per annum. The figure dropped again, before growing in the noughties and the 2010s as those who were born in the previous boom became the parents of a new generation, thirty years later.

With a downward trend in the number of deaths, the natural increase in the population has therefore grown in recent decades. In the 1970s the annual increase was more than twice that of the 1920s and 30s. In the late noughties the growth was more than three times higher.

Over the past 20 years the contribution of greater natural increases and increased immigration to our robust population growth has been roughly equal. Half our recent growth has been due to declining deaths and more babies, and half has been due to Irish people returning from overseas and new migrants arriving for the first time.

Population by province, 1926–2016

SOURCE: CENTRAL STATISTICS OFFICE

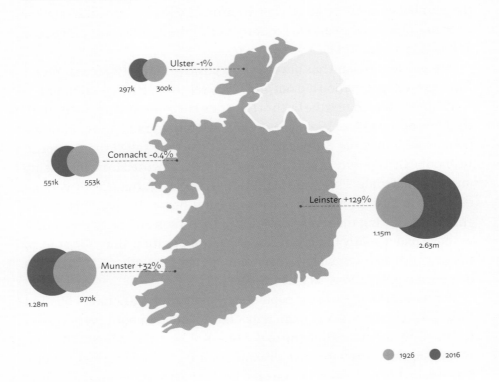

That growth has not happened equally all over Ireland, however. Like every other country on the planet, the trend has been unequivocally towards urbanisation. It has resulted in the population of Leinster growing unabated throughout the past century to become the dominant province. It has more than doubled in size to 2.6 million, making Dublin the fastest growing of all European capitals since the turn of the century.[1]

Munster has also grown. Its population decreased by more than 100,000 until the mid-1960s, since which it has grown by over a third to reach a record 1.28 million. The populations of Connacht and Ulster, however, have not changed at all. Despite Ireland gaining an additional 1.8

million people over the past 90 years, the population of the two provinces nowadays is precisely the same as it was back in the 1920s.

The changing nature of employment is a critical factor. When the State was founded, most of the available jobs were in agriculture in the countryside. One hundred years later, most of our jobs are in services in urban areas. We have consequently changed from being predominantly a rural country to being an urban one.

 ## We Have More Than Halved Our Death Rate

The number of people who died in that year per 1,000 of population

SOURCE: CENTRAL STATISTICS OFFICE

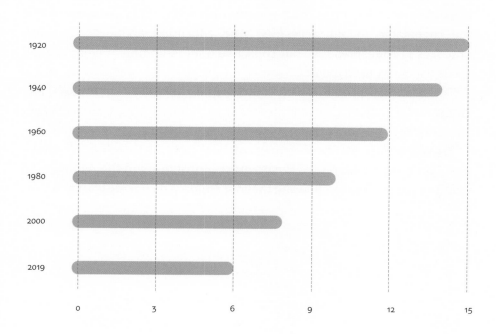

Throughout the first three decades of Irish independence, your chances of dying remained essentially unchanged. Fourteen or fifteen out of every 1,000 people died each year. Men, women and children passed for every reason imaginable: illness, accidents, old age. Little or no progress was made in tackling these causes up until the early 1950s.

Then the Great Big Miracle of Human Progress began to take effect. The death rate began to fall. On average, we have managed to save the life of one additional person out of every thousand in each subsequent decade.

Many things contributed to this. The spread of infectious diseases was reduced through improved living conditions and less overcrowding, alongside improved water and sanitation provision. Access to medical services was transformed, particularly for those who would not have had the income to pay for them in the past. Advances in medical treatment have been extraordinary, such as the development of antibiotics, chemotherapy and cardiac interventions. Huge public health initiatives were put in place, for example for immunisation, infection control and antenatal screening. Nutrition has been transformed – our diets today would be unrecognisable to our ancestors. And education about good health practices is widespread, so our collective understanding of what is good for us has never been greater.

Today, only six people in every thousand fail to see the year through. The chances of you dying this year are less than half what they were 100 years ago. Now that's what I call progress.

We will explore advances on many of these fronts in this chapter and the next. Let's start with one of the greatest contributors to the reduction in deaths – our success in ensuring that our children do not die young.

3 The Likelihood of a Child Surviving Their First Year Has Improved 25-Fold

Deaths of infants under one year of age per 1,000 births, 1922–2019

SOURCE: CENTRAL STATISTICS OFFICE

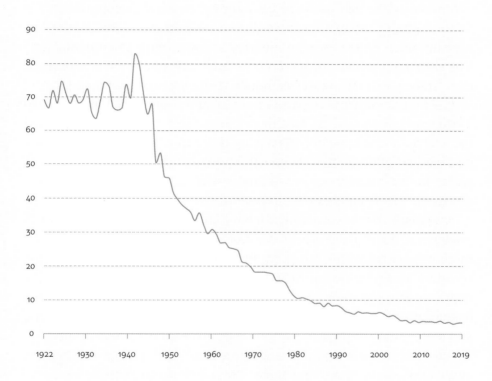

Infants under one year of age had to endure a battle for survival in the early years of the Irish State. Right up to the 1940s, seven in every 100 children – that is, one in 14 – died before their first birthday.[2] Astonishingly, the death rate for 'illegitimate' children born outside of marriage was one in three.[3] It is hard to imagine the scale of the trauma for parents and for the siblings left behind.

Those born in the early years of the State's independence faced significant challenges, most particularly poverty. Larger families lived in much smaller spaces and ate far less well than today. Disease passed easily from person to person in confined surroundings and amongst those too nutritionally weak to fight them off. And many of the advances of preventative medicine had yet to be made.

Starting in the mid-1940s an unrelenting, continuous improvement in infant mortality began. Children's allowances were introduced for the first time in 1944 with the express aim of reducing poverty in large families.[4] The cost represented an increase of over one-quarter in government expenditure and took place even though World War II was ongoing.

The first standalone Department of Health was created in 1947 with a dedicated minister. The Health Act introduced that same year paved the way for a new approach to tackling tuberculosis and other infectious diseases by offering free diagnosis and treatment and allowances to sufferers. It aimed to secure cleanliness in the handling and sale of food and the fixing of proper nutritional standards.

When Noël Browne became Minister for Health in 1948 he sought to implement the Act's provision for free, state-funded healthcare for all mothers and their children aged under 16 without a means test. This so-called 'Mother and Child Scheme' ran into deep opposition from doctors in private practice and from the hierarchy of the Catholic Church. Church leaders claimed that the scheme would interfere with parental rights and feared that the provision of non-religious medical advice to mothers would lead to birth control. Under pressure, the government backed away from the scheme and forced Browne's resignation as minister. As a result, Ireland adopted a two-tiered health system of public and private provision rather than the national health service which Britain implemented at this time.

Nevertheless, government expenditure on health doubled in the following five years. Free ante-natal care for women and free hospital services to those on lower and middle incomes were introduced in the 1950s.

Child mortality halved in just ten years from the mid-1940s to the mid-1950s, and it halved again by the early 1970s, when it dropped below

2 per cent for the first time. Continued improvements in incomes and housing raised living standards and made a significant contribution. More notably, there was huge progress in disease prevention. Vaccination was introduced in the 1950s and 60s and successfully eliminated several debilitating and killer diseases.

If you were born in 1970 you had a 98 per cent chance of surviving your first year. For those born just ten years later the survival rate reached 99 per cent. By the early 2000s 99.5 per cent of children were guaranteed to live through their first year. And now fewer than three in every 1,000 children will die each year.

We have improved the likelihood of our children surviving their first year 25-fold in a century. An incredible achievement. This year alone nearly 5,000 infants will not die because of the leaps forward that we have made over the past 70 years. Ireland is one of the safest countries in the world for a child to be born in today.

Yet just as childbirth bore great risks for newborns a century ago, so the lives of delivering mothers were in equal peril.

 ## Maternal Death During Childbirth Has Been Eliminated

Our first year of independence was a dangerous year to be giving birth: nearly 0.6 per cent of all births resulted in the death of the mother. With women having an average of about five children, mothers had a significant chance of dying in childbirth.[5] My great-grandmother died giving birth to my grandfather, and he was only her second child.

The mortality rate fluctuated between 0.4 and 0.5 per cent for the remainder of the 1920s and into the 1930s. However, sustained improvement began in the mid-30s, and in just a decade the rate halved to below 0.2 per cent. It continued to decline decade after decade until an astonishing milestone was reached.

In 1995 no mother died giving birth anywhere in Ireland. A Great Big Miracle. From 370 deaths in 1922, we had reached the point where not a single one occurred.[6] Although further deaths did occur in the years after 1995, the zero figure was achieved again, once in the noughties and twice in the 2010s. Each decade continues to be safer for mothers than the previous one.

Maternal deaths per 100,000 live and stillbirths, 1922–2019

SOURCE: CENTRAL STATISTICS OFFICE

Many of the developments that we have outlined as benefitting newborns equally assisted in reducing maternal deaths. The introduction of blood transfusion and antibiotic therapy in the 1940s was important. But perhaps the most critical factor was the change in where births occurred. As late as 1955, 34 per cent of births took place at home. By 1970 the figure was 3 per cent. By 1991 this had fallen to just 0.3 per cent.[7] Hospital births were unequivocally safer.

Those who are critical of our health service should pause for thought. It has provided the women of Ireland with remarkable care. The tragic deaths of women such as Savita Halappanavar, Sally Rowlette and Karen McEvoy are all the more tragic because they are the exception to the norms that we have come to expect. The call for mandatory inquests into every maternal death is both a reasonable means of highlighting where further improvements could be made and an indication of how far we have come.

 5 ## Work-Related Fatalities Have More Than Halved in the Past 20 Years

Work-related fatalities rate per 100,000 workers, 1996–2019

SOURCE: HEALTH AND SAFETY AUTHORITY

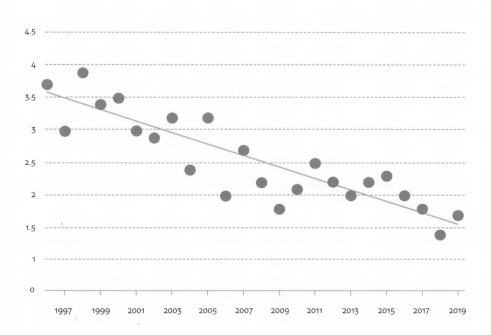

One of the places where men are far more likely to die than women is in the workplace. Forty-seven people were killed in work-related accidents in 2019 and all but two of them were male.

I have to admit to being cynical about those fire-alarm drills in the office. The ones where you're in the middle of a long-scheduled phone call – or worse, a group video conference – and then the fire alarm goes off unannounced. You just know it's bound to be a drill. But annoying as they are, these safety precautions do have a genuine benefit. There was no Health and Safety Authority in the early years of the State's existence to give us a measure of work-related fatalities back then, but the data from just the past 20 years shows that the chances of you being killed in your place of work have more than halved. It is now at its lowest-ever recorded level.

The two sectors with the highest fatality rates are farming and construction. Progress in reducing farming fatalities has been made as the sector has increased in scale and professionalised and as safer technologies have been deployed. Nevertheless, the chances of someone losing their life on a farm remain five to six times higher than in any other workplace.

Dr Sharon McGuinness is Chief Executive of the Health and Safety Authority (HSA), which was founded in 1989. She points out that it is easy to discuss health and safety with a farm that is being run as a professional business, but a challenge remains in tackling smaller farms, which are increasingly run by ageing farmers. 'We are seeing farmers aged over 60, over 70, over 80, and even over 90, which tells you that farming isn't a career only for those between 18 and 65 with a beginning and an end. Farming tends to go on forever. It's your life. So that brings a huge challenge: how do you talk to someone [about workplace safety] where their farm and their home is very much one?'

Construction remains the second most deadly sector in which to work, but one that has made great strides in recent years. 'If you think about construction now versus construction in 1989, it's chalk and cheese,' says McGuinness. 'If you look at early reports [of the HSA], construction fatalities were huge. Now we're down to five deaths a year. When you walk past construction sites and you see the level and size of machinery, the numbers of people, the things they're doing, the heights they're building, you just go "that's quite incredible".'

There is a lot more understanding about health and safety as the sector has been modernised and the workforce educated. Perhaps the single most important initiative has been the Safe Pass health and safety awareness training programme that was launched in 2000. The programme was born out of the Construction Safety Partnership established by the Irish Congress of Trade Unions, the Construction Industry Federation and the Health and Safety Authority in recognition of the seriousness of the issue.

The one-day course is a requirement for all personnel and must be refreshed every four years. 'You can't get on site unless you have that,' says McGuinness, 'so that upped the level of knowledge and expertise.' Although we were not the first country in the world to introduce such a mandatory scheme, we were early adopters of an approach that has paid strong dividends in reducing the number of fatalities in the sector even as employment levels grew rapidly pre-Covid.

Of course, the very nature of work itself has changed radically over the past century. What was predominantly manual labour has transformed into predominantly non-manual work in service sectors. Such work inherently poses far fewer risks to body and soul.

Technology also enables one person to do a lot more than a single individual could have done in the past. Fewer people are required in manufacturing and mining to produce the same output, thereby reducing the potential for fatalities, even as the machines themselves are increasingly designed with safety in mind.

The next time you are tempted to complain about over-the-top health and safety measures at work, think again. Your chance of being killed in your workplace is less than half what it was when you were 20 years younger, incredible as such progress may seem in such a short period of time. 'Over those years, people started to see health and safety as something that makes sense for them personally and for their business and their workers. If you've a good, safe, healthy place that people want to go and work in, then you'll get a lot more productivity – it just makes total sense,' concludes McGuinness.

6   The Likelihood of Dying on the Roads Has Been Reduced by Three-Quarters over the Past 40 Years

Number of road deaths, 1922–2020

SOURCE: ROAD SAFETY AUTHORITY, WIKIPEDIA[8]

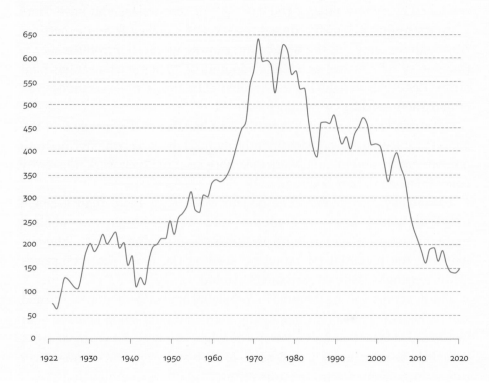

The first car to appear on an Irish road was a Benz Velo, manufactured by a forerunner of Mercedes-Benz, in 1898. It was 1906 when the number of vehicles passed the 1,000 mark and 1914 before there were 10,000 cars on our roads.[9] As the number grew, so too did the death rate of drivers and pedestrians alike. Fifty-one people were killed in 1922, rising steadily throughout the 1920s and 1930s. The outbreak of World War II and the reduced availability of petrol resulted in a welcome pause in the growing numbers killed, but the unrelenting increase resumed in 1946 and reached a peak in 1972 when 640 people lost their lives on Ireland's roads.

In the early 1970s most people driving on the roads had never taken a driving test – the requirement to pass one before being granted a licence only became a requirement in 1964. Nor were they wearing seatbelts. In the early 1970s my mother drove me and my sister around in her NSU Prinz, a forerunner of the Volkswagen Polo. It wasn't just that there weren't any seat belts for us in the back seats – there wasn't even one for the driver! The requirement for cars to even have seatbelts in front seats only came into force for new cars in 1971. But even then, there was no requirement for drivers to use them – that was not mandatory until 1979.

The most exciting aspect of our road trips in the Prinz was watching the road go by – through the holes in the floor on each side of the driver's seat. Yes, the undercarriage had corroded so badly that my parents had to cover the holes with wooden blocks in case one of us gave into temptation and lost a hand or a leg by putting it through them at high speed. Still, in the absence of a National Car Test (NCT), the car was probably worth the £20 my mother paid a neighbour for it.

The good news is that things have become a lot safer since then and the number of road deaths has declined hugely. In the last few years, fewer than 150 people were killed on our roads each year. While the figure remains too high, these are the lowest numbers since 1945. Even though there are four times as many cars on our roads today, the number of people killed is less than a quarter of what it was in the early 1970s. This represents a remarkable reduction in the death rate – for every car on our road the chances of death are now just one-sixteenth of what they used to be. With 29 road deaths per million people in our population, our roads are now the safest in all of the EU.[10]

One of the things that helped us achieve relative road safety in such a quick timeframe was that we could look to other countries that have been on this journey longer than us and see what worked and didn't work for them. For example, one of Ireland's innovations has been to deploy hard-hitting advertising showing the realities of the death and injury that poor driving behaviour can cause, mirroring what had been done success-fully in Australia. 'We were the only ones across Europe doing advertising like that,' says Brian Farrell, Communications Manager at the Road Safety Authority, who has been involved in road safety for the past two decades.

The campaigns were initiated in the 1990s by the National Safety Council and the Department of the Environment in Northern Ireland as joint North–South campaigns. 'I think they're what helped put road safety on the map as a major social issue in this country – those hard-hitting ads, which beamed in the reality that was happening on our roads on a daily basis and really shocked people into acknowledging and realising what was going on and, critically, that what was happening was far from accidental: they were by and large as a result of our own behaviour,' says Farrell.

In 1998 the government launched its first-ever road safety strategy. This led to the introduction of the NCT in 2000 in an effort to take dangerous and unroadworthy vehicles off the roads. This was followed in 2002 by the introduction of the penalty points system to discourage speeding, resulting in an automatic disqualification from driving if anyone attracted too many points.

2006 witnessed the introduction of mandatory alcohol testing, often referred to as random breath testing, and the establishment of the Road Safety Authority (RSA) as a super-agency. As Farrell tells it, 'you had the National Safety Council responsible for education, you had the National Roads Authority building roads and responsible for road safety research, you had the Gardaí conducting enforcement, the Department of Transport was responsible for driving licencing and testing, and then you had a number of government agencies responsible for various aspects of road safety as well, so what they looked to do was to bring as many of these key components together as possible under the one umbrella'. Coalescing these functions into one agency enabled more effective delivery of further initiatives.

Penalty points were expanded to cover additional offences such as not wearing a seatbelt and mobile-phone use. Legally acceptable blood alcohol levels were decreased and the penalties for exceeding these were increased. Speed detection cameras were deployed nationwide. Graduated driver licencing was introduced, distinguishing learner and novice drivers. And a patently safer motorway network was put in place through consistent investment in national roads infrastructure throughout the 1990s and 2000s.

The number of road deaths halved again in just six years from 2005 to 2011. However, the decline then halted, something that Farrell attributes to a near-halving in the numbers in the Garda Traffic Corps, leading to lower levels of enforcement.

The downward trend was re-established in 2017 with a new low death level achieved. Subsequent legislation brought in an automatic driving disqualification for those drink-driving and made it an offence for anyone to let an unaccompanied learner driver use their vehicle. Despite complaints from rural representatives of overly strict regulation, the reality is that the destruction of many families' lives has been prevented by these measures.

The European Transport Safety Council tracks progress across all European Union member states and they hand out an annual award to acknowledge progress. Ireland won the inaugural award in 2010 for the progress we achieved then, and we were awarded it again in 2019 – the only country to yet receive the award twice. 'It's a great acknowledgement for the public because the government agencies can only do so much,' says Farrell. 'We cannot make this happen unless there's a public willing to change behaviour, to accept the road safety messages, and to accept and support high levels of enforcement.'

So by how much can we reduce the annual death tally? Is it feasible to get it below 100 people a year? Yes, it is. Norway, a non-EU member, is already at 20 road deaths per million population so a further one-third reduction is clearly achievable. We can reasonably aspire to be the safest country in all of Europe, given the scale of our recent success.

The Suicide Rate Has Declined to Its Lowest Level in 30 Years

Suicides per 100,000 of population, 1980–2019

SOURCE: CENTRAL STATISTICS OFFICE

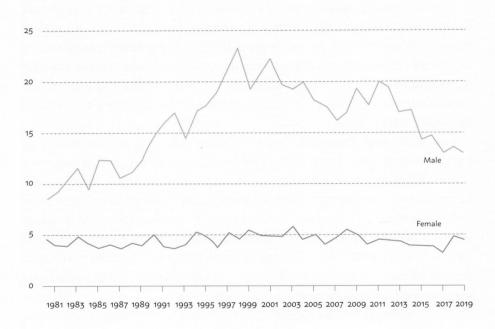

Undoubtedly one of the saddest occurrences is when an individual chooses to end their own life.

Did you know that before 1993 it was illegal to take your own life in Ireland? When the State was founded, we inherited the ancient common law of England, which deemed it to be such. And up until 1823, believe it or not, it was the practice in England to bury suicide victims at a crossroads with a stake through their heart. A law had to be introduced to stop that.[11]

Did the illegality of the act stop people taking their own lives? Or did the refusal of the Catholic Church to allow them Christian burials give reason to misattribute such deaths? Our suicide rate was historically very low. According to Dr Paul Corcoran, Head of Research at the National Suicide Research Foundation, 'it was so low you couldn't really believe that that was true'.[12] Efforts were made to improve the accuracy of the statistics in the late 1960s and the figures started to increase, year after year.

Corcoran believes that by 1980 the figures were a more reliable reflection of the truth. Although the numbers of women recorded as committing suicide levelled off at that time, the numbers of men continued to increase through the 1980s and 90s to reach more than four times the numbers of women. 'More women present to hospital having engaged in suicidal behaviour than men so it's not that suicidal behaviour is more common in men,' Corcoran explains, 'it's that deaths are more common in men due to their use of more lethal methods.'

So what contributed to this increase in male suicide? Rising unemployment and difficult recessionary times during the 1980s were factors. Escalating alcohol consumption is believed to have played a major role later, especially when unemployment rates began to fall in the 1990s but the suicide rate continued to increase.[13] However, there was also a growing belief that young men in distress were becoming more likely to opt for suicidal behaviour. 'The strict sense that it was the worst thing in the world to do – a huge taboo, a huge stigma for the family – was gradually loosening over a number of decades, and with that comes the acceptability that it is an option,' Corcoran says.

In 1993 Ireland decriminalised suicide. It was perhaps a case of the law catching up with the changes that had already happened in society. The social and religious stigma was passing away, and there was a growing recognition of suicide as a mental-health issue. The report of the first national task force on suicide, in 1998, called for a mental-health programme to be introduced in schools, for restrictions on paracetamol sales to one pack per person and for the appointment of trained suicide-prevention experts throughout the country's health boards. 'By putting these resource officers for suicide prevention in place, suddenly there was a real sense that there was somebody dealing specifically with suicide in every area in the country. It was being tackled now for the first time,' recalls Corcoran.

More importantly, 1998 was a landmark year because it marked when the tide began to turn on suicide. It was the peak year for male suicide. From then on the rate gradually, if inconsistently, declined. The new suicide-prevention initiatives, declining alcohol consumption and better economic prospects all came together at once to bring this about. We are now experiencing some of the lowest rates of suicide for both genders since the 1980s.

'We're in a relatively good place in terms of suicide prevention in Ireland,' Corcoran says. But we are on a journey rather than having arrived at our destination: 'Why does England have a consistently lower suicide rate? Is it to do with their mental health services, their accessibility through a national health service providing a service to everybody? We have a lot less investment in mental health here than in the UK – in proportion to our GDP it's half the investment level.'

There has been a sea change in our attitudes and approaches to suicide over the decades, and that has begun to pay dividends. Increased investment in our mental health services will be essential if we are to continue to make progress, particularly as our population grows inexorably in the decades ahead.

We Live 25 Years Longer Than Those Alive in 1922

Given all the progress we have seen in reducing the death rates of children and adults, it will be no surprise to report that each of us now lives longer than any of those who came before us. On average, we each live nearly 25 years longer than those who were alive when the State won its independence. We have added one whole generation to our lives.

It is sad to think that those living in the early 1920s had a life expectancy of just 57 years. A minority of people lived long enough to complete their working lives, assuming they were still healthy enough to work. Although couples married and started their families at a younger age, the opportunity to enjoy family life and to see your children and grandchildren raised was severely curtailed.

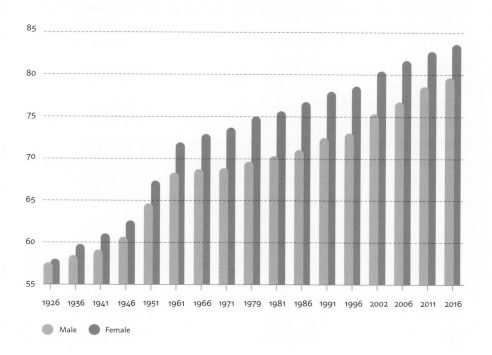

Average life expectancy, 1926–2016

SOURCE: CENTRAL STATISTICS OFFICE

We have completely turned that around through the Great Big Miracle of Human Progress. Today you can typically expect to live to 82 years of age. On average, women will live two years longer than this and men two years shorter, although that gender gap has been narrowing recently.

The greatest increases were experienced in the late 1940s and early 50s as infant deaths and maternal mortality tumbled. Life expectancy for females increased by nearly one year per year during the course of a whole decade.

Some of the relatively poor performance of male life expectancy during the 1950s, 60s and 70s was due to the differential impact of coronary heart disease, which peaked during this period. Its subsequent steady decline has had a great impact on reducing male death rates and contributed to the contraction of the gender gap.

Advances in life expectancy for those aged 65 and over were negligible for many decades. It took until the 1970s before older women started to experience longer lives than their parents, and it was not until the 1990s that older men started to experience similar gains. In contrast to the earlier years of the State's existence, it is gains among older people that have accounted for over half of the increase in overall life expectancy since the mid-1980s and three-quarters of it since the mid-1990s.[14]

Our life expectancy now exceeds the European average and is higher than that in the UK. On a global scale, the Irish are the sixteenth longest-living people in the world.[15] We live only two years less than those with the greatest longevity, the Japanese. Quite an achievement, given where we started. A scientific and medical miracle, surely, but part of the secret of our success is the fact that we are also living healthier than ever before.

(2)

Living Healthier

THE GREAT BIG MIRACLE OF HUMAN PROGRESS HAS
ELIMINATED DISEASES THAT WERE COMMONPLACE KILLERS A
CENTURY AGO. WE KNOW WHAT CONSTITUTES GOOD HEALTH
BEHAVIOUR NOWADAYS, AND WE ARE INCREASINGLY LIVING IT.
SO MUCH SO, THAT THE IRISH ARE AMONGST THE HEALTHIEST
PEOPLE ON THE PLANET TODAY.

YOU COULD VIEW our encounter with Covid-19 through two different lenses. One lens will tell you that this was just a warning shot – if we continue to mess with nature then the human race will be entirely overrun the next time and all our lives will be brought to a horrible and premature end.

The other lens will tell you that this was a particularly virulent disease but that human ingenuity came to the fore and we defeated the threat in record time – just as we will with the next one.

While we need to protect against the distant possibility that we could lose the battle against disease, the reality is that we have had success after success in reducing and eliminating diseases over the past century. In some instances, the war is well and truly over.

We Have Eliminated or Hugely Reduced Nearly All the Leading Diseases of 1922

The leading diseases causing death in 1913–22 and their prevalence today

SOURCE: CENTRAL STATISTICS OFFICE[1]

	Disease by rank	Annual Average Number of Deaths 1913-22	Annual Average Death Rate 1913-22	Number of Deaths in 2018	Death Rate in 2018
1	Tuberculosis	5961	1.89	19	Eliminated
2	Heart disease	5025	1.59	6818	1.40
3	Bronchitis	4040	1.28	13	Eliminated
4	Pneumonia	2823	0.89	1058	0.22
5	Cancer	2611	0.83	9258	1.91
6	Influenza	2143	0.68	149	0.03
7	Premature birth and congenital debility	1992	0.63	131	0.03
8	Cerebral haemorrhage	1399	0.44	415	0.09
9	Violent or accidental deaths	1275	0.40	954	0.20
10	Kidney disease	1126	0.36	17	Eliminated
11	Diarrhoea and enteritis	750	0.24	0	Eliminated
12	Other respiratory disease	740	0.23	292	0.06
13	Whooping cough/pertussis	432	0.14	0	Eliminated
14	Measles	350	0.11	0	Eliminated
15	Diphtheria	260	0.08	0	Eliminated
16	Diabetes	240	0.08	534	0.11
17	Ulcer of stomach or duodenum	226	0.07	51	Eliminated
18	Typhoid/enteric fever	173	0.06	0	Eliminated
19	Cirrhosis of the liver	158	0.05	96	Eliminated
20	Appendicitis	137	0.04	1	Eliminated

The death rate is the number of deaths per 100,000 people. A disease has been deemed 'eliminated' where its rate has dropped below 0.02 per 100,000 people. Note that the medical definitions and accuracy of diagnosis have changed over the century, making the comparison indicative. Over 25 per cent of deaths in 1922 were uncertified so the rates for this period are likely to be somewhat underestimated.

My grandfather was born in Belfast but his first cousins lived on a farm in County Derry, from where the family originated. There were ten children in that family. In the two decades from the mid-1910s to the mid-1930s, six of those ten died. They were variously aged from two to 28. The tragedy is that all of them died of diseases that we can cure today: tuberculosis, diphtheria and a kidney infection. I can only imagine the heartbreak for their parents and their surviving sister and three brothers.

The top twenty illnesses causing death in the decade running up to Ireland's independence in 1922 are listed in the table. You can see the number of deaths annually from each of them, as well as the rate of death per 100,000 people. The incidence of the same illnesses is then shown for the latest available year, 2018.

Of the twenty most fatal illnesses one hundred years ago, eleven of them have been effectively eliminated altogether. Six more have been hugely reduced. We have made enormous advances in neonatal care, in surgery, in rehydration, in antibiotics and in vaccination, all of which account for the improvements.

The most fatal disease a hundred years ago was tuberculosis, which accounted for nearly one in eight of all deaths. Although there still remain a handful of cases today, it has been practically eliminated thanks to vaccination. Vaccines have also entirely eradicated other bacterial diseases such as whooping cough, measles, diphtheria and typhoid. Diarrhoea is no longer a killer thanks to advances in rehydration. Appendicitis is easily dealt with through routine surgery. Stomach ulcers can be treated by antibiotics.

Only three diseases have failed to show significant improvement. The rate of fatal heart disease has remained essentially unchanged, although it did in fact get a lot worse before we began to turn the tide in recent decades.

The rate of diabetes has increased as we migrated from being a society that was physically active with widespread malnutrition into one of greater inactivity and calorie excess.

The rate of cancer has more than doubled, making it the greatest single cause of death today. This is partly a function of people living longer, as most cancer patients are aged over 50 years, but it is also due to poor health behaviour such as the increase in the numbers smoking in the 1960s and

70s. There are, however, reasons for optimism here too, as survival rates have improved sharply in recent decades.

The single most successful driver of disease elimination has been Ireland's adoption of childhood vaccination. Immunisation is credited with saving more lives than any other public health intervention throughout the world apart from the provision of clean water.[2] Professor Denis Gill, formerly of Temple Street Children's Hospital, previously chaired the National Immunisation Advisory Committee: 'I was born in 1943. Five hundred children were dying every year from vaccine-preventable diseases at that time.'

Although the anti-tuberculosis BCG vaccine had been available in Ireland since the 1930s, there was no programme in place to ensure that a sufficient number of people received it to manage the disease's prevalence. The first nationwide TB vaccination programme was planned in 1949; a vaccine against diphtheria, tetanus and whooping cough (pertussis) was introduced in 1952; and an oral polio vaccine was introduced in 1957. As Gill recalls, 'People have forgotten about diphtheria – it was the worst death imaginable, by slow suffocation. Polio was very scary and people were terrified of it.' The uptake of the vaccines was therefore strong and within ten years TB, polio and diphtheria were wiped out.

A rubella vaccine was introduced in the 1970s, one for measles, mumps and rubella (MMR) in the 1980s and one for meningitis in the 1990s.

Vaccination must be widespread to be effective. Ninety-five per cent of people need to be vaccinated in order to prevent a disease finding enough hosts to persist and to therefore entirely eliminate it from the population. Adoption of the MMR vaccine dropped below 75 per cent in the early 2000s following false claims of a link between its use and autism in children. Extensive research has shown that there is no link whatsoever. However, children suffered and died as a result of the lower vaccine adoption. 'I worked in Temple Street [hospital] when we had an outbreak of measles in Dublin in 2000,' Gill recalls. 'We had 300 children admitted, we had thirteen in intensive care and three deaths over three months.'

'Parents today do not realise what measles, whooping cough and diphtheria were like – they have no experience of them – and some think that the vaccination is worse than the disease. It's rubbish, they are totally wrong,' concludes Gill. Vaccines saved the lives of hundreds of thousands of people in Ireland over the past century, well before Covid-19 struck. They are the most precious gift of preventative medicine that any parent can give their child. Don't let anyone tell you otherwise.

Ireland led the world in preventative medicine when it introduced the first national newborn screening programme in 1966.[3] A few years previously a doctor in the United States had developed a test to diagnose the disorder phenylketonuria using a heel-prick blood sample from newborn babies. Although it can be easily treated by dietary modifications, the disorder causes profound intellectual disability if it is not identified early.

Doctors at Temple Street Children's Hospital convinced the Department of Health to fund a nationwide programme for Ireland. Seven other disorders have been added to the screening process since that time, including a thyroid disorder and cystic fibrosis. All the conditions can cause disability or death, but they are preventable if identified in time. The programme saves around 100 children every year from such a fate.

There has never been a safer time to live in this country. The Great Big Miracle continues its progress.

 ## Cancer Mortality Rates Have Been Declining for the Past 30 Years

Although cancer is our number one cause of death today, we are making good progress in reducing its impact. The National Cancer Registry assesses the prevalence of cancer in Ireland. As its recent director, Professor Kerri Clough-Gorr, puts it, 'mortality rates from cancer as a whole are now lower than they were in the late 1950s. For Irish men, total mortality rates from cancer increased between 1950 and the early 1990s by about 50 per cent overall, and then declined by about 30 per cent by 2015. For Irish women, total cancer mortality rates showed a less marked increase of about 20 per cent between 1950 and early 1970s, then showed little change up to the late 1980s, then declined by about 25 per cent.'

Age-standardised cancer mortality per 100,000 of population, 1950–2015

SOURCE: INTERNATIONAL AGENCY FOR RESEARCH ON CANCER, WHO[a]

The increasing trend from the 1950s reflected both an increased rate of some cancers and improvements in diagnosis. The increases seen in lung cancer mortality clearly reflected earlier increases in smoking, but improvements in diagnostic capability likely accounted for increases in breast cancer rates.

Men are more likely than women to die from cancer. In part this difference reflects the fact that men develop more cancers – they are far more likely to develop lung cancer, for example, due to their greater prevalence and frequency of smoking. In part it is also because men are more likely to die of cancer once it is diagnosed – tumours may not be spotted as early as they are in women and men's overall health may not be as good, thereby impairing their ability to fight a tumour successfully.

Regardless of gender, each of us is now more than 30 per cent less likely to die of cancer than we were just three decades ago, and the rate is continuing to decrease. As more of us are living into old age, the number who will contract cancer is set to increase in the years ahead. But that is simply because there are more people aged 50+ living amongst us. For anyone who is unfortunate enough to be diagnosed with cancer, their chances of surviving it have never been greater. Up until the turn of the century, a cancer diagnosis could legitimately be considered a death sentence: the majority of those diagnosed with an invasive cancer were destined to live no longer than five years more. Today, nearly two-thirds of those with a similar diagnosis will survive longer than five years.

What has brought about this great improvement? 'A combination of greater availability and more widespread use of effective treatments or diagnostic methods,' says Clough-Gorr, 'improvements in health service organisation [through increased specialisation and centralisation] and public health initiatives aimed at raising awareness of risk factors, in particular tobacco smoking.'

1996 could be identified as the milestone year in Ireland's battle against cancer. The first-ever national cancer strategy was published. 'It led to a big increase in the numbers of consultant oncologists working in public hospitals,' says Clough-Gorr. 'This consolidated the downturn in cancer mortality rates already evident since earlier in the 1990s, but accelerated further improvements through treatment improvements and other initiatives, including the introduction of breast screening.'

The follow-on 2006 strategy led to the centralisation of cancer treatment in a limited number of hospitals, rather than expecting every hospital in the country to be able to treat it equally well. Would you prefer to be operated on by a local doctor who only does ten breast cancer operations a year, or in a dedicated facility where the doctor carries out 200 of them? This resulted in new treatment centres with deeper expertise and a higher standard of patient care. While some people pine for local facilities, you are more likely to live longer if you are treated in a large centre of excellence – even if it means travelling further from home for the privilege.

Greater availability of treatments and their improving effectiveness have played their part. There were major increases in the number of patients receiving chemotherapy between the mid-1990s and early 2000s, for example. Cancer screening programmes have also had a significant impact in catching diseases earlier, making their treatment more effective. There were no national screening programmes in place before the 2000s. The breast cancer programme began on a regional basis in 2000 and coverage extended gradually, reaching nationwide coverage in 2008. The programme for cervical cancer was introduced the same year. Screening for bowel cancer was introduced in 2013.

International studies show that the greatest advances in the battle against cancer are due to reductions in lung cancer in men thanks to the reduction in smoking in recent decades.[5] Ireland has truly been a world leader in the area of tobacco control, and we can expect to see further reductions in cancer deaths over the coming decades as a result.

 ## Smoking Is in Rapid Decline

Cigarettes smoked daily per capita in various years

SOURCE: DEPARTMENT OF HEALTH AND THE REVENUE COMMISSIONERS

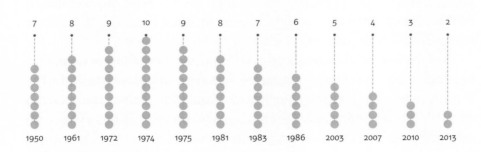

The graph shows the average number of cigarettes consumed every day per person aged over 15 years in the population in the specified year.

Cigarette smoking peaked in Ireland in the mid-1970s and has been declining ever since.

Irish men did not start smoking in any great numbers until the time of the Second World War. Disposable incomes did not leave much over for tobacco, and smoking was a fire hazard in our rural economy. However, tobacco sales increased by three-quarters over the course of the 1940s and smoking truly became popular.

The uptake amongst women lagged but tobacco marketers spotted the growth opportunity. New products were introduced with 'feminine' appeal: slim cigarettes, pink cigarettes, menthol cigarettes. Targeted advertising leveraged the promise of freedom, equality and even sexual liberty.

It worked well. From the late 1950s and into the 1960s smoking amongst women took off. The market boomed. By 1974 there were ten cigarettes smoked daily in Ireland for every man, woman and child aged over 15. Given that half the population didn't smoke at all, that was an average of twenty cigarettes a day for every person that did.

My father ran his own graphic design company for many years. One of his biggest clients in the early 1980s was P.J. Carroll & Co. cigarette manufacturers. His job was to make the packaging as attractive as possible to tempt smokers to purchase Carroll's brands. Meetings in their offices were literally in smoke-filled rooms – with free cigarettes on hand for anyone who hadn't brought their own. As a smoker himself, I think Dad quite enjoyed it all at the time.

Dr Paul Kavanagh is the lead public health adviser to the HSE's Tobacco Free Ireland Programme and an Honorary Clinical Lecturer in the Royal College of Surgeons in Ireland. 'When I was a kid growing up in Walkinstown in the late 1970s and 80s, the John Player *Tops* variety show television programme aired on a Sunday night,' Kavanagh recalls.[6] 'I can remember myself and my siblings used to lie on the floor in front of the fire and my parents would be sat in the armchairs and would we watch that together. Both my parents were smokers. You can guess what brand they smoked. Both of them passed away in their 60s and the fact that they had been smokers for long parts of their life probably contributed to their premature demise. So I have a bit of skin in the game. To be able to take up a pen and write how this story ends is a hugely motivating thing.'

Kavanagh is unequivocal that 'there is very little that we have created as humankind that has had greater potential to destroy human health than cigarettes'. It took a while for medicine to prove the point as it was not until the 1950s and 60s that the health consequences began to be identified.

Anti-smoking campaigns began alongside regulation. Government restrictions in the 1970s prohibited cigarette advertising on TV and outdoor posters; advertisements in newspapers and magazines could no longer glamourise smoking; the amount of money tobacco companies spent on sponsorship was limited; and sponsorship of youth events was prohibited altogether.

By the mid-1980s, cigarette consumption had fallen by one-third. Dublin Bus introduced a ban on smoking upstairs on double-decker buses on Ash Wednesday 1988. Tom Darby, the general secretary of the National Busworkers' Union, claimed it would be unenforceable: 'when gangs get on the buses at night-time, the conductors can't even get the fares from them and if Dublin Bus think a conductor is going to go upstairs to make them stop smoking, they have another think coming'[7]. But people generally complied.

Confidence in the ability of regulation to make a positive impact was growing. Legislation banned smoking in public places and public buildings in the 1990s, putting an end to the commonplace practice of smoking in cinemas and theatres. The dirty, foul-smelling ashtrays in the arms of cinema seats began to disappear.

'The other thing that happened during the 1980s and 90s was accumulating evidence that if you are not a smoker yourself, but if you are exposed to second-hand smoke, that can actually have quite a significant impact on your health,' says Kavanagh. 'If you can remember yourself being in pubs back when there was smoking – whether you were a smoker or not – when you came home in the evening you certainly felt the worse for wear, even if you weren't drinking!'

In 2004 the Irish government implemented a world-first national ban on smoking in the workplace, including in restaurants and bars. 'The bit of the jigsaw that really brought this to a tipping point was the question of workers and workers' rights to have their health protected when they were in the workplace,' recalls Kavanagh.

It required a degree of courage for the Health Minister, Micheál Martin, to pursue the initiative. But we were a country that was doing well economically – the 'Celtic Tiger' was winning us international renown. National confidence was high. We were not afraid to be leaders.

Some predicted doom and gloom. A British tour operator said that it would destroy the atmosphere in Dublin's pubs and drive away tourists in their droves. The hanging smoke added ambiance, apparently, albeit somewhat lethally. But the ban turned out to be a huge success, one that has been followed by more than 85 countries across the world.[8] It also resulted in a steep decline in cigarette sales, prolonging the lives of tens of thousands of people over the course of one generation.

In 2009 Ireland became the first country in the EU to remove all tobacco advertising from retail outlets. Tobacco products in shops had to be stored out of view. Self-service vending machines were generally prohibited. In 2011 graphic health warnings became mandatory on packets. In 2017 we were the third country in the world, after Australia and the UK, to introduce legislation requiring standardised, plain packaging for all cigarettes.

Today only two cigarettes are sold daily for every man, woman and teenager – a decline of almost 80 per cent from the high of 40 years ago. The World Health Organization has presented awards to Ireland in recognition of the strides that we have made in tobacco control. 'It's part of our psyche not to take praise very well or not to focus too much on achievement and there has been a lot of achievement in tobacco control,' says Kavanagh, 'but we need to balance that with not being complacent; we need to move on and identify the next thing we can do.

'Despite all of the progress that we have made, smoking continues to be one of the leading preventable causes of ill health, disability and premature mortality in Ireland. Each week in Ireland over 1,000 hospital admissions are attributable to smoking and second-hand smoke. Each week there are over 100 deaths attributable to smoking and second-hand smoke. It's avoidable tragedy for individuals and their families.'

The economic cost of smoking has recently been quantified as an astonishing €10.7 billion a year.[9] That includes direct health care costs to the State, loss of productivity for employers and loss of welfare payments to people who die prematurely. We are still paying the price today for poor health decisions made by individuals three or four decades ago.

The State has the declared ambition for Ireland to be effectively tobacco-free by 2025 – meaning that fewer than 5 per cent of people will still be smoking by then. 'I may be live on *Morning Ireland* in 2025 trying to explain why we haven't gotten there,' says Kavanagh. 'The odds are against us in terms of reaching it, but we'll certainly get to a better place in terms of the stretch we feel because of it than we would get to if we set ourselves a target that was more achievable. It is the right ambition.'

 ## Death from Heart Disease Has Decreased by Two-Thirds in the Past 40 Years

Deaths from diseases of the circulatory system per 100,000 of population, 1980–2018

SOURCE: CENTRAL STATISTICS OFFICE

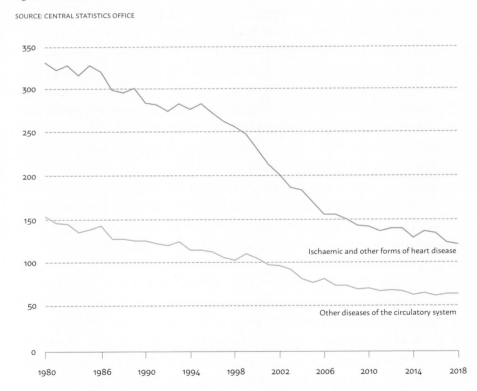

Here is a surprising fact. Life expectancy in middle-aged men in Ireland did not improve one bit between 1922 and 1981. The improvement in life expectancy over the past century was enjoyed first and foremost by young children as the battle against infectious diseases was won, and then by pregnant women as safety in childbirth improved. Men who survived into their 50s were likely to die in their mid-60s, just as their fathers had before them.

What they died of, however, did change. Professor Emer Shelley is the Dean of the Faculty of Public Health Medicine in the Royal College of Physicians of Ireland and President of the Irish Heart Foundation. As Shelley explains, 'what happened was that the very high death rate from infectious diseases like TB was replaced by a high death rate from coronary heart disease'. That rate rose steadily from the early 1950s through to the mid-70s and then plateaued at that high level through to the mid-80s.

My grandfather died of massive heart failure at the age of 58. John Henry was a self-employed graphic designer, like my father, and often worked from home. My uncle went to fetch him for dinner one evening only to find him collapsed at his drawing desk. John was a heavy smoker and this undoubtedly contributed to his passing. It is, therefore, not without irony that my father undertook that graphic design work for Carroll's cigarettes in later years.

But perhaps it was his dinner plate that did John the greatest harm. The Irish diet was not designed for long life for much of the twentieth century. Food was typically fatty: fatty meats and fatty spreads, accompanied by a poor intake of fruit and vegetables.

'We had very low intake of vegetables, we didn't really appreciate them, we had a poor selection of them, and we boiled them to bits and took all the vitamins and poured them down the sink,' Shelley reminds us. 'So when you asked what was for your dinner you were told there was pork or beef or chicken, no one said "oh and broccoli".'

'Even when people had a salad it was limp lettuce, half a tomato, a few slices of cucumber, a slice of ham with a thick rim of fat on it, a hardboiled egg and salad cream full of saturated fat. Olive oil was something you put on sunburn or to get the wax out of your ears – it wasn't something you used as food!'

We were encouraged to eat as much as we possibly could as well. 'If you were thin, you were suspected of maybe having TB so no one would marry you if you were a young woman,' Shelley says, 'and if you didn't finish everything on your plate you were reminded that your ancestors had starved to death.'

Smoking and alcohol consumption also increased greatly, which added risk factors to our high-in-saturated-fat diet, causing heart disease to really take off. Exercise for the benefit of your health was still an alien concept. 'If you were out jogging back in the 1980s they'd probably send for the local mental health services for you – this was not what normal people did!' declares Shelley.

At its peak, half of all deaths were cardiovascular (related to the heart or blood vessels) and half of those in turn were due to coronary heart disease. The inflexion point came in the mid-1980s. It started to become accepted that we could – and probably should – start to do something about the problem.

Dr Risteárd Mulcahy was a leading cardiologist in Saint Vincent's Hospital at the time, and a founding member of the Irish Heart Foundation. He lobbied the Department of Health to start funding interventions to address the issue. The Minister of Health of the day, Barry Desmond, allegedly stopped off to see him one morning on his way to work to hear what he had to say. Mulcahy pitched him the establishment of Ireland's first project for the prevention of heart disease, to be centred on Kilkenny, and Desmond committed to funding it on the spot.

This became the Kilkenny Health Project, established in 1984. One of the most concerted health promotion initiatives ever undertaken in Ireland took place in the county over the next five years. Articles were published in local papers. Leaflets were printed and distributed. Health messages were broadcast on local radio. Community meetings were held with a wide range of organisations. Health education programmes were undertaken in secondary schools. A Quit Smoking competition was organised. A 10K road run took place.

And it worked. Local people's knowledge about the factors associated with heart disease went up. They changed their diets. Cholesterol levels dropped. Blood pressure declined. Smoking decreased. The project's ultimate legacy was Ireland's first national cardiovascular health strategy, subsequently developed in the late 1990s, which recognised the vital importance of prevention.

It was from 1986 that the death rate from cardiovascular disease began to decline at pace. Incredibly, the death rate has fallen by two-thirds over the past 40 years. Changes in people's behaviour accounted for about half of the reduction, with the other half due to better medical treatments.[10]

What caused Ireland to change its behaviour? Shelley points the finger at our expanding horizons as economic wealth began to grow. 'People started to travel and they discovered when they went on their holidays to Spain that people there ate broccoli and it didn't kill them!' We were increasingly exposed to a greater diversity of healthier foods. And as we went into our local shops and bought a wider variety of foodstuffs so they started stocking a wider variety.

Eating habits changed. 'My parents would have remembered a time as marrieds in the 1940s and 50s that they had a fry every morning for breakfast,' Shelley recalls, 'and then later they only had a fry on a Sunday morning, then later again they only had a fry on Christmas morning, and then they didn't have a fry any morning.'

As the Department of Health ran health promotion campaigns for the general public, so our health education levels rose. So too did our general education levels, providing the means for more people to earn a better living that could sustain a higher standard of health care.

Medical treatments have improved, of course. Although I have focused on coronary heart disease, there have been significant declines in the death rate from stroke too.

The Irish Heart Foundation undertook the first-ever national audit of stroke services in the mid-2000s and concluded that the services were so poorly organised that they were largely ineffective.[11] As Shelley puts it, 'there was this sense that "oh, it's stroke" and the poor person was put in the corner and there wasn't a whole lot done'.

That situation has been transformed over the past decade and a half. Dedicated stroke units have been established in hospitals throughout the country, operating 24/7. Ambulance crews conduct diagnostic tests in transit and will be met at the door of the hospital by a nurse to do a triage. CAT scans are used to establish the appropriate treatments, and priority cases can be fast-tracked to specialist hospitals to have the clot vacuum-sucked out of the patient's body. A follow-up audit by the Heart Foundation found that our death rate from stroke had been cut by more than a quarter in just seven years.

As a result of all our progress, the proportion of deaths assigned to cardiovascular disease decreased from 50 per cent in the 1980s to less than 30 per cent today. However, heart disease remains as great a cause of death today as it was 100 years ago and the rate of progress has started to slow down in recent decades. An undoubted factor is our obesity epidemic – an area in which we have little to be proud of. Rising weights and increasing diabetes will lead to more heart disease and stroke in the future. As Shelley concludes, 'on the building sites we're back into the breakfast-roll era so the notion that all this has gone away would be a false notion'.

Public Health Spending Has Increased 14-Fold over the Past 50 Years

The Great Big Miracle of Human Progress comes at a cost. Although we read media reports about the underfunding of our health service, I maintain that the Irish State has generally risen well to the challenge of providing an ever-more sophisticated health service.

Government health spending has increased at an astonishing rate over the past fifty years. Back in 1970 the State spent the equivalent of €1 billion in today's money on funding national health care. That was around €363 for every man, woman and child in the country at the time.

A steady increase in funding saw that figure grow nearly five-fold by the end of the 1990s. Then expenditure truly shot up. Between 1999 and 2018 it tripled again, even allowing for a stalling of growth during the austerity years of 2011–15. There has been a fourteen-fold increase in real spending on public health over the past fifty years. Even allowing for our expanding population, nowadays the State spends over €3,000 per person every year. No wonder we are living longer and healthier than ever.

So what has it all been spent on? A huge change in Irish health care took place in 1970 when the government created regional health boards. Previous to this, the health-care system was organised as a voluntary system with the Catholic Church retaining ownership of hospitals and health institutions. Doctors acted as sole traders. The State took few responsibilities beyond the provision of health care to the disadvantaged, which was generally organised at a county-level.

Government health spending in real terms, 1970–2018

SOURCE: OECD[12]

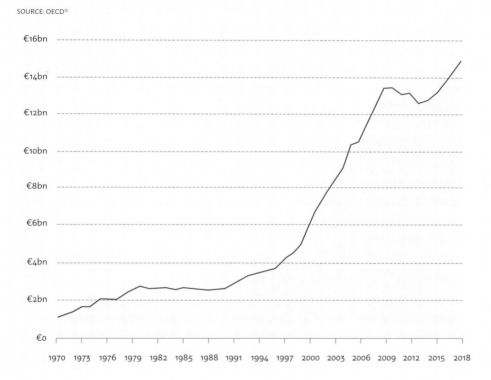

The 1970 Health Act changed all that. Eight health boards were created to cover the country with the aim of ensuring a common standard of care throughout the nation. The remit of the Department of Health was expanded to allow it to oversee the boards' performance and to develop national health policy. The government committed to paying for the health and well-being of all its citizens.

Two years later a new scheme was put in place to ensure public patients had access to free GP services. The General Medical Services Scheme represented a radical new approach. It facilitated treatment of public patients alongside private patients and allowed public patients to choose their own doctor. The numbers in possession of a free 'medical card' grew strongly over the years. The introduction of free health care for children under the age of six in 2015 further boosted the number of people covered by the scheme. Today there are more than 2.1 million of us – that's more than four in ten – entitled to GP care at the State's expense.[13]

We are, of course, living longer too. Given that we are less likely to drop dead on the spot from heart disease or to lose a battle with incurable cancer, we can be expected to require more health treatments over the additional decades that we will live to enjoy.

Just as the State is paying for the health care of more people for longer, it is also providing more and more services. Alan Smith is one of the country's Deputy Chief Medical Officers in the Department of Health. 'Undoubtedly we are able to do more, so we are expected to fund more: more GP services, more GPs, more vaccination programmes, more cancer screening programmes – the breadth of service provision has increased,' Smith observes.

'It has become the norm for hospital consultants to train here and then to go abroad for specialist study. They come back with enormous expertise so suddenly a health intervention that nobody ever thought of is available. Somebody doesn't have to travel abroad for a certain operation any longer because it can be provided here,' says Smith. 'In the 1940s and 50s, in our parents' and grandparents' era, what we're doing now was the talk of science fiction.'

The miracle of modern medicine is increasingly sophisticated but is therefore increasingly expensive for that very reason. The rising cost of treatments has been identified as being behind the vast bulk of growing health-care costs.[14] Diagnostic machines are high-end technologies that need to be updated and replaced periodically. Medicines are increasingly expensive to research and develop. Consultants are increasingly specialist. Surgical procedures are increasingly complex.

The State's increased investment has ensured that the quality of care available has improved significantly. Despite growing demand resulting in long waiting lists for some treatments, most people have only good things to say about their experience of the health service and about the quality of the staff and the treatment that they receive. Medical treatments have never had more of an impact in improving the quality of our lives, and the number of people receiving them has never been greater.

 ## Hospital Treatments Have More Than Doubled Since the Turn of the Century to Reach Record Levels

Day cases and in-patient numbers at publicly funded acute hospitals, 2000–18

SOURCE: DEPARTMENT OF HEALTH

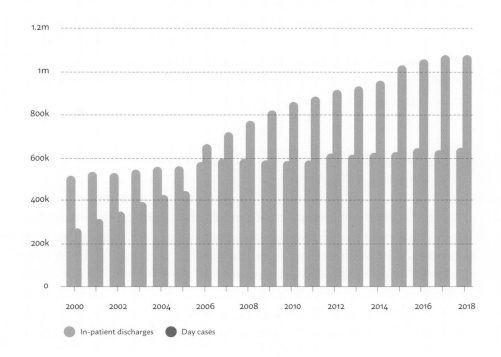

In-patient discharges   Day cases

Over 1,700,000 patient treatments take place in our publicly funded hospitals annually. That number has more than doubled in less than two decades.

The huge increase has been led by growth in day case treatments, rather than those requiring a patient to be in hospital overnight. At the start of the 2000s most patients were admitted to hospitals for an overnight stay for treatment. As Alan Smith recalls, 'if you were having an operation, you'd come in a couple of days beforehand, and we'd keep you for a week just to make sure that you were fine. [Since then] it's been about shifting to day surgery admission: you don't need to come in beforehand – all your blood tests, X-rays, etc. can be done on an outpatient basis – so that hospital treatment is reserved for the most complex cases.'

Between 2000 and 2018 the number of day cases increased nearly four-fold from just over a quarter of a million a year to well over a million. In-patient treatment has increased as well, if far more gradually. Just over half a million patients in publicly funded hospitals in 2000 has become over 640,000 today – an increase of nearly a quarter.

The face of the Irish health service has transformed rapidly in a very short period of time, and it is set to continue to do so. As Smith concludes, 'we're continuing to shift the care of patients out of hospitals and into the community and with GPs. If you need a blood test you shouldn't have to toddle into a large tertiary hospital in Dublin to do it.'

The Irish Consider Themselves the Healthiest People in Europe

It is a testament to our lifestyle choices and to the quality and investment in our health service that Irish people feel so positive about their health. The percentage who describe their health as 'good' or 'very good' is the highest of any country in the European Union at 84 per cent.

However, our positivity is influenced by our youth. Ireland has the lowest average age of any country in Europe, and the younger we are the more positive we are about our health. It will be a challenge to retain such high ratings as our population ages and the number of us living with chronic diseases increases.

Percentage of the population reporting good or very good health in 2019

SOURCE: EUROSTAT[5]

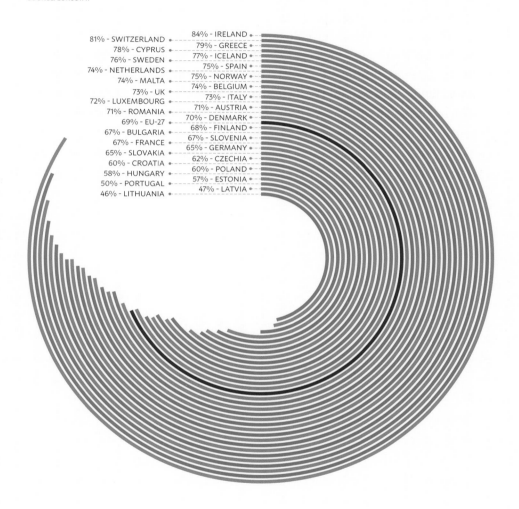

81% - SWITZERLAND
78% - CYPRUS
76% - SWEDEN
74% - NETHERLANDS
74% - MALTA
73% - UK
72% - LUXEMBOURG
71% - ROMANIA
69% - EU-27
67% - BULGARIA
67% - FRANCE
65% - SLOVAKIA
60% - CROATIA
58% - HUNGARY
50% - PORTUGAL
46% - LITHUANIA

84% - IRELAND
79% - GREECE
77% - ICELAND
75% - SPAIN
75% - NORWAY
74% - BELGIUM
73% - ITALY
71% - AUSTRIA
70% - DENMARK
68% - FINLAND
67% - SLOVENIA
65% - GERMANY
62% - CZECHIA
60% - POLAND
57% - ESTONIA
47% - LATVIA

We are nevertheless well positioned to remain amongst the healthiest places in Europe. Uniquely, many of the health advances we have made have been driven by clinicians, i.e. doctors who have direct contact with patients. The HSE coordinates programmes across more than 30 different domains in which doctors identify how best to care for patients. As Smith describes the programmes, 'they're researching best practice and developing a model of care to empower GPs and communities to look after patients with these conditions. It's an Irish innovation.'

Through a health service designed by experts, supported by evidence-based policies, we have successfully curbed tobacco use, reduced heart disease, improved cancer care and eliminated diseases through nationwide vaccination. We have shaped ourselves into a healthier nation. The healthiest we have ever been. I consider that to be a little miracle.

Eating Better

WE ARE EATING BETTER, MORE NUTRITIOUS FOOD AND
YET SPENDING LESS ON IT THAN EVER BEFORE. AS A
COUNTRY, WE PRODUCE FAR MORE FOODSTUFFS NOWADAYS,
YET UTILISE LESS LAND AND LESS MANPOWER TO DO SO.

 ## We Have Hugely Increased Our Production of Food

We Have Increased Our Crops by Two-Thirds over the Past 60 Years while Using One-Third Less Land

WE CAME FROM A challenging starting place. A report by a visiting New Zealand grassland expert in the 1940s concluded that while 'there is no area of comparable size in the Northern Hemisphere which has such marvellous potentialities for pasture production as Eire undoubtedly has … I saw hundreds of fields which are growing just as little as physically possible for the land to grow under an Irish sky'.[1] In the vivid words of Agricultural Minister James Dillon, Irish grass 'would fill a cow's stomach and yet let her die of starvation where she stood'.[2]

Index of area harvested for crops and the tonnes produced, 1961–2019

SOURCE: FOOD AND AGRICULTURE ORGANIZATION OF THE UNITED NATIONS

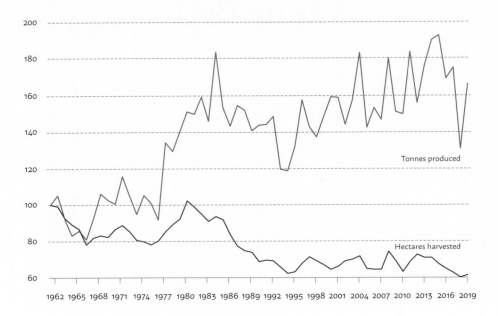

Improving soil fertility was therefore one of the primary tasks given to the Irish agricultural research institute, An Foras Talúntais, when it was established in 1958. Irish soil becomes naturally acidic because the rain washes out the calcium, meaning that crops cannot grow easily unless this balance is restored. An Foras Talúntais, and its successor, Teagasc, helped farmers to address this through the deployment of fertilisers in the 1960s and 70s, supported by the use of pesticides to control weeds, pests and disease.

Importantly too, as Professor Frank O'Mara, Director of Research at Teagasc, points out, what we are growing today are not the same varieties of crops that we grew fifty years ago. 'There's genetic improvements in the varieties, and new ones are continually being introduced, so there's a gradual rate of increase in the yield of the crops over time.'

Do you remember Mendel from your secondary school curriculum? 'Mendel started the science of crop breeding by crossing different plants with each other and selecting out the best-performing offspring,' O'Mara reminds us. 'In Ireland we have a very particular set of diseases that can affect crops because of our moist, temperate climate. They'd be a very different set of diseases than French cereal growers would be encountering, for example. So in Teagasc we work with European crop breeders and provide them with feedback as to how their varieties are working in our climate.' A new variety will be adopted if it shows a sufficient improvement in yield or in pest resistance, thereby increasing the amount that a single plot of land can produce.

We have significant plant-breeding programmes for just three crops in Ireland – but three that are of strategic and historic importance: grass, clover and potatoes. 'Ninety per cent of our agricultural land area is grass so there's a strategic national interest in having a grass-breeding programme to help breed the best varieties for an Irish environment. The same goes for clover. We're interested in things like spring growth and autumn growth: when the weather is cooler can the crops grow and give us a good long grazing season? In Ireland we want to get out grazing as soon as we can, whereas in countries such as Finland or the Netherlands the cows are indoors most of the time so it's overall yield that is important to them.'

Despite the fact that we breed and grow our own potatoes, you might be surprised to read that we import half of the potatoes we eat! O'Mara explains: 'We grow nearly all of our own table potatoes, but then there's an awful lot brought into the country as frozen chips or for processing – to put the topping on your packaged shepherd's pie. We produce virtually none of those.' It's a question of scale. 'We produce about 300,000 tonnes of potatoes here. In the Netherlands they produce 20 to 25 times more: about 7 million tonnes. We just don't have the land availability in tillage to do that.'

In fact, the amount of land we have in tillage has decreased by about a third over the past sixty years. It's primarily due to economic reasons. The profitability of a hectare utilised for tillage is lower than one given over to dairy. In particular since the abolition of milk quotas in 2015, there has been increased demand for grazing land and a corresponding reduction in the amount used for tillage. Tillage also requires expensive, modern machinery to farm in a way that grassland does not.

Of course, technology is one of the greatest changes we have witnessed in agriculture over the past century. We were still cultivating our land with horses a century ago. It was not until the 1950s and 60s that they were practically entirely replaced by tractors. The increasing power and output from machinery over subsequent decades has enabled us to produce all this food with a tiny fraction of the manpower that it previously did.

We Have Increased Our Meat Production Four-fold in 60 Years

Since the early 1960s, the number of cows and pigs in Ireland has increased by half. Yet, incredibly, the amount of pigmeat we produce has doubled and the amount of beef we produce has quadrupled! How is this possible?

As with our crops, the answer is that today's animals are not the same ones as those that populated the Irish farms of the 1960s. They are of a different breed. Our traditional Hereford and Aberdeen Angus cattle have been replaced by ones from the European continent that are much bigger, resulting in much more meat from each animal.

Ireland is practically unique in producing so much beef as a percentage of our total meat output. However, it is actually poultry that has grown the most since the 1960s in percentage terms. We produce 14 times more chicken meat nowadays. 'The growth in poultry meat around the world has far outstripped the growth in any other meat for the last 50 years so we're no different,' Professor O'Mara explains. 'Consumers like it: it's low fat, it's very easy to cook, it's very versatile, so it's made chicken very popular.'

More than two-thirds of Ireland is covered by natural or agricultural grasslands, meaning that Ireland has the highest proportion of natural vegetation of any country in Europe.[3] That grass is of no use to pigs or chickens, so our livestock is primarily cattle. 'That's why we have such a big beef industry and quite a big dairy industry: we're a grass farming country. That's our unique selling point,' explains O'Mara. 'Other countries' meat and milk are produced through a mix of forage and concentrate diet.'

Tonnes of beef, pig and poultry meat produced, 1961–2019

SOURCE: FOOD AND AGRICULTURE ORGANIZATION OF THE UNITED NATIONS

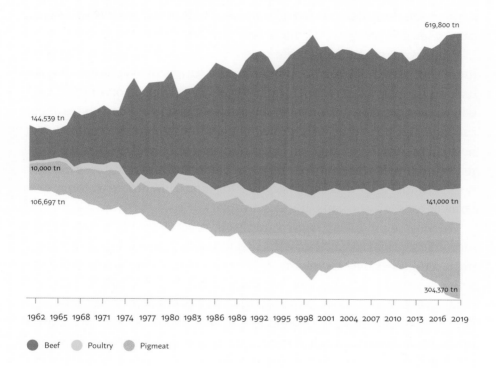

619,800 tn

144,539 tn

10,000 tn

106,697 tn

141,000 tn

304,370 tn

1962 1965 1968 1971 1974 1977 1980 1983 1986 1989 1992 1995 1998 2001 2004 2007 2010 2013 2016 2019

● Beef ● Poultry ● Pigmeat

Our grass farming approach has its roots in our environment and in our culture. Environmentally speaking, we get a lot of rain. 'Our climate is really suited to grass: the continuous rain. If you want to grow grass, you need rain all the time. Tillage crops generally like long dry summers and Ireland doesn't give us those.' Then there is the land itself. Our stony and wet soils can often be unsuitable for heavy tillage machinery but perfectly fine for a wandering cow. And, finally, there's our culture of small land holdings. Although the average farm size has more than doubled from 15 hectares around the time of independence to over 32 hectares today, that is still insufficiently large to make crop growing profitable.[4]

We produce so much beef that the vast majority is exported. 'Irish consumption is almost immaterial as we export about 90 per cent of our beef – so we're 1,000 per cent self-sufficient! Even if the Irish stopped eating beef altogether, we would only have to grow our exports by 10 per cent to sell everything we produce,' says O'Mara.

While we are producing more food than ever before, we have become more specialised. We are not producing the variety of vegetables that we used to, for example. O'Mara recalls: 'If you went back 30 or 40 years ago, when I was growing up, the vegetables on your plate were carrots, turnips, cabbage and peas that were grown widely throughout the country. But now there's a whole range of vegetables that you can buy that we can't really produce in this country, and we're producing less than we were. Our horticultural industry is very specialised around a few products: tomatoes, strawberries, mushrooms. It's less diverse.'

We may be producing fewer varieties of vegetables, but we are eating more of them and eating less of the meat that we produce. I gave up eating meat altogether over 35 years ago. Famine struck Ethiopia in the early 1980s and ultimately claimed the lives of more than a million people. I realised then that I could help in a small way to improve the world's food supply if I cut out meat (which requires a huge amount of food just to fatten up the animals) and switched to a less intensive, plant-based diet. I like to think that the number of animals that I haven't eaten in that time adds up to something quite significant: surely, it'd be hundreds of cows and pigs and thousands of chickens.

Now that the detrimental climate impact of meat production is fully understood, it appears that more and more of us are choosing to change our diets and to realise the environmental and health benefits of increasing our vegetable intake.

Irrespective of the choices we make, nowadays we have more than enough food to feed ourselves. Aside from our increasing tillage and meat production, our dairy output has grown by approximately two-thirds since milk quotas were eliminated. It is therefore unsurprising that Ireland has been rated as the second most food-secure nation on the planet.[5]

We Eat Twice the Amount of Vegetables & Fruit Than We Did 60 Years Ago

Kilograms of meat, seafood and fruit & vegetables available for consumption per person per year

SOURCE: FOOD AND AGRICULTURE ORGANIZATION OF THE UNITED NATIONS

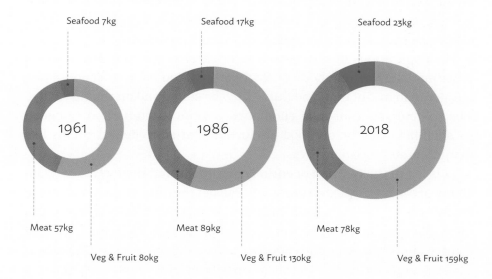

Seafood 7kg Seafood 17kg Seafood 23kg

1961 1986 2018

Meat 57kg Meat 89kg Meat 78kg

Veg & Fruit 80kg Veg & Fruit 130kg Veg & Fruit 159kg

Not only are we producing more food than ever, but we are also eating more food than ever.

The typical Irish person consumed 144 kilograms a year in 1961. By 2018 it had reached 260 kilograms. Our consumption of meat increased by more than three-quarters, before reducing in recent years. Our consumption of vegetables and fruit has doubled, and our consumption of fish has more than trebled.

If there is one foodstuff that is associated with the Irish no matter where in the world I go, unsurprisingly it is the potato. The Famine of 1845–49 radically altered our ancestors' eating patterns, however, and by the time of independence many people's diets were far worse than they had been a hundred years before.

'In the early decades of the nineteenth century a large part of Ireland's population was existing on pure ingredients – things with very little processing involved – primarily potatoes and some sort of milk,' says food historian Regina Sexton, based in University College Cork. 'The post-famine period sees a lot of the population launched into this period of processed foods. You have the substitution of potatoes with wheaten bread or, in urban areas, factory-made bread. It is highly processed, and it is being eaten with cheap factory-made spreads like margarine or lard or else sweet spreads like cheap jams with a lot of sugars in them.'

The applications of science and technology began to transform food consumption. New methods of food preservation such as canning and refrigeration meant that foodstuffs could be stored and distributed wider. The pasteurisation of milk eliminated harmful bacteria and extended its shelf-life. And factory food production started to deliver things like margarine and chocolate bars.

This led to the creation of entirely new foods and the increased availability of others, as Sexton explains: 'You get the diversification of all the food staples. Breads become breads and biscuits and cakes; meat becomes meat that you can put in cans or freeze or preserve in different ways; and you get things like jams and chocolate and golden syrup and OXO cubes.' These new goods heralded a transformation in Irish people's relationship with food. Instead of it being something that you produce yourself, food became something that you purchase from others who produce it for you.

By 1922 the typical Irish diet was a combination of traditional ingredients like meat and fish, wheat and oats, and some limited fruit and vegetables, with an increasing amount of processed foods. The forms of some of these foods would not be familiar to us today. Some of them we might not be happy to eat at all. 'If you look at the meats that were being consumed, there was an awful lot more offal items that we now would be reluctant to consume. Innards like the heart or the kidneys, things like beef tongue, these were viewed as being almost exquisite parts of the animal.'

The eating habits of people in rural Ireland contrasted significantly with those of city-dwellers. 'In rural Ireland you still had a pattern where they're food producers for the most part and there's a balance between home production and shop-bought goods. They might buy flour, sugar, the odd bit of cheese. Self-reliance was still going strong by producing their own chickens, eggs, pork, bacon and garden vegetables.'

In contrast, the urban poor relied mainly on breads and spreads for their calorie intake. 'Eating these poor foods led to all sorts of nutritional problems and the health problems associated with that,' says Sexton. 'The tenement dwellings in Dublin, in particular, were one of the worst nutritional and social environments for the poor in all of Europe at that point.'

Would any of us want to go back to the food choices of 1922? There were some positives. As Sexton points out, 'We would have had more knowledge and understanding of how food is produced and where it comes from, and we would have had that security of production as a nation. But then if you did find yourself back in 1922, I wonder would you be yearning for the diversity of food choice that we have today?'

As Ireland opened up to the world in the 1960s, so we began to explore and to expect greater diversity in our food consumption. 'People became more curious because of their access to education. They wanted to engage with this globalisation of culture. People wanted to have connections with new foods like Italian or Chinese.' The growth in supermarkets in the 1970s and 80s facilitated an explosion in the range that could be made available to shoppers, in contrast to what could fit on the shelves of a small corner shop. 'I think if you brought someone from the 50s and put them in a supermarket today, they'd be staggered. If you put them in the cereal aisle for example: breakfast cereals didn't exist! You had porridge or eggs and maybe a bit of bacon, and now the variety is mind-blowing.'

What has transformed our diets for the better over the past sixty years has been a doubling in the amount of vegetables and fruit. 'Historically the consumption of fruit and vegetables in Ireland was quite low. Coming up to the 1950s and 60s what you had available were things like cabbage, kale, turnips, parsnips, carrots, and potatoes,' says Sexton. 'Then you had the introduction of all of these diverse foods and the variety takes off because Irish people now have access to many of them for the first time.'

Our consumption of meat increased significantly from the 1960s through to the 90s, although, as Sexton explains, 'we have become blander in our consumption patterns. So even though we're eating more quantity, we're eating less variety: lean beef, lamb, and the big one since the 1970s is the huge increase in the consumption of chicken that's perceived to be a healthier approach to meat-eating.' That growth trend has recently been reversed, however, and meat consumption has declined. It's not all down to me. 'That's to do with health and sustainability and ethics and morals – the whole injection of responsible consumption.'

Seafood has not formed a large part of the Irish diet despite us being an island nation. One reason is that fish was historically deemed to be a penitential food. It was something eaten on a Friday when meat was forbidden by the Catholic Church in order to encourage worshippers to express sorrow for the sins they had committed. It was not something that you were meant to indulge in or to enjoy. The reversal of that association has seen fish-eating increase considerably, although the variety has narrowed in recent decades in line with changing tastes and as a result of unsustainable fishing of some species.

The growing number of women at work has played a part in changing how we prepare food; and how we prepare food nowadays has played a part in enabling more women to work. In the early part of the of the twentieth century, as Sexton explains, 'women were in the home, especially married women, and domestic refrigeration comes in later so they're shopping on a daily basis and dealing with fresh produce all the time. They're cooking that from scratch and that's going to take some time. It's not always the leanest of meat – chicken was unavailable – so it's a different cooking approach that's more time-consuming.

'What disrupted all of that was the changing role of women and the fact that the industry has sold us the idea of convenience. It's the industry that's preparing the food now. We pay for convenience to bring down the cooking time down to 15 minutes. Furthermore, the types of dishes that we prepare now are things that our parents or grandparents would never have heard of: Italian style-dishes, stir-fries, and other things that can be done very quickly.'

No generation has had the opportunity to eat as wide a variety of healthy foodstuffs as ours. We are better nourished than any that have come before us, and we have seen the benefit in additional years added to our lifespans. It is also costing us less than ever before to do so.

18　We Spend Less on Food

Percentage of the average household budget spent on food, 1922–2016

SOURCE: CENTRAL STATISTICS OFFICE⁶

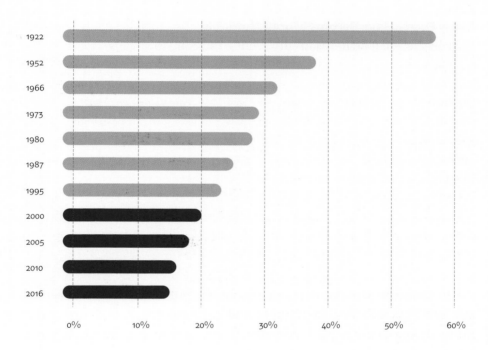

The main factor that has enabled our high levels of food consumption nowadays is its relatively low cost. In 1922 more than 50 per cent of the average household spend was on food and non-alcoholic drinks. Today that figure is less than 15 per cent even though we are purchasing far more.

Major events in European history helped to make that happen. As Regina Sexton explains, 'After the Second World War European leaders come together to say "we don't want to ever go back to a situation where our populations almost starve due to rationing". In 1957 the Treaty of Rome was signed [to create the EEC] and part of the thinking was food security.'

Those founding nations started to use science and technology to boost productivity, deploying new practices from which Ireland also benefited. 'What happens as a result is that the price of food comes down because you have so much food circulating,' says Sexton. 'The obvious consequence is that people have better spending power so they can buy more and they can consume more.'

Many Foods Have Become More Affordable

Cost of selected food items in euro / cents, 1922–2019

SOURCE: CENTRAL STATISTICS OFFICE[7]

Food Item	Weight	1922	2019	Price Multiple 2019 v 1922	
Potatoes	7.5 kg	11c	€7.79	73	More expensive
Sirloin steak	1 kg	20c	€14.18	72	More expensive
Cheese	1 kg	20c	€9.92	50	Similar
Bread	800g loaf	3c	€1.30	49	Similar
Fresh milk	1 ltr	3c	€1.03	39	Cheaper
Eggs	1/2 dozen	5c	€1.42	32	Cheaper
Butter	1 lb	11c	€3.04	28	Cheaper
Sugar	1 kg	9c	€1.21	14	Cheaper

The Central Statistics Office and its predecessors have been collecting information about the cost of staple foodstuffs since the foundation of the State. On the face of it, food seems much more expensive now given that a litre of milk only cost the equivalent of 3 cents back in 1922. However, when you account for inflation it turns out that a litre of milk is now significantly cheaper than it was 100 years ago.

All told, the cost of goods increased 53-fold between 1922 and 2019. A shopping basket that cost you just €1 in 1922 would set you back €53.10 in 2019. Our 3 cent litre of milk should therefore cost €1.59 today if its price increased in line with inflation. In fact the average price is only €1.03, so milk is more affordable nowadays.

As the table shows, eggs, butter and sugar are all significantly more affordable now than they were in 1922. If the cost of butter had kept pace with inflation then it would cost twice as much as it does today, and sugar would be nearly four times as expensive.

The price of cheddar cheese and a loaf of bread have more or less kept pace with inflation so they remain equally affordable. Potatoes and sirloin steak, on the other hand, are more expensive now than they were – they both cost just over one-third more to purchase. However, as I will show later, our disposable income has grown by a far greater amount over the century so the affordability of all of these goods has improved, contributing to food's declining share of our household budget. A calorie has never been so affordable.

 ## Our Alcohol Consumption Is in Decline

Litres of pure alcohol consumed per adult per year

SOURCE: REVENUE COMMISSIONERS[8]

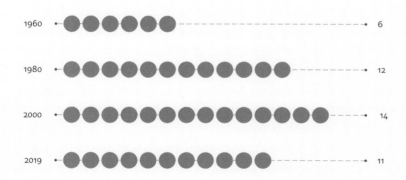

I have had the great privilege of attending St Patrick's Day parades all over the world. Every parade varies in how formal it is, how long it is, who organises it and who participates. Most of them are all-embracing, joyful celebrations of all things Irish. But have you ever seen St Patrick's Day portrayed in an episode of *The Simpsons*? It always ends up in a drunken street brawl! We may have a bad reputation for alcohol consumption, but it is one that is increasingly undeserved.

Ireland reached peak alcohol in 2001. The average Irish person drank 14.3 litres of pure alcohol that year. Since then, however, the typical person's consumption has been declining. By 2019 that figure had fallen to just under 11 litres.

What does 11 litres of pure alcohol look like? It is equivalent to drinking 41 bottles of vodka or 116 bottles of wine or 445 pints of beer in a year.[9] But as one in five of the adult population abstain from alcohol completely, the figures must be adjusted upwards. Each drinker in Ireland consumes an average of 46 bottles of vodka, 130 bottles of wine, or nearly 500 pints of beer a year.

Our drink of choice has changed a lot in recent decades. Beer accounted for more than 70 per cent of all the alcohol we bought in the early 1980s but its share has fallen to under 50 per cent. Wine has seen huge growth – from close to only 5 per cent of purchases in the early 80s, it now accounts for nearly 30 per cent. Growing consumption among women and growth in off-licence purchases for drinking at home contributed to these shifts.

There has traditionally been a strong link between economic wealth and alcohol consumption. As the money in our pockets increased so did the amount we spent on alcohol. At the start of the 1960s we consumed only six litres. As the economy grew throughout the 60s and 70s so did our consumption and it had effectively doubled by the end of the 70s. The economic woes of the 1980s saw consumption fall again, but the arrival of the Celtic Tiger in the mid-1990s corresponded with strong growth.

In recent decades, the link between rising incomes and consumption has been broken. Our disposable incomes grew throughout the Celtic Tiger era, yet our alcohol consumption peaked in 2001 and we now consume roughly a quarter less alcohol than we did back then despite having more euros in our pockets now.

The efforts to eliminate drink-driving may be having an impact, but increasing health consciousness, particularly amongst young people, seems to be fundamentally changing our attitudes towards alcohol consumption. 'There's a well-being culture that's emerging and alcohol is a bit of a no-no in that context,' says Regina Sexton.

So is our international reputation for heavy drinking deserved or not? Ireland does have a high rate of alcohol consumption by international standards, but we are not the greatest drinkers. The most recent data for advanced economies show Lithuania topping the list followed by Austria, France, the Czech Republic and Luxembourg ahead of Ireland.[10] However, the average consumption across most developed nations is 8.9 litres, meaning that the Irish typically drink 20 per cent more than most other nationalities.

If every Irish person adopted the Department of Health's guidelines on maximum alcohol consumption, taking into account that a fifth of us do not drink at all and that those under 18 should not be consuming any amount, then our level of per-capita consumption should be no more than seven litres per person per year.[11] We will need to reduce our current drinking levels by a third to achieve that measure of safety. I suspect, though, it will take a generation or two before the 'drunken Irish' stereotype is supplanted in the minds of many overseas – particularly as alcoholic drinks remain one of the exports for which we are best known.

 We Are Taller Than Ever (by 11 to 12.5 Centimetres)

The fact that we are eating more food than ever before, are drinking less alcohol than we used to, are increasingly health-conscious and are better at managing disease has had very visible benefits. We are significantly taller than our ancestors!

Women are an average of 11.1 cm taller than they were a hundred years ago. In fact, women nowadays are only about one centimetre shorter than men were back then. Men have gained 12.5 cm over the century, thereby increasing their height advantage over women by one-and-a-half centimetres. They are nearly 14 cm taller on average nowadays.

Height is a predictor of success in life, believe it or not. On average, taller people have higher education, higher earnings and better social positions. They generally live longer and are less likely to suffer from heart disease and stroke. Taller women and their children are less likely to have complications during and after birth.[12]

Average heights of Irish men and women aged 18 in centimetres, 1914–2014

SOURCE: NCD RISK FACTOR COLLABORATION[15]

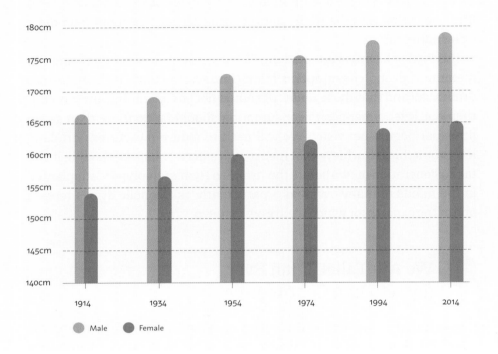

Male   Female

How high can we go? The height increases that we have experienced from decade to decade are beginning to slow down. Nevertheless, we have some way to go to catch the Dutch. The Netherlands is home to the tallest men and the second-tallest women in the world. The men average 182.5 cm and the women 168.7 cm – roughly three and a half centimetres more than us for both genders. That suggests that we can keep on gaining height for another thirty years or more at our current pace of growth, assuming our genes are not radically different from the Dutch. Let us hope our national success and improved health continues to grow along with our average stature!

Bring warmth and elegance to every room. With Elegante.

Meet the Elegante butane room-heater. The heater that warms your home in elegance and style. As good to look at as it is to sit by.

But the Elegante isn't just a pretty face. It's a powerful, effective heater that throws out about twice as much heat as conventional butane heaters. The patented burner design and special mirror-chrome reflector sees to that.

And the Elegante saves you money too, because it has three heat settings. So once your room is warm, you can turn down the heat — and the room will stay warm for little more than $\frac{1}{2}$p an hour! The Elegante is safe. It's tested to Irish Institute of Industrial Research standards. So you can move it from room to room on its super-smooth castors and never have to worry! One more thing. The Elegante costs less than ordinary heaters, because it's made right here in Ireland. Enough said?

Drop into your local gas stockist. Ask to see the Elegante. Alternatively just fill in the coupon and we'll send you a full-colour leaflet by return.

Elegante

I want to know more about the Elegante. Please send me your full-colour leaflet

Name

Address

To: Irish Raleigh Industries Ltd., 8 Hanover Quay, Dublin 2.

④

Living Easier

THE CONDITIONS IN WHICH WE LIVE TODAY ARE UNQUESTIONABLY LUXURIOUS COMPARED TO THOSE OF A HUNDRED YEARS AGO. OUR HOMES ARE MANY TIMES LARGER AND THE FACILITIES INSIDE THEM WOULD BE UNRECOGNISABLE TO OUR ANCESTORS. BUT EVEN WHERE THOSE HOMES ARE LOCATED HAS CHANGED MARKEDLY.

-----

21 We Have Transformed from a Country That Was Two-Thirds Rural to One That Is Two-Thirds Urban

POTENTIAL TOURISTS TO IRELAND I speak to invariably have an image of the country that is predominantly rural, of lush green landscapes and a rugged coast. I venture that if you asked most Irish people to conjure up an image of the place, they would plump for something quite similar. Yet Ireland is not a rural country anymore.

The percentage of the population living in Dublin, another urban centre or a rural location

SOURCE: CENTRAL STATISTICS OFFICE[1]

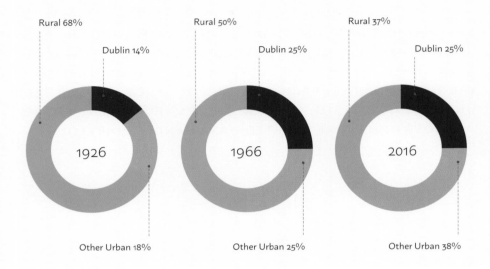

One hundred years ago it was true: over two-thirds of the population lived in rural places – in villages and in the countryside – while one-third lived in Dublin or another urban centre. But the flight from rural Ireland that had begun with the Famine in the mid-nineteenth century continued into the twentieth century. While there were massive outflows to Britain and North America, there was relatively little movement from the countryside to local towns. Those who chose to remain in Ireland, or who could not afford to travel abroad, headed for Dublin – it was the only county to experience an inflow of population from the rest of the country.[2]

By the mid-1960s Ireland had become an urban country. Less than half the population remained in rural surroundings, while a quarter lived in Dublin and a quarter in other urban locations. As the country's population has grown in subsequent decades, it is urban Ireland that has accommodated practically all of that. Although a quarter of us still live in Dublin, nearly four in ten now live in another urban area and fewer than four in ten live in rural Ireland.

Dublin city and county was home to half a million people at the time of independence. Now it is home to 850,000 more. Half of all the growth in population that Ireland has experienced in the past century has been absorbed by County Dublin alone. Our other cities have kept pace with Dublin's growth, but it has been the 'commuter towns' in rural County Dublin and in the neighbouring counties where the growth has been most extreme as suburban living sprawled beyond the capital city. These are places such as Swords and Balbriggan in Fingal, Navan in County Meath, Naas and Celbridge in County Kildare, and Greystones and Bray in County Wicklow.

Housing this growing urban population was not a priority for the country's first independent government. Dr Ellen Rowley is an archi-tectural historian and author based in University College Dublin. 'The urban housing is appalling,' says Rowley, 'but because of the 1916 rising, because of World War I and then the War of Independence, all of that reform gets pushed back. Especially Dublin, which was completely ransacked and destroyed. [The focus is on] reinstating public structures like our courts and Custom House, and evolving Dublin Castle into a centre for bureaucracy ... You've got all these bureaucrats camping out in the National Museum and the National Library and they've no offices. So housing is put on the back burner.'

Yet Dublin's housing stock was coming under continuously increasing pressure from the relentless drift of people from the countryside. Conditions were deteriorating. Something had to be done.

It took the arrival of the pro-public-spending Fianna Fáil government to instigate Ireland's first large-scale urban slum clearance and social housing building drive. An average of 12,000 new houses were built annually between 1932 and 1942, compared to just 2,000 per year between 1923 and 1931. The majority of these were built by local authorities. In fact by 1940 41 per cent of the country's housing stock had been built by local authorities – far higher than the 25 per cent in neighbouring England and Wales.[3] The outbreak of World War II put a halt to housing development for nearly a decade, but the building boom recommenced in the late 1940s.

The top 25 urban centres and their population growth, 1926–2016

SOURCE: CENTRAL STATISTICS OFFICE[4]

City or Town	County	1926	2016	Growth Multiple 1926–2016
Dublin city and county	Dublin	505,654	1,347,359	3x
Cork city and suburbs	Cork	78,490	208,669	3x
Limerick city and suburbs	Limerick	39,448	94,192	2x
Galway city and suburbs	Galway	14,227	79,934	6x
Waterford city and suburbs	Waterford	26,647	53,504	2x
Drogheda	Louth	12,716	40,956	3x
Swords	Dublin	839	39,248	47x
Dundalk	Louth	13,996	39,004	3x
Bray	Wicklow	8,637	32,600	4x
Navan	Meath	3,652	30,173	8x
Kilkenny	Kilkenny	10,046	26,512	3x
Ennis	Clare	5,518	25,276	5x
Carlow	Carlow	7,163	24,272	3x
Tralee	Kerry	10,533	23,691	2x
Newbridge	Kildare	2,249	22,742	10x
Portlaoise	Laois	3,374	22,050	7x
Balbriggan	Dublin	2,281	21,722	10x
Naas	Kildare	3,442	21,393	6x
Athlone	Westmeath	7,540	21,349	3x
Mullingar	Westmeath	5,293	20,928	4x
Celbridge	Kildare	643	20,288	32x
Wexford	Wexford	11,879	20,188	2x
Letterkenny	Donegal	2,308	19,274	8x
Sligo	Sligo	11,437	19,199	2x
Greystones	Wicklow	1,594	18,140	11x
Total Population		**2,971,992**	**4,761,865**	**1.6x**

Although it was building most of the homes in the country, the State also encouraged the purchase of them by their tenants. As Rowley says, 'In the 1930s, 40s and 50s there isn't free education; the healthcare provision is from the church, and so the welfare state is in the form of housing. You're given handouts and loans for housing. Our welfare state was property-based until the 1970s.'

Most of Dublin's newly built housing during this period involved the creation of new suburbs on greenfield sites. People wanted to get away from the city centre's grim housing, and Dublin Corporation found it more cost-effective to build afresh. A move to the suburbs met the needs of the city-centre dweller who craved more space for their family and fulfilled the desire of the former countryside resident for a touch of rural living. The new suburbs were part-urban and part-rural.

By the end of the 1950s the State's investment in housing development was largely seen as complete. Taoiseach Seán Lemass concluded that the government needed to move away from providing jobs through home building to attracting foreign investors and growing our exports. Development was increasingly left to the private sector, which, for the first time in the 1960s, delivered more homes than the local authorities. In the following decade there were almost three times more private house completions than there were public ones.[5]

As the nation's population began to grow from the 1970s, so city suburbs were extended, small towns and villages grew and rural housing was built to accommodate the expanding population. New towns were developed in west Dublin – Tallaght, Lucan, Clondalkin and Blanchardstown – and Dublin's northern and southern suburbs expanded. Most of these new homes were built or purchased by the people who lived in them. Home ownership continued to rise steadily throughout the twentieth century and was amongst the highest anywhere in the developed world, peaking at 80 per cent in the early 1990s (compared to the UK at 65 per cent and Sweden at only 39 per cent).[6]

All this suburban house building allowed bigger homes to be built than if they had been located in existing urban centres. Yet our family sizes have decreased over the decades and our homes no longer need to accommodate as many people as they did 100 years ago.

22 Our Houses Have Never Been Bigger and the Number of People in Each Has Never Been Fewer

Number of rooms and the average number of people per household, 1926–2016

SOURCE: CENTRAL STATISTICS OFFICE[7]

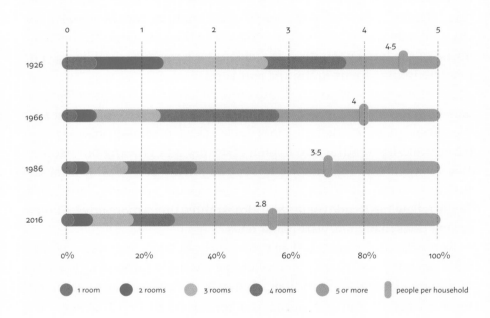

A quarter of all households in 1926 lived in accommodation that comprised only one or two rooms. A further quarter, roughly speaking, lived in three-room accommodation. Yet the average household consisted of four-and-a-half people at the time. The next quarter lived in four-room accommodation. And the final quarter lived in five or more rooms. These are not the number of bedroom: these are the total number of rooms in the flat or tenement or cottage or house in which the entire household had to live.

Forty years later, by 1966, there had been quite a transformation with only a quarter – rather than a half – of households now living in units of one, two or three rooms. A third of households were in four-room units; and four in ten households were in units of five or more rooms.

Fifty years further on, in 2016, only three in ten households were in accommodation of four rooms or less. Seven in ten of us were living in five-or-more-roomed accommodation. And there were fewer of us living in each place, as average household size had dropped to fewer than three individuals.

Over the course of the century, therefore, we have progressed from having more people in each household than the household had rooms to a situation where we have twice as many rooms in each household as there are people living there.

The residents of newly independent Ireland started off in poor circumstances. The majority of the urban working classes lived in makeshift homes, overcrowded cottages or, in the case of Dublin, the decaying former homes of the wealthy, which were subdivided as tenements and let on a room-by-room basis. Slum conditions of squalor and overcrowding existed in all of Ireland's cities and towns, although most evidently in Dublin, where they were frequently compared to those of Calcutta.[8]

When the State's house-building programme got underway in earnest in the 1930s, Dublin Corporation started building four- or five-roomed houses with two or three bedrooms in each. When the second wave of building got underway after World War II, the typical council house was built with four bedrooms. Private developers tended to follow the councils' lead by building houses with a similar number of rooms but bigger in size.

Inevitably, as the State's housing stock gradually expanded over time so the average number of rooms in each household grew. The preference for construction in greenfield suburban sites, and more recently in commuter towns adjacent to County Dublin, has enabled the ongoing addition of large dwellings that continue to push our average number of rooms up and up.

Although, traditionally, we have been obsessed about owning a place with our own front door, I believe that is about to change. Now that people are living longer, they are destined to enjoy several decades of life after raising their children and they don't need to remain in the same large home. Family sizes are, themselves, shrinking too. As our average household size therefore continues to decline, there is no reason to suspect it won't come to match the European Union average of 2.3 persons or even the German average of just two people.[9] We are simply not going to need such big houses in the future.

One study has estimated that at least two-thirds of Irish households will comprise just one or two people in 2080.[10] On this basis there is no need for any new family homes to be built to house three, four or five people. We have enough already. What we will need to build is apartments – 25,000 of them every year for the next six decades to meet the country's future housing requirements.

The trend of increasingly larger housing that we have experienced over the past century is about to go into reverse. But with increasingly fewer of us living in each one, we should not mind a bit.

23 Our Home Comforts Have Never Been Greater

There isn't a house in Ireland today where living conditions resemble those at the start of the twentieth century. At that time, most people had to use a local water pump for their supply – only in newly built houses was running water beginning to be provided. Toilets were outside in their own outhouses, with only the well-off enjoying indoor lavatories.[11]

Houses did not have bathrooms. A galvanised-steel bath was filled with heated water from the range for bathing. Either a cast-iron range or an open fire was used for cooking as well as for heating the kitchen area, while open coal or turf fires were used in other parts of the house. The fuel was stored in an outhouse or, in older urban houses, in cellars accessed from the street by coal-holes. Oil lamps and candles provided lighting, with gas or locally generated electricity available in urban locations.

Most people experienced little change in the first half of the century. The 1946 census revealed that less than a quarter of houses had an indoor lavatory and only 15 per cent had a fixed bath. A sharp divide was evident between urban and rural areas. More than a third of all dwellings in urban and suburban areas had a fixed bath, but that compared to just 4 per cent in rural areas. Over half of all urban households had an indoor lavatory by this time, but less than 7 per cent of rural-dwellers did – although urban households were more likely to share their facilities with another family.

The percentage of households with various utilities in each decade

SOURCE: CENTRAL STATISTICS OFFICE

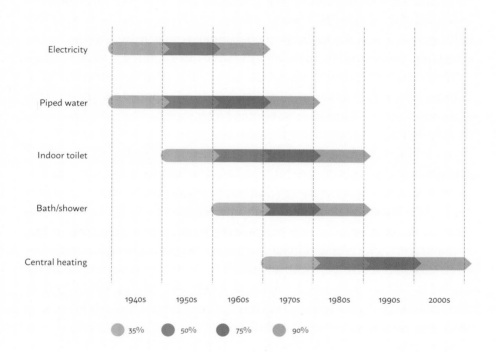

Why are these conditions so entirely unfamiliar to us today? It is due to the 'barely discernible but relentless' improvements in living standards over many decades, as Ellen Rowley puts it. The infographic shows that the vast majority of households lacked electricity, piped water, an indoor toilet, a bath and central heating in the 1940s. It was not until the 1950s that more than half of households acquired electricity and piped water.

Although practically all households had an electricity supply a decade later, it was not until the 1970s that nearly all had piped water.

Most houses had indoor toilets by the 1960s but it was not until the 80s that nearly all did; similarly with a fixed bath or shower. Central heating is a relatively new phenomenon: it began to appear in a large number of houses in the 1970s but it was into the 2000s before nearly all houses had this in place.

'The Dublin artisan housing that developed at the turn of the twentieth century and into the 1910s had toilets out in the yard,' explains Ellen Rowley. 'When the big housing programme got underway from 1932 through to the 1940s, all of those were built with an indoor toilet but no sense of an indoor bathroom. There was a tin bath stowed under a table in the kitchen.' It was only after World War II that bathrooms were incorporated in new housing.

There was no national electricity service before independence. Local authorities and private companies generated and supplied electricity in the main urban areas. Only 45,000 homes had a service when the Electricity Supply Board (ESB) was established in 1927.[12]

One of the first major initiatives of the newly formed Irish Free State was aimed at delivering energy independence. The decision was taken to harness the energy of the River Shannon by building a hydroelectric power plant. The Shannon scheme, commonly referred to by its geographical location at Ardnacrusha, was sufficiently large to meet Ireland's entire national electricity demand in its early years of operation and to make our electricity sector 100 per cent renewable.[13] Once it was up and running, the ESB had a transmission network ready to transfer the electricity nationwide. This gave Ireland the first fully integrated national electricity service in the world.

Although electricity connections had reached 240,000 by the mid-1940s, the vast majority were in urban areas. Practically none of the country's 400,000 rural dwellings had any service.[14] A determined effort was undertaken to electrify the entire country with the introduction of the Rural Electrification Scheme in 1946. It took twenty years to extend supply to every parish. However, it was not until the 1970s that 90 per cent of rural homes were connected and the total number of houses and businesses on the national grid exceeded one million for the first time.[15]

Increasing building standards over the decades ensured that what were once luxuries became commonplace. By the 1960s new houses were obliged to contain a separate bathroom with a toilet, hot-water facilities, proper insulation, lighting, ventilation, laundry and cooking facilities and adequate storage and shelving. Central heating then became the norm in houses built from the 1970s.[16]

Our homes have never been more comfortable. We no longer need to brave the elements to fetch water or fuel for the fire or to go to the toilet! But these are not the only technologies that transformed our homes and what we do with our time in them – what followed was the rise of the household appliance.

We Own More Time-Saving Appliances Than Ever

The arrival of electric-powered household appliances has transformed our lives in the past half-century. How we store and prepare food, how we clean our clothes, how we communicate with each other and how we access information and entertain ourselves have been transformed beyond all recognition.

Fifty years ago, only half of all Irish households had a fridge. Many households had to buy their food fresh and consume it within a day or two, before going shopping again for the following day's dinner. Great strides were made, however, as the electricity network expanded nationally. By the end of the 1970s more than eight in ten households had acquired a fridge and by the end of the 80s it was ubiquitous. This transformed food shopping from a daily affair to a weekly one. In turn, this encouraged the growth of supermarkets at the expense of specialist stores such as butchers or fishmongers, which only provided items for a meal or two.

The time required to cook food also reduced dramatically with the introduction of the microwave. The technology became affordable in the late 1980s and half of all households had one by the mid-1990s. (I admit to being initially cautious about standing in front of our new microwave when it was in use, just in case some of those waves escaped and inadvertently cooked my kidneys!) Their adoption stimulated the development of prepared meals that could simply be heated in the microwave and were then ready to eat. This reduced the average meal preparation time by about a third, freeing us up for other things.[17]

Percentages of households without various appliances over time

SOURCE: CENTRAL STATISTICS OFFICE

No refrigerator	No microwave	No washing machine	No tumble dryer
1987 – 3%	2000 – 29%	2000 – 7%	2006 – 35%
1980 – 14%	1995 – 53%	1987 – 23%	2000 – 58%
1973 – 46%	1987 – 94%	1973 – 56%	1980 – 85%

No telephone landline	No mobile phone	No home computer	No internet access
2000 – 11%	2016 – 3%	2016 – 19%	2016 – 13%
1987 – 46%	2000 – 56%	2005 – 44%	2005 – 55%
1973 – 79%	1995 – 96%	1987 – 94%	2000 – 80%

The acquisition of washing machines followed closely behind refrigerators. Most households did not have one in the mid-1970s but nearly all did by the end of 90s. Tumble dryers were a much more recent invention. Although they were available to purchase in the 70s, most households still did not have one in the early noughties and the most recent figures suggest only two-thirds of houses contain one today.

The impact of automating clothes cleaning on the time spent on housework was dramatic. Although we do not have extensive data for Ireland, research in the USA shows that the time women spent on household chores dropped hugely as these new technologies were adopted.[18] The time spent on core housework more than halved between the mid-1960s and today, freeing up time for women to devote to childcare, shopping or getting jobs outside the home.[19]

Person-to-person communication is so extraordinarily easy nowadays that it is hard to appreciate how unconnected most people were throughout the twentieth century.

The first telephone exchange was opened in Dublin in 1880 with five subscribers. That number had grown to 12,500 by the time of Ireland's independence in 1922, half of them outside of Dublin.[20] The system was entirely manual, requiring operators to sit in local exchanges waiting for callers to ring and ask to be connected to another named subscriber. An automatic exchange system was introduced for Dublin in the late 1920s, but it was not until the 1960s that the rest of the country was automated and the job of telephone operator was entirely eliminated.

Businesses were the first to adopt the use of telephones so residential lines were few in number for many decades. By 1950 just 2 per cent of households had a connection. The total number of phone calls made in the country equated to just 23 per person per year – an average of one call per person every fortnight![21]

The analogue phone system was not sophisticated. You had to hang up the phone at both ends to disconnect a call, for example. I can clearly remember my father yelling down the phone to a fellow graphic designer trying to get his attention. The caller forgot to hang up his phone after the call and proceeded to work away with music blaring in his studio, so he couldn't hear my dad shouting. Someone had to be sent around in person to knock on his door and to get him to hang up the phone so that my father's company line was free to accept calls again!

Nine in ten households had a landline by the turn of this century, but then the numbers started to go in reverse. Who wants to use a shared line in a household when you can have a personal phone that allows someone to reach you wherever you may be? The rapid growth of mobile telephony is making residential landlines redundant.

No household technology has been adopted as fast as mobile telephones. In 1995 there was a mobile phone in less than 5 per cent of households. Just five years later, nearly half of households had a mobile (or more than one). Today, they are entirely ubiquitous.

The initial impact of having a phone with you at all times was to increase the number of calls we made to each other and to boost written communication through texts. However, the introduction of smartphones has transformed how we use them and impacted on many other areas of our lives. Our mobile phone is now our camera, our alarm clock, our watch, our calendar, our diary, our wallet, our newspaper, our games console and our portable TV. And it is reducing our interest in buying all of these other devices for ourselves and for our homes.

Mobile phones and tablets are also impacting on ownership of another household technology: the home computer.

The first organisation in Ireland to acquire a computer was the Irish Sugar Company, which bought one in 1957 to calculate the annual payments it made to sugar-beet growers.[22] It took until the early 1980s for computers to arrive in the home in the form of Commodore's VIC-20 and Sinclair's ZX Spectrum. They were initially positioned as teach-your-kids-programming devices, although they became increasingly popular as games consoles.

Only 6 per cent of households had a computer in 1987, but as their functionality and ease of use increased significantly, so ownership took off. Most homes in Ireland had one by the early 2000s and more than eight in ten households had one by 2016. However, at least before Covid-19, ownership had begun to decrease as mobile devices – and dedicated games consoles – can deliver similar functionality.

The one modern 'utility' that feeds our home computers, mobile devices and increasingly our TVs and other household devices is broadband internet access. Although the internet is over 50 years old, household internet access only became available in the mid-1990s. In just over a decade, more than half of our homes were connected. A decade later, only one in ten households were left unconnected.

With so many devices now relying on our internet connection for increasingly complex services that use more and more data, it is no surprise that access to high-speed broadband has become an issue of concern to so many. And just as with electrification in the 1950s, rural access to this modern 'utility' will require political will and government investment to ensure access for all.

We discovered during the Covid lockdowns that we no longer need to leave our houses for anything. Everything you need to look after yourself and to be entertained is either already there or can be ordered on your internet-connected device and delivered to your door. Many of us were educated and worked without having to walk out the front door. That would simply not have been possible twenty years ago. We have undergone a truly remarkable transformation.

Having said that, we are able to travel far further and far easier than our ancestors were ever able to. And we generally choose to do so.

We Have Never Been More Mobile

The number of motor vehicles on Irish roads has never been greater. More than a quarter of a million vehicles are registered for the first time annually. We are not yet back to the peak year of 2007 when over 300,000 vehicles were registered, but the pre-coronavirus trend was a restoration of the consistent and unrelenting growth seen since the 1950s.

Transport in Ireland was predominantly undertaken by rail, by city trams and by horse and cart at the time of independence. An increase in the number of motorised vehicles, however, required the new Free State to introduce a uniform code of hand signals for police and motorists in 1923 and standard road markings and signage in 1926.

Henry Ford had opened his first European factory on the site of an old racecourse in County Cork in 1917. His father hailed from nearby Clonakilty. Originally manufacturing tractors, from 1921 the factory started building cars as well.

When Ireland's trade disputes with Britain boiled over into an economic war in the early 1930s, Britain slapped tariffs on their cars, and the number of imports to Ireland fell dramatically. Motor dealer Frederick Maurice Summerfield suggested to the Irish government that it should respond by incentivising car assembly here and stimulating an entirely new industrial sector.

New Cars on the Road Have Increased Ten-Fold over the Past 60 Years

Number of vehicles licensed for the first time, 1954–2020

SOURCE: CENTRAL STATISTICS OFFICE

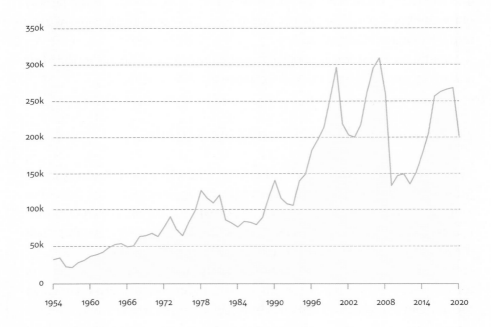

Tax concessions were introduced and within six months there were 13 assembly plants operating. They imported cars in completely knocked-down form, with the components taken from the manufacturing line overseas and shipped here for assembly. In this way, Ireland became the first-ever place of manufacture outside of Germany for the Volkswagen

Beetle in 1950. (Car assembly continued as an industry here up until the 1980s when the Volkswagen and Ford plants closed. It ultimately became more cost-effective to construct cars in larger factories servicing entire continents rather than single countries.)

By the onset of World War II there were just over 95,000 private cars registered – one for every 44 people.[23] It was in the 1950s and 1960s that our motoring boom really got underway. Leanne Blaney has written about the growth of Ireland's car culture: 'Rural Ireland in particular entertained a romanticised notion that cars could provide their owners and passengers with a form of escapism from the drudgery of daily life on farms and in small communities. Young people and women availed of the opportunities presented by cars to travel greater distances than previously possible and to enjoy the relative freedom that independent motorised transit offered – much to the chagrin of authorities in the Catholic church, who feared immorality would ensue.'[24]

Growth in car ownership facilitated the growth of city suburbs. Areas that were previously hard to get to became easily accessible. The capacity of a car boot made weekly grocery shopping more practical. But the car more fundamentally transformed the retail sector: the 1960s saw the development of the first shopping centres in Stillorgan and Cornelscourt in County Dublin, designed specifically to be accessed by car.

In 1996 the total number of licensed private cars reached the one million mark. Less than two decades later, in 2014, it reached two million.[25] Have we too many cars in Ireland nowadays? By European standards, Ireland still has room for growth. We have 444 passenger cars for every 1,000 people in the country today, but the European Union average is 15 per cent higher.

The increasing awareness of cars' negative environmental impact, in terms of both carbon emissions and air quality, may slow their growth in the coming years. I expect that the rising popularity of car-sharing and the introduction of self-driving cars will remove the need for many of us to ever own another car at some point. So although the adoption of personal motor transport has undoubtedly transformed Irish society over the past century, the shape that this will take in the future appears uncertain. But whatever happens, we are unlikely to surrender any of the increased mobility that we have come to value so highly.

26 Our Leisure Time Has Grown Enormously

Number of visitors to Dublin Zoo to the nearest 100,000 people,
1922–2019

SOURCE: CATHERINE DE COURCY, DUBLIN ZOO: AN ILLUSTRATED HISTORY

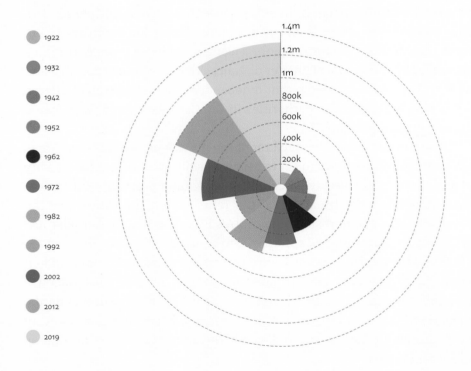

With our household appliances hard at work on our behalf and meal preparation time only a fraction of what it used to be, we have never had more time for our leisure pursuits. And with the ability to travel anywhere parked right outside our front door, it is no surprise that we are increasingly going places to keep ourselves amused.

We do not have to look far for evidence of that. Who doesn't have a fond childhood memory of visiting Dublin Zoo? The zoo is Ireland's leading domestic tourism attraction. It has added approximately 100,000 annual visitors in each decade for the past hundred years.

Dublin Zoo opened for business in 1831, making it the fourth-oldest in the world after the ones in Vienna, Paris and London. Zoos were initially established as genteel pleasure gardens where the wealthy could 'promenade' and socialise with their peers. Dublin Zoo took a more egalitarian approach from its earliest days and admitted the general public for a penny on Sundays.

'In the 1920s most of the visitors were very much the same as they are now: families from Dublin and from around the country who had come up for the day,' explains Catherine de Courcy, who has written the definitive history of Dublin Zoo.[26] 'At that point the zoo had a good range of animals including lions, tigers, chimpanzees and elephants. The big difference between then and now was that young visitors could ride on the elephant, play with the lion cubs and feed the chimpanzees!'

Most days, access was limited to the members of the Royal Zoological Society of Dublin and their guests. In the late nineteenth and early twentieth century, members were predominantly from the professional and wealthier classes, many of whom were Protestant. The members of the zoo's leadership council were noticeably loyal to the British Crown – at one point they even discussed the idea of raising a statue of Queen Victoria on the grounds – so they found the establishment of an independent Ireland very concerning. However, the Minister for Agriculture and the Minister for Local Government of the new Free State, Patrick Hogan and Ernest Blythe, both made a point of becoming members, the small government grant was continued, and Dublin Zoo was welcomed into the fabric of the new State.

Visitor numbers trundled along at between 150,000 and 200,000 a year throughout the 1920s and 1930. Surprisingly, it was the turbulence brought on by World War II that started to see visitor numbers rise sharply in the early 1940s. 'It's a phenomenon of zoos,' says de Courcy, 'people turn to [them] when there's chaos. You are there with the animals and you really forget about all of the other distressful things that are going on.' Fuel rationing probably helped too – the zoo became one of the most accessible places for a family day out for Dubliners.

The following decades were a golden age of growth as Dublin Zoo set about acquiring animals that they knew the public would want to see such as sea lions, giraffes, rhinoceros, monkeys and snakes. Tea parties on the lawn were organised for young chimpanzees. Giraffes, tigers and a rhinoceros named Ringo were born. And the opportunity for an elephant ride was still there.

Ireland's growing Catholic middle class began to change the composition of the Society's membership and the focus of Dublin Zoo. 'A parent now joined as a family member in order to bring the kids to the zoo regularly,' explains de Courcy. 'They weren't wealthy families – they would have come for a half day or brought their own picnics. They had no interest in the whole society scene.' The strawberry breakfasts, garden parties, dances and fêtes finally fizzled out in the 1970s.

Visitor numbers declined during the 1980s, the first decade in which there had been a decrease. 'Old-fashioned enclosures were no longer adequate and zoos were expected to create habitats that allowed for the animals' natural instincts. Dublin Zoo simply did not have enough money to do much with the animals' enclosures,' says de Courcy. Overcrowding became an issue.

The financial outlook was bleak too. Costs were rising faster than gate receipts and it had no other source of income. The zoo was heading towards closure. By December 1989 there was not enough money to pay the wages.

Bertie Ahern saved Dublin Zoo. As Minister of Finance, he provided sufficient funding to pay off debts and to keep it going. A redevelopment plan for the rescue of the zoo was drafted and Bertie ensured that the government provided £15 million (€19 million) to fund it in 1993. One condition was attached: the Royal Zoological Society of Ireland had to drop the word 'Royal' from its name, 71 years after Ireland's independence from the UK.

The space problem was resolved a few years later. The official residence of the President of Ireland, Áras an Uachtaráin, was right next door. The residence had a large lake and extensive grounds for the relaxation of the President. Bertie, now Taoiseach, secured the transfer of these lands to the zoo in 1997 with the support of President Mary McAleese, nearly doubling its size.

The new land allowed the Zoo to provide its animals with the space they needed and to build state-of-the-art habitats for them. The first of these, the African Plains, opened in 2000 with gradual development of new habitats over the next decade. Visitor numbers grew again as the new facilities were unveiled. The western lowland gorillas were the last of the African animals to move in in 2011. The number of visitors that year exceeded one million for the first time.

Ireland was in the midst of a deep recession at this time, yet visitor numbers were reaching new heights. As de Courcy pointed out, zoos can often be a place of solace during times of turbulence. But there were other factors at play: 'The first baby elephant was born in 2007, the second was born in 2008. And there were baby rhinos, baby giraffes, baby tapirs and others. Now there was a different sort of excitement and interest for families visiting: young, exotic animals living in natural social groups in naturalistic settings.' When people had to cut back on their international holidays, the zoo was well placed for a domestic leisure trip.

Visitor numbers in 2019 were more than 12 times greater than they were back in 1922. And if Dublin Zoo was amongst the world's first, today it is amongst the world's best. 'Zoo professionals now come to Dublin to look at the animal care, the habitat design, the management of the zoo and how Dublin Zoo has implemented a conservation strategy at every level of its operation.'

Its growth in visitors and its change in membership reflects the changing nature of wealth in the country and the increasing leisure time at our disposal. Its world-class status reflects our excellence in infrastructure development and the education level and professionalism of our people.

Learning More

IRELAND HAS UNDERGONE NOTHING SHORT OF AN EDUCATIONAL REVOLUTION OVER THE PAST CENTURY. IF I HAD TO CHOOSE JUST ONE REASON WHY IRELAND IS AS SUCCESSFUL AS IT IS TODAY, THIS WOULD BE IT. EACH GENERATION HAS BEEN EDUCATED LONGER, AND TO A HIGHER STANDARD, THAN THE PREVIOUS ONE.

I LIKE TO THINK of our progress as being on the 'education escalator'. Primary schools, secondary schools and universities all existed 100 years ago. But although as many children as today were getting on the first steps of the escalator to begin their educational journey, back then they nearly all got off at the first floor. Few took the escalator on to second level.

Our success has been firstly in terms of getting more and more children to take the escalator to the next level. It has also been to get more of those children who stepped onto that escalator to stay with it until it reaches its final destination, and not to jump off early.

So few children went on to third level a century ago that you could hardly think of there being an escalator to it all. It was more like a badly lit back stairwell. Building that escalator to connect second and third level over the past four or five decades has been revolutionary. It has resulted in the Irish being amongst the best-educated people on the planet. The beneficial effects have been experienced both in our national economic performance and in individuals' life satisfaction. Yet I believe we are only at the beginning of seeing how this education revolution will unfold.

So what did education in Ireland look like back in 1922 and how has it changed since?

 The Number of Children in Second-Level Education Has Soared

Full-time student enrolments in primary and second level, 1925–2015

SOURCE: CSO, DEPARTMENT OF EDUCATION[1]

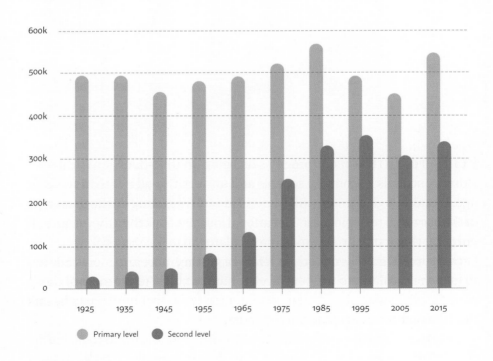

You might be surprised by the fact that the number of children enrolled in primary schools has remained roughly the same throughout the past century, even though our population has increased hugely in recent decades. There were just under a half a million children enrolled in the early 1920s and there are just over a half a million enrolled today.

Free primary education had been introduced in the nineteenth century and enrolment was compulsory up until the age of 12. However, children could remain in primary school until the age of 14 if their parents could afford not to have their teenage child bring in an income for the family. All children from 5 to 11, as well as many 12- and 13-year-olds, were therefore included on the primary school rolls back in the 1920s. Enrolment was not a guarantee of attendance, mind – only around two-thirds of children attended on any one day.

One of the greatest differences between primary schooling then and now lies in the number and the size of schools. 'There were 6,000 national schools in 1922 and today we only have 3,000,' explains Professor Áine Hyland, who led the School of Education in University College Cork. 'Because of the lack of transport, schools were much closer together and therefore much smaller with only two or three teachers.'

The churches owned and ran the schools, although the State funded them. Around 95 per cent of national schools were under the patronage of the Catholic Church on the foundation of the State, with the balance predominately run by the Church of Ireland.

The numbers who continued on the educational escalator to second-level education grew slowly. It was the 1940s before a third of primary school pupils progressed to second level, and by the early 1960s it was around 60 per cent. Aside from the fact that pupils had to pay to attend, there were simply not that many secondary schools in places – making it hard for pupils to get to one, even if they could afford to. This was mainly because the Catholic Church viewed secondary education as a means of preparing young men for the priesthood and, to a lesser extent, young women for religious life. The bishops set up schools in their diocese for this purpose and were very protective of them.

The Catholic Church's control of the educational system ran deep. The government's 'Council of Education' report on the primary school curriculum in 1954 emphasised the religious purpose of education. The first purpose of primary school, it said, was to assist parents in their duty 'to train their children in the fear and love of God'.[2] The Council's 1962 report on secondary schools similarly concluded that the 'ultimate purpose of secondary schools in Ireland is to prepare their pupils to be God-fearing and responsible citizens'. So much for providing children with the skills they would need to earn a livelihood!

This religious-influenced conservatism went further in seeking to restrict the equality of opportunity for Irish citizens. At a time when free second-level education had become the norm in other European countries, the Council's report dismissed the suggestion that it be implemented in Ireland, describing this as 'utopian'.

But you can't hold back the hopes and aspirations of a nation. The need for radical change was increasingly evident. The 1950s were an economic disaster for the country and emigration reached extraordinary heights. Sending our people out into the world made it self-evident that we had become educational laggards amongst our European neighbours. 'By the mid-60s, more than half of our young people had left school by the age of 15 and most of them had emigrated to low-level jobs,' points out Hyland. 'That's the generation that, very sadly, ended up in parts of London and New York with the men working on building sites and the women as domestics who had very deprived lives. We certainly failed at least half of our population during the 1940s and 50s compared to other countries.'

When Seán Lemass became Taoiseach in 1959, he brought a new economic vision of export-led economic growth. Professor Hyland was part of the team that produced a seminal 'Investment in Education' report in the mid-60s, which for the first time comprehensively analysed the status of Irish education. 'The statistical analysis pointed out that if we continued as we were in education then there would be a serious shortfall of qualified young men and women to work in these industries even if we succeeded in attracting them. That is what woke up the government to rethink what education was about.'

'Education, from then on, was seen as an investment in Ireland's future and in Ireland's economy – the thinking changed completely.' The government decided, for the first time, to invest directly in establishing a new type of secondary school: so-called 'comprehensive schools' aimed to combine both academic and vocational training under one roof, initially in thinly populated rural areas. The Catholic bishops objected vigorously, calling the initiative a 'revolutionary step'.[3] Yes, indeed it was. And thankfully the government proceeded regardless. Four of these new schools opened in the 1960s, laying the ground for the introduction of 'community schools' throughout the country from the 1970s.

Arguably the most transformative decision of all was made by Minister for Education Donogh O'Malley in 1966. Some say that he didn't tell anyone what he was planning before he announced it. He certainly did not tell his fellow Cabinet members or officials in the Department of Finance. At a weekend seminar of the National Union of Journalists in Dún Laoghaire, O'Malley made a sweeping commitment to provide 'full educational opportunity' for all children from primary to university level, and he announced the introduction of free second-level education to at least Intermediate (Junior) Certificate level by September of the following year.

The Secretary of the Department of Finance, T.K. Whitaker, was furious and complained to Lemass about O'Malley's disregard for official procedures. His department fought to modify or delay its introduction, but the Cabinet endorsed O'Malley's unauthorised initiative and went even further, also approving a nationwide free transport scheme to ensure that all children could get to their school.

There was no longer a fee to use the education escalator to access second-level education. Nearly 90 per cent of secondary schools offered free education for the 1967–8 year and the impact was immediate. The total pupil enrolment in secondary schools surged from 103,600 in September 1966 to 118,800 in September 1967 – an extraordinary increase of over 15,000 in a single year and more than double what the Department of Education had expected. This accelerated rate of expansion was sustained for the remainder of the decade. In just three years, the secondary school population grew by nearly 40 per cent.

Change was implemented in the primary sector too. The 'Investment in Education' report revealed that three-quarters of primary schools taught fewer than 100 pupils and that more than 700 schools had just a single teacher. The benefits of consolidation were self-evident and the government adopted a policy of the amalgamation of small schools. Once again, several Catholic bishops opposed the move and the Minister for Education was labelled 'a dictator'.[4] Nevertheless, 1,100 small schools were closed within a decade.

More fundamentally, the primary school curriculum was revolutionised for the first time since independence. Rather than turning children into infant Irish nationalists or putting the fear of God into them, the aim was to equip each child for further education – i.e. for progression up the education escalator. It provided a wider range of subjects, with a greater focus on social, environmental and scientific education, the arts and physical education.

The number of students in primary school peaked at 568,000 in 1987 as the 1980s baby boom reached its zenith. Today we are experiencing the 'echo' of that boom as those children have grown up to be parents in turn and primary school attendance has risen again to match its previous peak.

Second-level attendance grew massively through the 1970s and 80s, driven by greater numbers of primary school students opting to avail of free secondary education, by more pupils remaining to complete their education up to Leaving Cert level and by the country's growing youth population. Our level of education was utterly transformed within just two decades of free education being introduced.

The size of our secondary schools has been transformed as a result. Before the introduction of free education, three-quarters of our secondary schools had fewer than 200 pupils. Today, fifty years later, merely one in eight of our schools are that small. Half of them now have over 500 pupils each.

Religious control of secondary education has changed radically too. In 1966–7, the year before free schooling was introduced, just less than half of all secondary school teachers were priests or nuns. By 1997–8, the last year for which figures were produced, less than 5 per cent of secondary school teachers were members of religious orders. The professional lay teacher had entirely taken over.

Utopia had arrived!

28 More Pupils Than Ever Are Being Taught in Irish

National school pupils taught in Irish, 1976–2016

SOURCE: CENTRAL STATISTICS OFFICE

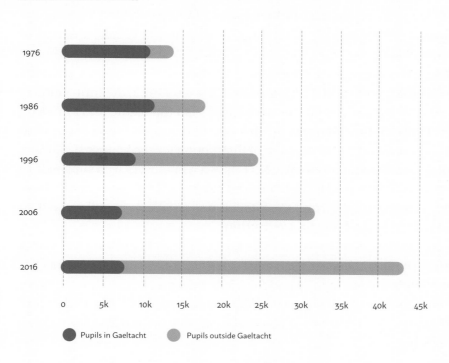

Despite 14 years of compulsory tuition in the Irish language in primary and secondary school, my grasp of it is appalling. When I finished my Leaving Certificate, I knew I had done well enough in all other subjects to secure a place to study psychology in University College Dublin. However, passing Irish – an entry requirement – was another issue.

On results day I joined the queue outside the headmaster's office to hear my fate. When my turn came he called me in, sat me down, opened his folder and proceeded to read out my grades, subject by subject, with his commentary on each grade. I wasn't listening. I leaned over and ran my eye down the page. Irish: a D grade on the pass paper. Mission accomplished!

I'm not sure I would have given me a pass mark if I had been the examiner, but I'd like to say a big 'thank you' to whoever gave me the benefit of the doubt. I know my experience with Irish is far from unique. Despite the best intentions of the State's founding fathers, making learning the language compulsory for most students has not delivered a nation of fluent speakers.

When the provisional government of the Irish Free State assumed responsibility for national education on 1 February 1922, they immediately issued new regulations on the teaching of Irish that came into force that Saint Patrick's Day. Henceforth Irish was to be taught for one hour each day and used as the sole medium of instruction for the youngest children in all national primary schools. 'No English whatsoever was supposed to exist,' says Professor Hyland, 'but the teachers themselves didn't have enough Irish to do that, and the families and the children still wanted an emphasis on English reading and writing.'

This promotion of Irish wasn't for the benefit of children per se – it was for the benefit of the State. As Taoiseach Éamon de Valera later said, 'We cannot fulfil our destiny as a nation unless we are an Irish nation – and we can only be truly that if we are an Irish-speaking nation.'[5] The curriculum was further reformed to emphasise Irish culture and history as well as the language.

Needless to say, De Valera's dream never came to pass. Schooling alone cannot change a culture and a society. There wasn't a broader buy-in from society as a whole, so there was very little else being provided through the medium of Irish. The educational aspiration was retained despite the reality, however. It was not until 1971 that the State withdrew the requirement to teach everything through Irish, even though it was being entirely ignored.

Parents who were committed to the language's survival responded by starting to demand a change in how their children were taught. 'I myself grew up in an Irish-speaking family,' says Hyland, 'but then there were no Gaelscoileanna [Irish-language schools], so I ended up having to go a school where in theory everything was taught through Irish but in practice it was taught through English. Families like that persisted into the second half of the twentieth century.' And they believed they could do things better, leading to a parental-led movement for change.

It took time to convince the powers that be that you did not have to be a religious organisation to run a school. The first multidenominational primary school in Ireland was founded by parents in Dalkey, County Dublin, in 1978. Others followed in the early 1980s and paved the way for a new approach to establishing schools. 'The Department of Education and the ministers of education finally conceded that it wasn't only the bishops who could be patrons of schools,' explains Hyland. 'You see significant growth in Gaelscoileanna from the 1990s because it's only then that the government agrees that the Irish language can have its own patronage system.'

A new organisation, An Foras Pátrúnachta, was established in 1993 to provide patronage for Irish-medium schools and to help parents establish Gaelscoileanna in their areas. 'It leads quite quickly to a growth in the number of Irish language schools. If you have staff whose job it is to encourage and support groups of parents around the country to set up schools then of course you will get a growth because the groundswell is there anyway, but it's very, very difficult for a group of parents to do that on their own.'

The number of primary school pupils attending Irish-language schools has more than tripled in just four decades. Amazingly, all that growth has come from schools outside native-speaking Gaeltacht areas. While only 8 per cent of primary school pupils today are taught through Irish, we must recognise that the enthusiasm and toil of parents succeeded where officials, ministers and Taoisigh before them had failed. Irish-language education has never looked so healthy.

29 Pupil-to-Teacher Ratios Have Never Been Better

Pupil-to-teacher ratios in primary and secondary level, 1970–2020

SOURCE: DEPARTMENT OF EDUCATION[6]

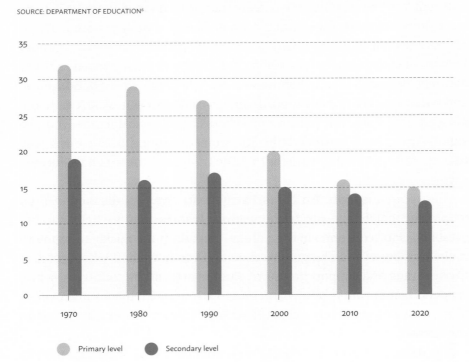

Primary level   Secondary level

Now that we have record numbers of students in our schools, what can we say about the quality of the education they are receiving? One way of assessing this might be to look at the number of students each teacher has to work with. Are class sizes sufficiently small to enable each student to get the attention they need to perform at their best?

For the State's first five decades the pupil-to-teacher ratio remained essentially unchanged. There were between 33 and 36 pupils for every primary school teacher.

That average, however, concealed stark variation. There were multiple small national schools with more than their fair share of teachers. As late as 1960 two-thirds of schools had only one or two teachers. And there were nearly a thousand schools with a daily attendance of fewer than 30 pupils. With fewer pupils for each teacher to look after in these small schools, it meant that large schools in urban areas had much greater numbers in their classrooms – many of them had classes of more than 50. The amalgamation of these smaller schools from the mid-1960s reduced the variations between institutions; and increased government investment in education began the process of reducing the average number of pupils per teacher.

Over the course of the 1970s and 80s the average primary school pupil-to-teacher ratio fell from 32 to 27 pupils. However, during the Celtic Tiger era, government investment in education grew hugely and the ratio fell to just 16 pupils for every one teacher by 2010. That is a remarkable doubling of teaching resources in just four decades.

Many of the additional teachers are not teaching mainstream classes but rather are providing support to select numbers of pupils who have special educational needs, who require English-language support or who benefit from Home School Community Liaison services. They are helping to make our educational system more inclusive for all. The average primary-school class size has remained virtually unchanged for the last twenty years at 24 or 25 pupils, after being reduced from more than 30 pupils in the 1980s.

Improvements in second-level ratios have been more modest although nevertheless important – from 19 pupils per teacher in 1970 to 13 today. While secondary schools were better staffed than primary schools to begin with, their student numbers have grown hugely since the 1960s, so to improve their ratio while taking in more and more pupils was a notable achievement. It is one that has been delivered thanks to large increases in government funding for second level.

So do we need to reduce our class sizes even further? Or have we reached the optimal pupil-to-teacher ratio? Professor Áine Hyland believes that we could probably reduce it a little further, though not a lot more improvement is needed. 'Below a certain level there is no evidence that reducing class size makes any significant different to pupil achievement [...] Ireland is a good example of that because, if you look at class size, Ireland has one of the biggest class sizes in Europe at primary level and yet we are one of the highest performing countries internationally. You come to a certain point where, quite frankly, no matter what the teachers think, there is no evidence that pupil performance improves.'

Ensuring that we have high-quality teachers is critical. 'If you do not have well-trained teachers, no matter how much money you put into education, it's not going to improve the situation.'

In that respect, we can be proud to say, Ireland is a world leader. 'We are probably the only country where the top 15 per cent of our Leaving Certificate students apply for primary school teaching. That is unprecedented. Our primary school teachers are among the most academically able in the world.'

One other factor that has contributed to the high quality of our education is a legacy of the Catholic Church's approach to organising schooling. 'Because of the Church control of schooling, our schools are very local. They have traditionally been parish schools and nowadays that is regarded as a very good way of running an education system,' says Hyland.

'Initially it was the parish priest who was the manager of the school, but since the mid-60s it's a board of management, which includes parents, teachers and local people with legal expertise, financial expertise and so on. All our boards of management are totally voluntary, that's something I think that no other country in the world has. The people who volunteer to run our schools are extraordinarily committed and able. A combination of a good school principal and a local board of management – which is looking out to make sure their own children are getting a good education – has worked very well.'

'Ironically, what we might have thought 50 or 60 years ago as being the undue control of the Church has had a very positive outcome: we have a very good structure and very high-quality education because of that.'

30 Second-Level Education Completion Rates Continue to Grow

Percentage of students entering secondary school who completed their Leaving Certificate, 1960–2010

SOURCE: DEPARTMENT OF EDUCATION[7]

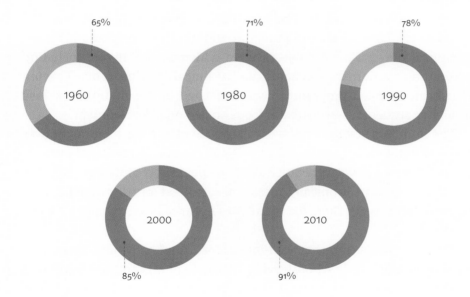

We have seen a huge growth in the numbers of children participating in second-level education over the past fifty years. But all those who started their second-level education did not actually finish it. A large number got off the education escalator before it arrived at the second floor.

Amongst those who started first year in a secondary school in 1960 – when it was still only the preserve of those who could afford to pay fees – a third did not complete their Leaving Certificate five or six years later. Those who entered vocational post-primary schools did not have the possibility of progressing past their Group Certificate (similar to today's Junior Cert).

Given that a large minority never made it past primary level at all, this means that fewer than one in five children completed their education to Leaving Cert level in the early 1960s.

The numbers of pupils increased sharply as free secondary education arrived in the late 1960s so a lot more children gained a Leaving Cert qualification in the 70s and 80s. However, the proportion of those who entered secondary school and saw it through to completion increased only slowly. Amongst those entering in 1980, three in ten still did not complete the exam.

Action had to be taken. The Leaving Cert programme was changed to make it more suitable to students' differing interests and abilities. Technical and practical subjects were added in the 1970s, including accounting, economics, mechanics and technical drawing. A new Leaving Certificate Applied programme was launched in the mid-90s for less academic students, with a greater focus on personal development.

The numbers staying on the escalator began to grow a bit faster over time, although partly inadvertently. As Professor Hyland explains: 'In the 1980s and 90s we were stuck at 80–85 per cent completion, and then the recession came. Ironically, recessions are good for education because there are no jobs out there for 15-, 16- or 17-year-olds who would have left school early.'

Then we discovered that well-intentioned unemployment assistance was encouraging early school leaving. 'We had a number of such incentives in the early 90s,' says Hyland. 'For example, a young person who left school early and went to a Youthreach programme would get £30 a week to attend; so, of course, they were dropping out of school good-o to go to these so-called training centres. There was very little training going on in them! I remember visiting some and the kids were sitting on the wall outside waiting for their envelopes to come on a Friday. It took a while for us to realise that we were inadvertently encouraging a certain amount of early school leaving – then some of those incentives were removed.'

Today, only 8 per cent of those who start in first year in secondary school fail to complete their Leaving Cert. We have the second-highest completion rate of secondary level education within the European Union.[8] That's hugely important for the country's economic development – as it is for an individual's life satisfaction – given that fewer than one in five jobs in the EU are filled by people who do not complete second level, and that proportion is dropping every year.[9]

 31 ## Half the Population Has Completed Higher Education – a Figure That Has Doubled in Just 20 Years

Percentage of adult population that has completed higher education, 1960–2020

SOURCE: BBVA, CSO[10]

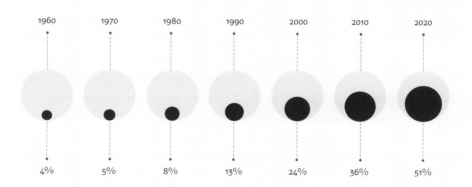

There is no graph that better communicates Ireland's educational revolution than this one. Higher education was only for a small elite fifty years ago. There was no working escalator that allowed pupils to access third level. Less than 5 per cent of adults had completed any form of higher education in 1970. Yet over subsequent decades, that number increased ten-fold! Half of all adults in Ireland today have completed some form of higher education. It is one of the highest figures of any country in Europe.

This didn't happen by accident. The government recognised that we needed to have a skilled workforce if we were to develop an export-orientated economy. The education escalator needed to connect to a new level.

'Up to the early 1960s, almost 90 per cent of entrants to higher education were attending universities. The smaller proportion were going to training colleges – theological courses for the priesthood and teacher education – but the proportion attending higher technical courses was very small,' explains Dr John Walsh of Trinity College Dublin, who has written about our history of higher education.[11] 'The policy-makers realised it wouldn't be possible to achieve the scale of participation they wanted through the universities alone and they wanted institutions that specialised in the higher technological space – what we'd now call STEM.' That's science, technology, engineering and mathematics.

The solution was to create an entirely new education sector: the Regional Technical Colleges (RTCs). Education Minister Donogh O'Malley was central to bringing this about. He established a Steering Committee on Technical Education in 1966 and ordered it to report within a year. It concluded that new colleges should be established to provide education for trade and industry over a wide range of occupations and opportunities for students in rural Ireland who had no real option to go to college unless they got a university scholarship. Everything moved with remarkable speed. The first college opened in 1969–70 and there were seven of them in operation within a decade.

The RTCs offered courses in science and engineering; however, the biggest growth area was in business courses, which, at the time, wasn't a discipline you could study at university. They attracted a rapidly growing proportion of students. 'By the mid-1980s, just 15 years after the first regional colleges had been established, the proportion of new entrants to higher education was evenly divided between the RTC sector and the universities.'

The number of students leaving secondary school who availed of further education grew immensely. 'The level of first-time entrants to third-level courses increased from 10 per cent of the school-leaving age cohort in 1965 to 28 per cent by 1985,' says Walsh.

The numbers attending third level continued to increase steadily. 'The expansion never really stopped. It slowed somewhat in the 90s as the birth rate was lower, but the slack was taken up by the creation of access courses and by the entry of mature students. Then, from 2008, applications again increase dramatically, reflecting the increasing birth rate but also the economic crash.' Recessions can be good for education, don't forget. With fewer jobs available, there are more reasons for students to invest in continuing their education.

The increasing education of the Irish handsomely achieved what the policymakers hoped it would. 'Much of the economic growth during the Celtic Tiger era has been attributed to our highly educated workforce,' says Walsh, 'and there's a lot of research showing that there are significant income benefits for individuals, and significant wider benefits for society.'

I believe that we are only at the beginning of realising the many beneficial effects of being a highly educated country.

6

Earning More

THE ONE REMARKABLE ACHIEVEMENT THAT HAS ENABLED
ALL THE POSITIVE CHANGE THAT I HAVE ILLUSTRATED IS
ECONOMIC GROWTH. IRELAND'S ECONOMIC PERFORMANCE
IN RECENT DECADES HAS BEEN ASTONISHING. THIS IS WHAT
HAS ENABLED US TO INVEST IN IMPROVING EDUCATION, IN
BETTER HEALTH SERVICES, IN UPGRADING OUR HOUSING AND
FITTING THEM OUT WITH THE MOD CONS.

Trailer: A Remarkable Story of Economic Growth

IRELAND'S REMARKABLE ECONOMIC progress has delivered a
higher standard of living for us than for any of our forebears. So time for a
little economic history. Don't let the sound of that put you off – this is the
extraordinary story of Ireland's swings and roundabouts. It's the ups and
downs that have seen us soar to incredible heights and become one of the
richest countries on the planet. Of course, we tripped and stumbled along
the way many times – spraining an ankle or two, bringing us to our knees
and giving us some deep cuts and bruises on occasion.

Let me tell the tale of our first century over six episodes – with a prerequisite cliffhanger at the end of each.

1922–1931 Joining the League of Nations

Attaining independence allowed us to take our place on the world stage. The break with the United Kingdom went smoothly and we joined the League of Nations as an equal partner, albeit one that still traded nearly exclusively with our former countrymen.

What we traded was overwhelmingly agricultural goods, mainly live cattle or beef and dairy. But that was a tough business to be relying on following World War I as global food prices fell sharply. There was no dividend from independence for the majority of the State's workers who were employed by the sector. And there were few opportunities for employment elsewhere. Two-thirds of the island's industrial output originated in what was now Northern Ireland.[1] The Irish Free State was left with just one in ten jobs in industry, and most of those were concentrated in food and drink production.[2]

We had joined a brave new, globalised world but we struggled to benefit from it economically. 'It might strike people as a little unusual: "hang on, wasn't globalisation a later phenomenon?" but there was a pretty deep globalisation that happened in the late nineteenth and early twentieth century that was undone by World War I,' explains Ronan Lyons, Assistant Professor of Economics at Trinity College Dublin. 'There was an attempt in the 1920s to rebuild this and Ireland, as a new country, was trying to take its part. We were very heavily reliant on the British market, but still we had open trade and labour and capital markets.'

While we were working out how to realise the benefits of globalisation, everything changed. The Great Depression started in the United States in late 1929 and became the longest, deepest and most widespread depression of the twentieth century. Worldwide gross domestic product (GDP) fell by around 15 per cent. International trade fell by more than 50 per cent. Unemployment soared everywhere.[3]

Countries turned inward and instigated protectionist policies to try to support their domestic enterprises. Ireland was far from the first to follow this path, but with little to show its citizens by way of the benefits of independence, the people rejected the government of Cumann na nGaedheal in the general election of 1932 and opted for the populist policies of Fianna Fáil, who promised economic self-sufficiency through nationalism. (Sound familiar?)

1932–1957 From Globalisation to Self-sufficiency

The new Fianna Fáil government, with Éamon de Valera as Taoiseach, chose to pick a populist fight with its main trading partner. Tariffs were introduced for a wide range of imported goods and the government stopped repayments to Britain of the loans that tenant farmers had received to purchase their land in the late nineteenth century. Britain retaliated with the imposition of a 20 per cent import duty on Free State agricultural products. Ireland responded in kind by placing a similar duty on British coal, cement, sugar, iron, steel and machinery. The Anglo-Irish Trade War was in full swing.

The UK was a large country with many trading partners. The Irish economy, on the other hand, was largely reliant on agricultural exports to Britain and was badly affected. The Great Depression itself may have had a smaller effect than this trade war that followed it, in the view of Lyons. Many farmers could not sell their cattle or could only do so at a lower price than it had cost to raise them. The government responded by paying bounties to farmers to slaughter their calves in the absence of any possibility of them being exported. They further encouraged a shift from pasture to tillage to drive greater self-sufficiency.

The Irish people may have suffered terribly, but Fianna Fáil benefited electorally from taking on the 'old enemy' and is generally reckoned to have won the war.[4] 'If you're going to act like a mad man, it helps to be a mad man all the way through the negotiations,' says Lyons. 'By sticking resolutely to "we don't care what the economic cost is domestically, we're not going to pay this", eventually Ireland got a pretty good deal out of Britain.' In 1938 the UK agreed to a £10 million lump sum settlement of the £100 million land-loan liability it was owed. Ireland also won the return of its remaining ports left under British control – which would shortly enable the country to remain neutral during World War II.

The rationale for introducing high import tariffs was to encourage the development of domestic industry. It worked in part. Many new manufacturing companies were established. A good number of them were British-owned firms that set up plants here to avoid tariffs that would have applied if they had shipped over the same goods from England. Ireland's textile industry got going during this period, for example. That helped to create new industrial employment, particularly in the cities and larger towns, but it was of insufficient scale to turn Ireland into an industrial powerhouse.

World War II hit households and industry hard as the availability of imports fell, restricting everything from materials for house construction to petrol for cars. The absence of British coal for heating and electricity generation was keenly felt and resulted in another effort at self-sufficiency with the wholescale harvesting of peat as an alternative fuel. Bord na Móna was founded in 1946 to advance this ambition.

Europe was obviously devastated by the war. However, a mammoth redevelopment effort was put in place to rebuild economies and livelihoods afterwards. The 1950s became a golden age of economic growth throughout Europe. But not in Ireland. 'Europe tried to create an open trading network,' explains Lyons, 'in order to prevent further war and to boost the living standards of Europeans. Countries opened up in order to reap the benefits of intra-European trade. Ireland, however, had a small and young industrial sector that had developed in the 1930s and it wanted to protect that in the 1950s, so it opted out and retained high tariffs on imports.'

While the rest of Western Europe emerged back into the sunshine, Ireland experienced a lost decade of darkness. Unemployment was high. Tens of thousands simply upped and emigrated every year due to the utter lack of opportunity. Then things went from bad to worse.

The Irish pound and the English pound were linked one to one, which meant that Ireland had to copy whatever the Bank of England did with interest rates. If the British rate was 5 per cent and the Irish rate was only 4 per cent, for example, then money would flow out of Ireland and into the banks and markets in London, chasing a better return. In 1955 the government here experimented by doing exactly that: it chose not to follow a British rate rise. The country started to run out of money.

The government increased taxes to try to keep more money in the country and managed to send it into recession instead. Employment fell. Our economic performance was one of the poorest of any country in Europe.[5] We were on the verge of bankruptcy.

A radical new plan was needed. Cometh the hour, cometh the man. Well, two men to be precise.

1958–1989: From Self-sufficiency to Globalisation

T.K. Whitaker was the youngest ever Secretary of the Department of Finance at the time. He warned the incoming Fianna Fáil government of 1957 that Ireland would be better off rejoining the United Kingdom if it did not face up to its failing economic policies.[6] Working with other civil servants, he produced a plan that called for a complete about-face: a total reorientation away from protectionism and towards internationalisation.

Instead of import tariffs, embrace free trade. Instead of focusing on production for the domestic market, focus on production for export markets. Instead of prioritising local companies, incentivise foreign investment. The government accepted the proposals (as if it had any choice) and incorporated them into the country's first ever Programme for Economic Expansion in 1958.

The second man in this double act, the one who had the means to deliver the plan, was the man who became Taoiseach the following year, Seán Lemass. Ironically, Lemass had been the man charged with implementing Ireland's turn inwards when he was Minister for Industry and Commerce in 1932. A generation later, here he was leading Ireland back out again.

Ireland sought to join the European Economic Community as early as 1963 but French President General Charles de Gaulle made it clear that France didn't want Britain to join and Ireland was not in a position to proceed without its largest trading partner. A second application in 1967 was again blocked by de Gaulle. Ireland and the UK had to wait until he retired to successfully conclude accession negotiations. A referendum was held in May 1972 to confirm our entry, with 83 per cent of voters endorsing membership. Ireland finally joined on 1 January 1973.

This was transformative. We gained access to the largest market in the world. In theory, if not immediately in practice, we no longer had to depend on the performance of the British economy for our own export success. While our agricultural produce could reach new export markets, our farmers also benefited straightaway from direct financial supports. Structural funding followed later to improve our roads and national infrastructure. And multinationals found Ireland to be an increasingly attractive base for their European operations.

It took our own politicians to mess it up right at the start. In a bid to return to power in the general election of 1977, Fianna Fáil promised voters the sun, moon and stars. Lyons describes their election manifesto as 'the epitome of reckless fiscal policy'. 'They said, "We're going to abolish property tax, abolish vehicle tax, lower income tax and we're going to increase wages in the public sector, increase public sector employment, and increase infrastructural investment by the government." What you're doing is reducing taxes and increasing spending and you're just creating a problem for future voters to have to pay for.'

The government deficit ballooned. A global oil crisis caused prices to spike in 1979 and the economy went downhill fast. Youth emigration, which had reversed following economic gains in the 1960s and 70s, returned to haunt the country once again in the 1980s.

1990–1999: The 30-Year Overnight Success Story
Ireland started the 1990s in poor shape, with high unemployment, low economic growth and a standard of living well below that of most Europeans. It was to end the decade as a global superstar.

A Social Partnership process was initiated in the late 1980s in an effort to bring government, employers and unions together to reach a consensus on how best to achieve economic progress. Wage growth was gradually brought under control, industrial disputes decreased, and the tax burden was reduced. Exceptional growth in employment followed.

The government committed the country to joining the single European currency. In doing so it agreed to abide by a strict set of Maastricht criteria, developed in 1991, that required inflation to be brought under control and budget deficits to be reduced. A new fiscal rectitude was mandatory.

Most importantly of all, the EEC decided it needed to go further in creating a proper internal market for goods and services. 'Ironically, one of the strongest pushers for completing the Single Market was Margaret Thatcher,' explains Lyons. 'Her view was that there's all these non-tariff barriers that are stopping British firms from selling into Italy or Germany or France – if we want to be a single European market then we need to get rid of all of these. [Irishman] Peter Sutherland was the person given the job of heading up the final push to the Single European Market. They picked 1992 as the year they were going to complete this, and by and large they did it.'

This further strengthened Ireland's attractiveness to multinationals seeking to access the re-christened European Union. The economy expanded at nearly 10 per cent per annum between 1995 and 2000. Full employment ensued. Wages and consumer spending shot up. Government debt fell. The fabled Celtic Tiger was born.

The country gave up its old punts in January 1999 and proudly adopted the euro as the new currency's poster child. A fairy-tale ending, perhaps, if it had all gone well from there.

2000–2010 Bubble and Crash

Joining the euro benefited us on many fronts. The elimination of multiple currencies and their associated transaction costs was a clear advantage for trade and exports. Being tied to such a big currency was going to help lower inflation. And then there was the promise of lower interest rates on borrowed money.

'The view was that having lower interest rates would help us to invest and would increase spending and make government borrowing cheaper,' recalls Dr Ella Kavanagh of Cork University Business School. 'In reality euro interest rates were too low for Ireland during the early to mid-noughties, given economic conditions.' They encouraged people to over-borrow. Inflation hit 5.5 per cent in 2000, yet people could borrow money at interest rates of just 4 per cent. You were effectively subsidised to take out a loan.

And what did the Irish spend the money on? The one thing that our history had taught us to value above everything else: security of homestead. A place we could call our own and that no one could ever take away from us. We poured our borrowings into property. Prices shot up. So we borrowed even more.

It helped the Celtic Tiger to roar ahead of itself altogether. 'You can look from the 1990s up until 2001 and describe that as largely driven by funda-mentals – largely "good growth" and "catch-up", in the view of Lyons. 'After 2001 it's very hard to argue that it's fundamental growth and much easier to argue that it's a credit-driven bubble.'

With fortunes being made in the private sector, public sector employees wanted in on the act. In light of perceptions that they were losing out in terms of pay and access to talent, a 'benchmarking exercise' was undertaken in 2002, which delivered large pay increases throughout the public service. 'It's one thing to give a windfall pay-out and say, "look, things are really good at the moment, they're not going to be this good in the future, so every public servant can get an extra 5 per cent or 10 per cent this year and just go and enjoy yourselves because it's not going to be like this forever,' says Lyons. 'But what the Irish government did was to take those increases and cement them into future increments in pay and to future pension liabilities. When they tried to reverse them when times did eventually become less good, there was an outcry that's lasted all the way through to the last couple of years.'

The government got carried away. As money flowed into government coffers, the tiger economy purred. And it used that money to further fuel the bubble. Public expenditure more than doubled in a decade. The government failed to apply the first lesson of national economics – or even household economics – save when the going is good so you can spend when the going is bad.

Just as we benefited from positive global trends in the 1990s, so we were at their mercy when they reversed suddenly in 2008. The global financial crisis, triggered by increasing levels of defaults in the subprime mortgage market in the USA and the subsequent collapse of investment bank Lehman Brothers, hit Ireland extraordinarily hard.

Financial institutions across the globe teetered on the brink of collapse as borrowing came to a screeching stop and people wanted their investments turned back into cash. The Irish banks had lent too much to survive without government intervention. As the recession hit and wages were cut and people lost their jobs, so many hadn't the money to pay back what they had borrowed. Those who had savings wanted them back as they feared the banks' collapse. The government was forced to guarantee bank deposits to prevent a complete run on the banks, but even that was insufficient to prevent deposits falling by a third.

Together, the failure of the banking system, the impact of the deep economic recession on companies and individuals, and the slashing of government expenditure united to make this one of the most difficult periods ever for the Irish Republic.

By November 2010 the government could no longer borrow the funds it needed to run the country at a reasonable price. It sought the help of the International Monetary Fund (IMF), the European Union and the European Central Bank (ECB) – the 'troika'. There was no other option. The country would have been bankrupt without them.

2011–2021 Bounce Back, then Whack

Ireland lost its financial sovereignty for three years, from December 2010. The government agreed to implement 270 different programme measures for the troika. While the measures were economically sensible – focused on restoring a balanced government budget and stimulating private sector activity – the impacts on individuals were harsh and they attracted the label of 'austerity' measures.

State spending was cut. The budgets of government departments and their agencies were hacked, public-sector employee wages were reduced and a pension levy applied, and social welfare payments such as child benefit and unemployment benefit were cut back.

Tax revenue was raised. New taxes were introduced such as the Universal Social Charge and property tax; existing taxes were increased; tax credits and bands were reduced.

The minimum wage was reduced. Third-level registration fees were increased. Those over 70 lost their automatic entitlement to a Medical Card. I could go on. It was tough.

Unemployment reached nearly 16 per cent in 2012, practically tripling in just five years. And that figure does not include those who left the country. Nearly 50,000 people emigrated in that year alone.

Yet we were lucky. Our reliance on multinational exports served us well. The US and the UK economies recovered quickly, and we experienced the benefits of that. In fact, the growth in the value of Irish exports only stuttered slightly in 2008 and 2009 before surging forward again.

In April 2013 I hosted a meeting of European tourist boards in Dublin's Docklands. There were representatives from Spain, Portugal, Greece – all of whom had their own deep difficulties with austerity. In my opening address I pointed out the window towards Google's HQ, then Facebook's, then Twitter's, then LinkedIn's. I told them there was no recession here. While many Irish people were suffering deep financial difficulties, those employed in these export-orientated technology sectors were doing just fine, thank you. The restaurants around there were still busy, and the cafés, and the convenience stores, and the gyms. And from there, Ireland's recovery would start.

That December Ireland became the first stricken eurozone state to exit its bailout rescue programme. Unemployment began to fall. The following year GDP growth exceeded 2 per cent for the first time since the start of the crisis. And our economic indicators improved year after year from there.

There was carnage left behind for many, of course. There were debts that had to be paid, and companies or individuals that could not pay them were forced into bankruptcy. There were legacies of the years of reduced spending and reduced lending, most particularly in the construction of new homes. It took the full decade for some of us to recover, but the vast majority found themselves in a much better position at the end of the 2010s than they had been at the end of noughties.

All in all, we were in the best shape of our lives when Covid-19 hit. Not perfect, of course, but back to fighting form and able to slug it out with the best of them. Having prepared to fight the Brexit battle, we were much better resourced and economically stronger than we had been when the previous crash occurred.

The Covid whack was intense. Unpredicted. Painful. Pervasive. But this time it is different. We are starting from a different place, and we know where we want to get back to.

'We don't want to go back to a life of 1980s Ireland,' says Kavanagh. 'We still want to be able to go out and to go to restaurants and to get take-aways. We want to have a certain lifestyle. People's expectations are much higher now and that will create demand for consumer goods and services and get people working again.'

If the world economy returns quickly then we will experience the benefits of that again. If the pharmaceutical and technology sectors are amongst the ones that come out of this crisis strongest then we will benefit disproportionately. If corporations decide that they will spread their global risk by locating operations in several regions around the world, then we are extremely well placed to win our fair share.

Let me turn to the remarkable economic progress of our first century, which, I am confident, we can restore and surpass.

 ## 32 Ireland's Economic Wealth Exceeds That of Most Countries

GDP per capita in constant $, 1920–2018

SOURCE: MADDISON PROJECT DATABASE[7]

We are earning more now than we have done at any time in our history. Practically all of that improvement has come in the last 30 years. In one single generation we leapt from being amongst the poorest countries in Western Europe to being amongst its richest. We have a lot to be grateful for.

The world's accepted measure of a country's economic activity is Gross Domestic Product (GDP). There's a formula: you add together the value of everything that individuals and the government purchased, along with the value of all the savings and investments they made; you then add the value of your exports and minus the value of your imports. As Ireland is a location for huge volumes of multinational exports, the value of our exports is an enormous contributor to our country's GDP. For that reason, it is not the best measure of what is happening in the domestic economy, but I will come back to that.

As a country that had such a poor economic performance for so long, it is truly remarkable that we are now in the top division. The graph shows the value of our GDP per capita, in US$ for ease of comparison, and strips out inflation so that the real underlying performance of the economy can be seen. Look at the large gap between our performance and that of the British economy, with which we overwhelmingly traded, right up until the late 1990s.

For a long time the average Briton was roughly twice as wealthy as an Irish person – and our economic policies did nothing to close the gap. As our exports took off in the 1990s we began to power ahead – very, very quickly indeed. Those Celtic Tiger years saw the value of our economy nearly triple. We didn't just catch up with Britain and the rest of Western Europe, we powered past them and aligned with the one of the world's wealthiest: the United States.

The graph also puts the Great Recession into perspective. It impacted on people much harder here than in Britain or other European nations, but the unwavering performance of our export sector meant that the value of our economy as a whole continued to outperform that of most others.

Our economy is now amongst the wealthiest in the world, at least if you measure it on a per capita basis. Here we are, hobnobbing with Luxembourg and Switzerland. Their GDP figures are similarly reliant on exports, but they are undeniably wealthy countries, and so are we now.

Ireland Is the World's Third-Wealthiest Country

GDP per capita in current US$ in 2020

SOURCE: INTERNATIONAL MONETARY FUND[8]

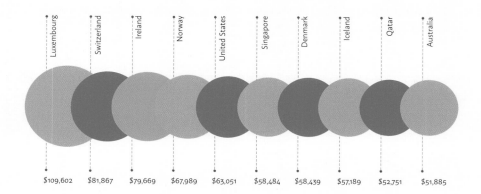

Luxembourg	Switzerland	Ireland	Norway	United States	Singapore	Denmark	Iceland	Qatar	Australia
$109,602	$81,867	$79,669	$67,989	$63,051	$58,484	$58,439	$57,189	$52,751	$51,885

As the value of our exports has grown, it has become harder and harder to judge the underlying performance of the domestic economy from our GDP figures. The 'export' part of the equation overwhelms that sum of the other elements. A new measure has had to be developed to track that: Modified Gross National Income (written as GNI*). It excludes the profits of multi-national companies and cuts out the big-ticket aircraft leasing sector, for which we are a global hub. It's therefore a better measurement of what is available to residents.[9]

Needless to say, our economy is appreciably smaller if we exclude the value of multinational exports. In 2018 our GDP was valued at €324 billion but our GNI* was only €198 billion – roughly 40 per cent less.[10] However, this is also true of the other countries in the 'rich list' so we remain amongst the top ten wealthiest countries in the world even with this revised measure.[11] And, positively, there is a strong correlation between GDP and GNI*: as our exports grow so employment is created and people have more money to spend and pay more taxes so the domestic economy benefits proportionally.

Whatever measure of economic performance you choose, it had never been as strong as it was before the arrival of Covid-19. Although the virus hit some sectors of the economy particularly hard, we were the only European country that saw our GDP grow regardless in 2020, thanks to exports of medical and technology products. Given that there was no country untouched by the impact of the virus, our prominent position will not have diminished at all.

 ## More People Had Jobs Than Ever Before

Number of people in employment to the nearest 100,000, 1977–2019

SOURCE: OECD

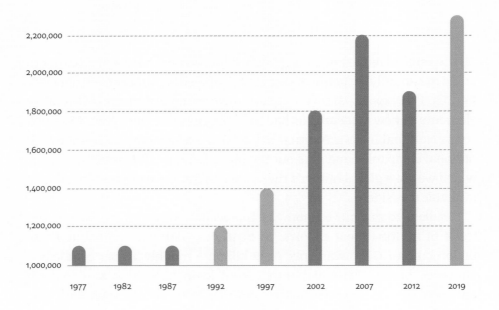

For most of our nation's short history, there were never more than 1.25 million people with jobs. That number held level through our experiment in self-sufficiency as a nation in the 1930s and 40s. Then, during the 1950s, the number of people in jobs started declining year after year. No wonder so many emigrated.

1961 witnessed the country's worst ever employment numbers: just over 1 million people held jobs that year. It was a further 20 years before the figure rose above 1.1 million. And then it just toddled along again until the 1990s. A pretty miserable performance – particularly given that the population was growing and there were more and more mouths to feed.

The transformation during the Celtic Tiger era was truly extraordinary. Having experienced no employment growth for 70 years, we managed to double the number at work in just 17 – between 1990 and 2007.

I have highlighted some of the factors that accounted for our growth at this time. Social Partnership between government, employers and unions. Government fiscal rectitude in preparation for joining the euro. The removal of barriers to European trade through the creation of the Single Market. The improvements in national infrastructure from billions of euros invested through the EU's Structural Funds.

We were lucky too. Economists label this period the 'Great Moderation' – a time of greater global stability characterised by positive economic growth, lower inflation and rising corporate investment. It coincided with the collapse of the Soviet Union and the end of the Cold War, which increased confidence in global trade and international investment. It was also the start of the global technology boom fuelled by the rise of the internet. Ireland was ready to claim its share of the thriving Foreign Direct Investment market, particularly from new technology companies. Our exports boomed. Jobs were created. Wages increased. Consumer spending increased. And that created more jobs. A wonderful virtuous circle.

When the crash came, the reverse happened. People lost their jobs. Wages decreased. Consumer spending dropped. And the number of jobs fell. Between 2007 and 2012, the number in employment fell by 15 per cent. A loss of 350,00 jobs. That was a painfully high number for our small economy.

Having experienced five years of declines, it took us five subsequent years of increases to get us back to where we were. As the recovery kicked in, by 2018 we had established a new record: more than two and a quarter million people were in employment for the first time in our history. There is no reason to believe that we will not reach that figure again once the economy recovers from the Covid crisis.

 ## Unemployment Was at an Historic Low

Percentage of labour force unemployed, 1923–2019

SOURCE: REBECCA STUART, CENTRAL STATISTICS OFFICE[12]

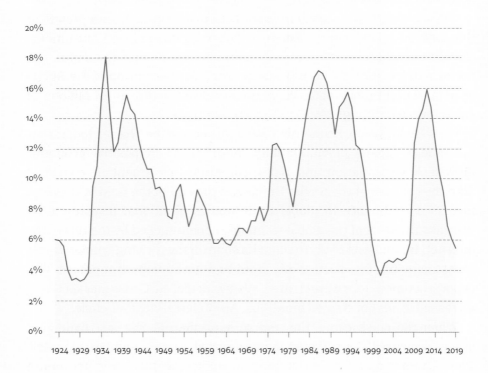

Despite the stability in the numbers at work, there was huge variability in the numbers out of work through the decades.

You can never get to zero unemployment. Some companies fail. Some people quit their jobs. Some people enter the workforce for the first time or return to it, perhaps after a period working in the home or after an illness. Allowing for this churn, economists consider full employment to be reached when unemployment falls below 5 per cent.

Ireland has achieved full employment three times in its history. The first was shortly after the foundation of the State: unemployment hovered at around 3 per cent in the late 1920s. The jobs available at the time were predominantly in agriculture. After a tough year in 1924 marked by bad weather and cattle disease, agricultural output grew over the rest of the decade, providing more jobs for labourers.

The other factor that kept unemployment so low – and actually prevented it reaching greater heights later on – was emigration. It was unemployment's pressure valve. The 1920s experienced an increase in emigration over the 1910s as the restrictions of World War I were left behind and as some moved away as a consequence of independence.[13]

The low figures did not last long. The Great Depression hit the United States at the end of 1929 and their government responded by halting immigration, cutting off the most popular emigration route for the Irish. As the Depression became global so the opportunities in the UK dried up too, leaving would-be emigrants stranded at home and pushing up unemployment.

This was exacerbated by the self-inflicted Anglo-Irish Trade War. Agricultural exports to our largest market were cut, prices fell, labourers had less work. Unemployment reached the highest level it was ever to experience in 1935 when 18 per cent of the workforce were unoccupied – nearly one in every five persons.

Although unemployment was to decrease through the 1940s and 50s, it was only because the pressure valve of emigration opened up full tilt. Twice as many people left Ireland in the 1940s as did so in the 1920s, and even more again in the 1950s.

The economically volatile 1970s and 80s saw Ireland's second-highest peak in unemployment reached in 1986 at 17 per cent. Ireland started the 1990s with the highest unemployment rate amongst the 12 member states of the EU. However, it ended the decade with the lowest rate amongst what had become 15 member countries. Ireland's second period of full employment was reached in 2000 thanks to our astonishing employment growth.

Just to prove that there's always unemployment, I managed to lose my job twice the following year. While Ireland was having its moment, in part due to the unprecedented growth in internet-fuelled tech firms, the dot-com bubble was bursting in the US. Online firms that had sucked up millions of venture capital dollars and floated on stock exchanges without making a cent of profit started going belly-up as their funds ran out. And when America gets a cold ...

I worked for the internet services firm ebeon, part owned by the former State telecoms company eircom. We built big corporate websites. One hundred staff were employed in Dublin and seventy more overseas. Everyone was called to the boardroom for a company-wide announcement. I had worked with the management team to try to develop a new business model for the firm as the bursting bubble hammered our income; with an inkling of what was to come, I slunk to the back of the room. Other colleagues were excited – it was payday after all, and this was clearly a big announcement.

The big reveal was that the company had run entirely out of cash. It wasn't yet profitable and eircom was no longer willing to finance its running costs. Colleagues were told to take their stuff and go. And, by the way, there wasn't any money left to pay this month's wages. I signed on the dole the following week.

In a time of full employment, it didn't prove too difficult to get another job. I became head of strategy for Webfactory, part of Horizon Technology Group plc. But the doubts that the burst bubble had raised in companies about investing in this new internet thing persisted – was it really going to take off? Within twelve months I was made redundant again as Webfactory implemented the downsizing plan that I had written for the company. A career in the public service began to look a lot more appealing after that.

Before we had our third period of full employment, we reached our third peak of unemployment. The economic collapse of the Great Recession saw unemployment rise sharply once again, reaching 16 per cent in 2012. It took seven years to return to full employment. Before the Covid catastrophe.

We have experienced some striking swings in our fortunes over the past forty years. But the unemployment levels we attained in the early noughties and again in the late 2010s were the lowest we have experienced since the early years of the State's foundation. Critically, we did not need the valve of emigration to achieve that. In fact, as I will show later, we turned that tide into one of net immigration on both occasions.

We are a small country. For all our obsession with regional differences, they pale in comparison to those seen in larger countries. We have the smallest regional variation in unemployment in Europe.[14] Denmark, Sweden and the Netherlands come close, but the regional variations experienced within Italy, Belgium and the UK are much, much greater. That aids our national cohesiveness and could count as a remarkable achievement in its own right too.

 ## We Have Transformed from an Agricultural to a Services Economy

Ireland may be well known for its food and drink exports, but we are far from an agricultural nation. Fewer than one in twenty people work in the sector today. Its share of employment has consistently declined, decade after decade, since the foundation of the State, at which time the majority (54 per cent) of workers were indeed agricultural. Nowadays, more than three-quarters of us work in services.

Each generation has experienced a radically different jobs market from the one before it. Think of the middle-aged folk amongst us who were raised on their parents' family farm and whose daughter now designs emojis for a living! What do the grandparents and grandchildren talk about when they get together for Christmas?

The first shift was from agriculture to industry. Between the 1920s and 60s the proportion of workers in industrial occupations doubled.

The government's protectionist policies stimulated some industrial development, and the first wave of foreign companies that established operations here in the 60s were all about manufacturing. Agriculture was also going through its own transformation as new technology and automation replaced manual labour. Tractors replaced horses. Combine harvesters replaced men. And fertiliser boosted productivity without a requirement for another pair of hands.

Proportion of all those employed in the agricultural, industrial and service sectors, 1926–2016

SOURCE: CENTRAL STATISTICS OFFICE[15]

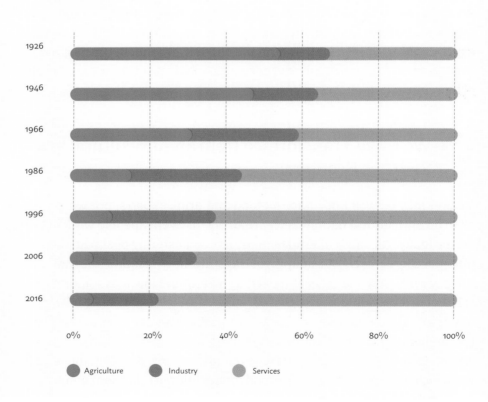

It was from the 1960s that the services sector began to grow its share, initially at the expense of agriculture but in recent years at the expense of industry too. As technology improved industrial productivity, so more jobs were created in management and clerical roles rather than on the factory floor. There were more jobs in education and health as the State provided better access for more citizens. Our standard of living increased and we began to spend more on days out with the family or nights out in a restaurant or at the cinema. That created more service jobs too. Then the internet turned everything virtual and manufacturing jobs started to be converted into digital services.

'If you go back to when we were at subsistence levels, very little of what we consumed was services. We had to build our own housing, food, clothing, all that basic stuff of our lives was close to 100 per cent of what we spent,' explains Ronan Lyons. 'What do you get someone as a birthday present or a Christmas present these days? Often you'll get them a voucher so they can fly somewhere or go out for a meal. I think that's a really nice feature of our lives: we're at a point now where we can think about unique experiences whereas most of our ancestors 100 years ago were worrying about much more basic things.'

More People Are Employed in High-Skilled Jobs

It is not inevitable that a shift towards increasing employment in services would be accompanied by a growth in high-skilled jobs, but that is what we have accomplished. In the last thirty years the number of people employed in high-skilled jobs – those that are deemed professional, technical or managerial – has increased by 150 per cent.[16]

That is a truly transformational number. It denotes a transformation of the nature of the work we do, of the structure of the workplace in which we work, of the complexity of the jobs we are asked to do, of the technology that is required to enable people to do their jobs, of the educational levels that people need to have to take up these jobs, of the extent to which people engage their brains in doing their work and of the contribution that people can make in the workplace.

The workforce as a whole has grown strongly over the past 30 years. However, the number of high-skilled jobs has grown twice as fast as the overall labour market, whereas the number of medium-skilled jobs has grown to a smaller extent and the number of low-skilled jobs has remained completely unchanged. As a result, the proportion of people in high-skilled jobs has flipped from having the smallest share to having the largest.

Percentage employed in high-, medium- and low-skilled jobs

SOURCE: CENTRAL STATISTICS OFFICE

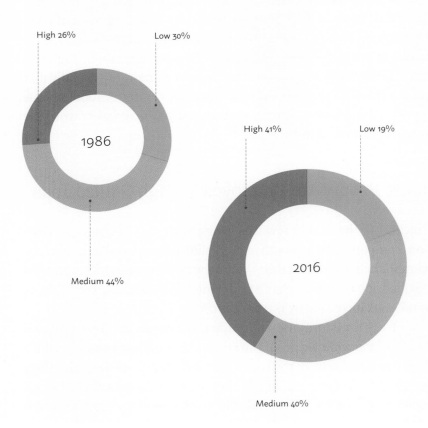

High 26%   Low 30%

1986

Medium 44%

High 41%   Low 19%

2016

Medium 40%

The stark change is enabled by many of the shifts in the sectors people work in and in the evolving nature of our export-orientated economy. As new technology automated aspects of agriculture so the number of low-skilled jobs there declined. As automation on the factory floor reduced the need for low-skilled operatives so it increased the need for supervisory and technical staff. As digitally delivered services substitute for manufactured products (think of streaming movies instead of buying DVDs) so high-skilled technical jobs replace those in production and shipping.

There is a symbiotic link to our rising educational standards. As we produce more highly skilled graduates they can take up more highly skilled jobs so we can attract more investment from highly skilled companies so we have the need for more highly skilled graduates. You could ask the classic chicken-and-egg question: which came first, the jobs or the graduates? The answer is neither. Or both. They are mutually beneficial, the presence of each reinforcing the opportunity for the other in a beautifully virtuous circle that has created new opportunities for the people of Ireland.

This growth in high-skilled employment offers us positive protection from the next wave of automation. It is not only the factory floor that will be at the frontline; it will also be financial services, customer service, sales, business administration, education, journalism and legal services. As digital technology plays an increasingly fundamental part in many jobs, so the opening for parts of those roles to be automated expands. Routine tasks can be increasingly automated by time-saving and error-minimising software. And isn't that to be welcomed, freeing us up as it does to spend more time on making a higher value contribution?

Technology will continue to complement the jobs done by humans, replacing some tasks and changing the nature of jobs, rather than replacing us all to the point of mass unemployment. Just as when automation hit agriculture and the factory floor, there will be a further employment shift towards higher skilled and technical jobs.

Feeding that beautiful virtuous circle of high-skilled jobs creation will be vital to our future success. Higher education will become even more critical for an individual's and the country's continued success. In fact, given the speed at which the next phase of AI-driven algorithmic disruption is arriving, lifelong education will become far more important than it was in the past. Having started our careers with one particular skillset and acquired another mid-career, we may end up retiring with an altogether different one.

 ## We Are Working 20 Per Cent Fewer Hours Than the Last Generation

Average hours worked per person employed, 1972–2010

SOURCE: OECD[17]

Average number of hours a year	Year	Average number of hours a week
2,300	1972	50
2,200	1978	48
2,100	1981	46
2,000	1992	44
1,900	2003	41
1,800	2010	39

It may or may not feel like it, but we are working fewer hours than the last generation. The average number that each employee spends working has dropped from 50 hours a week at the start of the 1970s to less than 40 today.

The change is partly related to the changing nature of the jobs that we do. Our working time has become less regimented as it becomes more service orientated. A service-sector job does not require the exact same number of hours from each employee every day in the way that a factory shift does. A services firm can achieve everything it needs to by spreading the work amongst its available employees, thereby enabling individual workers to dial up or down their hours as their motivation and personal circumstances allow. A job can even be shared across different people working different days or times. And that's what more and more people are doing.

Growth in part-time working accounts for a significant element of the changes in working hours. The number of people working two or three days a week has doubled over the past two decades. The number working four-day weeks has tripled.[18] It is not that the five-day week is becoming any less popular – the proportion working 35 or 40 hours has held steady – but the proportion who work more than 45 hours a week has dropped.

The other critical factor in reducing our weekly hours was the implementation of the EU's Working Time Directive in 1997. This prohibited a regular working week that exceeded 48 hours, which was precisely how long the average employee worked in the 1970s. It also increased the minimum amount of paid holidays that employees were entitled to from three to four weeks. We have added three public holidays since the 1970s too. With the addition of New Year's Day in 1974, the October holiday in 1977 and May Day in 1994, we now enjoy an annual total of nine days off.

Yet it probably does not feel like we are working fewer hours. You cannot milk the cows from your couch. You cannot manufacture curtains from your kitchen. There is a definite end to the working day for many jobs. But you *can* catch up on your emails from your bedroom at midnight and check your day's appointments in the bathroom first thing in the morning. If there is one thing that the Covid pandemic proved, it was that many of those in the service sector can work entirely from home at all hours of the day if needs be. The consequence is that 'always-on' technology is facilitating a bleeding of some people's working lives into their personal ones. This occasional work-dipping is not easily captured in the official statistics.

Are we also losing some of the time we're gaining from a reduced workday to our commute? For most people there has been little change in commuting time or distance in recent decades. A significant minority have experienced a deterioration, however – most particularly those living in the commuter belt in the counties neighbouring Dublin for whom it typically takes the longest to get to work and whose commute increased notably as traffic volumes returned after the last recession.[19]

Post-pandemic, many will undoubtedly hold out hope that the pressure to commute will soften as it becomes obvious that homeworking can be as effective as time spent in the office thanks to the changing nature of our work and the technology at our disposal. That will gift us even more time with which to better manage our work–

life balance (as long as we can keep away from the temptation to check up on the work phone after hours).

 ## Ireland's People Are the Most Productive in the World (by some measures)

GDP per hour worked in US dollars, 2019

SOURCE: OECD[20]

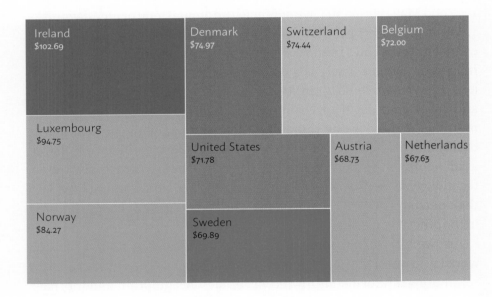

The fact that each of us is working fewer hours on average but that the GDP we produce per head is increasing leads to one conclusion. We are becoming more and more productive. For each hour we work, we are generating an increasing amount of revenue for our organisations and for the Irish economy. So much so that we are now the most productive people on the planet.

Well, by some measures at any rate. The Organisation for Economic Cooperation and Development (OECD) collects data on 36 of the world's wealthiest countries and they place us at number one.[21]

The OECD uses GDP as its financial metric, so that includes the value of all our multinational exports as well as our domestic economy. Undoubtedly this boosts our productivity figure hugely. An hour spent working for Apple, Google or Facebook creates more financial value for those firms than an hour spent working for an indigenous Irish company in a more traditional sector. But then that is also true of firms in other export-orientated countries such as Luxembourg, which sits behind us in second place.

The good news is that even if we endeavour to strip out part of the multi-national sector by using Gross National Income (GNI) instead, the result is not hugely different. Ireland ranks as the second most productive country then, only falling behind Norway.[22]

Given where we have come from as a nation, to top a list such as this – even with caveats – is nothing short of an outstanding performance.

 ## Our Indigenous Companies Are Amongst the Most Productive in Europe

Another way of measuring productivity is using Gross Value Added (GVA), which puts a financial value on the goods and services produced and then minuses the cost of the inputs and raw materials required to produce them. Ranking European countries by the value added per employee once again results in Ireland being placed significantly ahead of every other country. The value produced by our technology and pharmaceutical multinationals is extraordinary.

If we set aside our multinational firms and only look at our indigenous companies, the result remains one that we should be very proud of. The value that each employee adds is well above the EU average and only significantly behind Luxembourg, Denmark and Belgium, whose national figures also include their fair share of multinational companies.

Manufacturing firms and information and communications firms are the greatest source of value add to the Irish economy. Then it's the retail and wholesale sector, then financial and real estate, followed by professional, scientific and technical firms.[23]

GVA per person employed in the EU, 2017

SOURCE: CENTRAL STATISTICS OFFICE.

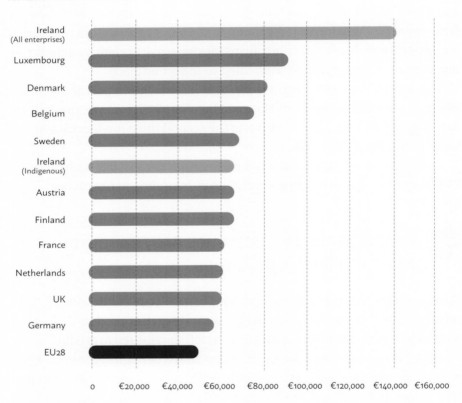

It is fair to recognise that the strength of our indigenous companies is, in part, driven by the multinationals who make use of their services. Those companies, and their well-remunerated employees, are customers for our food and drink, for financial products, for property and for professional and legal services, amongst others. The success of both sectors is mutually beneficial.

Our Companies Are Leaders in Selling Online

Percentage of enterprises in EU countries selling online, 2019

SOURCE: EUROSTAT[24]

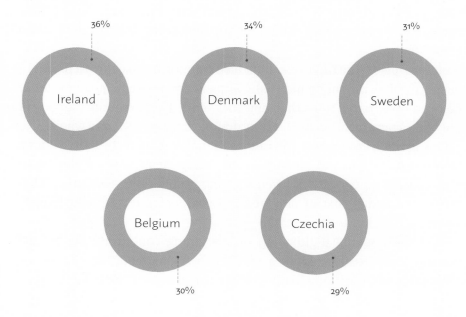

36% Ireland

34% Denmark

31% Sweden

30% Belgium

29% Czechia

The fact that so many of the multinational companies in Ireland are tech firms has the benefit of increasing Ireland's digital capability. It also fosters the development of the digital capability of indigenous firms, either by encouraging them to be early adopters of the online platforms provided by these tech firms or by raising the competence of the workforce at large.

The digital leadership of Ireland's enterprises is real. A third of our firms sell online, the highest proportion in the EU. That is higher than our Nordic neighbours in Denmark and Sweden and significantly higher than the UK, where it is only a quarter. When the coronavirus lockdown came, our firms were therefore better prepared to meet the needs of those of us trapped at home.

The country took a Great Digital Leap during lockdown. We leapt into home working, home schooling, online exercise classes and remote socialising. And we gleefully leapt into the world of e-commerce to acquire our essential – and not-so-essential – items: school books and uniforms, basketballs and bicycle pumps, garden furniture and three-course meals. Having emergency deodorant supplies dropped to my door was a first for me!

But even before the Digital Leap enabled many firms to keep their revenues flowing through the pandemic, Irish companies generated a greater share of their turnover from e-sales than anywhere else. They accounted for 34 per cent of company turnover here, nearly double that of the EU as a whole.

This is not a case where the multinationals are distorting the picture. Amongst our small and medium-sized enterprises (those employing 10 to 49 people), 29 per cent of revenues were from e-commerce sales. That share was double that of similar-sized companies in the next biggest countries, Czechia and Denmark.

With the ongoing digitisation of everything continuing apace, and probably even accelerated as a result of the pandemic, our firms are remarkably well positioned to avail of the opportunities ahead.

The Number of Strikes by Workers Is at an All-Time Low

As a kid in the 1980s I remember often seeing strikes featured on the 6 o'clock news. Men (yes, they were nearly always men) marched back and forth in formation, striding around an invisible circuit, raised placards in hand. There always seemed to be a postal strike. Or else it was the buses. There was even an occasional teachers' strike, although I can't remember being lucky enough to have them close down my school.

Strikes used to be a thing. Now they're not. The 1970s and 80s were bad times for industrial relations. Ireland experienced its greatest number of strikes in 1974, when 219 took place. Only a few years later, in 1979, nearly one and a half million working days were lost through industrial action, surpassing the total in every year for the previous four decades. The number of strikes has since plummeted to just ten a year in recent times. (Climate strikes are not included, despite that being quite a noble reason for closing a school down these days.)

Can the reduction in strikes be considered an achievement? Yes, if it signifies improved pay and conditions for workers. Yes, if it signifies improved worker and employer relations. Yes, if it signifies the growth of alternative means of addressing grievances that are less disruptive to a firm's customers.

Number of strikes, 1984–2020

SOURCE: CENTRAL STATISTICS OFFICE[25]

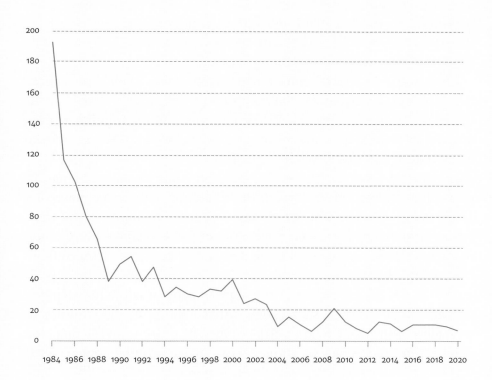

So what's the story here? What underlies this staggering decline?

The first factor at play is a declining number of trade union members. Union membership increased from the 1930s as the numbers at work in industrial sectors grew steadily. It peaked in the early 1980s when more than six in ten of all of those at work were members of unions. In recent years it has fallen to less than a quarter, the clear majority of which are in the public sector. [26]

'Up until the 1960s, trade union membership was by weekly contribution, rather like if you're a practising Christian you renew your faith every week by going to church,' explains labour historian Francis Devine.[27] 'You handed over your subscription to a shop steward or a branch collector who entered it into a little book, and that gave you an opportunity to complain about the union or raise a case.' That enabled a strong bond between the worker and their union. 'As payment systems changed, we moved to "check-off" deduction at source – in other words, your union contribution was deducted from your wage packet by the employer. So there was no longer an organic link between the member and the union.' Relations between worker and union weakened.

Changing industrial relations practices also saw workplace grievances increasingly referred outside the workplace to arbitration or to the Labour Court. A vicious circle ensued. As fewer workers saw the benefits of trade union membership the numbers of members reduced, so the power of the union reduced, so fewer workers signed up.

Legislation – and the threat of legislation – has also played a part in controlling strikes. These days, most strikes only involve members of a single union. Workers who are members of different unions in the same organisation tend not to join them. All-out pickets, where every union member follows each other out the door in sympathy, were much more frequent in the past.

'One of the longest strikes in the State's history was the maintenance workers' strike in 1969,' says Devine. 'At the end of it, the government threatened legislation to control picketing. In order to avoid that, the Congress of Trade Unions instituted a two-tiered picketing system. What that says is that you can have a strike on your own anytime you like, as long as you go through your own procedures. However, if you want others in the factory who are members of a different union to obey, then you have to go to Congress whose Disputes Committee make a decision as to whether to allow an all-out strike or not.' Unsurprisingly, the number of all-out strikes fell.

One of the most noteworthy parallels with the decline in strikes was the growth of Social Partnership. Starting in 1987, and continuing for 22 years, there can be little doubt that the bringing together of unions, employers and government to agree multi-annual programmes for the benefit of workers and citizens negated the need, or the appetite, for many local disputes.

'When I was starting out as a trade union official in the 60s and 70s, one of the models that was held up to us was Scandinavia,' says Devine. 'In countries like Sweden you pay a high rate of tax, but the government provided a fantastic range of services. When Social Partnership was at its height, we actually had delegations from Scandinavia coming to look at Ireland.'

One way in which Ireland was different from Scandinavia was the fact that we did not have social democratic governments. In fact, there wasn't any prospect of such a government here, given the relatively low levels of support that the Labour Party attracted. Yet, despite that, national agreements were put in place that unquestionably aimed to deliver on social democratic ambitions for better pay, reduced working hours, a fairer tax system and initiatives to tackle homelessness and disadvantage. 'The trade unions were treading a fine line: to exchange the negotiating power we had at the Social Partnership table for moves on tax, social welfare and other non-wage issues that we didn't have the possibility of doing in government,' explains Devine. 'In that sense, it was unique.'

Social Partnership provided stability and certainty for employers and government and played a part in enabling the Celtic Tiger to roar. It delivered improvements in workers' gross pay, in their real income after taxes were deducted and in what they could purchase for themselves and their families. Ironically, its successes may have contributed to the decline in the membership of the very unions that were delivering these benefits for workers. 'A lot of people saw their wage packets increase, but often an employer would put a little note in saying *We're pleased to inform you that we're bringing you the next phase of the current national agreement* and therefore they didn't necessarily associate the wage increase with their membership of a union at all.'

Two decades of Partnership broke down with the economic crash in 2009. Employers, in particular, believed the agreements to be too restrictive when they sought to tackle their mounting losses through significant redundancies and pay reductions. Yet strikes did not return to their previous levels. Partly because most union members are in the public sector and, there, national agreements continued to be negotiated. We have had the Croke Park Agreement, the Haddington Road Agreement and the Lansdowne Road Agreement. Even through the worst of times, public employment has been protected and commitments to pay restoration have followed unavoidable cuts.

Perhaps the most significant factor that explains our absence of strikes is that there is less and less to strike over. Remuneration and working conditions are generally better than they ever have been, even though we are only a decade on from a formidable economic collapse. Employer–employee relations are arguably also much more equal and mutually respectful than they were in the past. The changing skill requirements of the workplace have played a role in that. An empowered workforce does not need to rely on a shop steward to argue their case for them. And Google can tell you everything you need to know about employment law.

The changing nature of employment itself also makes unionisation more difficult than before. Think of those working in the gig economy, on short-term contracts and doing freelance work. How can you organise people that are in precarious employment or are forcibly self-employed, as many in the construction industry are?

As memorable as strike action invariably is, perhaps the amount of attention it attracts is unwarranted. 'We get very concerned publicly about strike figures and at certain times in Irish history, such as in the 60s and 70s, there was endless commentary about the need to curtail strikes,' explains Devine. 'Yet more people are off work through dental ill health every year than through strike action!' Yes, you read that right. The need for urgent fillings and fixing cracked teeth adds up to more lost workdays in any 12-month period than strikes ever did.

42 We Are Earning Five Times More Than Our Grandparents

Average weekly industrial wage in real terms, 1940–2020

SOURCE: CENTRAL STATISTICS OFFICE[28]

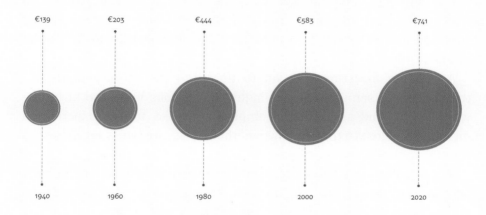

| €139 | €203 | €444 | €583 | €741 |

| 1940 | 1960 | 1980 | 2000 | 2020 |

Those in employment have never been as well paid as they are today. Really.

The cost of everything in an economy rises from year to year, as we know, but the average wage has consistently increased above the rate of inflation year after year, decade after decade. So in *real* terms – stripping out inflation – workers today are paid more than five times what their grandparents received in the 1940s. Those in industrial employment at the start of 2020 earned an average weekly wage of €740. The like-with-like comparable figure in 1940 was only €140.

Wages increased relatively slowly in the post-World War II period. Despite, or indeed because of, our protectionist drive for self-sufficiency there was little notable growth in our industrial sector. It was only when we began to attract foreign direct investment that wages started their nearly unremitting rise. Real average weekly earnings have increased by over 2 per cent a year since then.[29] Only during the recessions of the early 1980s and the late noughties was there a notable period of decline. On both occasions it took only three years of subsequent wage growth to recover all the loss of income.

So why have wages increased so strongly? Prior to the 1960s, cheap labour was plentiful. Emigration was widespread simply because there were not enough jobs to go around. There was little need for employers to increase wages to attract the staff they needed – they could offer a job at any price and be sure of filling the role. In the absence of free second-level education, most of the workforce were not highly educated and there wasn't a need for a lot of skilled labour to do the available jobs.

As foreign investment began to flow into the country thereafter, the number of semi-skilled and highly skilled jobs increased at higher wage levels. And as industrial employment rose, unions experienced membership growth that empowered them to secure real wage increases through national pay-bargaining.

The figures I have shown are only for those in industrial employment because they stretch back the furthest. The proportion of workers in the industrial sector peaked in the 1970s and early 80s, however, and it has been the services sector that has stormed ahead since then. Unsurprisingly, the largest average pay packets today are all to be found in service sectors: financial, information and communications technology, education, and professional and technical areas.

The disposable income that we have today would make us look like millionaires to our ancestors. Of course, there are things we consider essential to modern living that they never had to think about finding money for: video-streaming services, seasonal fashion trends or foreign holidays, for example. But it is the very fact that earnings have increased so much that has caused us to consider such things indispensable.

Remember too that food prices have generally decreased over time. These strong increases in real wages therefore result in the actual cost of feeding ourselves shrinking hugely. Hence, we spend far less of our income on sustenance these days than previous generations, and yet we can afford far more exotic and nutritious foodstuffs. And it is not just food that is increasingly affordable: most basic goods are too once we account for the impact of inflation.

Price Inflation Is at an Historic Low

Average annual changes in consumer prices, 1923–2020

SOURCE: CENTRAL STATISTICS OFFICE[30]

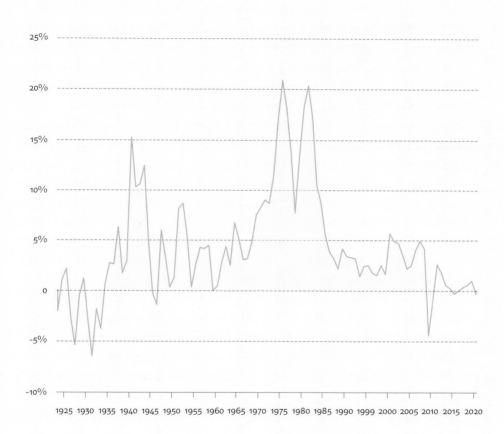

I am sure some of you are old enough to remember the burdensome inflation levels of the 1970s and early 80s. We had two periods of annual inflation in excess of 20 per cent, when the average price of goods went up by a fifth in a single year. Between 1973 and 1978 prices doubled; and then from 1979 to 1984 they did it again! The prices that people had to pay for their weekly shopping quadrupled in a decade. It sounds like the travails of a failing South American state.

To be fair, it wasn't our fault. In the main.

'We were a small, open economy and a price-taker so we imported pretty much all our inflation,' explains Dr Ella Kavanagh. From the foundation of the State right through to the 1970s, the vast majority of our trade was with the UK. With the value of the Irish pound linked to parity with sterling, there was little we could do to avoid mirroring whatever happened to the British economy. Consequently, Irish inflation rates merely tracked those of the UK.

We experienced a bout of high inflation during the World War II even though Ireland remained neutral. Wartime shortages pushed prices up, and in its immediate aftermath the population tired of austerity and sought pay increases to cover the cost of living.

The peaks of the 1970s were also due to global factors well beyond our control. According to Dr Kavanagh, 'The 1970s is the decade of oil crises, the first in 1973 and again in 1979. Oil production was cut and oil prices rose dramatically. This increase in costs led to higher prices more generally and higher unemployment. Governments responded by increasing expenditure, further contributing to a rise in price inflation.'

As consumer prices increased, so workers started agitating for larger wage increases to cover their rising bills. 'In the National Wage Agreements of the 1970s, expectations of higher price inflation were factored into higher wages. As well as that, a lot of wages were indexed to actual price inflation so as inflation was rising, wages were increasing in line with that,' says Kavanagh.

Entirely reasonable as it is to sustain people's standard of living, the impact of putting more money into people's pockets is to perpetuate price increases as people have the means to cover rising costs in the year ahead. A vicious circle develops whereby large pay increases enable greater spending, allowing companies to increase their prices, resulting in workers seeking further increases to cover those rises, and then forcing companies to raise their prices again to generate the revenue to pay higher wages.

It was a tricky time for the global economy as a whole, but Britain and Ireland suffered more than most. Our inflation rate was twice that experienced by the United States and three to four times that experienced by Germany during the same crises.

There was a recognition that we were not benefiting by being so closely linked to Britain. Having joined the EEC in 1973, we had the option to join the newly created European Exchange Rate Mechanism (ERM) in 1979. We seized the opportunity to break the Irish pound's link to sterling for the first time since independence and to link it to a basket of European currencies instead. The government's mismanagement of the economy at the time delayed the immediate realisation of its benefits, but by the late 1980s Ireland finally achieved inflation rates of 2–3 per cent for the first time in twenty years.

Despite the economy roaring ahead at a world-beating pace throughout the Celtic Tiger years, the transition of the ERM into the euro helped ensure that annual inflation only once tipped above 5 per cent.

The subsequent crash brought the opposite problem. Something we hadn't experienced since the end of World War II: falling prices. Not inflation, but deflation. 'What fell quite strongly was housing, water, electricity and gas,' says Kavanagh. 'Oil prices fell quite dramatically with the reduction in global demand so that reduced the cost of electricity and some utilities. Lower interest rates, as Central Bankers responded to the crisis, and falling house prices meant that mortgage interest repayments declined significantly. The price of food and clothing went down as well due to the widespread recession.'

Although inflation returned again in 2011, it has remained at a remarkably low level. For the past eight years it has not exceeded 1 per cent per annum. For all intents and purposes prices are at a standstill. That provides citizens, employers and government with a bedrock of stability. Although government and economists now worry that inflation is too low, and therefore could easily tip again into deflation, the era of historically low price increases could yet be here for some time to come.

Products with the Greatest Price Increases and Decreases

Nominal changes in consumer prices over the past 25 years

SOURCE: CENTRAL STATISTICS OFFICE[31]

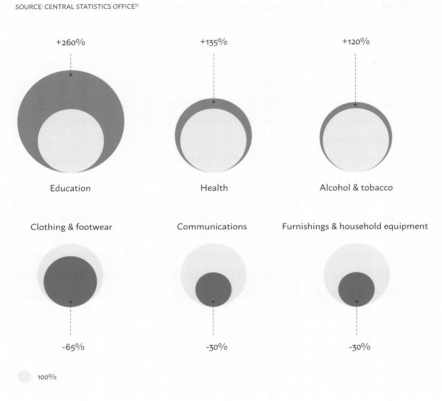

+260%

Education

+135%

Health

+120%

Alcohol & tobacco

Clothing & footwear

−65%

Communications

−30%

Furnishings & household equipment

−30%

100%

The reported inflation rate is an average, based on the price for a basket of consumer goods that the CSO tracks monthly. But the average price hides huge variations in different types of goods. And there have been some astonishing changes in a relatively short time.

Since 1996 the real cost of clothing and footwear has plummeted by two-thirds. That's right, buying a pair of shoes today will cost you only a third of what it cost your parents to buy an equivalent pair twenty-five years ago. Asking someone who was visiting the US to bring you back a pair of jeans to save a few bob is now entirely unnecessary. (Yes, that used to happen.)

The price of furniture and household appliances has fallen by 30 per cent. As with our clothing, the benefit of globalisation is realised in our pockets. Buying clothes made in Bangladesh and fridges made in Turkey is saving us all a hell of a lot of money. Our open economy has ensured that we have benefited to the greatest possible extent.

The cost of communications has similarly fallen by nearly a third. Telecom Éireann had a virtual monopoly on telecommunications services back in 1996. Not only has competition grown hugely, but the option of connecting with someone over broadband has driven the cost of calling the other side of the planet to close to zero.

What is increasing most is the things that cannot be automated or easily outsourced to countries with lower labour costs. Education and health services have more than doubled in price. These are people-intensive sectors in which higher wages are required to cover the cost of skilled employees. They are also sectors for which our appetite has grown hugely: we are progressing to higher levels of education, are increasingly learning throughout our lives, and are living longer with the help of medical advances. The fact that the government has raised the prices of alcohol and tobacco, frankly, plays a positive role in helping us to live longer too.

With inflation now at such low levels, any increase in our income can contribute meaningfully to improving our quality of life rather than merely covering the increasing cost of standing still.

The Proportion of the Population on Lower Incomes Is Declining and the Middle Class Is Growing

Can it really be any surprise to learn that Ireland's middle class is growing and that the proportion of people on lower incomes is declining? Given all the achievements that I have highlighted?

You are defined as being middle class if your after-tax household income is not less than two-thirds the national median average and not more than double it. Household size and composition is taken into account as larger households clearly need more income than smaller ones to sustain a middle-class lifestyle. A single person with an after-tax income of between €16,500 and €50,000 was therefore counted as middle class in 2018. A household with two adults and two teenage children, in contrast, needed between €41,500 and €125,000.[32]

Percentage of the population in the upper-, middle- and lower-income brackets

SOURCE: CENTRAL STATISTICS OFFICE[33]

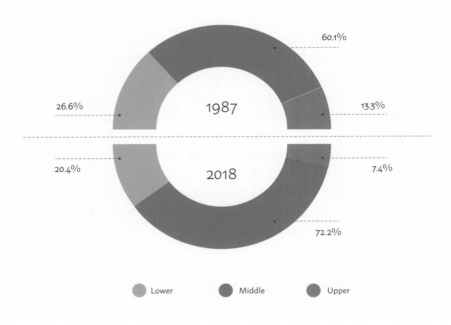

Look back to 1987 and six in ten of us were in the middle-income category, while more than a quarter were in the lower-income bracket. Jump forward to 2018 and the middle-income group has grown significantly to nearly three-quarters, while the lower income group has shrunk to one fifth.

In fact, Ireland has seen the biggest expansion of the middle class among Western European nations over recent decades. At a time when a lot of developed countries are experiencing a shrinking middle class, we have bucked the trend.[34] But it is not just that the proportion earning middle-incomes that has grown – the average income level itself has increased sharply. Today incomes are 70 per cent higher than they were in 1987, even after stripping out inflation.

One factor that has assisted in reducing the proportion on lower incomes was the introduction of a national minimum wage in 2000. Initially set at €5.58 an hour, it had risen to €10.20 by 2021. Allowing for inflation in the intervening years, that represents a real increase of nearly one-third. We can be proud of the fact that Ireland's rate is the second highest in Europe, only beaten by Luxembourg. Someone on the minimum wage will earn close to half the median national income. However, our European rank slips back to sixth place when you take account of the fact that the cost of living in Ireland is more expensive than in some other countries.[35]

Growth in personal wealth engenders political stability. We have lived through one of the most rapid advancements of any Western European nation in the past fifty years. Is it reasonable to suggest that the support of the majority of Irish voters for centrist politics over many decades has been underpinned by their experience of improving living standards? Those improvements have surely provided a bulwark to the rise of extremism on the far left or the far right.

Of course there are those still in poverty who need greater support, but our economic transformation has benefited huge numbers of people, not a few. We can easily envisage that improvement by contrasting our own lives with those of our parents and grandparents when they were our age.

The path has not always been a straight upward one either. Talk of the 'squeezed middle class' in other countries concerns the declining proportion of middle-income earners, under pressure from a growth in the number of both higher and lower earners. In Ireland it's different. Our 'squeeze' was the deep and widespread impact of the Great Recession.

'The last recession caused a profound shake-up in Irish society,' says Professor Christopher Whelan, the former head of the School of Sociology at University College Dublin. 'People saw the values of their property collapse, they saw the value of their savings eroded, in the public sector they saw large reductions in their salaries, they saw swinging increases in their taxation, and so suddenly they went from relatively comfortable lives to really being under pressure. People who would normally be considered to be middle class simply had problems paying the bills.'

The impact was disproportionately felt by those on middle income.[36] 'You can say the people at the bottom suffered as well – of course they did, I'm not suggesting for a moment that they didn't – but the level of absolute change in their living standards was different than for many of these middle-class people. If you were in public housing then your housing wasn't affected, and welfare benefits weren't slashed that much, so there was a buffering effect for those at the bottom.'

Those in a higher social class typically have the benefit of savings and assets, of a supportive family and network, that lower-income earners do not have. 'During the recession, these weren't operating at the same level. People's assets were now liabilities, their feelings of security were greatly reduced, their parents weren't in the same position to help them as they might have been before.'

'Who were the people who were kicking up the most? They were teachers, nurses, guards – these were the guys who were feeling screwed,' says Whelan. You could argue that, compared to the worst off in our society, they had no right to be complaining. But it was more of a crush than a squeeze for many in Ireland's middle class. And it took them several years to recover, for those that did so.

The shake-up resulted in lots of top-income earners losing out. According to the Revenue Commissioners, more than four in ten of those who made up the top 10 per cent of earners before the recession experienced income drops so significant that they dropped out of that category. But it also saw many lower-income earners benefit as the recovery got underway. More than three-quarters of those in the bottom 10 per cent rose out of that group in the early years of the recovery.[37]

All of this points to very fluid social class membership. It is entirely possible for people to work their way up from one class to the next, but also for those in higher classes to drop down. After all, the proportion of higher-income earners has nearly halved over the past thirty years – partly due to the strong increase in average incomes sweeping the lower echelons of the 'upper class' into the middle-class net, and partly due to the disproportionate hit that upper-income earners took during the recession.

It is not the case in Ireland that if you are rich then you are guaranteed to stay rich. Or that if you are a lower earner, you are destined to remain so for good. There is an equality of opportunity in Irish society that is to be welcomed.

45   Household Wealth Is at an All-Time High

The assets owned by private citizens have never been worth more than they are today. Irish households are wealthier than ever. Net household wealth – that is, households' assets minus their liabilities – totalled €855 billion at the end of 2020. Spread amongst 1.7 million households, that equates to an average of more than €500,000 per household.

Not every household is wealthy, of course. There are many with no assets at all and others who have net liabilities. But, as a country, we exceeded the previous heights of the Celtic Tiger in 2018.[38] Irish households are twice as wealthy now as they were twenty years ago.

Property constitutes the largest single element of most households' wealth. The bricks and mortar they occupy is what most of them will spend twenty or thirty years paying to own. When the mortgage is finally sorted, the value of that house or apartment is likely to be the single most valuable thing the householders own. It will also be worth a lot more than they originally paid for it, all going well.

The bad boom years pushed property values through the roof – unsustainably. The utter mania of the market is evident in the Central Bank's statistics. In just five years, from 2002 to 2007, the value of household property assets doubled! Speculation over proper valuation.

Things reversed very quickly during the crash. By 2013 our property assets were back at 2002 values. The collapse caused devastation to the property development and construction sectors, leading to a dearth of new housing for the best part of a decade that has had implications for today's young adults. 'Clearly a lot of wealthy people are older people who have houses and have paid off their mortgages,' explains Professor Christopher Whelan. 'Whereas a lot of younger people don't have these kinds of assets and are now facing a housing situation where it's almost impossible for them to get a foot on the ladder.' It's creating a wealth inequality problem for the future.

Household wealth and liabilities, 2002–20

SOURCE: CENTRAL BANK OF IRELAND[39]

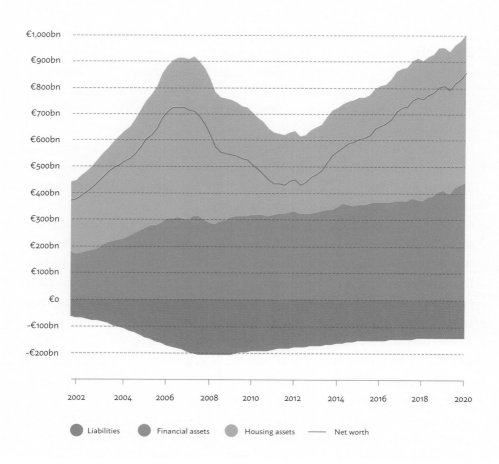

Liabilities   Financial assets   Housing assets   —— Net worth

Property asset values are not yet back to the highs of the Celtic Tiger era, but they are getting close. That is good news if you own a property today, but bad news if you want to acquire one – just as it was fifteen years ago.

It is, however, steady growth in the value of financial assets – people's pensions and insurance – that have underpinned the record wealth levels of recent years. Their value was barely impacted by the crash; their growth merely stalled temporarily. The increase is welcome, but we have a long way to go yet. 'What people don't have here – apart from public servants – is pension wealth,' says Whelan. 'In Germany and in the US, for instance, a lot of your wealth is in your pension fund, which is one of the reasons people get really upset with declines in the markets. Everybody there knows that their living conditions in retirement are very strongly tied to what goes on in the stock market, and that's not true of all that many people in Ireland.'

This is gradually changing. Success would be a sustained increase in household wealth over the next couple of decades as people invest more in financial assets to prepare for their future retirement and to buffer them against an unforeseen change in their personal circumstances.

Poverty Is in Decline

Close your eyes for a moment and think back to your history textbook from your school days. Conjure up a memory of one of those black-and-white photographs illustrating life in Ireland in the early twentieth century. It might be a farmer and his large family standing outside their small thatched cottage. Or ragged, barefoot children gathered on the streets of Cork or Dublin in front of their tenement buildings. It doesn't take much effort to reflect on how far we have come in a century. The poverty that was so evident and so prevalent has effectively been eliminated.

But that change came slowly, says Professor Christopher Whelan. 'Even in the 1950s people lacked what would now be considered minimum facilities. Families living in older buildings in the cities would have had to share their bathroom. Talk to people now about not having a bathroom!'

Working conditions in the dominant agricultural sector and in the growing industrial sector were relatively tough. Wages were low and people survived from week to week. Family sizes were much larger, so those low wages had to cater for more mouths.

State welfare support was extremely limited. The Free State inherited the Old Age Pension from the British government. From 1909, those aged 70 and over, of low or moderate incomes, were able to avail of a weekly payment. A form of unemployment assistance was also in place for those in industrial occupations. With health and education provision predominantly controlled by the Catholic Church, the State's primary welfare investment in its early decades was in public housing provision.

Percentage of population experiencing consistent poverty, 2003–19

SOURCE: CENTRAL STATISTICS OFFICE

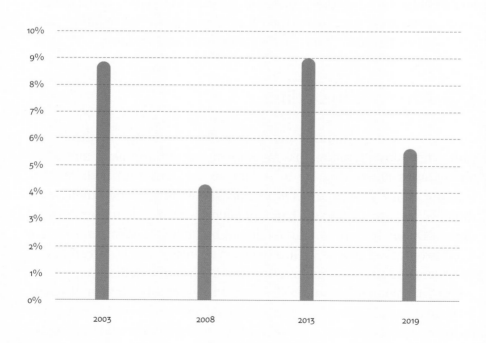

The first Fianna Fáil government, however, specifically sought to address rural poverty through the introduction of national unemployment assistance in 1933. This replaced locally administered schemes and covered those in agricultural employment and domestic service for the first time. The children's allowance followed in 1944 to reduce the risk of poverty amongst large families. Initially applied only to those with three or more children, it was extended to cover the second child in the 1950s and the first-born in the 1960s.

Other supports were few and far between. Even if it had had the ambition to do more, the State lacked the financial resources. It was not until we opened ourselves to the world again, and realised the economic benefits of doing so, that we had the resources to meaningfully improve living standards and address poverty.

'My wife is from Headford in Galway. In the early 70s, when I was going to Headford, you were aware of the local hierarchy, which was the bank manager, the doctor and the parish priest,' says Whelan. 'Farming was still hugely important and small businesses, such as shopkeepers, were really important. That huge traditional occupational structure was still there, while the professional and managerial group was rather modest.'

The new opportunities created by our economic growth swept that structure clean away. Opportunities opened up that never existed for previous generations. And the inevitable consequence of that is greater social mobility, which in turn has a large impact on reducing poverty and inequality.

'The occupational structure changed dramatically over a relatively short period of time,' points out Whelan. 'If you look at the UK, they have problems to do with the fact that they were an advanced industrial nation quite early on. So the changes in their workforce occupations are often to do with loss – the decline of mining, the decline of shipbuilding, the decline of traditional engineering – which accounts for part of their political problems. It's related to their north-south divide and to the way their class divisions have emerged.' Our situation is different because we never had those industrial jobs to begin with. We didn't have to deal with deindustrialisation as Britain and many other countries did.

Our increasing investment in education also played an important part in empowering people to make the most of the changing landscape of work.

'When the crash came in the 1980s, lots of kids in England were leaving school aged 15 to go to jobs which were there. Those kinds of jobs for young working-class people simply weren't there for our kids so a lot of them stayed on in education. That turned out to be significantly to our advantage later on.'

Joining the European Community provided economic benefits that enabled the government to tackle poverty through the introduction of new social welfare supports and to provide relatively high levels of benefits. It also opened us up to what was happening elsewhere in Europe and to how we measured up. The first comprehensive survey of poverty in Ireland was undertaken in 1987 with funding from the European institutions, and in 1994 a pan-European household survey commenced that provided comparisons across the Continent for the first time. 'The European notions of social exclusion began to percolate the public sector. But it wasn't just that the idea spread, it was often that there were European requirements that they reported on social progress in certain areas.'

Poverty can be measured in absolute or relative terms. In absolute terms, how many people do not have enough income to maintain a basic standard of living that enables them to feed and house themselves and their family? In relative terms, how many people are in the bottom income bracket and receiving significantly less than the average national income?

As societies become wealthier, the aim should be to reduce the number experiencing absolute poverty while acknowledging that only in a very equal society can there be no one in the relative poverty bracket. Those in absolute poverty are, by definition, suffering deprivation in some aspect of their lives. 'When unemployment went up very substantially in the 80s, relative poverty levels didn't vary very much but deprivation levels shot through the roof. Then, later on in the 90s, the issue was the opposite as employment picked up and again the relative poverty position didn't move very much but the deprivation levels dropped dramatically.'

So what is the best way of measuring poverty in a meaningful way that reflects these dramatic changes in individuals' lives? Whelan, together with Brian Nolan in the Economic and Social Research Institute, developed a measure of consistent poverty. It identifies the percentage of people who are suffering from at least two forms of material deprivation in their lives. This may mean that they cannot afford to keep their homes adequately warm, that they cannot afford to buy new clothes, or that they cannot afford a decent meal every couple of days.

In 2019 one in twenty of our citizens found themselves in the sad situation of consistent poverty. They were more likely to be lone parents, the unemployed or those who weren't at work due to illness or disability.

When we think back to those old school textbooks, we must take some comfort from the fact that the figure has declined to this level. Nineteen out of every twenty of us do not lack the means of providing food and shelter for ourselves and our loved ones. Good progress was made during the Celtic Tiger years in reducing consistent poverty to just 4.2 per cent. The subsequent crash saw that figure more than double so that one in ten were experiencing consequential poverty by 2013, before solid progress was made in reducing this again before the Covid crisis. The government will have to work hard to prevent a retrenchment and to progress poverty elimination.

So how low can consistent poverty go? Whelan and his colleague incorporated some softer measures of deprivation in order to give a broad indication of social exclusion. 'We put in things like "being able to have friends over for dinner once a month" and "being able to buy presents for family or friends". The problem with that is that it becomes practically impossible to get to zero. I'd be astonished if consistent poverty ever fell below 3 per cent unless you changed the measures to reflect something quite different.'

We were closing in on that level. That said, there is clearly more that we can do. Our proportion of consistently poor people is lower than that in Spain and Italy, similar to France and Belgium, but not yet as low as it is in the Netherlands or in the Nordic countries.

Income Inequality Is Decreasing and Is Less Than Elsewhere

There has been a growing debate about inequality in Irish society over the last few years. Such a debate is one to be welcomed. It can helpfully guide the hand of government, of non-governmental organisations and of individuals who can act to abate the negative impacts of inequality. But it is important that the debate is informed by the facts.

The good news is that inequality in Ireland is not growing. It is, in fact, declining somewhat and had reached the lowest level recorded in recent times before the Covid crisis. The equally good news is that inequality here compares favourably to that in other countries. We are a more equal nation than most.

That is a remarkable achievement. Successive governments have acted responsibly in sharing the benefits of the country's economic rises and protecting those less fortunate from the economic falls. Of course more can be done to engender greater equality, but we are not in a bad place and have been travelling in the right direction.

Income inequality (Gini coefficient percentage), 2004–19

SOURCE: CENTRAL STATISTICS OFFICE

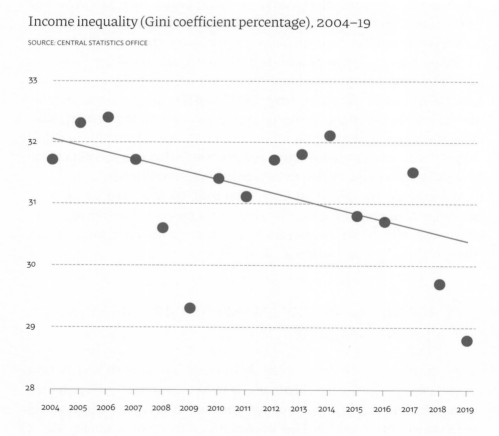

How is inequality measured? The globally accepted metric is the Gini coefficient, named after the Italian statistician who developed it. It gives a percentage score for how equal income distribution is in a country. A country in which every resident has the same income would have a score of 0 per cent, while a country in which one resident earned all the income – and everyone else earned nothing – would have a score of 100 per cent. So lower scores denote greater equality. Our scores have edged downwards from 32 per cent in the mid-noughties to around 29 per cent today.

How does this reconcile with the inequality apparent throughout Irish society? Some people clearly earn a fortune while others are entirely reliant on State support – not just for a temporary period, but for a large portion of their lives. The answer lies in our taxation and welfare systems. When you look at gross incomes – the amount everyone gets before taxation and welfare supports kick in – then we are, indeed, a highly unequal society. There are people earning enormous amounts and there are people literally earning nothing. However, our tax system does a great job of ensuring that higher earners pay more, and our welfare system does a great job of ensuring that those earning nothing have the resources they need.

No other tax system in Europe does more to reduce income inequality than Ireland's.[40] We are a leader at taxing people's incomes in a fair and progressive manner. Our highest rate of income tax comes into effect quite early on, for levels of pay that other countries would consider moderate. The Universal Social Charge (USC), in addition, is a broad-based progressive tax, which ensures that practically every income-earner makes some contribution towards the government's funding of social services. It is common to hear political parties promise to reduce or abolish USC at election times, but to do so would increase inequality. Is that really the best outcome for society?

Our pension and welfare benefits systems are also effective in supporting a large number of people with low or no income, and providing them with respectable rates of welfare payments. One of Ireland's distinctive characteristics is the number of people with no incomes at all who are entirely reliant on State support. We have the highest percentage of adults of working age, living alone, who are permanently disabled or unfit for work in all of Europe. We also have the highest percentage of single-parent households in all of Europe, and the lowest percentage of those single parents who work outside the home.[41]

So what can be done to help these families to boost their income? 'The only thing you can do, long-term, is what the Danes and the Swedes have done: to say "we have to find ways of getting these people into the labour market", which might involve drastically improving the child support services available to them,' says Whelan. This is not about forcing anybody to do anything. Rather, by supporting people to obtain skills and by improving childcare options, increasing numbers will have the opportunity to boost their income through paid employment when it suits them to do so. The more people that avail of such opportunities, the more inequality in society can be further reduced.

It is entirely natural for Irish people to compare themselves to our nearest neighbour and to the other English-speaking country with which we have the greatest affinity, namely the United Kingdom and the United States. But to do so for income inequality is perilous. Those two nations are outliers amongst developed nations. Inequality soared in both countries during the 1980s in a way that it didn't elsewhere. The legacies of President Ronald Reagan and Prime Minister Margaret Thatcher remain evident today.

Income inequality in selected countries

SOURCES: CSO (IRELAND), EUROSTAT (EU COUNTRIES), WORLD BANK (USA)[42]

Country	Gini measure of income inequality
United States	41.4%
United Kingdom	33.5%
Italy	32.8%
EU average	30.2%
Germany	29.7%
France	29.2%
Ireland	**28.8%**
Denmark	27.5%
Norway	25.4%

Ireland is much more equal than both of those countries and more equal than most places in Europe. Why did we not follow in the footsteps of our Anglo-American cousins? Four factors have contributed to our fundamentally different outlook: our politics, our education, our uniformity and our history.

Like it or not, centrist politics have stood us in good stead. We did not have political parties with deep ideological differences who might demonise sections of the population from which they did not draw their support. 'A significant reason has been the dominance of Fianna Fáil, the classic catch-all party with its roots in small farming and the working class,' says Whelan. 'It was never profitable for them to go down that road.'

Our education system is more universal and more Christian. Nearly everyone receives the same education at primary and secondary level, irrespective of their social background. Limited numbers of children attend private schools and, even when they do, the schools are often run by religious orders. Christian principles, with an emphasis on charity towards those less fortunate, therefore helped shape the worldview of our social and civic leaders – again, like it or not.

We are a relatively small and, until recently, homogeneous community. We don't suffer from great social class differences. We don't have great ethnic divides. And for all the talk of rural versus urban Ireland, there aren't significant differences between our regions in comparison to the UK or the US or Germany or Italy. Your accent matters a lot less here than in other places.

Finally, our history of national poverty is entrenched in our psyche and embedded in our school history curriculum. Most of us can talk about the struggles of our grandparents or their parents. 'If I should fall from grace with God,' as the Pogues might have put it.

Together, these factors create a supportive culture that enables greater generosity for those who need our support. 'You can look at the structure of [welfare] benefits and in that respect the Irish system still mirrors a lot of the UK,' says Whelan. 'But if you look at the actual levels of benefit and the way in which the systems are implemented, they are very, very different.'

So where do we go from here? The surge in Covid-related unemployment has, once again, put enormous pressure on our social welfare system. The radical change in many people's circumstances will make it very difficult to prevent rises in consistent poverty and inequality over the next year or two. But even as we turn our attention to addressing the short-term challenge, we must also consider where the longer journey is taking us. If we want to further reduce inequality, then how are we going to pay for that? Are we prepared to all make a greater financial contribution towards becoming a more socially democratic state?

We need a serious debate on how to bear the cost of the growing public services that the Irish people want for themselves and their families. Social partnership benefited Irish society in the 1990s and 2000s. Another coming together of our civic and political institutions could design a new social contract to get us to where we want to go in the 2020s.

We Have Changed from a Net Beneficiary of the European Union to a Net Contributor

Do you recall the time when every major road in Ireland had a large metal sign along it announcing it was 'part-funded by the European Union'? Maybe you are too young. When I was in my teens they seemed to be everywhere. You could recast the puzzle that James Joyce set in *Ulysses*: can you cross Dublin city without passing a pub? Only, it would have been: can you cross through County Dublin without passing a 'funded by Europe' road sign?

European Union membership transformed Ireland's fortunes. From the year we joined, in 1973, we received back far more in direct financial assistance than we paid in our membership fee. That annual funding kept growing, year after year, for more than twenty years. In 1997 we reached a peak of €2.7 billion net benefit. Allowing for the inflation in subsequent years, that's equivalent to over €4 billion in today's terms.

The initial beneficiary was the agricultural sector. Gerard Kiely was the Director of the European Commission's Representation in Ireland until recently. As he recalls it, 'there were huge grants at the farm level and at the industry level. Larry Goodman's empire today was built on EU grants, as it was for Dawn Meats and any of the meat or dairy industry leaders.'

In combination with that was the opportunity to develop new markets for our agricultural produce and to diversify away from our reliance on Britain as our dominant customer. Being a member of the EEC gave our producers not only access to European countries but also the opportunity to partake in the Community's export schemes to more distant markets.

Ireland's receipts from the EU minus payments made, 1976–2019

SOURCE: EUROPEAN COMMISSION

Structural Funds to modernise our national infrastructure flowed in significant quantities from the 1980s. They accounted for more than 3 per cent of the country's Gross National Product (GNP) at their height.[43] 'Everything that was built in Ireland in the 80s and 90s was EU-funded! There was some level of grant in there,' claims Kiely. Hence all those road signs.

But it was also funding for rail: new Intercity trains, the extension of the Dart line and constructing the Luas, for example. For ports and airports: the redevelopment of Cork, Killybegs and Rosslare ports to accommodate larger ships, and extensions to the terminals and runways at Dublin, Cork and Shannon Airports. For tourism sites such as Brú na Bóinne, Kilkenny Castle, the Irish Museum of Modern Art, the National Museum in Collins Barracks and the Museum of Country Life. For water and sewage treatment plants. And for new telecommunications and energy infrastructure.[44]

'After the Big Bang of European enlargement in 2004, you had a lot of similar-sized countries looking at Ireland as *the* example of how to use the Structural Funds. The Commission was telling these countries "go look at Ireland, they're a good example of how to go about it". It was well managed and thought out.'

As the benefits of our enhanced infrastructure began to pay economic dividends, in particular by enhancing our attractiveness as a location for foreign direct investment, so the amount we paid to be part of the Union increased. 'You pay into the budget more or less 1 per cent of GDP so if your GDP is growing you'll pay more in absolute terms. You get back a share of what you contribute under the different programmes.' While we no longer receive the high levels of Structural Funds that we did in the past, in agriculture and other areas the funding levels are similar. What has changed is that we have become a wealthier country and therefore our contribution has markedly increased.

In 2009 Ireland paid more into the European budget than it received for the first time – albeit fleetingly so, as the Great Recession then took hold. It is only since 2016 that we are now consistently paying out more to help other less developed European nations and beginning to repay the moral debt we owe Europe for our own advancement as a nation.

A focus on the financial transfers to or from Europe could, however, obscure the greatest benefit of membership. It isn't the amount of money we receive; it is how much we can earn with access to one of the most lucrative markets in the world: a single market of nearly 500 million people. As Kiely sees it, 'foreign companies aren't coming here because of the weather! They're not coming because of the corporation tax either – it's icing on the cake but that isn't the primary reason anymore. It's for access to the [European] internal market.'

There have been many non-financial benefits of European membership as well, of course. Most of our environmental regulation would not be in place today without the EU. Likewise, much of our equality legislation has originated in Europe – initially preventing discrimination by gender and subsequently by age, race, religion, disability and sexual orientation. 'There isn't one area of your life in day-to-day living that isn't influenced in some way or other by the EU, directly or indirectly,' concludes Kiely.

Being a member has helped open Ireland to the world, and it has also helped open the world to Ireland. Being part of such an important bloc gives us an enhanced status on the world stage that we otherwise would not have. And that has enabled a wide range of additional, remarkable achievements.

(7)

Opening to the World

IRELAND IS ONE OF THE WORLD'S LEADING EXPORTING
COUNTRIES. THE VALUE OF THE GOODS AND SERVICES WE
EXPORT EXCEEDS THE VALUE OF EVERY OTHER PART OF OUR
ECONOMY.[1] THIS A RECENT DEVELOPMENT – SINCE 2010 – BUT
WE ARE NOW ONE OF ONLY A HANDFUL OF COUNTRIES FOR
WHICH THIS IS TRUE.[2] WE HAVE BECOME ONE OF THE MOST
OPEN COUNTRIES IN THE WORLD.

 ## 49 We Export More Goods Than Ever

THE VALUE OF the goods we exported barely registered before the
1970s. Steady growth in the 70s and 80s was eclipsed by staggering
growth throughout the 90s when export values more than tripled in ten
years. Growth stagnated during the noughties before rocketing again in
the 2010s.

Most of this export growth has been created by foreign multinationals.
'Today, foreign multinationals account for over 80 per cent, maybe 90
per cent, of Irish exports. So the huge export-intensive nature of the
Irish economy is very much part of our story of attracting foreign multi-

nationals,' explains Frank Barry, Professor of International Business & Economic Development at Trinity College Dublin.

While our low corporate tax rate undoubtedly influences the value ascribed to goods by multinational firms, there is little doubt about the genuine benefit that their export orientation brings the people of Ireland. More jobs are directly or indirectly attributable to exports here than in any other developed economy. The majority of all the jobs done by men, and over 40 per cent of all the jobs done by women, are dependent on export sectors.[3]

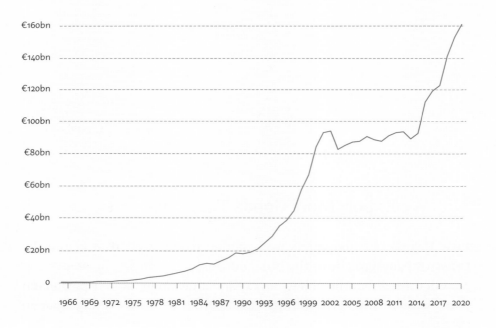

Value of goods exports, 1965–2020

SOURCE: CENTRAL STATISTICS OFFICE

'We are more export-oriented than most other small economies such as Greece, Portugal, Netherlands or Belgium. But we always have been, even when we were entirely reliant on agriculture: the agriculture we produced was always oriented towards the British market. Small economies are export-oriented and we are particularly export-orientated.'

The profile of our exports at the end of the 1940s could hardly be more different from today. Live cattle accounted for more than one-third. Horses, for breeding or racing, accounted for nearly a tenth. And so did fresh eggs. Beer was next on the list.[4]

As late as 1973, when we joined the EEC, most of our exported goods were agricultural. It was then that the diversification really occurred. Not only did it open up new markets for those traditional goods, but it also increased our attractiveness as a location for new foreign industries and for expansion by those foreign firms that had been attracted here since the late 1950s.

The 90s boom was greatly facilitated by the completion of the European Union's Single Market initiative. 'This had hugely important effects for Ireland that people were not predicting at the time. It was a large part of the Celtic Tiger boom,' explains Barry. 'It made restrictive public procurement policies illegal. Up until the Single Market, France could say to a multinational company "unless you come and produce your pharmaceuticals in France, our health system is not going to buy them". That was all made illegal. That freed up multinationals to locate where they wanted to locate and to export out of those locations.' And Ireland benefited enormously.

I explored how Ireland's Celtic Tiger was initially jump-started by our export boom but then became a 'bad' boom in the noughties, driven by excess borrowing. Policymakers and commentators at the time seemed to have failed to notice that our export growth had stalled. Ironically, it was the very success of that export-boosted boom that made it difficult for growth to continue.

'If one sector increases dramatically then it exerts cost pressures on other sectors and they can't expand as dramatically. We had a big domestic boom and a large share of the workforce got sucked into construction,' explains Barry. 'You can't have the construction sector running at full tilt and all other sectors of the economy running at full tilt as well.' A labour shortage for export firms ensued and wages shot up, limiting firms' ability to invest in growth.

Exports led Ireland's recovery from the subsequent crash. The converse happened as all that labour became available again, wages and other costs fell and export-oriented sectors were able to return to growth. Today, nearly a third of the goods we export are pharmaceuticals. A fifth of them are organic chemicals (as ingredients for medical, pharmaceutical, or biochemical products). One-tenth are medical devices.[5]

'We were a poor country in 1956, we had pretty much nothing going for us, and we stumbled on this policy that has proved highly beneficial. Being export-oriented is a better strategy because the higher the number of markets you export to, the more your risk is minimised. If one market goes belly-up, there are other markets you can turn to.' Ireland's unusually high degree of export orientation diversifies our economic risk and provides greater stability than a strategy that relies more on the performance of our small domestic market.

In a post-Covid-19 world, where companies will want to better manage their operational risk, there is arguably an even greater opportunity for Ireland to benefit from multinational investment as firms seek to further diversify their global presence to protect against the risk of a future epidemic halting their operations in some part of the world. Ireland is, furthermore, extremely well positioned in terms of the sectors that dominate our export economy: pharmaceuticals, medical devices and IT services are all likely to be areas of increased investment. Could we be any better positioned for a bounce back?

 ## We Are Leaders in Food and Drink Exports

Our food and drink exports account for a tenth of the value of all the goods we send overseas. And because we need to import very little to produce them and the realised profits are not subsequently repatriated to an overseas headquarters, the sector accounts for up to 40 per cent of the net earnings Ireland makes from goods exports.[6]

Dairy products and ingredients constitute over one-third of what we send overseas, meat and livestock is just under one-third, prepared consumer foods are around a fifth, and beverages constitute roughly a tenth. Seafood and horticulture complete the picture, but account for tiny amounts.[7] 'We export 90 per cent of what we produce and that is almost a unique ratio globally,' explains Helen King, until recently Director of Strategic Insight & Planning at Bord Bia, the Irish food board. 'I don't believe any other country comes near us with that.'

Notable facts about Ireland's exports

SOURCE: SUSTAINABLE FOOD SYSTEMS IRELAND, BORD BIA[8]

We are the largest net exporter of beef in the Northern Hemisphere

We produce over 10% of global infant formula

Our agri-food exports increased by 67% from 2010 to 2019

Irish Whiskey exports have nearly quadrupled since 2010

The world's first country to implement a national sustainability programme for agriculture and food: Origin Green

For a very long time our agricultural history has been about producing food to feed Britain. In the nineteenth century Ireland was referred to as Britain's 'breadbasket' in light of how much of our grain production was exported to feed their fast-growing industrial cities.[9] Our cross-channel trade in livestock was similarly well established for many decades before Irish independence.[10]

Our ability to expand our export markets beyond Britain was limited before we joined the European Community. That dependency had a downside: 'they could turn on and off the tap at will,' notes Professor Frank

Barry. 'They could say one year, "we're not going to take any more powdered milk from Ireland". So joining the EU is hugely significant to [Irish] firms. We became part of a rules-bound system and that allowed the stability for companies to start planning over a 10- or 20-year time horizon, rather than a one- or two-year time horizon.' It enabled our food and drink sector to start planning expansion into new markets. Market diversification, as I have highlighted, increases opportunity and reduces risk.

The last decade was an extraordinarily successful one. Our agri-food exports increased in value by 67 per cent from 2010 to 2019 to reach €13 billion.[11] What we are selling changed and where we are selling changed.

Dairy products, for example, nearly doubled in value in the decade. 'A big part of that was the lifting of the milk production quota in 2015. Since then, the amount of milk produced annually in Ireland has increased more than 50 per cent,' explains King. 'There has been massive growth in global demand for high-quality dairy products, which Ireland is well positioned to supply, and there has been opportunity to increase value growth ahead of volume growth through branded differentiation.'

The story of butter encapsulates all of those elements. The value of our butter exports nearly tripled to reach €1.1 billion. 'That was underpinned by an 85 per cent increase in the volume of butter being exported, but it was substantially driven by having people willing to pay more for Irish butter – a great example of this is Kerrygold in the US – and by a significant rise in the global commodity price for butter as more and more people start using it in their cooking or consuming products that are made with butter.'

We have been a leading beef exporter for many years. But did you know that we are the largest net exporter of beef in the Northern Hemisphere? Not on a per capita basis, but in the actual tonnes of weight that we ship overseas each year.

'When you take the export volume of beef and subtract imports, the only countries in the world that are larger net exporters of beef are Brazil, Argentina, India, Australia and New Zealand,' says King. 'We have a population of five million. Brazil and Argentina have a combined population of two hundred and fifty million!'

We have increased the value of our beef exports by doing more and more processing at home. Decades ago, our exports took the form of ships full of live cattle that were sent to the UK for slaughtering, processing and packaging. The meat processing companies have taken back all that added value to Ireland over the past 25 years. The exports leaving Ireland nowadays are the final packaged product destined directly for a supermarket shelf or a food-service provider.

Alcoholic drink is yet another sector that has been transformed. Twenty-five years ago it was mainly Baileys and Guinness that was being exported. Spirits have increased dramatically since then. Whiskey exports nearly quadrupled in the 2010s, driven primarily by Jameson.

It may be hard to believe that at the start of that decade there were only two whiskey distilleries in Ireland: the French company Pernod Ricard owned Irish Distillers and distilled their spirits in Midleton in County Cork, and the Irish-owned Cooley Distillery started operations in County Louth in 1987. By the end of the decade, however, there were thirty-one distilleries in operation![12] They have brought strong new Irish brands onto the market in recent years. That has stimulated innovation in how the whiskey is casked, how long it is matured and how it is branded, which is contributing to driving the strong growth.

But the foundation stone of the category's growth has been the success of Irish Distillers in their sales and marketing of Jameson. 'Whiskey was previously perceived to be quite an older man's drink,' says King. 'Jameson have done a fabulous job, particularly in the US, of having a brand that does exceptionally well in the younger age group that can also compete as a luxury drink. That eruption in exports over the last ten years is primarily due to Jameson, with the smaller brands adding on top.'

Aside from what we are exporting, it is also where we are exporting to that has profoundly changed. Our reliance on the British market has been in constant decline since we joined the EU and diversified within Europe. In the past decade that market diversification has expanded much further. The value of our food and drink exports to Asia, for example, quadrupled to €1.4 billion. 'The needs of the Asian middle class are evolving. They're looking for a more diverse range of foods. China and Southeast Asia typically did not eat beef or dairy but because of their increased wealth, because of their changing tastes, they're now increasing their consumption per capita in both beef and dairy at a pretty high rate.'

Our success with infant milk formula paved the way in penetrating Asia. Remarkably, Ireland is the source of more than 10 per cent of the world's formula. We exported just under 150,000 tonnes of it in 2019. Our biggest market is China, which receives over one-third, followed by the US and then Europe.

'Wyatt have the most premium brand of infant milk formula that is sold in China and Southeast Asia. A tin of infant milk formula here sells for €12. The Wyatt equivalent in China could sell for up to €100 for that. It's Irish grass-fed, premium milk that's going in. It's something to be really proud of. For their strong brands, they chose Ireland because of the quality of our product and its sustainability credentials.'

It will be a challenge for the Irish food sector to keep on growing at this pace. Can we really produce that much more food on our small island? 'Our benefit to the world is our small family farms. While that has huge benefits in terms of the care and the attention to the animals and its sustainability, the downside to that is we don't have scale so it's very difficult for us to compete on price,' says King. 'That's where the whole idea of Origin Green came about: how do we differentiate Irish food and drink if it's not going to be on price? We can do it through our sustainability credentials.'

Origin Green was the world's first national sustainability programme for agriculture and food production. Launched in 2012, it put in place standards and measurements to substantiate our claim that we are sustainable and green. 'It's at farm level, it's at processing level, and we have a programme for retailers. Farmers set benchmarks on all different aspects of the environment, animal welfare, energy usage and biodiversity,' explains King. 'Teagasc advisors audit the farms and then go back 18 months later, audit them again and look to monitor their progress towards a reduction in carbon footprint and energy usage.' A decade after its launch, 95 per cent of our dairy farmers and 85 per cent of beef farmers are in the programme.

The programme was ahead of its time. Consumer demands for sustainable food production and reductions in carbon emissions have increased markedly since it commenced. That provides us with a basis for increasing the value of our food exports, even if volume increases will inevitably become harder to achieve. We can play to our strength as a small island nation with a reputation for natural, organic food in order to command a premium price. The opportunity for continued value growth in the decade ahead is there.

 ## 51 Our Exports Travel Further Than Ever Before

Destination of goods exported, 1940–2020

SOURCE: CENTRAL STATISTICS OFFICE

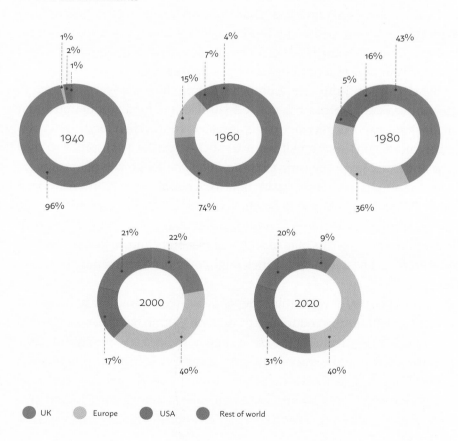

A central element of the story of Ireland's first century has been that of increasing economic and social independence from the United Kingdom. Ninety-six per cent of our exported goods in 1940 were destined for Britain, and that figure was still three-quarters of everything we exported in 1960. The explosive growth of the 1990s saw the UK's share fall to less than one quarter by the year 2000 as Europe's share grew to 40 per cent. Nowadays less than 10 per cent of our goods end up in the UK; three times as many are shipped westwards to the United States.

But our main indigenous sectors, both food and tourism, rely to a greater extent on the British market. As Helen King points out for the agri-food sector, 'our dependency on Britain has decreased, but still it's up at around 30 to 33 per cent overall. The biggest sectors impacted would be beef, cheese and mushrooms.' Half of all our beef, half of all our cheese and 90 per cent of our mushrooms cross the water to Britain.[13]

The UK's exit from the European Union has not yet resulted in substantive change. Britain is not self-sufficient in food production and it will take time to get other trade deals agreed to source their food elsewhere. Furthermore, consumers will want to stick with the Irish produce they know and trust for some time to come. 'The challenge will be if retailers decide to complete the shortfall in their Irish supply with South American beef or Polish beef, which will be *much* cheaper. But the challenge for the retailer is: will the consumer accept products that they don't believe are of the same quality in terms of food safety, traceability and sustainability?' In the short term perhaps not, but they might over time as Britain pivots to a wider world.

Ireland's journey of economic independence will ultimately be hastened by Brexit. It will further reduce our trade with Britain, whether we like it or not. Given how big a market the UK is, and how close it is, it may not make sense for us to aim to reduce our export trade much further. However, for some sectors such as food and tourism we have yet to reach an optimum level of independence that minimises our risk of being overly reliant on a single market and maximises the export revenue potential we can achieve for our nation.

52 We Export More Services Than Goods

Value of goods and services exports, 2003–19

SOURCE: CENTRAL STATISTICS OFFICE

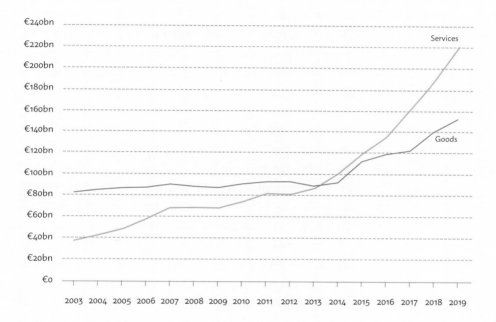

If I asked you to conjure up an image of a typical Irish export, what might it be? A bottle of Jameson on a supermarket shelf somewhere in Britain? An Avoca cardigan on the back of a recently returned American tourist? Or maybe a packet of Viagra from Pfizer's Cork factory hidden in a sock at the back of a chest of bedroom drawers?

None of these are typical Irish exports anymore because today's typical Irish export isn't a physical thing. It's a service.

The last decade saw a huge shift in the nature of what we export. Yes, goods exports increased sharply, but that was nothing compared to the growth in services exports we experienced. They effectively tripled in value. Since 2014, the value of the services we export has exceeded the value of all the goods. Services exports as a share of all our exports are now amongst the highest of any country.[14]

So what constitutes a service export? It could be a financial service, business advice, access to intellectual property, a software licence, a lease for an aircraft, or scientific research for an international client. None of them involve something being wrapped in a package, a label applied and a call to a delivery service. An email or conference call might be all it takes to 'export' the service to someone overseas.

I was a devoted Talking Heads fan when I was a teenager. The only way to get hold of their rare early vinyl releases was to buy *Record Collector* magazine monthly and to send off a postal order on trust to a record dealer somewhere in England who stocked the promised rarity. And then wait. Usually for a few weeks. Eventually, a masking-taped cardboard package would arrive containing the rare plastic pressing and the promised joy of music heard for the very first time. It was worth the wait.

All those LPs are now stored in my shed, even though I don't have a turntable anymore. It took so much effort to collect them, I just can't let them go. But now I can get every song ever released by Talking Heads – and practically every other artist there has ever been – on my mobile phone for less than the cost of getting one of those old vinyls shipped to me each month. It's mind-blowing.

The internet has truly revolutionised our world. It has also changed all those goods exports I was receiving into services exports. The same music, the same pleasure, but delivered digitally instead of physically, changes it from a good into a service. This shift is what underpins our explosive growth in services exports. 'The big IT companies used to export their programmes on CD ROMs so that counted as a merchandise good export,' explains Professor Frank Barry. 'When's the last time you saw a CD ROM when you got a new computer? They don't exist anymore. These are now exported over the internet.'

Growing digitisation has also allowed companies to structure themselves differently. Spotify can be based wherever it wants – no one is needed to run down to the CD archive in the basement to locate that obscure track in order to fulfil a listener's request. And its customer service agents and finance team can be located on the other side of the world if that is what works best.

IDA Ireland has been notably successful in attracting many of these corporate subsidiaries to establish operations here. The services provided by their agents and accountants are legitimate exports if they are charging an overseas firm or parent company for them. And Ireland benefits from the employment and the tax revenue.

We Are Amongst the Best in the World at Attracting Investment from Foreign Companies

It may be obvious that Ireland has had great success in attracting foreign direct investment (FDI) over many decades. Measuring the extent of that success is, however, more difficult than you might imagine. The official statistics on international investment flows include a lot of cross-border corporate mergers and acquisitions. There may be no job creation or facilities investment associated with any of that. How can you narrow the measure of FDI to only that which kindles genuine economic activity?

The IBM Institute for Business Value has pioneered a way. It tracks every corporate announcement of a new facility or a planned expansion everywhere in the world. It tallies the totals for every country every year to calculate the genuine job creation and economic development occurring in that place.

Their figures show emphatically that Ireland is one of the very best countries at attracting job-creating foreign investment. Accounting for the size of every country, Ireland has been the second best in the world at attracting this valuable type of investment over the past decade. We are the only Western European country to feature in the top ten.

The quantity of jobs created is a very useful indicator. But the quality of those jobs is equally important. 'In mature economies, where you have lower unemployment, people are more interested in the quality and value of those jobs,' says Jacob Dencik, who leads the Economic Research function at the IBM Institute. 'For every project we record we therefore assess the knowledge-intensity, the skills requirements and the salaries associated with those type of projects, and apply a value to each job announcement. That allows us to assess each country on the average value of the project they receive. On that metric, Ireland has come out on top every year.'

Average number of jobs created through foreign investment for every million residents per year, 2009–18

SOURCE: IBM INSTITUTE FOR BUSINESS VALUE[15]

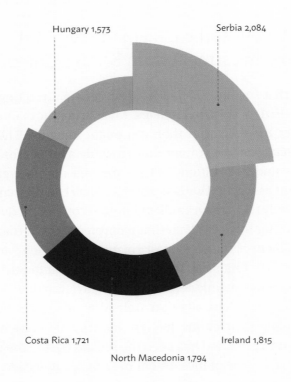

Hungary 1,573

Serbia 2,084

Costa Rica 1,721

North Macedonia 1,794

Ireland 1,815

That is to say, the jobs generated by foreign investment here have been worth more than those generated in any other country on the globe every single year for the past decade. 'Ireland receives a lot of R&D investment in IT and in life sciences, and there is also some investment in regional headquarters, so it is those higher quality functions within high-value sectors that combine to give Ireland a very high score.'

Ireland's performance in those high-value sectors is incredibly strong. The top five global software companies are located here. Nine of the top ten US technology companies. All of the world's top ten pharmaceutical companies. Fourteen of the top fifteen medical technology companies. Eight of the top ten financial services companies.[16]

Dencik also credits Ireland's investment in education as paying strong dividends. 'In the last 10 or 20 years what has been key is the way you approach skills development and make sure that you have a strong talent pool for those sectors that are important for the economy. The needs of business are fed back into how you design your education and skills policy. That's an important element that is less well developed in other countries.' It has helped Ireland increase the value it can offer firms that locate here and, in return, the earnings we can generate from being employed by them.

'Ireland started off as one of the lower-cost but lower-quality locations in Western Europe. It was the low-cost proposition that was attractive to companies and Ireland used that to attract investment. Over the last 40 years Ireland has improved its quality as an FDI location through investment in education, through investment in infrastructure, through the maturity of the research and innovation environment, and improvements in the business environment. Ireland has shot up to become a really prominent high-quality location. You can justify the higher salaries and the higher costs that you have because of that higher quality. It is a remarkable shift [...] compared to other countries.'

The policy of encouraging inward investment, consistently pursued by every government for many decades, has proved a winning formula that continues to bring the country rich rewards. 'There is a common assumption that because we have a low rate of corporation tax, we don't collect much corporation tax. In fact, we collect *vast* amounts of corporation tax,' says Professor Frank Barry. 'Interestingly, when we started out on this export strategy in the 1950s the tax receipts were of no interest to us – there was a zero rate of corporation tax on exports for a while – it was employment we were concerned with.' This, too, has been delivered in spades. The bulk

191

of our export-related employment is underpinned by foreign firms that typically pay higher wages than indigenous Irish companies.[17]

Is there a risk that we are now overly dependent on foreign businesses? 'We have been relying on foreign direct investment firms for 60–70 years now and there has never been the kind of catastrophe that people are always saying is possible, "oh, they might get up and leave overnight",' says Barry. 'It hasn't happened yet, and it doesn't look to me like it will.'

As other countries learn to copy Ireland's success, can we continue to win as high a share of global FDI in the decades ahead? If we continue to develop the skills necessary to attract it, then yes. Dencik cites the IT industry as an example. 'Their skills requirements are changing rapidly and one thing that Ireland has been very good at is thinking ahead and saying "OK, we're now seeing AI [Artificial Intelligence] changing the IT industry – how can we ensure that five or ten years from now we have the skills in our economy that will ensure we remain attractive to inward investment?"'

These foreign companies have themselves been great training grounds for generations of Irish workers. They have helped to widen our horizons and develop our global business expertise. That, in turn, has strengthened the skill base available for Irish firms to pursue international expansion.

Irish Companies Are Amongst the Leading Creators of Jobs Overseas

For every job created in Ireland by a foreign company, Irish domiciled companies create more than one elsewhere in the world. We have become a source of significant foreign direct investment ourselves.

The IBM Institute for Business Value's analysis shows that over the course of the past decade Ireland has been amongst the top five nations in the world creating overseas jobs, once you allow for population size. We have been the leading country in the European Union, despite the figures encompassing the years of the Great Recession.

We have many Irish corporate successes to celebrate. Kerry Group is a leading player in the global food and beverage industry with manufacturing locations in 32 countries and over 26,000 employees.[18] Smurfit

Kappa's packaging operation has production sites across 35 countries with over 46,000 employees.[19] CRH's building materials business has a presence at 3,100 locations in 30 countries and employs 77,000 people.[20] These are homegrown companies whose continued overseas expansion is a tangible benefit to our economy and creates high-skilled jobs here.

Average number of jobs created through international investment for every million residents per year, 2009–18

SOURCE: IBM INSTITUTE FOR BUSINESS VALUE[21]

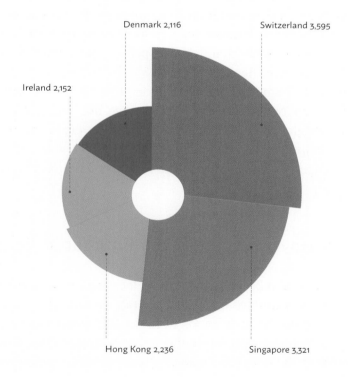

Denmark 2,116

Switzerland 3,595

Ireland 2,152

Hong Kong 2,236

Singapore 3,321

Multinational companies that have located their corporate headquarters to Ireland are also counted as Irish, even if the vast majority of their activity take place elsewhere. Did you know that Accenture, for example, is headquartered here? The business services firm is listed on the New York stock exchange, has annual revenues of over $44 billion and employs more than 500,000 people.[22] The company relocated to Ireland from Bermuda in 2009. Every time Accenture creates 1,000 jobs overseas, it counts as job creation by an Irish firm.

They are not alone – the last decade has seen an assortment of large American firms relocating their HQ here. Medtronic is a medical device company. Its 'inversion' from an American to an Irish company in 2018 was the biggest in American corporate history and saved it paying billions of dollars of tax in the US. Yet Ireland accounts for less than 0.1 per cent of Medtronic's sales.[23] Have you heard of Johnson Controls, which produces safety and security equipment for buildings? Or Eaton Corporation, which is a power management company? All three of these Irish firms employ more than 100,000 people each – but very, very few of those jobs are located here.

Regardless of whether the expansion stems from the success of an indigenous firm or a multinational enterprise, our national reputation as a location for global business is enhanced with every job announcement. And that helps create opportunities for the next wave of Irish firms and Irish business leaders that follow in their footsteps to flourish on the world stage.

We Have Eliminated Our Emigration Tradition

Ireland's success in becoming a leading location for the export of goods and services has enabled us to turn the tide on our other great export – our people. From the early 1920s until the end of the twentieth century roughly 1.5 million people left independent Ireland.[24] One of the reasons our population did not grow for so long was because so many people were leaving. When emigration reached its peak in the 1950s, the number of emigrants equalled the number of births in some years.[25]

Our emigration tradition has distant historical roots. When I represent Ireland at European meetings, I invariably get seated next to the representative from Iceland. Their tourist board's chief executive was a qualified geneticist. As she put it to me, most Icelandic men have DNA that originates in Norway, and most Icelandic women have DNA that originates in Ireland. That's an emigration story worth telling, but perhaps not one the participants willingly engaged in!

Net number of people emigrating from, or immigrating to, Ireland, 1951–2020

SOURCE: CENTRAL STATISTICS OFFICE[26]

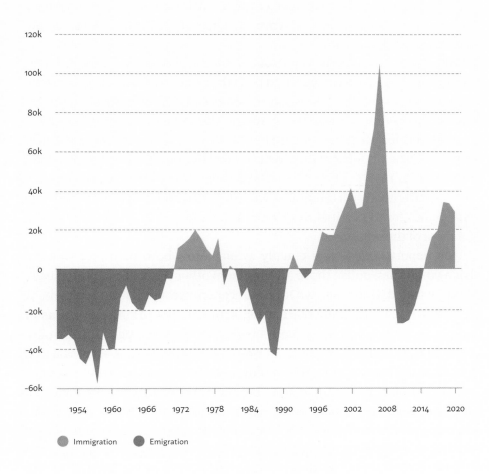

You might have expected that the achievement of independence would have given potential emigrants pause for thought – why leave now in search of a better life when we can finally control our own economic destiny as a country? 'The lesson that became obvious fairly quickly in the 1920s was that, even with a new State, you couldn't control emigration,' says Enda Delaney, Professor of Modern History at the University of Edinburgh and author of *Irish Emigration since 1921*.[27]

The economic benefits of independence took many decades to realise and the very creation of the Free State was a reason for some unionists and former republicans (who opposed the establishment of a state consisting of only 26 counties) to up and leave. One in every ten people departed the country in its first decade.[28]

The 1920s also marked the start of a radical shift in the destination for emigrants. The United States had been the principal destination since the Famine. However, the US began to restrict immigration with the introduction of quotas for each country and the requirements for sufficient capital and for an American citizen to act as a guarantor for each new arrival. As the US fell into the Great Depression, emigrants turned instead to Britain as their leading destination. From the 1930s onwards, roughly three-quarters of Irish emigrants were destined for Great Britain and only one-eighth for the United States, with Canada and Australia accounting for most of the remainder.

Job opportunities were equally available for both men and women. Irish emigrants, unlike those arriving from other countries, have typically demonstrated gender parity. Our rural economy provided less employment for women and originally there were plenty of opportunities overseas in domestic service and shop work overseas. 'What happened in Britain, particularly from the 1930s and into the Second World War, provided a lot of employment for females in munitions work, factories and nursing,' explains Delaney. 'The fact that Ireland was obviously a very closed, patriarchal society is part of the explanation for female emigration but there is very little evidence of people citing that as the primary reason they go.' Economic opportunity is the main driver.

The nadir of Irish emigration was reached in the 1950s. Incredibly, one in every three males and females who were under the age of 30 in 1946 had left the country by 1971.[29] 'Whereas in most societies emigration is abnormal behaviour, in Ireland *staying* becomes abnormal. Bizarrely, there is a sort of stigma about people who stay – perhaps they don't have the get up and go to emigrate. The question is asked: "what's wrong with them?"'

As farming became mechanised, employment opportunities for labourers disappeared, with few industrial jobs to replace them. 'The highest emigration rates tend to be from very rural places with very little available in non-agricultural employment,' explains Delaney. 'The midland counties are the ones that really suffer from the mass exodus of young people.'

Given the lack of free secondary level education at the time, most of these emigrants had few qualifications. Unsurprisingly, this restricted their employment opportunities and many of the men ended up in unskilled, heavy-labour jobs such as those in the construction sector. However, there was also a brain drain of highly educated people. Over two-thirds of those who graduated from medical schools after 1950 are believed to have emigrated by 1966 due to a lack of employment, for example.

There was a growing sense that the creation of an independent state had failed its people entirely. The July 1956 cover of the satirical *Dublin Opinion* magazine featured a cartoon map of Ireland and the caption, 'Shortly Available: Underdeveloped Country. Unrivalled Opportunities. Magnificent Views, Political and Otherwise. Owners Going Abroad'. The resulting political pressure was an undoubted factor in the adoption of the new export-orientated government policy of the late 1950s. The explicit ambition underpinning the government's first Programme for Economic Expansion was the desire to create sufficient employment to reverse the tide of emigration. In that, it succeeded.

It took time, of course, but the 1970s witnessed the first wave of net immigration that Ireland had ever seen. The reason was abundantly clear: the creation of new employment opportunities ensured that people did not have to leave the country to find work, and it even enticed back from abroad some of those who had previously left. The majority of the immigrants were returning emigrants, some of whom returned with their foreign-born children in tow.

Their return had an impact on Irish society. It challenged the status quo in several respects. 'They brought back a restlessness with the existing social order in Ireland. If you were a labourer's son in Britain no one cared, but if you were a labourer's son or daughter in rural Ireland that was a huge social class distinction. People who were at the top of the pile in rural Ireland resented what they saw as their social inferiors going to Britain, earning money and having a good lifestyle with that, so it upset things a bit.'

The return of large numbers of highly skilled women, such as the nurses that had worked in Britain's National Health Service, had perhaps the greatest impact. 'Second-wave feminism, as it develops in Ireland, is profoundly influenced by these large numbers of women who come back,' explains Delaney. 'They bring with them the views they've imbibed in Britain about equal pay and gender equality which helps shape Ireland in the 1970s in particular.'

The economic difficulties of the 1980s saw emigration return quickly enough. Although this time, the emigrants were different. There had never been a more educated generation of young people. That challenged the stereotypical image of the Irish as lowly, unskilled labourers. They were more likely to be bankers than builders this time.

The Celtic Tiger's economic boom transformed Ireland in so many ways, but perhaps one of the most unanticipated changes was how attractive this made the country as a destination for economic immigrants. For the first time in its history, Ireland attracted non-Irish immigrants in large numbers to help service the growing economy. At its peak in 2007 more than 100,000 people settled here in a single year. This was five times greater than the number who had settled here during the peak of the previous immigration wave in the mid-1970s.

Roughly one-third of these were returning Irish emigrants of the 80s and 90s. A further third hailed from the European Union, including the dozen member states that had joined during the noughties, and the final third hailed from North America and the rest of the world. Population growth, employment numbers and tax revenues boomed as a result.

The subsequent crash resulted in five years during which mass emigration returned once again. Positively, however, the return of net immigration from 2015 saw the number of immigrants in the second half of the decade exceed the number who were forced to leave in the earlier part.

We have turned the tide very decisively on forced emigration. As we are a small island with an open economy and full membership of the European Union, there will inevitably be a significant movement of people in and out of the country forever. However, we all want that movement to be volitional rather than forced. That is, to be because someone wants to go and experience life elsewhere for educational or work or family reasons, rather than because there are simply no prospects for them at home. That is what we have now achieved.

The legacy of so many years of forced emigration has been the dispersal of Irish citizens throughout the globe. The Department of Foreign Affairs calculates that there are in excess of 1.7 million Irish citizens resident outside of the island of Ireland today.[30] The majority live in Britain, with roughly one in five resident in the United States, a further one in five in Continental Europe and other developed nations, and perhaps one in ten in more far-flung locations.

'Emigration is generally seen in a negative light, but there is a form of soft power that comes from the fact that huge proportions of Irish people end up living elsewhere,' points out Delaney. 'That gives Ireland a voice in Irish America and other places. You can draw on these resources, whether it's for the peace process or whether it's during a European debate.' We have been so successful in attracting foreign investment precisely because of our diaspora in the United States.

The eyes and ears of our citizens overseas furthermore opened our minds to current affairs and cultural developments across the globe. Their influence has helped to raise our expectations of what our country can achieve and to modernise it. It is arguably because of our history of emigration that Ireland is such an open and successful country today.

We Have Never Been So Multicultural

Percentage of the population born outside of Ireland, 1950s–2010s

SOURCE: CENTRAL STATISTICS OFFICE[31]

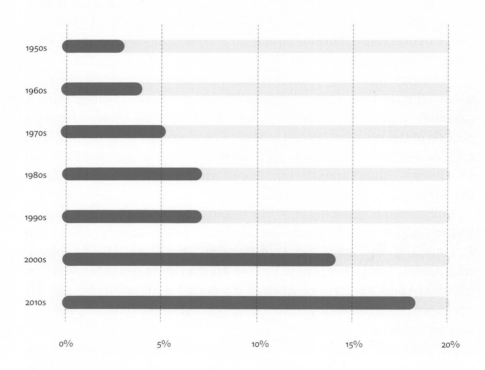

Nearly one in five residents of Ireland today originally hailed from somewhere else. We have opened ourselves up to welcoming the world in.

Most of these are immigrants or their families who have availed of the economic opportunities that modern Ireland offers. Some are the children of returned Irish emigrants, born when their parents were overseas. Others were immigrants here at one point in their lives but are now naturalised Irish citizens.

Can we now say we are a multicultural society? Look at the variety of places where people were born. Aside from those from our nearest neighbour, four of the top ten countries are Central or Eastern European nations, two are Asian, one is African, one is South American and one is North American. What a spread!

Top ten countries of birth of non-Irish-born residents

SOURCE: CENTRAL STATISTICS OFFICE[32]

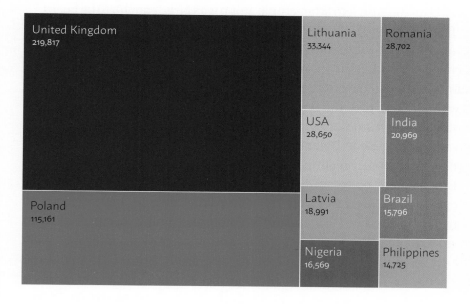

Although the number hailing from some countries is relatively small, the total percentage of our residents born elsewhere ranks our population as amongst the most diverse in Europe.[33] We are more multicultural than France, Belgium, the Netherlands and even the United Kingdom on this measure.

We have taken a three-step journey to multiculturalism. It is fair to describe Ireland as monocultural from our foundation through to the 1970s. No more than 5 per cent of the population was born outside of the country, and those born in Northern Ireland constituted one of the largest groups within these.

You could say we became stereocultural from the mid-1970s through to the mid-90s as that figure grew to around 7 per cent. Although we began to see a rapid increase in Europeans after we joined the EEC, it was from a very low base. The significant increase was the near doubling in the number of British-born residents who constituted the majority of the non-Irish at that point. If your left ear was hearing RTÉ, your right ear was most likely picking up the BBC. No other ethnic group was large enough to be heard.

That all changed in the mid-90s as the Celtic Tiger roared. In just twenty years the number of non-Irish more than doubled. Those of British origin increased by half, and those from the United States doubled, but the number from all other countries increased ten-fold to dwarf them. This is when Ireland took the final step towards the multiculturalism we have today. 'Future historians will say this has been a significant development,' says Professor Enda Delaney. 'The influx in the late twentieth and early twenty-first century really has changed Ireland, completely, forever.'

Employment opportunities are, of course, the primary motivator for people to come here. But Delaney believes that there is another factor at play: 'There is a sense that Ireland is a more welcoming society than some other European countries. Far right, anti-immigration politics is really the preserve of the nut jobs in Ireland, whereas in Britain, Germany, the Netherlands and other places, these are serious political movements.' It would be nice to think that our long history of emigration has increased our empathy for the plight of immigrants.

Those arriving here span the full spectrum of education level and skills. On balance, they are more likely to hold a third-level qualification than the Irish themselves.[34] But there are many who find less glamorous employment, filling the jobs that people born in Ireland don't really want to do. 'I welcome the very high rates of third-level participation now, but that means that other opportunities, primarily manual work or apprentice-ships, have become less desirable. There is a sort of historical irony in that: that the new immigrants who have come here have ended up doing the sort of jobs that the Irish would have done elsewhere in earlier generations.'

As many of our immigrants put down roots and become naturalised citizens or have Irish-born children, we have had to rethink the very concept of what it means to be Irish. We now accept that 'new Irish' do not need to be white and Catholic; they can equally be black and Muslim.

'In the due course of time, the changes that have taken place in the last 25 years will be seen to be very, very important for what it means to be Irish and for what Irishness looks like,' says Delaney. 'Ireland, unlike other European countries, hasn't demanded that people strip themselves of their identity. It's not saying that there's a formula for Irishness and you have to conform to that. We seem to be open to Irishness coming in very different shapes and forms.'

Our openness as a society, supported by our welcoming sense of community, has attracted talented individuals with the full range of skills that we need for our country to flourish. Their arrival has helped us to become an even more diverse and modern place. That we have achieved that transformation in such a short period of time without any consequential social backlash is something to be proud of.

Irish Residents Send $1.7 Billion in Remittances Overseas

Irish emigrants used to be an important source of income for the relatives they left behind. Our nineteenth-century emigrants to America would typically send back money they earned to fund the journey of others to come and join them. As travel became more affordable in the twentieth century, and as more emigrants headed the short distance to Britain instead, these financial remittances became more about assisting the family at home.

It has been estimated that almost £3 billion was sent from Britain to Ireland between 1939 and 1969 through official means such as telegrams and money orders.[35] The total was undoubtedly much higher as this figure cannot count the cash sent buried inside an envelope with a Christmas card or the money passed hand to hand when emigrants returned home on holidays or when Aunty came to visit them. Such remittances are believed to have constituted around 3 per cent of the country's national income in the 1950s and 60s.[36] This was roughly the same sum spent by the State on old-age pensions at the time.

Countries to which Irish residents send the greatest remittances

SOURCE: WORLD BANK, PEW RESEARCH CENTER[37]

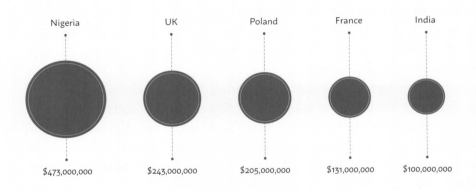

Nigeria	UK	Poland	France	India
$473,000,000	$243,000,000	$205,000,000	$131,000,000	$100,000,000

Remittances declined dramatically in the 1970s as the living standards here improved. Nowadays Ireland is one of the least reliant countries on inbound remittances in all of Europe.[38] Remarkably, we have become a significant *source country* for emigrants' remittances as some of our recent arrivals follow the same well-trodden path of sending home a portion of their earnings to help the relatives they left behind.

Residents send in the order of $1.7 billion abroad every year. The leading destination countries include Nigeria, Poland and India, which are amongst our foremost sources of immigrants. You might be surprised to see the United Kingdom and France on the list, in light of their relative wealth – however, funds may be sent back to pay off mortgages or student loans still held at home, for example.

Now that we have attained the status of a source of remittances, we are likely to retain it. The number of foreign migrants here is forecast to increase a little more over the next 30 years.[39] Nigerian, Polish and British nationals will remain amongst our most prominent migrant groups, ensuring continued outflows of cash to help build better futures for them and their kin.

 58   We Receive Record Numbers of Tourists

Number of overseas tourists to the nearest million, 1960–2019

SOURCE: CENTRAL STATISTICS OFFICE[40]

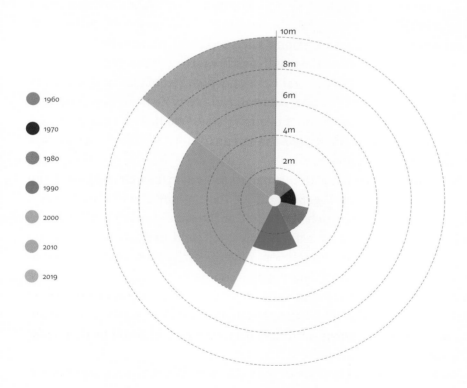

Did you know that visits from overseas tourists count as exports? When visitors spend their pounds or dollars or euros here that is deemed export revenue for the country. It sounds counterintuitive – have we not 'imported' the visitor here for the duration of their stay? But their hard-earned money is being taken out of their home economy and poured into Ireland so, in that sense, it is generating export earnings in the same way as if they had stayed home and ordered a buffet of Irish beef and salmon and Aran sweaters for all their neighbours.

Tourism was a slow burner at first. We welcomed 1 million overseas visitors for the first time in 1961. It then took more than 25 years for that number to double to 2 million in 1987. Yet, just three years later we added our next million. Irish tourism exploded in the 90s as numbers doubled and we welcomed 6 million visitors in 2000. By 2019 we had reached a record high of 9.7 million. That was two visitors for every resident. We had, by then, built a hugely professional and successful industry that benefited communities throughout the length and breadth of the country.

Ireland had a strong cultural base on which to build. The diaspora in Great Britain, the US, Canada, Australia and New Zealand have a natural affinity with the country and a desire to visit 'one day'. As our air travel connections grew and prices fell, that dream could be fulfilled not just once in a lifetime but multiple times.

A cultural connection with Germany was born in the late 1950s with the publication of *Irisches Tagebuch* ('Irish Journal') by one of the country's foremost writers, Heinrich Böll. Böll spent time on Achill Island and wrote imaginatively about the people there and of Irish society in the 50s. The book touches on religion, poverty, emigration and a culture of drinking and caring. (*Peig Sayers* for Germans, perhaps.) It has sold more than two million copies and unquestionably influenced perceptions of Irish life for decades. Böll was subsequently awarded the Nobel Prize in literature. His cottage on Achill has been converted into a guesthouse for visiting artists.[41]

As for France, did you know that the most popular rousing finale at French weddings is the song 'Les Lacs du Connemara'? It's the equivalent of 'New York, New York' at an Irish shindig. Released by Parisian crooner Michel Sardou in 1981, the million-selling single spent 18 weeks in the

French Top 20. The lyrics evoke desolate scenery, silent stoicism and some suggestive skinny dipping! It has done wonders to drive generations of French tourists to the west in search of 'scorched earth', 'stony moors' and a half-naked Maureen dragging herself out of a local lake.

Ryanair's explosion of route connectivity in the 1990s opened up Ireland for all these dreamers to come and experience the place for themselves. The young airline adopted their low-cost model in 1990 when they flew 750,000 passengers. After a decade of expansion that initially created a comprehensive UK–Ireland network, followed by flights connecting half a dozen continental European countries, the airline was flying 7 million passengers by 2000.[42]

Did Ireland's wins at the Eurovision Song Contest help tourism? Without any doubt. Five wins in a decade, from 1987 to 1996, including three of them back to back. A show broadcast live on the main TV networks of 30 countries into hundreds of millions of homes. Was there a soul in Europe who didn't associate the country with musical talent and entertainment by the end of our run?

And let's not forget the dancing. *Riverdance* the show, born from the interval act at the 1994 Eurovision Song Contest, has been experienced live by over 28 million people worldwide. It is one of the most successful dance productions in the world and has unquestionably brought Irish dancing global fame.

With the IRA ceasefire reducing visitors' concerns about the safety of travelling here, the 1990s was Ireland's first golden era of tourism. Coinciding with our export boom, we were a nation beginning to feel confident. We wanted people to come and see how we were doing because we were proud of the way things were going. We had a success story to share at last, and we were more than happy to entertain them with it.

The early 2000s proved a great deal more troublesome. Covid-19 was not the first virus to close parts of Ireland's tourism industry. The highly infectious foot and mouth disease, which affects cattle, pigs, sheep and goats, closed parts of Ireland in 2001. Following an outbreak in Britain in February, travel from the UK was actively discouraged. The St Patrick's Day festival was cancelled. Troops were deployed to Dublin Port to keep stowaway cattle out.

When our one and only case of the disease appeared in Louth in March, rural Ireland closed down. National parks, national monuments and heritage centres shut their doors. Public buildings, schools, offices and supermarkets installed unavoidable disinfectant mats to ensure the virus wasn't carried on your shoes. Hotel bookings fell by double digits.

By mid-May the health emergency was declared over and life returned to normal in time for the summer season. Dublin's Saint Patrick's Day parade went ahead in warm summer sunshine. But everything changed again with the terrorist attacks on New York's Twin Towers on 11 September. It took four years for tourism numbers to return to what they had been, and six years before we would see as many Americans again.

Subsequent steady growth throughout the decade was wiped out again by the Great Recession and Ireland's economic collapse. We started the 2010s with fewer international visitors than we had a decade before.

The decline was not entirely surprising. Cheaper is better in a recession, but by the end of the noughties Ireland was an expensive place to visit. The Irish were throwing money at their spa breaks and fine dining, so hotel and restaurant prices were adjusted accordingly. The result was that 41 per cent of foreign visitors rated the country as poor value for money.[43] Remember the talk of 'rip-off Republic'?

But tourism bounced back as prices readjusted and the word got out. Annual visitor numbers jumped by nearly 4 million during the 2010s. The number who were here for a holiday doubled. That created lots of jobs quickly, making a significant contribution to increasing employment and helping to put the country on the road to recovery. We didn't win the Eurovision – half the time we didn't even qualify for the finals – but lots of other things went our way.

One of our largest-ever tourism initiatives took place in 2013. Communities throughout Ireland were asked to reach out to the diaspora and to invite family and friends to come over and visit for 'The Gathering'. Perhaps you were one of the tens of thousands of people who helped organise one of the five thousand events that ranged from family reunions and clan gatherings to festivals and sports fixtures. We had just come through a terrible economic downturn, so the 'can do/will do' spirit of individuals and communities was on fine display. People wanted to make a contribution to the country's recovery and here was a way that they could practically do so. More than 250,000 incremental tourists visited Ireland as a result.[44]

Filming the world's biggest TV series and the world's biggest movie franchise on the island also helped enormously. All eight seasons of *Game of Thrones* were partly filmed in Northern Ireland. With more than 30 million viewers per episode, unsurprisingly it wasn't long before 'set-jetting' tourists arrived in search of the real-world locations.[45]

Star Wars: The Force Awakens became the third highest grossing movie of all time on its release in 2015.[46] (Spoiler alert: the big reveal was Luke Skywalker hiding out on Skellig Michael all these years.) It further enhanced Ireland's screen appeal: landing a seat on one of the boats to the island became harder than securing tickets to *Hamilton* on Broadway.

Ireland is now one of the best countries in the world at promoting itself as a tourism destination. I would say that, wouldn't I? Factually, the World Economic Forum ranks us as the third best country at destination marketing and branding.[47] Supported by the expanding route networks of Ryanair, Aer Lingus and the Middle Eastern airlines, Ireland became a holiday destination for people from every corner of the globe.

The diversity of our tourism source markets has changed completely. Just as with our other exports, our reliance on the British market has decreased. Nearly nine in ten overseas visitors in 1960 were British. Today it is one in three.

In fact, we are attracting far more British visitors today than we did back in 1960 – more than four times as many – but the growth from other places has been even more dramatic. We welcome more visitors from Continental Europe now, and although there are only half as many Americans, they come for longer and outspend every other nation.

Before Covid-19, people were beginning to ask if we had reached a limit – had we too many tourists? The 'overtourism' associated with Barcelona and Venice felt equally apparent to those who had to elbow their way to a prime photo spot at the Cliffs of Moher or who had to join the snaking queue in the rain outside Trinity College's Old Library to see the Book of Kells. Dublin hotels were experiencing the highest occupancy rates of any European capital city – even greater than London or Paris.[48] Voices clamoured for 'sustainable tourism'.

Where our overseas tourists hail from, 1960–2019

SOURCE: CENTRAL STATISTICS OFFICE

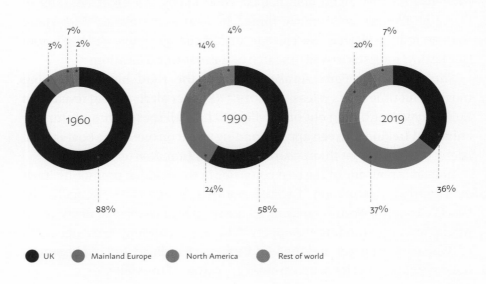

Few sectors were impacted harder by the pandemic than tourism and hospitality – well over 100,000 jobs were lost. Overtourism will not be with us for a few years to come. The issue will inevitably arise again, however. Our tourism sector will roar back into life. International travel is on a global growth curve that is set to see it double in size by 2050.[49] Managing our share of that growth and ensuring that we have an industry that is sustainable economically and environmentally will be the challenge.

59 The Cost of Travelling to and From Ireland Has Plummeted

Air travel has become marvellously more accessible within our own lifetimes. What was a business perk has become mass transit. It is cheaper to fly somewhere nowadays than it used to be to take the ferry there, never mind the huge time saving it also offers. We are an island nation to which you cannot get by car or train, so this increase in affordability has made us more accessible for both inbound tourism and outbound travel.

Price of a Dublin–London return flight in real terms

SOURCES: BARRETT, ROSEINGRAVE AND FARECOMPARE[50]

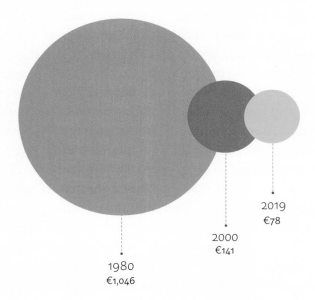

1980
€1,046

2000
€141

2019
€78

Air connectivity has grown globally, needless to say, but Ireland was an early beneficiary. Ryanair was one of Europe's first low-cost airlines. Today it is the world's largest low-cost airline and attracts more passengers than any other airline in the world outside of the United States.[51]

The standard non-restricted fare for a flight from Dublin to Heathrow Airport was a fixed IR£208 in the early 1980s. It did not matter whether you chose to fly with Aer Lingus or with British Airways, the price was the same. That might not sound like a huge sum but when you correct for inflation and convert it into euro, that is equivalent to €1,046 in today's money. You read that right: more than €1,000 for a return flight to London. No wonder so many took the boat instead.

In 1986 the brand-new Ryanair obtained permission from the regulatory authorities to challenge the British Airways and Aer Lingus duopoly. The service started with two 46-seater turbo-prop aircraft that flew from Dublin to London Luton. Their launch fare of IR£99 was less than half the price of the incumbents.[52] Both British Airways and Aer Lingus began to drop their prices in response to the increased competition.

Within fifteen years of Ryanair's successful launch on the route, by the year 2000, average fares had fallen to just €141 in real terms. A whopping reduction of 85 per cent and a great boon for attracting tourism in the 1990s. Fares were down to nearly half that figure again by 2019 at just €78. So a cross-channel flight today costs you only 7 per cent of the price you would have paid forty years earlier. No wonder the worldview of today's young adults is so entirely different from that of those who came before.

The Ryanair low-fares model we are familiar with today was not the airline's initial business strategy. As travel journalist Eoghan Corry explains: 'Ryanair saw it was very easy to undercut Aer Lingus, because Aer Lingus was ripping people off, but it wasn't a particularly low cost airline at the start. It was Michael O'Leary's arrival in the early 90s that changed it. There was a massive row between [founder] Tony Ryan and Michael O'Leary – the stuff of legend – when he suggested things like removing the free cups of coffee. Tony Ryan thought that would sink the airline!'

Ryanair expanded its route network into destinations that had never been considered destinations before. 'Ryanair generally found an airport that was newly vacated by the end of the Cold War, that used to be military, and now had nothing to do. They generally found a friendly local tourist authority and hoteliers who wanted to get business and were prepared to give marketing money: "how much is it worth to for us to fly to your airport?" They started doing deals and opened up airports that weren't in the game in countries that weren't in the game." It resulted in Ireland being one of the very first countries in Europe to benefit from a truly low-cost airline.

You had to book a Ryanair flight through a travel agent in the 1990s. There was no online booking option. The agent received a commission for every flight sold. In an effort to further reduce their cost base, Ryanair reduced the commission available to agents in the late 90s. 'The agents – illegally – said they would boycott Ryanair and not take any bookings. "You need us more than we need you!" Well, we all know how that worked out,' says Corry. An investigation by the Competition Authority and High Court proceedings against the Irish Travel Agents Association put an end to the threat of a boycott. Shortly afterwards, Ryanair put a booking engine on their website so customers could purchase directly – with no commission payable to any intermediary. The website was handling three-quarters of all their bookings within a year.[53]

The September 11th 2001 terrorist attacks in the United States were catastrophic for the airline industry. Demand for air travel took a sharp dip, forcing Swissair to seek bankruptcy protection and Sabena, Belgium's national airline, out of business. Incongruously, the sector's travails benefited both of Ireland's airlines. Ryanair used the depressed market to negotiate rock-bottom pricing for an order of 155 new aircraft from US manufacturer Boeing. Timing is everything.

'Ryanair before 2001 was a very struggling airline. They were desperately short of cash. Aer Lingus weren't tremendously worried about them,' claims Corry. 'That all changed with the arrival of the new Boeing aircraft that Michael O'Leary purchased in the wake of 9/11. The figures aren't public, but it has been said that the airline got them at such low prices that, after working them for three years, they were selling them second-hand for more than they paid for them!'

The collapse of Sabena and Ryanair's bullish expansion plans brought home the challenge of business sustainability to the incoming CEO of Aer Lingus, Willie Walsh. He concluded that they had to follow suit: to cut costs and to switch to a 'no frills' lower-fare model. Jobs were lost, the aircraft fleet was streamlined, and business class was eliminated on short-haul routes. They were huge changes, but ones that saved the company. 'Aer Lingus had always lost money and it always had a government to prop it up. Everyone in Aer Lingus would say that the reason that it's an airline surviving and thriving today is the fact that it had Ryanair to compete with. It's no coincidence that two airlines that didn't run to the local government office for aid during the Covid pandemic were two Irish airlines.'

The growth strategies of these two airlines, combined with their aggressive focus on delivering cheaper air fares to consumers, has boosted air passenger traffic in and out of Ireland to record levels. And that has been to the immeasurable benefit of the country as a whole. Ireland's exporting success would not be as strong as it is without our powerful air connections.

The sector faces an enormous challenge in reducing its contribution to climate change over the coming decades. Nevertheless, it is poised to restore much of the connectivity that was destroyed by Covid-19 within a few years, and to resume its unrelenting global growth trajectory from there as the global middle class grows and as people in new places benefit from the declining cost of air travel.

That continued growth in aviation will require more aircraft to meet demand. Ireland is a world leader in meeting that demand – not in manufacturing them, of course, but in leasing them. Ireland is the world's aircraft-leasing nexus. Well over 50 per cent of the world's leased fleet is owned or managed from Ireland. That is one in every five aircraft taking off somewhere around the globe today. Fourteen of the world's top 15 leasing companies are headquartered here.[54]

How on earth did that come about? It was all down to that enterprising man Tony Ryan – the very same one who founded Ryanair. He worked for Aer Lingus for two decades before ending up charged with leasing an under-utilised Boeing 747 for them in the early 1970s. He found a willing lessor in Air Siam in Thailand.

'It was very simple economics: we've got an aircraft that we can't fill, and they're short at this time of the year, so let's send it down to them,' explains Eoghan Corry. Ryan was struck with the realisation that much of aviation is caught by this cyclical thing, so why can't somebody lease aircraft to those that need them for when they need them?

He established Guinness Peat Aviation (GPA) as a separate leasing company in 1975, backed by Aer Lingus and the Guinness Peat Group, a London-based financial services company. Over the next 15 years Ryan built GPA into the largest aircraft lessor in the world, worth $4 billion at its peak. However, the decision to float the company on the stock market in 1992, during an aviation industry downturn following the 1991 Gulf War, proved disastrous. International financial institutions refused to buy shares. The company was plunged into crisis with some $10 billion in debts.[55]

Part of GPA was rescued by a subsidiary of General Electric, GE Capital Aviation Services (GECAS), which purchased some of its aircraft and took over the operational management of its fleet. Through a series of mergers and acquisitions, the balance of GPA became AerCap. Before Covid struck, GECAS was the world's largest aircraft lessor and AerCap was the second largest.[56] They have since agreed to merge, with the resultant Dublin-head-quartered company set to control half the world's fleet of leased aircraft.

So how does Ireland benefit from being at the centre of this global sector? 'How many people does it employ? Diddly squat. How much tax does it pay? Diddly squat. Having a Dublin address on their website – what does it actually do for us? Maybe a little bit of prestige. But what it does is it keeps a very healthy relationship with the aviation industry which does our travel and tourism sector no harm,' concludes Corry. 'It means that we are never going to be in a situation where our link with the aviation industry is severed to such a degree that we end up with connectivity problems.' For an export-orientated island nation, that is an important benefit.

 ## 60   Everyone in Ireland Now Takes a Foreign Holiday (On Average)

Number of overseas holidays taken as a proportion of the population, 1992–2019

SOURCE: CENTRAL STATISTICS OFFICE

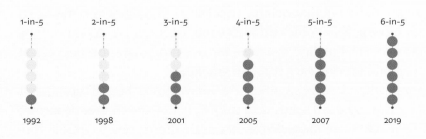

As recently as 30 years ago, the vast majority of people in Ireland did not take holidays overseas. Fewer than one in five were able to afford such a luxury. Like so many other areas that I have explored, this changed rapidly in the 1990s as our wealth increased, our horizons broadened and our air connectivity expanded. But there is a clear date when international travel first started for the Irish.

'The 1958 centenary of the Lourdes Apparition was the invention of Irish tourism,' claims travel journalist Eoghan Corry. 'It was down to a guy called Michael Walsh, who had a travel agency in Dublin. As a young man he had run pilgrimages for Holy Year to Rome in 1950 and chartered aircraft and persuaded people to come up with money. Because Ireland in the 1950s wasn't particularly well off, and holidays were regarded as being something hedonistic and a waste of money, he identified 1958 as a time when he would offer these package holidays to Lourdes. And people went in large numbers.'

Those early travellers paved a pilgrim path for others to follow. Trips to Lourdes became a thing. 'A local priest would decide that a delegation would go, and parishioners would put aside seven shillings and six pence a week. They all went as a group and they really had a brilliant time. Hard to believe, but Aer Lingus' original continental European programme involved aircraft flying to Lourdes and then on to wherever they were supposed to go.'

The Michael Walshes of the world then saw the opportunity to upsell by combining a week in Lourdes with a week in the sun afterwards. You could justify the hedonistic aspect of your holiday because you had offered your prayers up in advance for the sins that you were about to commit!

The package holiday market, kick-started by religion, developed from there into the more familiar holiday trip. But sky-high prices remained a barrier for most people. A flick through a tour operator brochure from the early 1980s reveals holidays available for IR£450 or IR£500 per person that convert into €2,000 each in today's money.

The prices fell and, more significantly, our wealth increased throughout the 1990s. 'You could tell we were getting richer by the charter departure slots we got. We were shovelled into a midnight or two-o'-clock-in-the-morning take-off in the early days because the Irish tour operators couldn't afford the slots that the Germans and the Brits could. But as affluence stalked the land, the Irish flights became more consumer-friendly and so did the apartment blocks we stayed in. By the late 90s and early noughties, we were pretty much up there,' says Corry.

Airlines began to realise that there was a lot of money to be made. From the mid-1990s, they started competing with the chartered airlines with scheduled flights. As travellers proved increasingly willing to book direct with an airline, the role of the travel agent and the tour operator diminished appreciably. 'In 2001 charters would still have played a major role: there were 1.1 million charter seats flying out of Dublin Airport. That's down to around 140,000 now,' explains Corry. The low-cost airlines offered greater flexibility and lower prices, and that enabled more frequent holidays.

2007 was a milestone year for Irish holiday-taking: for the very first time, there were more overseas holidays taken by Irish residents then there were Irish residents. In other words, on average, absolutely everyone in Ireland took an overseas break. Needless to say, in reality some people were taking three or four breaks a year while others were taking none. But it is a milestone nevertheless: noteworthy progress in the democratisation of foreign holiday-taking. No longer only for the wealthy, as they were in the 1970s and 80s, holidays had transitioned from the luxury category to being accessible – and maybe even a necessity – for many.

The subsequent recession ensured that this milestone wasn't long-lived. People had to cut back. But by 2017 we had achieved that level of holiday-taking again. And by 2019 we had well surpassed it. That year we took an average of 1.2 foreign holidays per person.

We are now amongst the greatest travellers in Europe. We spend twice as many nights abroad each year as the average European.[57] That's more than the average German or Belgian or French or Danish person. And don't forget we're an island! It is harder for us to get places than it is for any of these.

61 Our Passport Is One of the Most Widely Accepted in the World

The Irish passport is one of the most widely accepted in the world. Out of 199 passports issued by countries and territories around the globe, the Republic of Ireland's ranks joint 11th in the freedom to travel that ours offers us. Our passport is accepted by 188 countries and travel destinations without the need for us to secure a visa before we travel. Japan, with the world's most accepted passport, enables visa-free travel to just five more destinations than ours.

Membership of the European Union plays a huge role in securing our freedom. Its member states occupy 13 places in the top 20, alongside our neighbours in Norway, Switzerland and the UK. A high ranking is, of course, evidence of relative wealth and political stability. The citizens of those countries topping the list are, therefore, amongst the most sought-after visitors.

Number of destinations passport holders can access without a prior visa

SOURCE: HENLEY & PARTNERS[58]

Rank	Passport	Visa-free score
1	Japan	193
2	Singapore	192
3=	Germany	191
	South Korea	191
5=	Finland	190
	Italy	190
	Luxembourg	190
	Spain	190
9=	Austria	189
	Denmark	189
11=	Ireland	188

The freedom to travel conferred on our passport is one that we value. 'When you're in a smaller country, on a smaller island, you're more aware of the outside world. When you're a country with a strong maritime and emigration tradition, you're even more aware of it,' says Eoghan Corry. 'We grew up with relatives in America. We might have been over to America for weddings and christenings. We might even have been getting postcards back from missionaries in Africa and India. So from a young age, we're aware of all these countries [...] and making the decision to go and see them isn't that big a deal.'

'When you live by the ocean, or the River Shannon, it's stretching out to the world. It's not confining. It opens, rather than closes, your borders and your aspirations. In our thought process, we are at the centre of the world.'

RTE GUIDE

PROGRAMMES SEPT. 25–OCT. 1 :: Vol. 13 No. 39 :: IRIS RADIO TELEFIS EIREANN, SEPTEMBER 24, 1976. PRICE 6p.

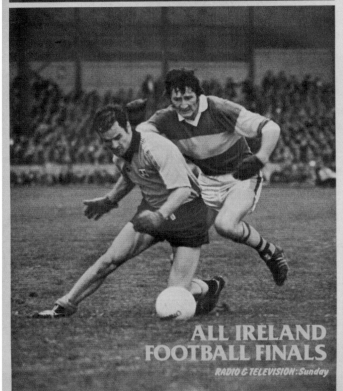

ALL IRELAND FOOTBALL FINALS

RADIO & TELEVISION: Sunday

AUTUMN/WINTER Television Schedule Starts

$$\binom{8}{}$$

Cultivating Culture
and Sports

FOR A SMALL ISLAND, WE HAVE A STRONG INDIGENOUS CULTURE AND STRONG SPORTING TRADITIONS THAT HAVE BEEN STRENGTHENED, NOT DILUTED, BY OUR GREATER ENGAGEMENT WITH THE WIDER WORLD.

THE MORE WE have opened up, the more the opportunities for our writers, musicians and actors to showcase their talents on the global stage have grown. And so our love for and our participation in our own native sports has strengthened.

62 Our Indigenous Sports Are Our Most Popular

It is a remarkable achievement that sports that we created for our own entertainment – and have in common with nowhere else in the world – have not only remained the most popular sports in Ireland over the past century, but have become even more favoured. Most people say that Gaelic games are their favourite sport (just ahead of those who pick soccer or rugby). More people attend Gaelic football and hurling matches than any others. More people volunteer to assist with Gaelic football than with any other sport. And the number holding membership of a GAA club is second only to the number with gym membership.

Support for Gaelic games

SOURCE: TENEO, SPORT IRELAND[1]

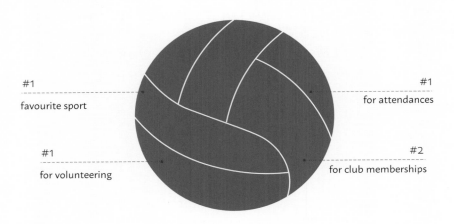

#1
favourite sport

#1
for volunteering

#1
for attendances

#2
for club memberships

The Gaelic Athletic Association started well. Founded as part of the Gaelic revival movement in 1884, the association was naturally at home in the new Irish Free State even if, as an all-island body, clubs in six counties found themselves in Northern Ireland. By the 1920s the GAA was already a prosperous organisation with its headquarters established in Croke Park. It had a presence in every corner of the new state, but it was still in the process of establishing its necklace of grounds throughout the country.

In contrast to the two established sports of soccer and rugby, it attracted a broad breadth of participation from the full social spectrum. 'It was a game that was really open to everybody,' explains Professor Paul Rouse of University College Dublin and author of *Sport and Ireland: A History*.[2]

'Soccer had established itself as the dominant game across working-class Dublin. Rugby was the game of the elite who went to fee-paying schools and it was the game of the professions in country towns. That left GAA in a very particular space. It developed as a working-class to lower-middle-class to middle-class sport.'

There was a hard core of nationalists within the organisation for whom the GAA represented a continuation of the fight to establish an independent Ireland with its own distinct culture and traditions. 'They were people who absolutely genuinely believed in the cultural revolution; who believed that they hadn't just fought a revolution so that they could paint the post boxes green or fly a different flag. They fought a revolution so that people would speak Irish, that people would listen to Irish music, that this would be a thriving country of Gaelicised culture.'

That meant the rejection of what they deemed to be non-Irish. A series of 'Ban Rules' were adopted by the organisation at the start of the twentieth century to reinforce its nationalist credentials. If you wanted to be a member of the GAA then you could not play or even watch a game of soccer, rugby, hockey or cricket. You couldn't even attend a dance organised by one of their clubs.

Enforcement of the rules was stepped up in the years after independence. The GAA established 'vigilance committees' that sent trusted members to soccer and rugby matches to spy on the crowds so they could suspend any members in attendance. There were no exceptions. Douglas Hyde was the first President of Ireland, a founder of the Gaelic League and a patron of the GAA. But that patronage was revoked after he dared to attend an Ireland-Poland soccer international in his official capacity in 1938.

The hard core further attempted to rewrite the organisation's history. 'The GAA set about obliterating all complexity from its records and inventing a history by which the organisation had been in step with the people from 1916 to '21, and that no GAA person had ever joined the British Army and fought in the Great War,' explains Rouse. 'The reality was that, when it came to 1916, there were more GAA members fighting in the British Army than there were in the GPO [General Post Office].'

It reached its height with the invention of the story that Hill 16 in Croke Park was built from the rubble of the GPO after it was destroyed in the

Easter 1916 Rising. That would be the most extraordinary achievement in Irish sporting history, considering the terrace was inaugurated in November 1915! In fact, before it was rechristened 'Hill 16', the stand was known as 'Hill 60' after an action involving the British Army's Connaught Rangers in the Battle of Gallipoli.

This may have all been done with the best of intentions, but their aspirations were ultimately unfulfilled. 'The ambitions of cultural nationalism foundered on the desires of so many members of the GAA who saw sport not as a badge of national identity, but as something to be enjoyed,' says Rouse. 'They didn't view someone as a lesser Irish person or a greater Irish person by virtue of the sport they played.'

Membership grew strongly. The GAA went from 1,000 clubs in 1920 to 2,000 by 1940 and 2,500 by 1960. So what was it that enabled Gaelic games to pull ahead of competitor sports? 'It offered sport that people loved playing, in a representational way. Because of their parish structure and their county structure, people could identify with a local area and local civic pride is important. So there's the love of playing the games themselves and there's a love of place, and those two things were accommodated in a structure of competition, supported by a growing physical infrastructure of playing facilities around the country, which allowed the GAA to develop as the biggest sporting organisation in the country.'

The GAA is sometimes portrayed as an organisation that is slow to embrace change. That has not been so in its adoption of modern broadcasting technology, in which it has generally led other sports. The first-ever live radio broadcast of a sports game in Europe was the 1926 all-Ireland hurling semi-final between Kilkenny and Galway. Once RTÉ television started broadcasting in 1960, the GAA adapted quickly again to ensure comprehensive coverage. However, the television era brought a new challenge for the organisation: it made a nonsense of the Ban Rules. 'I could go to Dalymount Park and watch the FAI Cup Final and get banned from the GAA,' explains Rouse, 'but I stay at home and watch it on telly and I'm grand.' The rules were repealed in 1971.

The ability to welcome a broader public into its fold allowed the organisation to reposition itself as a community organisation in the 1970s and 80s. 'It reinvented itself by building clubhouses as community centres around the country.'

Ninety years after the GAA was founded at a meeting held at the Hayes' Hotel in Thurles, County Tipperary, the Ladies' Gaelic Football Association was founded in the same venue in 1974. The GAA took until 1982 to recognise the new association. 'The fact is that men walked on the moon before women played football in Croke Park,' says Rouse.

The growth in participation in, and support for, women's football has been particularly strong over the last twenty years. There is much further to travel, but Ireland can already assert a claim to be a global leader in female sport. The 2017 All-Ireland Senior Ladies' Football Championship Final was the best attended women's sports final of 2017 anywhere in the world. The 2019 final was eclipsed only by the 2019 FIFA Women's World Cup Soccer Final.[3]

One hundred years after independence, we continue to embrace our own sports and to drive them to new heights. The GAA claims in excess of 500,000 members in over 2,200 clubs in Ireland and 400 others around the world.[4] 'The GAA is absolutely thriving,' concludes Rouse. 'It has enhanced the lives of huge swathes of the Irish population, and to me, that is the ultimate starting point for judging something's social worth.'

Its games are patently adored. The inclusion of women means that it is more of a family organisation than was ever the case. And it has a network of facilities unrivalled by any other competitive sport. The GAA is exceptionally well placed to retain its popularity into the next century.

63 We Are a World Leader in Horse Racing

Facts about Ireland's horse-racing industry

SOURCE: HORSE RACING IRELAND[5]

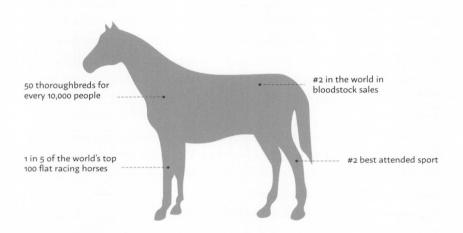

50 thoroughbreds for
every 10,000 people

#2 in the world in
bloodstock sales

1 in 5 of the world's top
100 flat racing horses

#2 best attended sport

Ireland is a small country so our expectations of achievements on the world stage of sport should be appropriately modest. We can claim occasional success in attaining the top rankings in rugby or golf, but there is only one sport in which we can claim to be consistently amongst the very best in the world. That is horse racing.

After Gaelic games, horse racing is the second most attended sport in the country, with around 1.3 million attendees annually. That is the largest number of horseracing fans in any country on a per capita basis.

But breeding thoroughbred horses is where Ireland truly excels. One in five of world's top flat racing horses are bred here – more than in any other country. We have 50 thoroughbred horses for every 10,000 people – twice the number than in Australia and ten times more than in Great Britain. And the value of Irish bloodstock sales is second only to those in the United States.[6]

Horse racing has a long-established history in Ireland. 'Hurling is often referred to as our national game but all the way through the 19th century everybody said that horse racing was Ireland's national sport. This was the sport that drew everyone together,' explains Professor Paul Rouse. 'From the inner-city kids who keep horses out to the people who live on big rolling country estates in Kildare, there is a grip that the horse has had on so many different generations of people since the foundation of the State. It's first of all a love of the animal and secondly the idea of racing it.'

But why does horse racing have a greater hold on Ireland than on other places? Partly because the sport here was deeply embedded from its very formation. So-called 'Jockey Clubs' were established in England and Ireland within a few years of each other in the mid-eighteenth century to formalise the rules and regulate the sport. Our proximity to Britain, long the world's largest horse-racing market until the Americans took over, was a huge advantage. And our abundance of land and grass and our mild climate made the country ideal for raising horses.

When World War I broke out, racing in England came to a halt but it was allowed to continue in Ireland. 'You got a decamping of a whole lot of English jockeys and horse owners and horses to Ireland. Now, they said it was for breeding purposes and to maintain the equine stock, but essentially they kept the sport going during this period,' says Rouse. 'During those four years [of the war] there were a whole load of fundraising events for the dependants of troops abroad or for disabled soldiers. But the minute the War of Independence ended, the minute the Truce was signed, there was a flip.'

'Horse-racing bodies accommodated themselves absolutely immediately to the new dispensation. They professed their great disappointment at the death of Michael Collins. They ran a race meeting in the Phoenix Park to raise funds for the dependants of injured or dead IRA men who had fought for independence.' The sport that was associated with the British military changed overnight to align itself firmly with the new Free State and continued on as if nothing had happened, retaining its place as one of the most successful sports in newly independent Ireland.

If there was one individual who transformed the Irish equine industry and who raised it to the world-beating level that it is at today, that is unquestionably trainer Vincent O'Brien. In a worldwide poll undertaken by the *Racing Post* at the start of this century, O'Brien was voted nothing less than the greatest influence in horse racing history.[7]

From humble beginnings in County Cork, he rose to become owner of the masterful Ballydoyle stables and a founding partner in Coolmore Stud. During a fifty-year career he trained six horses to win the Epsom Derby, won three British Grand Nationals in succession, and trained the only British Triple Crown winner since World War II. Despite being based here, he was twice proclaimed British champion trainer in flat racing and also twice in national hunt racing the only trainer in history to have been champion under both rules.[8]

'What you're dealing with there is a genius. Not just a once-in-a-lifetime, but a once-in-an-epoch kind of quality of individual, who was so utterly brilliant at what was his job as well as his love that he transformed perceptions of the sport as well as perceptions of what was possible within that sport,' says Rouse.

Sustained State support for the sector has also been a critical factor in its success. 'Horse racing remains the sport that the State gives most money to, because it's both a sport and an industry, and equine exports are worth a lot of money to the country.' Through direct funding and tax incentives, the State has incentivised owners, trainers and jockeys to compete here and to use the country as a base for international competition.

The sector's success mightily enhances our reputation as a nation abroad. As champion jockey Ruby Walsh put it, 'Irish racing people, when they travel abroad, are respected like the All Blacks are when they travel abroad.'[9] That's a powerful achievement.

64 We Are Amongst the World's Leaders in English Literature

Ireland has the most winners of the Nobel Prize in Literature and the Booker Prize per capita

SOURCE: AUTHOR'S CALCULATIONS FOR COUNTRIES WITH OVER ONE MILLION INHABITANTS [10]

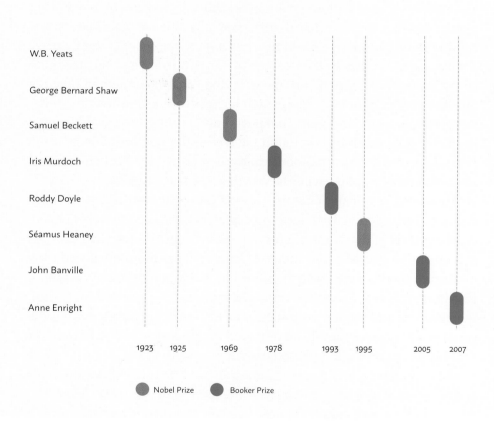

We are justifiably proud of our four Nobel Prize winners for literature. These poets, playwrights and novelists have given us the distinction of

being the home of more winners per head of population than any other country (setting aside the tiny countries of Saint Lucia and Iceland, which produced one winner each).

Since its establishment in 1969, the Booker Prize has become the world's most esteemed literary award for the best novel written in the English language. Ireland's four winners have again enabled us to capture the title of the country with the greatest number of wins per capita (albeit that American authors were not eligible for the prize until recently).

Our list of Nobel Prize wins is bookended by two great poets, W.B. Yeats and Seamus Heaney. They are amongst only eighteen poets to have ever won it. 'There is some truth in that jokey phrase that everyone in Ireland is coming down with poetry,' says Fran Brearton, Professor of Modern Poetry at Queen's University Belfast. 'Some of it is to do with a strong tradition of myths, legends, storytelling, and talk. And some of it is actually just the absolute centrality of W.B. Yeats to modern poetry over the last 130 years.'

Yeats may be Ireland's national poet, but he is deeply embedded in an English poetic tradition. He found his feet in the literary saloons of the late-nineteenth-century decadence movement in London. He helped found the Irish Literary Society while he was there, but he did not speak Irish.

His status as our national poet stems not only from his great work, frequently inspired by Irish locations or events, but also from his re-conceptualisation of the country. Through his influence on the Gaelic revival movement he crafted a new image of Ireland. The country was to be one of ancient spirituality, mysticism, romance, sociability and a closeness to nature. It was a deliberate counterweight to the perceived industrial, materialistic and modernistic society in Britain. This positioning of the country was one embraced and nurtured in turn by the bodies of the Free State and became our foundational myth.[11]

For all their Irish origin, it is notable that our first three Nobel laureates spent a great deal of their lives outside the country, as arguably Heaney did later as well. 'It's not exile,' explains Brearton, 'but dual placement can be a virtue when an audience outside – as well as inside – Ireland is a measure of your success. Shaw was a London-based, commercially very successful playwright, and Yeats has a huge audience in the States as well.'

While Yeats' poetry conjures up images of Sligo and Coole Park, he spent a lot more time in Dublin and London. 'It feels like he was here more than he was in reality because he was imaginatively here, in a sense, all of the time.' When he wrote in the 'Lake Isle of Innisfree' of standing 'on the roadway, or on the pavements grey' it was likely the grey pavements of London on which he found himself. 'Very embarrassingly, when he got married, he rowed his wife out to see Innisfree and he couldn't find it! They rowed around for ages in this boat and he's just like "I give up!"'

The 150th anniversary of Yeats' birth was celebrated with events throughout 2015 and I was honoured to serve on its advisory committee. A special boat trip was laid on for us to voyage out to see the Lake Isle for ourselves. It is a tiny, nondescript island scattered amongst several others in Lough Gill. There isn't space to land a boat on it, never mind for building a small cabin there. It certainly speaks to the imagination of the poet more than its potential as a tourist attraction. Even if it was better signposted.

The dual location of our leading writers also provided them with one further important advantage: the ability to avoid stifling Irish censorship laws. No less than a 'Committee on Evil Literature' was established by the Free State government in 1926. New censorship laws were enacted which prohibited any book deemed to be obscene. 'It could expand to almost anything that contravened largely Catholic principles,' explains Brearton. 'Anything that touched on adultery, divorce, contraception, homosexuality, masturbation – all of that was banned.'

'It was not just about censoring work by Irish writers, which was done and which therefore pushed them to an audience outside here, but primarily it was censoring what was or wasn't allowed to be brought in, and that was invisibly policed at the point of import. It was trying to censor how people thought through what was not brought in here, what was not available to a public to read, what was not available to be taught.' The list of the authors whose works were banned over the decades is shocking. Two of our Nobel prize winners, Shaw and Beckett, are alongside many, many others including James Joyce, Seán O'Casey, Seán O'Faoláin, Kate O'Brien, Edna O'Brien and John McGahern.[12] It wholly undermined the development of a new literature for a newly independent Ireland.

One positive arising from this blanket suppression was the literary response it spurred. 'The resistance to an idealised depiction of the Free

State at the hands of the authorities actually generated some really interesting mid-century realistic fiction. People like Seán O'Faoláin and Frank O'Connor at the time were pushing back against those kinds of restrictions and saying, "This is the reality of provincial Ireland. It's not what you say it is."'

Four decades of strict censorship waned by the 1960s as Ireland began to open itself to the world. The introduction of free second-level education widened the pool of potential writers and readers, and the State finally began to support writers financially through the Arts Council in the 1970s. The conditions were finally right for the emergence of our first Booker Prize-winning author who was entirely of, and resident in, Ireland – namely Roddy Doyle in 1993. John Banville and Anne Enright, similarly, emerged to claim the same prize in the following decade.

Seamus Heaney received his Nobel Prize in 1995. 'Heaney outsells most other poets in English put together. There's a persona in Heaney's work that people feel they know and love. There's a wonderful kind of Irish voice there, but it is more than just that. The technique, the inspiration, the expansiveness of Heaney's imagination – it is the complete achievement.'

So is there something unique about how Irish writers express themselves? 'There is a distinctive Irish English,' in the mind of Brearton. 'There's a richness absorbed from dialect. It's there in Heaney. It's even in Beckett. You could read scrupulously through *Waiting for Godot* and say "what is there that is remotely Irish about that text?" but when the characters meet, one says "get up till I embrace you" and you'd never hear that phrase outside here.'

But the borders of 'Irish English' and Irish literature do not neatly mirror those of government. I am counting Heaney in my list even though he was born, educated and buried in Northern Ireland. Yes, he held Irish citizenship and lived most of his adult life in the Republic, but much of his inspiration stemmed from his time north of the border. Should I not also count Belfast-born Anna Burns, who won the Booker Prize in 2018 for her Troubles-era novel *Milkman*?

'If Heaney is of Ireland then they're all of Ireland. In fact, it's exclusions other than nationality that have become more important. Irish writing is fundamentally still fairly white, middle class and quite male. The voices that are missing are probably to do with gender and Black, Asian and minority ethnic voices.'

Our past Nobel prize winners were all from minority groups. 'From a country that, in the census in the 1920s, identified as 93 per cent Catholic, there is only one Catholic in there, which is Heaney, and he is also from the North so he's from a minority in another way too.' It is the literature of these minorities that we now prize as being amongst the very best that the nation has produced. Taking an expansive view of our literature and encouraging more minority voices to emerge will strengthen our global contribution in the century ahead.

65 Ireland Has Won More Eurovision Song Contests Than Any Other Nation

Leading Eurovision Song Contest winning countries

SOURCE: EUROPEAN BROADCASTING UNION[13]

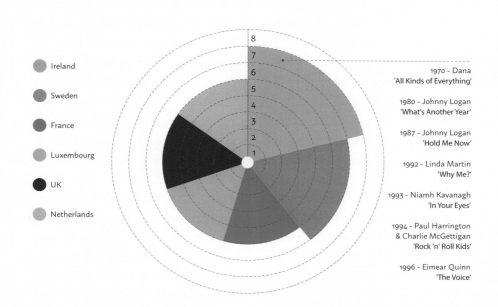

Ireland

Sweden

France

Luxembourg

UK

Netherlands

1970 - Dana
'All Kinds of Everything'

1980 - Johnny Logan
'What's Another Year'

1987 - Johnny Logan
'Hold Me Now'

1992 - Linda Martin
'Why Me?'

1993 - Niamh Kavanagh
'In Your Eyes'

1994 - Paul Harrington
& Charlie McGettigan
'Rock 'n' Roll Kids'

1996 - Eimear Quinn
'The Voice'

It is not just the written word: in the singing word too Ireland can stake a claim to excellence. Does our record number of Eurovision wins provide sufficient evidence of this or not? We can lay claim to more wins than any other country. We are the only country to have won three times consecutively. And Johnny Logan is the only performer to have won the contest twice.

All but one of the wins were in the 1980s and 90s. What was going on at that time that resulted in such an incredible run? 'We had some very, very good songs,' says musician and broadcaster Philip King. 'At that particular time, Eurovision was about good songs. Now, it's about something else.' The move from jury panel voting to televoting from the late 90s changed the dynamic entirely, resulting in far greater focus on the performance and the popular appeal of songs rather than their lyrical and musical craftmanship.

A competitive advantage that Ireland had until 1999 was the requirement that a country's entries had to be performed in its official language. Singing in English made our songs inevitably better understood and appreciated by audiences throughout Europe. Since this requirement was lifted, the vast majority of the winning entries have been sung in English but by artists from countries where this is not their national language. The playing field has been levelled.[14]

More fundamentally, the contest is more competitive now than ever before. Johnny Logan only had to compete against entries from 18 other countries in 1980. Today, more than 40 countries participate in the contest annually. The centre of gravity for the contest has shifted eastward as practically all of the additions are former Eastern Bloc communist states. However, accusations that 'political voting' results in a disadvantage for Western European nations do not stand up. Most of the winners over the past decade have been Western nations, including Sweden (twice), Denmark, the Netherlands and Portugal.

The 1980s and 1990s witnessed a much wider explosion of Irish music onto the world stage. U2 and Enya achieved global stardom. The Cranberries and the Corrs were close behind. Boyzone, Westlife and B*Witched stormed the singles charts in the 1990s and into the twenty-first century. 'U2's success had a profound influence because the international record companies began to look here for the next big thing.'

Success breeds confidence too. Our musical and economic successes as a nation engendered greater self-belief. 'We were beginning to be a little bit more comfortable in being Irish. We were beginning to appreciate we were good at stuff. We were little by little beginning to get over our post-colonial hangover,' says King.

We had come a long way from dancing at the crossroads and in each other's houses. That was where the action was in the early decades of independent Ireland. 'The ordinary people of Ireland gathered at crossroads and somebody came and played a box or played an accordion and people danced. Or you'd have a house dance once a month with a busker in the corner and somebody'd bring over a barrel of stout. That was where traditional music flourished in the form of jigs, reels, polkas and slides.'

The desire of the Catholic Church to control every aspect of the lives of its parishioners took its toll on these traditional entertainments in the 1940s and 50s. 'They didn't control it, and people might be getting up to things in the bushes, and they didn't like that sort of thing so parish halls were built where a supervised engagement could take place. And these then became sources of income for the church as well.'

It fundamentally changed the role of the musicians as much as the experience for the audience. Community musicians were replaced by céilí bands. The stage separated them from the crowd, who now had to pay to get in for a dance. And the whole thing was supervised by the priest.

It's hardly surprising, therefore, that trad music went out of fashion with the next generation. 'As Ireland developed and became more outward-looking, many people looked at traditional music and said, "We need to be cooler, we need to be more outward looking, we need to be more rock and roll." Much of traditional music was seen as redolent of failure and backwardness.'

Yet the very American and British music that we wanted to mimic had itself been deeply influenced by Irish traditional and folk music in a manner that was underappreciated at the time. 'Irish music left here in the heads and the hands and the feet of emigrants who arrived in the great cities of America and many of them found themselves, like many other migrant or economic migrant groups, in ghettos. But they began to play their music for their own community,' explains King. 'And once the method of recording that music was invented, some businessperson saw a chance and said, "We could record this music and we could sell it. All the Irish people would buy the Irish music, and they can then have a house dance at home without a musician and put on the record and they can actually get the musician to play the same thing over and over again, perfectly!"'

The music of Ireland was right there in the mix at the very foundation of the professional music business. The writers of Tin Pan Alley in New York City were reworking old Irish tunes and churning out new ones for their Irish-American audiences from the end of the nineteenth century into the early decades of the twentieth. 'We left an indelible thumbprint on the making of the American songbook,' contends King. These works can be found in the catalogues of Bing Crosby, the Everly Brothers, Pete Seeger, Bob Dylan, Simon and Garfunkel, Johnny Cash, Bruce Springsteen and many others.

It is not only American music that the Irish influenced – the same is equally true in Britain. 'There is no what I would call "pure pop for now" people in England without the influx of Irish migration that filtered into the DNA of what English music sounds like and without the black influence from Jamaica, the West Indies, and Africa. Those two things together give us what we call English music,' King says. The line of influence can be traced through to Dusty Springfield, the Beatles, the Kinks, Dexy's Midnight Runners, Elvis Costello, Boy George and Morrissey, for example.

These familiar roots of contemporary American and British music arguably paved the way for the success of modern Irish artists to be so well received there. But can we identify anything that is truly distinctive about the music from this place? Imagination and passion are what set us apart, King thinks. 'We have a natural resource of imagination that informs a hugely diverse musical lingua franca that influences and has been influenced by so many things, but at its core there is something woven into the DNA of people in Ireland that is profoundly musical. We have a very rich musical asset base.'

'I would also say it's spirit. Luke Kelly would be able to stand up and deliver a song with such power and spirit that he inhabited the song. The song sang him. Bono at his best is like that, he is consumed by the song. There's no halfway house with this thing. There is great power in it. There's great passion in it. And I think Irish music at its best has that.'

Musical entertainment was one of the sectors hardest hit by Covid-19. As we lost the opportunity to experience and create live music together, perhaps we came to recognise its value and its power in a way that we had not beforehand. 'At that time of anxiety and isolation, and almost a digital loneliness, we understood the profound necessity that music gives us a human, tactile, powerful engagement with others,' concludes King. 'As things fell silent, we began to understand what it was that we might be missing in those communal gatherings where we're joined together to raise our voices to sing – whether it's at weddings, wakes, funerals or concerts.'

Needless to say, our imagination and spirit did not dissipate in any respect. Our talent will shine on through and be recognised once again. And, no doubt, it will in time secure us another Eurovision win.

 ## Irish Actors Have Won More Oscars Than Those from Any Other Nation

(On a Per Capita Basis, If We Claim Daniel Day-Lewis as Our Own)

Ireland can lay claim to some very talented, truly world-class actors. The five Academy Award wins for acting clocked up by Barry Fitzgerald, Brenda Fricker and Daniel Day-Lewis mean that Irish actors have won more Oscars per capita than those from any other country.

Is including Day-Lewis a stretch, given that he was born in England? His father was Irish, he has Irish citizenship and his home is in County Wicklow. But even if he is excluded, our two other wins are enough to put us in third place for acting Oscars, behind only the USA and the UK when you allow for population size.

'We have a strong acting tradition in this country, although not acting for screen so much as acting for theatre,' says Dr Ruth Barton, Associate Professor of Film Studies at Trinity College Dublin and author of *Irish Cinema in the Twenty-first Century*.[15] 'We produce many, many actors. They can get much more money in one film than working for the other 40 weeks of the year on stage, so there is a constant drift from theatre to film.'

The other advantage our actors have is that they are English-speaking – a huge plus that allows them to easily transition to Hollywood films.

Roll-call of Ireland's Oscar-winning actors

SOURCE: WANDERU[16]

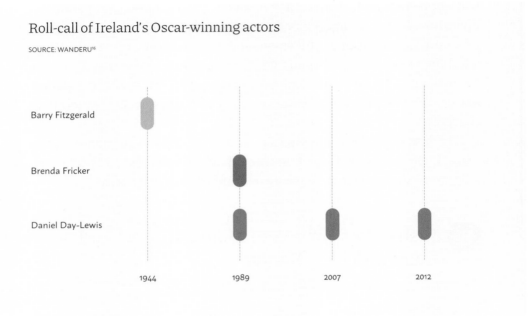

Barry Fitzgerald

Brenda Fricker

Daniel Day-Lewis

1944 1989 2007 2012

Barry Fitzgerald was our first winner, in 1944, as Best Supporting Actor alongside Bing Crosby in *Going My Way*. Fitzgerald was the stage name of William Joseph Shields. 'He was somebody who came through in the founding years of the Abbey Theatre; then he got the opportunity to go to America, and he jumped ship because he could make money,' explains Barton. 'He was somewhat typecast in American cinema because he wasn't exactly glamorous – he could never play the romantic lead! But he played a role that Irish actors have made their own, which is the priest.' His hugely successful career saw him appear in over forty Hollywood movies across three decades from the 1930s to the 1950s.

Fitzgerald could not have been a successful film actor at home because there were few films produced in Ireland throughout most of the twentieth century. That was for two reasons. 'One was economic: filmmaking is expensive and the country was reluctant to spend its small budget on that,' says Barton. All European nations had to support their film sectors financially because they could not compete with the commercial movies originating from Hollywood.

'The other reason was a deep suspicion in the church-ruling party dyad of film as a contaminating influence on the purity of the Irish nation that was being constructed by the often Fianna Fáil, but also Fine Gael, government. The Catholic Church was very, very suspicious of cinema and blamed it for all kinds of things, even for emigration.' With the country not open to the idea of a national cinema supported by government funding, the only films about Ireland were therefore made by outside filmmakers from the US or the UK.

'*The Quiet Man* is the one that everybody returns to over and again for producing an image of Ireland that was very much directed towards the diaspora. That had all those diasporic themes: the return home, the dream, finding the Irish Colleen, set in this beautiful remote part of Ireland, becoming part of a charming community, and so on,' explains Barton. 'A lot of the British films were much more about the Irish tendency towards violence – films like the 1940's *Odd Man Out* – and portray the Irish as rebellious. The idea was that the Irish were natural fighters. They were fighting because they were inclined to fight, not because they had a cause.'

The images depicted of Ireland were not those that indigenous filmmakers were likely to have opted for, if there had been any. The representation of the nation was in the hands of people who had quite different agendas. That finally began to change in the 1970s. Thanks to funding available, not from Irish sources but from British organisations such as Channel Four and the British Film Institute, small-scale, avant-garde movies began to be made here.

The government was embarrassed into establishing the Irish Film Board in 1980 to fund productions. However, the model was one that provided loans rather than grants to filmmakers. 'Well, that doesn't work because nobody ever makes money from films, or at least they never admit they do!' says Barton. 'So no money came back. Because of that, Charles Haughey suspended it [in 1987].'

That did not diminish the ambition of up-and-coming film-makers who sought out partners in the UK and the US to fund their big projects. It was Jim Sheridan and Neil Jordan who succeeded in bringing Irish film to the world stage. Ireland's second-ever acting Oscar win was Brenda Fricker's for Sheridan's directorial debut feature, *My Left Foot*, in 1989. Daniel Day-Lewis received his first Oscar for the same film.[17] Three years later, Neil Jordan's *The Crying Game* won the Oscar for Best Original Screenplay.

Irish film was having a moment in the sun – yet none of the credit could go to the Irish State, which had done nothing to support these productions. Pressure was building on the government to change its approach. 'There was also a financial imperative because *My Left Foot* was massively, massively commercially successful but none of the money came back to the country because it had been funded from the UK.'

Michael D. Higgins was appointed Minister for Arts and Culture in 1993 and he promptly re-established the Irish Film Board as a grant-giving organisation to support new film. He also introduced a tax credit for film production. Anyone who invested in making a movie could get a portion of their money back in tax credits, irrespective of whether it was any good or not. This resulted in a large number of productions being relocated to Ireland, even though they were not set here.

Braveheart is amongst the most prominent examples. Those were not, in fact, Scotsmen who raised their kilts and waved their bare asses at their English opponents before battle, but rather 1,500 members of the Irish Army Reserves who went the extra mile for their country – as well as 15 seconds of fame and a Hollywood pay cheque.

I was equally excited at the prospect of my 15 seconds and volunteered as an extra on one of the most expensive films ever produced in Ireland: Jordan's *Michael Collins* back in 1996. I turned up at the grounds of Bray Wanderers FC dressed in a tweed waistcoat and cap to join hundreds of others in a mass pitch invasion as we fled the fire of 'British armed forces' in a recreation of the Bloody Sunday atrocity of 1920. (Sad to say, no matter how many times I viewed the DVD frame by frame, I just could not catch a glimpse of my supposed big screen debut!)

These large-scale productions benefited our indigenous industry by providing world-class training for the technicians who worked on them, and opportunities for local actors. The tax incentive, furthermore, succeeded in the objective of enabling smaller Irish productions to get themselves a budget, supported by grants from the Film Board. There was a sudden, huge increase in the number of films being made. The greater availability of funding coincided with the decreasing cost of filmmaking as digitisation made expensive 35-millimetre analogue film redundant.

The 2007 movie *Once* is an exemplar of the change. Made for a budget of just €112,000, 75 per cent of which was funded by the Irish Film Board, it generated $23 million in box office receipts and an Oscar for Best Original Song.[18] It projected a far more modern image of Ireland. 'It's an urban image, but there's still a lot of traditional Irish stuff: the music and the community. It made a huge impact globally: a feel-good film, a romance, a musical, and it probably changed the way people thought about Ireland.'

Our expectations of higher-quality productions have increased in recent decades. We now want our movies to be as sophisticated as those originating from any other country. And that can only be achieved with large budgets, which often must be drawn in from funders from other countries.

'If you want to make a film now in Ireland, unless it's mini-mini budget, it has to be a co-production. The politics and finance of co-production mean that most 'Irish' films are transnational because they're co-produced with others from France or Germany or wherever,' explains Barton. 'But that allows for us to have a film industry.' Without it, we would not be able to afford to produce the quality of cinema that Irish and global audiences expect.

It is a model that is working well for us. The most successful independent Irish film at the box office so far, *The Guard*, was an Irish-UK production. *Room* was an Irish-Canadian-British-American co-production and received four Academy Award nominations including for its Irish director, Irish producer and Irish screenwriter, even though it was not filmed or set here. Similarly, *The Favourite* was an Irish-British-American co-production, resulting in nine Academy Awards nominations, including for its Irish producer and Irish cinematographer.

'It's a good moment for Irish cinema: there's money, there's good producers, there's been some successes,' concludes Barton. 'The films that reach a bigger audience are often films that touch on universal themes without abandoning their Irishness, and I think that's what the big successes do.' To successfully embody such universal themes will require greater diversity both in front of and behind the camera, reflecting the changes evident in Irish society and beyond. As Irish actors continue to flourish on the world stage, there is every prospect that our next Oscar winner will be a woman of colour.

 ## Irish Pubs Have Colonised the Globe

I recall attending a European tourist board gathering in Budapest. After a full day discussing European Commission funding and strategies to promote cross-border adventure tourism, we walked from the meeting venue to our dinner location. As we passed the front door of the inevitable Irish pub, I turned to the crowd of international colleagues and shouted, 'Look, it's the Irish embassy!'

That got a knowing laugh because Irish pubs are *everywhere* and, yes, they are great places to engage with Ireland and Irish culture. We have exported our famed hospitality and colonised the globe.

So how many Irish pubs are there in the world? Nobody knows. Irish Hospitality Global (IHG) has a membership network of nearly 5,300 pubs beyond our shores. But their 1,400 members in the USA are only a fraction of the estimated 4,000 Irish pubs there. And Mel McNally, the founder of the Irish Pub Company, points out that his firm alone has designed and fitted out around 7,000. The total must be comfortably in excess of 10,000 so.

IHG's membership gives a good flavour of the huge geographical spread. The bigger numbers are nearer to home with more than 1,100 pubs in Britain, over 400 in Germany, 350 in France and in Canada, nearly 200 in Russia, and around 150 in Spain and in Italy. But the network spreads out from there to encompass more than 80 countries. There's one in the Faroe Islands and Bolivia and Trinidad and Zambia and Iran and Nepal, just to name a few. A modern global social empire on which the sun never sets!

Number of Irish pubs per continent

SOURCE: IRISH HOSPITALITY GLOBAL[19]

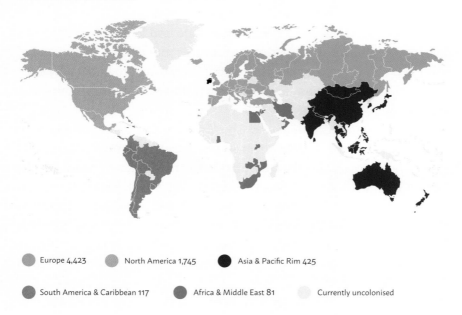

Europe 4,423   North America 1,745   Asia & Pacific Rim 425

South America & Caribbean 117   Africa & Middle East 81   Currently uncolonised

There were always Irish pubs outside Ireland, of course, whether established by our diaspora in honour of their ancestral heritage or by more recent emigrants creating employment for themselves wherever in the world they happened to settle down. However, it was the creation of the Irish Pub Company in 1990 that provided the blueprint for our global conquest.

It had its roots in a college project that McNally completed with fellow students. 'We wanted to investigate why some of Dublin's pubs are so beautiful. It went against the grain for the tutors, but it turned out to be a great success and was actually exhibited in the Mansion House back in the 1970s.'

McNally started his own architectural practice after graduating and had success creating Irish-style pubs in the UK. That brought him to the attention of Guinness, which had come to the realisation that one way to increase sales abroad was to have more Irish establishments which would, inevitably, stock the iconic drink. They asked McNally if it was possible to create a range of different Irish pub styles that could be exported and fitted out overseas.

'I said, "I don't know, but I need a year to go and look." I had about 25 people in my architectural practice. I took aside four of them with me and we decided to look at every pub in Ireland! We wanted to know why each pub was working, what was different about it, and what cultural stamp you would give it.'

The team identified four styles: the 'Country Cottage' typically with white-washed walls and timber beams, the 'Brewery Pub' with brick-wall interior and decoration that emphasised the brewing process, the 'Victorian Pub' with stained glass, bevelled mirrors, elaborate tiling and decorative brass, and the 'Shop Pub', which often doubled as a grocer and featured cabinets of goods for sale with plain wooden tables and benches. 'We added another one, which was the 'Celtic', to reflect Gaelic folklore and mythology. We couldn't find any like that but, in my heart and soul, I couldn't let that pass.'

'We formed a roadshow with Guinness and we did roadshows for investors for two and a half years all over the world,' explains McNally. 'The first one [we installed] was in Germany under a railway station. Then we moved to Estonia which had just gotten its independence. On the day it opened, there was a bomb in the building next door! I was wondering would we get paid?'

The Irish Pub Company (IPC) expanded hugely – 80 people were employed to do the designs as every location required a bespoke solution. 'From '96 onwards we were working hell-bent in America, we were all over Europe, we went to South Africa, we went everywhere.'

Imitators sprang up. A few Irish companies started to offer a similar service to IPC and planted flags for the Irish empire in new territories. And Belgian bars tried to copy the model and exported themselves, although with more limited success.

So what is the secret of Irish pubs' appeal? Why have so many been established in such far-flung places and proved such successes so far from home? 'It's conviviality. I go back to the reasons why we all love our pubs:

in most towns it's the epicentre of activity and social gathering.' McNally's research identified that this was a central element of how pubs in Ireland were designed that was not the case elsewhere. 'Simple things like the snug were never really used in the UK because it was a private area for the ladies in Ireland. Gathering at the bar was always important in our Victorian pubs but wasn't elsewhere.'

And our sociability embraces all ages. 'You can go, I can go, my son can go, all on the same night, into an Irish pub. But in other places, that's not necessarily so. If you are in a different age group you might have different tastes, but you can have all the tastes you want in a great Irish pub.'

The power of the global pub network is that it conveys a warm message about the conviviality of the Irish and gives a good sense of the place, building positive associations and helping to improve the standing of 'brand Ireland' in customer's minds. 'A great pub built with authentic snugs and flooring and joinery can really give you a feeling and the atmosphere of an Irish pub. If you're in a city overseas and you find one of that standard, you say "wow, it's a fantastic premises" and you get that warm feeling "I am in Dublin" or Cork or Limerick or wherever.'

The initial boom of Irish pub exports is behind us. The peak years of the 1990s and the early noughties were followed by more modest numbers of exports as Guinness' strategy moved away from supporting the establishment of new pubs. A constant flow of business has ensued for IPC, however, and McNally anticipates a second wave coming. 'There's potential in America in the smaller towns and the Chinese were starting to come here to do their research in big numbers before Covid, so they'll be back.'

In surveys of potential tourists, practically nobody says that they choose Ireland as a holiday destination because the people are friendly. They expect that alright, but they come to see our stunning landscapes and experience our culture. However, when people are interviewed on their way home after their holiday here, the number one thing that they say exceeded their expectations is the friendliness of the Irish. They come with high expectations, yet we surpass them. Our conviviality and engagement are truly different from what people experience in other countries they visit.

We should be very proud that we have exported some of that to the world. We have given them a bit of Irish culture and helped create a bit of happiness. In return, 'Irish' has become a by-word for friendliness and good times, and that has helped build goodwill and affinity with our small country. Let's hope our global social empire has further to expand yet.

Strengthening Society

AS OUR STANDARD OF LIVING HAS RISEN SO OUR SOCIETY HAS STRENGTHENED, RATHER THAN SPLINTERED. WE ARE MORE TRUSTING AND SUPPORTIVE OF EACH OTHER, AND WE ARE MORE COMFORTABLE IN ALLOWING OUR FELLOW CITIZENS TO HAVE THEIR FREEDOMS.

IRELAND IS ONE of the longest continuously established democracies in the world. By the mid-point of World War II, just twenty years after the Irish Free State came into existence, there were no more than a dozen democracies left in the entire world.[1] At that point, Ireland was the youngest of all of them. But as the ranks of democratic nations swelled in the decades after the war, we became part of the oldest cohort.

We haven't just sat back proudly content with the designation 'democratic', we have nourished that status and evolved in line with contemporary understandings of what a strong democracy should look like. Today we are considered one of the most democratic countries in the world, and as strong a democracy as we ever have been.[2] We are not flawless, but we have fewer flaws than nearly every other place.

68 Satisfaction with Our Democracy Has Never Been Higher

Satisfaction with democracy, 1973–2019

SOURCE: EUROPEAN COMMISSION[3]

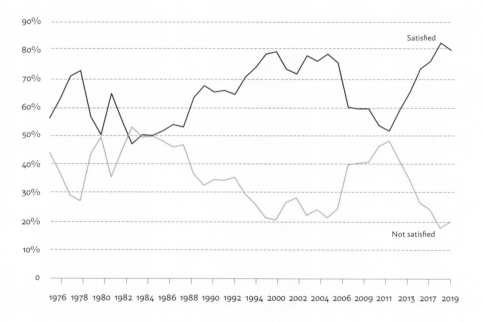

As a people we are very satisfied with where we find ourselves. More than eight in ten of us say we are very satisfied or fairly satisfied with the way democracy works in Ireland. The figure has never been higher and the trajectory over the past fifty years has been one of generally increasing satisfaction, albeit not without fluctuation.

There have been times when our democracy was under great stress. The early 1980s saw the only period when there were more of us dissatisfied than not. As the country got to grips with its economic woes and mismanagement, and in particular as the Celtic Tiger began to roar, satisfaction rose strongly again. The subsequent recession saw another rise in dissatisfaction, albeit one that fell short of the previous peak and was strongly reversed thereafter.

These are very impressive figures. In fact, we have the fifth highest level of satisfaction with our democracy of any country.[4] The United States ranks 34th and the United Kingdom is 43rd by comparison.

'We take it for granted in this country that we live in one of the most benign democracies in the world,' says Shane Coleman, presenter of Newstalk radio's breakfast programme and author of four books on Irish politics. 'When it comes to things like civil liberties, freedom of expression, freedom of the media, the freedom of elections, the rule of law, it is extraordinarily benign. Even when compared to our nearest neighbours that are strong democracies too – the likes of the UK, France, and other European countries.'

This is not to suggest that Ireland is some kind of utopia and that we do not have problems or that there are not improvements to be made. Of course there is more to do. But we are working from a place of strength. 'The State and the government are very reluctant to be seen to be coming down heavy on an individual. In fact, they do everything in their power to avoid that. People who take constitutional court actions rarely have to pay their costs, to pick a very small example. I'm not sure that happens in too many countries in the world!'

Our colonial history played a role in setting the tenor of the new Free State. Our country was now to be ruled by the Irish people for the good of the Irish people. Authoritarianism was what we had experienced at the hands of Britain, in the eyes of the country's founders, and was the very antithesis of their republican ideals. From 1922 onwards, no government wanted to have the same style and modus operandi as what had gone before.

'There was such a determination, after taking so long to win that democracy, that whatever needed to be done to protect it would be done,' says Coleman, 'whether that was protecting the country during the Second World War or facing down the IRA in the 1970s.' Ireland was not yet 17 years old when World War II broke out, don't forget. It was a young teenage thing trying to find its place in the world and to assert its own presence. Is it any surprise that we opted to be neutral?

For the full 100 years our governments have been led by one of the two political parties established in the aftermath of independence and the subsequent Civil War. Is it reasonable to conclude that Civil War politics have therefore proved to be a virtue for Ireland, not a problem? Their centrist economic policies have generally provided stability and certainty for citizens and businesses alike. Yes, we can certainly agree that economic mismanagement in the early 1980s and again in the 2000s caused huge damage to the lives of many people. They are the occasions when satisfaction with our democracy has been at its lowest. But the policies pursued by subsequent governments in righting the economy on both occasions were, if anything, more moderate and centrist and the evidence here is that they proved to be the right course of action.

'It's almost become a truism in this country that if Fine Gael and Fianna Fáil could merge, we can finally get that left-right divide in Irish politics – and people see it as a virtuous thing. I have never ever seen it like that,' says Coleman. 'When we look at events in Britain and events in the US, I think that is the *last* thing I want to see. We don't have a hugely ideological politics and I think that's a good thing.'

It amazes me that American politicians can portray the country as a leading democracy when the distortions in their system allow someone to be president when most citizens voted for the other candidate. In Britain, similarly, the electoral system grants huge majorities to parties with a minority of the votes and supresses the prospects of any mid-sized or small party making inroads.

That is not the case in Ireland. Our proportional representation system using the Single Transferable Vote (PR-STV) approach ensures that if 20 per cent of people vote for a certain party then that party is very likely to end up with 20 per cent of the parliamentary seats. It can't be said that the voice of the voter is not heard. Yes, it leads to a far more fragmented political landscape, but there is strength in diversity. It forces different parties with distinctive policy platforms to come together and agree on common programme for government that can reflect the best of both.

The votes of the public have resulted in more coalition governments than single-party governments in our hundred-year history. The last time we elected a single party into power with a majority in Dáil Éireann was in 1977. In light of the performance of the country since then, it is fair to conclude that we have been stronger for the diversity that has ensued.

Being a small country also helps. Our leaders are close to the electorate, and close to their problems. 'It's easier if you're a prime minister of Britain or of France to have strong leadership. When you have a population of 50 or 60 million, it's easier to shut down a hospital in Lyon than it is in Roscommon and maybe that's the right policy decision. But in Ireland, because the country is so small, because we have that system of PR-STV, every government always has to bring as many people on board as they possibly can with nearly every key decision they make.'

'It can lead to us constantly putting decisions on the long finger, but it does lead to a gentler, kinder state.' Of course, that is not to say that our State is always kind to all people. Given the range of choices it must make with limited resources, it probably never can be. However, relative to other countries, more of us are satisfied with how the state does its business here than the citizens of nearly anywhere else.

Why then do we occasionally hear some media commentators and opposition politicians decrying the country as a 'failed state'? Perhaps because they don't read books like this! Again, that's not to say that the State hasn't failed some individuals in different ways at different times. Democratic government is a creation of imperfect human beings – it is bound to fail from time to time. But when it works, it works well, and our democracy is working very well at the moment.

'If you look at where we were back in 1922, by any indicator you want to take, whether it's wealth, whether it's education, whether it's personal freedoms, whether it's the extent of our democracy, our levels of compassion, I just don't understand how people can say we're a failed state,' says Coleman. 'We have a pretty modern, progressive, liberal democracy.'

The battle is never won, though. We will never arrive at some utopian end game of 'mission complete'. We must nurture and enhance what we have. All the more so when democracy in our major cultural and trading partners is judged to be in peril – both from forces within and from anti-democratic foreign foes. It would be naive to think that Ireland is immune.

The unmoderated growth of social media can be identified as a significant threat to our democracy. 'It makes debate very simplistic. It's black and white. Nuance is completely lost. And you're on one side or another side,' says Coleman. 'It has the potential to create a politics that is more divided, that is much more hostile, more aggressive. I worry that we will lose the ability to listen to the other side and to other arguments, and that we will just go into our own echo chambers that confirm our views about things and confirm our views of people on the other side.'

We need to be mindful of where we could end up by driving division through simplistic and aggressive characterisation of political opponents. 'I think it will lead to even greater populism. There's a smugness here about Trump: "That could never happen here." I don't see any sign of a right-wing populist emerging in Ireland, but I see plenty of signs of hard left populism emerging and, to me, they're just two sides of a coin. I think they're equally dangerous.'

The centre ground can hold only by continuing to deliver on the needs of its citizens. Failure to adequately address the current housing crisis, for example, is excluding many people from getting their foot on the property ladder. Alienation from the political establishment will invariably follow. However, successfully addressing such challenges will sustain the high levels of confidence in our democracy and its institutions and thereby enable our continued progress.

69 Our Trust in the Institutions of State Is Nearly at an All-Time High

The majority of Irish people have trust in the majority of the institutions of state. Three-quarters of us trust the Gardaí, two-thirds trust the justice system and public administration, more than half trust the European Union and the press. Just less than half trust the parliament and the government. Trust in all of these institutions took a battering during the economic crash but has since rebounded.

This is a glass-half-full take on the figures. We can take comfort in the fact that just over half the people of Ireland trust the press, to pick just one example, or we can lament the fact that nearly half do not. There is undoubted value in examining the figures from both perspectives.

Public trust in various institutions

SOURCE: EUROPEAN COMMISSION[5]

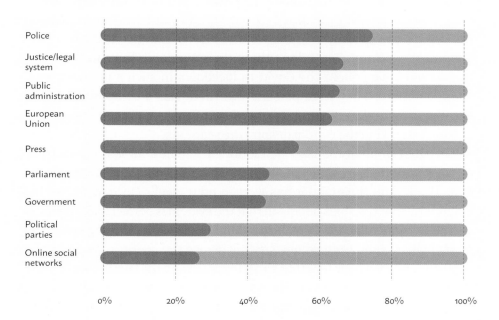

We can, however, be unequivocally positive about the fact that the trust in all of these institutions has been growing over the past decade and has reached a point where it has rarely – or never – been higher. We can also be positive about the fact that the levels of trust that the Irish people have in their institutions of state are generally higher than those of most other Europeans.

'I think in the vast, vast majority of cases the Irish State tries to do the right thing by its citizens,' says Shane Coleman. We saw the State step in quickly and comprehensively during the Covid pandemic in endeavouring to protect both the lives of its citizens and their livelihoods. It was generous in its financial support, gentle in its application of restrictions, and positive in its spirit of Meitheal.[6] It is impossible to get everything right in such pressurised circumstances, but ours was a country that chose to prioritise the population's health over economic wealth. Nor did it leave people to fend unassisted when circumstances forced them out of employment. The State stood by us well in a time of great need.

'It's kind of staggering that the confidence levels in the Gardaí are so high given what has come out over the last 20 years from corruption in Donegal to the treatment of the whistle-blower Maurice McCabe – it is genuinely shocking. Yet, I don't think there's a police force in the world that would have policed the Covid-19 lockdown in such a nuanced way,' adds Coleman. 'They were present, but there was a compassion there; there was an understanding. It's because of their approach that people still have a trust in the Gardaí despite the scandals.'

The trust in justice is also well founded. 'There's almost no evidence of any corruption in our legal system. There's been some miscarriages of justice but, in the main, it has worked pretty well.' Once again, let me emphasise that this does not mean that the system is perfect and that there isn't more work to do. As Coleman highlights, 'I have a difficulty with how many judges come from so few schools across the country. And I have a huge difficulty with the fees that barristers earn and the lack of competition in that area.' And high fees reduce the accessibility of justice for all.

It is in parliament, in government and, especially, in political parties where a trust gap becomes evident. Most people say they do not trust these institutions. Why, despite all the successes they have delivered for the country, is this the case? Unlike the State as a whole, people do fall foul of the government. With limited resources and a policy programme that results from compromise, it is simply impossible for government to keep all of the people happy all of the time. Their actions will inevitably go too far for some voters and not far enough for others.

'I wouldn't underestimate the impact of the economic crash as well,' says Coleman. 'You had the banking collapse and this perception that there was a cosy insider club and the bankers and politicians were all in cahoots together. I've never been a fan of those kind of theories, but I think there was a widespread perception that that was the case.'

This is not to ignore the fact that there have been examples of corruption that have undermined faith in politics and in individual politicians. However, we have taken steps to ensure that much of that has been consigned to our history. The public's acknowledgement of improvement has surely contributed to institutional trust growing to such high levels today.

70 Ireland Is One of the Least Corrupt Countries in the World

SOURCE: TRANSPARENCY INTERNATIONAL

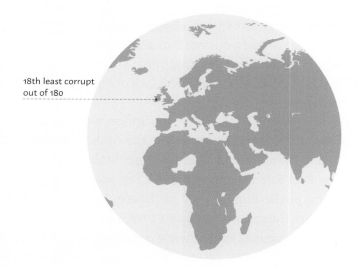

18th least corrupt
out of 180

Ireland is rated as the 18th least corrupt country in the world.[7] That puts us in the top 10 per cent of 'cleanest' countries, an undoubted improvement on where we were 20 or 30 years ago.

Shane Coleman co-authored a history of Irish political scandals since independence in *Scandal Nation*.[8] 'There was a newspaper headline a few years ago – "The most corrupt country in the Western world" – but I've never bought that even at the worst of times. I think what goes on in other countries, even other established democracies, is much worse. Scandinavian countries are standard-bearers in terms of clean politics but we are in the next group after them and, if anything, that has strengthened in recent times.'

We had problems for sure – *Scandal Nation* would hardly have warranted the title without them! 'During the 1960s a clique of politicians emerged that were overly close to business, that were willing to cut corners and, in a small number of cases, that were looking to line their own pockets,' says Coleman.

'The "cute hoor" kind of culture, that kind of "bend the rules a little bit", was a factor in that, particularly when you look at planning. There is always going to be a problem in any system that allows people to get incredibly rich by the stroke of a pen. Human nature being what it is, that's a huge temptation. We had a system that allowed that for a very long time and gave incredible power to a very small group of people. There was a lack of regulations, and there was a complete lack of enforcement of whatever regulations were there.'

Persistent allegations of planning corruption were investigated by a Tribunal of Inquiry, commonly known as the Mahon Tribunal after the name of its last chairman, Mr Justice Alan Mahon. The inquiry was established by Dáil Éireann in 1997 and it ran until 2012, making it the longest running public inquiry ever held here. It was one of the most expensive too, with the cost exceeding €130 million.[9]

Its investigation focused on planning permissions and land rezoning issues in the Dublin County Council area in the 1990s. After 16 years of work, although it found that various payments to councillors were corrupt, almost no one was prosecuted. However, the careers of several politicians were destroyed. Former cabinet minister Ray Burke was sent to prison for six months for tax offences. Former Taoiseach Charles Haughey had to pay €6.5 million in taxes and penalties for undeclared donations and was forced to sell his estate in north County Dublin to pay for his legal fees. Most prominently, revelations forced the resignation of serving Taoiseach Bertie Ahern in 2008.

Was the Tribunal worth all that for such little return? 'The real benefit of the planning tribunal is that it showed that people were not above the law, and it showed that there's a very good chance that if you try and diddle the system, you will get found out and you will be exposed.'

'Nobody wants to go through what happened to Charlie Haughey or to all the other politicians, even right down the scale to some of the councillors who were exposed as taking a few grand here and a few grand there. I think there was a lesson there for anyone who might be tempted to see politics as a gravy train. And so I think it served as a marker, as a warning.'

The surrounding controversy resulted in a fundamental change to political funding. In 1997 State funding of political parties was introduced. There was no longer any necessity for politicians to seek donations from businesses or wealthy sponsors. The State would cover their reasonable costs in proportion to their electoral success. The quid pro quo was that the value of any other donations they could receive was severely limited and election spending limits were introduced.

'Our funding rules are probably the strictest anywhere in the world. The amount of money I can give you if you are standing for office is negligible. The amount of money a business can give is very small. Look at American elections or in the UK – politics is funded by big business. And if you get a donation, you're beholden in some way,' says Coleman. 'We have taken the brown envelope out of politics.'

So does corruption still exist in Ireland? 'Of course it does. There isn't a country in the world where corruption doesn't exist. But twenty or thirty years ago, the dogs in the street knew that planning was dirty – I don't see a standout area like that. Politics is cleaner now than it has *ever been* in the history of the State.'

 ## 71 We Have Become a Safer Place in which to Live

We are a very safe country to live in. Our crime levels are not high by international standards, and they have declined in recent decades.

The spillover of the conflict in Northern Ireland resulted in some significant loss of life in the 1970s and 80s. The deadliest attack of the entire Troubles took place in the Republic with the coordinated bombings of Dublin and Monaghan in May 1974. Three bombs exploded in Dublin during the evening rush hour and a fourth exploded in Monaghan almost ninety minutes later. Together, they killed 33 people and a full-term unborn child, and they injured almost 300. They remain the deadliest attack in the Republic's history.

Terrorism fatalities in the Republic of Ireland, 1970s–2010s

SOURCE: GLOBAL TERRORISM DATABASE[10]

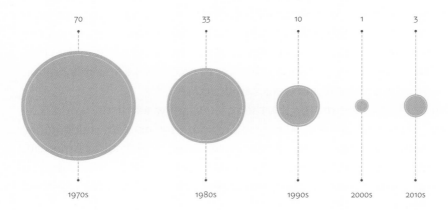

| 70 | 33 | 10 | 1 | 3 |
| 1970s | 1980s | 1990s | 2000s | 2010s |

Reprisals and targeting of British interests took place here too. The British ambassador was assassinated in Sandyford in Dublin in 1976. Lord Mountbatten, uncle of the Queen of England's husband, Prince Philip, was murdered aboard his fishing boat in Sligo in 1979.

And the IRA and INLA murdered public representatives and officers of the law. Senator and former TD Billy Fox was shot dead by the IRA in County Monaghan in 1974. Two gardaí were killed by the INLA during a bank robbery in County Roscommon in 1980. A guard and an army private were shot by the IRA during a kidnapping in County Leitrim in 1983. In total the IRA killed six gardaí and the INLA killed four during the years of the Troubles.[11]

The Northern Ireland peace process of the late 1990s helped to bring peace to the Republic alongside the North. While dissident republicans accounted for a handful of deaths in subsequent years, Ireland is now rated as the eighth most peaceful nation on the planet by the Institute for Economics & Peace.[12]

Remarkable as that achievement is, I had hoped to illustrate a different point for you – namely that crime rates in Ireland have been decreasing for the past couple of decades and that we are becoming a safer and safer place to live. That appears to be the case, but the statistics available from An Garda Síochána are so flawed that they cannot be relied on. The Central Statistics Office, which is responsible for publishing them, has placed the figures 'under reservation' because their quality does not meet normal statistical standards.

'The nineteenth-century crime statistics are better than the twenty-first century ones,' in the view of Ian O'Donnell, Professor of Criminology at University College Dublin. 'We have no idea what the guards do with reports that are made to them.'

What can we conclude about crime over the past hundred years then? The good news is that the data was collected consistently up to about the year 2000. They show that there were never more than 20,000 indictable offences a year until the mid-1960s (indictable offences being those more serious charges, which can or must be tried before a judge and jury). Most crime is against property but, given the basic living conditions of the majority of people in Ireland's early years, there wasn't a whole lot worth stealing.

'Sometimes people look at Ireland in the 50s and say, "Oh, halcyon days! That was a crime-free era." Maybe it was, but there weren't so many opportunities to steal and at the same time there was huge migration,' explains O'Donnell. Given that young men are responsible for the greatest proportion of crime, the continuous large-scale emigration of young people in Ireland's early decades literally meant that we were exporting our crime problem. 'There were more Irish-born men being sent to prison in England in the 60s than in Ireland. And you'll find in the newspapers from time to time district court judges giving a person the option of the emigrant boat or doing their time here.'

As households benefited from the nation's burgeoning economic wealth in the 1960s, and as the flow of emigration was stemmed for the first time, so crime rates rose. Dramatically. The number of indicatable offences doubled between the mid-60s and the mid-70s. Then they doubled again in the next decade, with the milestone of 100,000 offences reached in 1983.

The return of youth emigration in response the economic hardship of the 80s may have had a beneficial side effect in crime reduction. The high rate experienced in 1983 proved to be a peak that has never been matched since. Despite all the extravagant wealth on display during the Celtic Tiger era, the crime rate continued to trend modestly downwards. Jobs were plentiful. Everyone was doing better. And when people have more money to spend, there's less motivation to acquire goods illegally that can be purchased legitimately.

However, the way in which people spend their money can generate crime. Increased consumption of drink and illicit drugs contributed to an increase in violent crime. As alcohol consumption initially increased with wealth, so public order offences and homicide increased sharply.[13] 'People drink and congregate in public spaces where there's a potential for flare-ups. So you get an increase in interpersonal violence at the same time as you get a reduction in property crime.'

The same is true, although the mechanics are different, for illicit drug use. 'The people who live in leafy suburbs and enjoy recreational drug use of one kind or another are creating the conditions for violent gang conflicts in areas of socio-economic deprivation,' says O'Donnell. 'This creates a market, and that market is attractive to people who take big risks for big rewards, but the risks sometimes result in death. There's a connection there that people sometimes want to ignore because it shows that their behaviour has consequences. A gang feud in a particular part of Dublin or Limerick might be driven by their behaviour.'

Violent crime constitutes a tiny element of the overall crime rate. Think about it: there might be 45 or 50 murder a year when the total number of indictable crimes could be 80,000 or 90,000. Our homicide rate is not high by any international standard, but it is violent crime that makes the headlines. And that can lead us to misjudge what is really going on.

'As the crime rate was heading for a peak in the early 80s, people weren't concerned about crime at all. In some polls [at the time], concerns about crime were in the low single digits. And even in one year, zero!' The more pressing issues on the public's mind were unemployment, emigration and the Troubles in Northern Ireland.

'Go forward a decade to the 1990s, and public anxiety peaked when the crime rate started to fall. And it's possible to pin that down to a series of events in 1996.' The year started with three separate killings in rural Ireland: two male farmers and a female shopkeeper. That shocked public perceptions that murder was only a problem for impoverished urban areas. But the main catalyst for hardening public opinion was the killing of Garda Jerry McCabe during an IRA post office robbery in County Limerick and, two weeks later, the murder of investigative journalist Veronica Guerin by Dublin criminals.

Opinion polls were transformed: nearly 50 per cent then considered crime and law and order the most critical issue facing government.[14] A raft of legislation targeting organised crime followed, including the establishment of the Criminal Assets Bureau.

At the heart of this paradox lie some of the reasons that we are not all optimists all the time. We are attuned, as a species, to perceive threat. As I will show later, psychological biases lead us to believe that things are getting worse despite the evidence of progress being there for all to see.

For the past two decades, our crime rate has been on a consistent downward trend and appears to have fallen by a third or more (only the inferior quality of Garda statistics prevents me from giving a definitive figure). There are a million more people living in Ireland now than there were at the turn of this century, yet the amount of recorded crime is significantly less. Headlines about criminal gang feuds are not a good measure of what is going on in the nation as a whole.

Is that why the Irish people hold the Gardaí in high esteem? More than seven in ten of us say we tend to trust the force today. It is an astoundingly high number that has been little dented by the scandals that have engulfed the guards in recent times: the appalling treatment handed out to whistle-blowers, the widespread improper cancellation of penalty points, the falsification of one-and-a-half-million breathalyser tests, the potentially illegal recording of phone calls at garda stations, the fabrication and planting of evidence by gardaí in Donegal. And that is far from the complete list.

O'Donnell finds the explanation in the history of the force's birth and early years. 'The way the police came into existence in the 20s really generated a huge amount of public goodwill. It was the first Garda Commissioner, Michael Staines, who said we're policing with the consent of the people who we're policing. I think the decision to have unarmed police in such a volatile context was really important.' Recall also that there wasn't much crime for the Gardaí to investigate before the 1960s. Maintaining good community relations was easy.

The public's experience with the Gardaí nowadays is very different, of course, and support for them is not uniform. 'It varies geographically, so you don't find that high degree of trust in heavily policed areas where the community relationship with the guards wouldn't be that fantastic. And it tends to drop once people have direct contact with the guards.'

If we are going to continue to become a safer place to live, then the guards will need to meet the challenge of our increasingly diverse population. 'In other countries where there have been difficulties with the police, they've often involved a perception of policing that was not racially fair. We have a population that's now as diverse as the UK in terms of the percentage of people that are foreign-born. But we don't have a police force that represents that diversity and that's a really big challenge.'

They will also need to meet the challenge of the changing nature of crime today. More and more of it is virtual – identity theft, virtual fraud, ransomware, child pornography, incitement to hatred. And the criminals behind it are often international. Greater specialist expertise and growing cross-border cooperation will be vital.

So too will be reliable crime statistics. It is unacceptable that a modern police force in this age of data is unable to provide the public with an accurate assessment of crime in the country. It limits policymakers' ability to prioritise the laws and enforcement measures needed to continue to make this country a safer place to live.

Despite all the challenges we face, it is important not to lose sight of the evidence: the crime rate is nearly always lower than you think it is, and all the evidence points to its ongoing decline.

Our Media Are Amongst the World's Freest

World Press Freedom Index 2021

SOURCE: REPORTERS WITHOUT BORDERS

Rank	Country
1	Norway
2	Finland
3	Sweden
4	Denmark
5	Costa Rica
12	Ireland
33	UK
44	USA

Countries with greater press freedom have lower incidences of corruption.[15] A free media keeps government and public officials in line, ensuring that wrong-doing and mistakes are exposed and addressed – reducing the chances of them reoccurring and thereby strengthening our democracy and our society.

Ireland's press is amongst the world's freest. The non-governmental organisation Reporters Without Borders, established to defend press freedom around the globe, rates Irish media as the 12th-freest out of 180 countries. Scandinavian counties top the table, but we are placed well ahead of the media in the UK or USA.

'From my thirty years working as a journalist, I think we've an incredibly free media,' says Shane Coleman. 'But the libel laws are extraordinarily onerous in this country, and that does bring restrictions on how journalists can go about their work in holding institutions to account.'

This is one of the two factors that Reporters Without Borders identify as holding us back from attaining the top tier of freedom. The first is the high quantum of damages awarded by Irish courts. Combined with the high costs of defending defamation suits, this can result in a climate of self-censorship in which prominent individuals, known to be litigious, become largely untouchable by the Irish media.

The second factor is the high concentration of media ownership in relatively few hands. Reporters Without Borders cite the dominance of Independent News and Media and RTÉ in newspapers and broadcasting, respectively. Having said that, our media consumption has never been more diverse. 'When I started working in journalism, there was *The Irish Times*, *The Irish Press*, *The Indo*, a couple of evening newspapers, and *The Examiner* was largely in Cork. There was RTÉ and maybe two other radio stations had just started up. There was obviously no online media. Contrast that to what we have now. You're as likely to see some political comment online from Joe.ie as you are from *The Irish Times*.'

In fact, this shift online is a threat to the freedom our media currently enjoy. Just a decade ago, if a corporate wanted to reach an Irish audience, they had to spend all their advertising monies in Irish publications and media channels. Nowadays, half of their monies will be spent with Facebook and Google to reach the same consumers. An increased number of indigenous media channels chasing half the advertising revenue inevitably leads to reduced profitability. Many have downsized as a result, employing fewer journalists and less experienced (and therefore less expensive) ones.

'I worry about the economics of the media and about the sustainability of newspapers and even radio stations. The importance of old-style journalism – properly trained journalists who have ethics and who are balanced and adhere to those ideals of journalism – has never been more important than it is right now, given what's happening in social media.'

We only have to turn west to the United States or east to Great Britain to see the danger that an aggressive, ideologically driven media brings in cheapening public discourse, sowing social division and undermining a shared democracy. In supporting and protecting our indigenous free press we are unquestionably, in turn, supporting and protecting our society and the freedoms that it offers to us all.

73 Our Personal Freedoms Have Increased

Support for liberalisation of divorce, abortion and same-sex marriage laws, 1980s–2010s

SOURCE: WIKIPEDIA. EUROPEAN VALUES SURVEY. MILLWARD BROWN IMS[16]

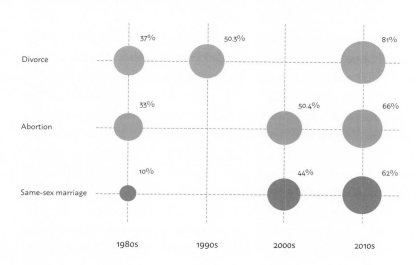

We have chosen, as the democratic will of the people, to increase the amount of personal freedoms and civil rights that we accord our fellow citizens. Within the last decade, significant majorities of us have voted to liberalise divorce, abortion and same-sex marriage laws. We were the first country in the world to legalise same-sex marriage by popular vote.

The country has come a long way in forty years. Two-thirds of the population opposed such liberalisations in the 1980s. Now, two-thirds support them.

The succession of votes for liberalisation delivered a lot of change in a short period of time. That does not mean that public support was quickly or easily won. As Ailbhe Smyth, co-director of the Together for Yes campaign on abortion and a founding member of Marriage Equality puts it: 'People used to say this to me after we won repeal or after marriage equality, "Oh, you did it all so fast." I'd say "Excuse me! Forty years of foot-slogging is half a lifetime!"'

There was a time when no one was thinking about these matters. 'I remember the 50s as being very difficult years in Ireland because people's living conditions were very poor. We didn't think about civil liberties and freedoms and we really didn't think beyond Ireland,' says Smyth.

Everything began to change in the 1970s. The government established a Commission on the Status of Women, whose reports in 1971 and 1972 recommended the implementation of equal pay and the removal of the 'marriage bar', which forced women to surrender their public sector jobs upon marriage. Shortly thereafter, as a member of the EEC, the government was obliged to introduce laws eliminating gender discrimination in employment and pay.

'The Commission on the Status of Women was an indication of changing thought and its report coincided, not coincidentally, with the emergence of the women's movement here at the beginning of the 70s. That was a huge breaking open, because what women in Ireland were asking for were our human rights and our civil liberties,' explains Smyth. 'You also had the recognition that there were international standards that we had to live up to. And if we wanted to be economically part of this wider world, we were actually going to have to look at issues of civil liberties.'

As the economy hit the buffers in the early 1980s, the movement for social progress was winded. The Eighth Amendment to the Constitution in 1983 enshrined the equal right to life of the mother and her unborn child in the Constitution – effectively putting a hard stop against any form of abortion. It was passed by a two-thirds majority. Three years later, a similar majority voted against the introduction of divorce.

The Catholic Church was a very vocal influence on both campaigns, providing clear guidance to the Irish public on how God wanted them to vote. Smyth has an unambiguous view of what the Church believed was at stake: 'If they lost control of women, they had lost control of the people, and they lost control of morality because women had always been held responsible for morality.'

Whereas Church and State had plotted together to affirm the ban on abortion, the government's proposals for divorce were a sign that the two were not entirely aligned. 'What the State and the Catholic Church didn't recognise was that they were on two very different courses. The Irish State was pursuing an economic course, inevitably towards an opening up and an acknowledgement that women were full citizens in their own right.'

The European Union played a direct role in defending freedom too. Its courts ruled in 1988 that the criminalisation of homosexual acts between consenting adult men was in breach of the European Convention on Human Rights. The State was slow to respond to the judgement, but homosexuality was finally decriminalised in 1993.

The Church's attempts to hold back social progress suffered a fatal blow in the early 1990s when the moral hypocrisy of its leadership was exposed to the Irish public. Serial sex abuse by priests started to be revealed after Father Brendan Smyth was arrested in Belfast in 1991. He fled to the Republic and was sheltered from the law by his religious order in County Cavan for three years before his arrest. He was able to abuse over 140 children because his superiors moved him from parish to parish as his crimes in each place came to light.[17] He proved to be merely the first of many clerical child sex abusers who would be identified within the Irish Church.

Then, in 1992, it was revealed that the Bishop of Galway Eamonn Casey had an adult son as a result of an affair in the 1970s. He resigned as a bishop but remained in the Church as a missionary and then a parish priest in England. If the churchmen couldn't sustain their own morality, who were they to preach to others?

'Both of these were foundational blows to the Catholic Church in Ireland – and they were in relation to children and to women,' says Ailbhe Smyth. 'You had women speaking up more and more, then you began to have people speaking up for children, and then the children who had themselves suffered began to speak up for themselves. That really destroyed the edifice of control, and of State and Church collusion, that had kept a firm grip on personal freedoms.'

In 1995 the people voted to introduce divorce. It could hardly have been tighter: 50.3 per cent voted in favour, 49.7 per cent against. Just 9,114 votes in the difference. But it was the first constitutional shift towards a more open and accepting society. Aside from the Church's loss of authority, the country's changing demographics were a factor: Ireland was getting younger.

'We had the largest youth population in Europe. Educationally, those young people may have been learning one thing from the nuns and the priests and the brothers in school, but it was being countered by what they were seeing on television. [...] The advent of television opened up young people to thinking about the world in very different ways, pushing in a much more open direction.'

Abortion remained a hugely divisive issue that was thrust to the fore in 1992 when the State secured an injunction preventing a 14-year-old rape victim, known only as 'X', from travelling to Britain to procure an abortion. The State argued that this would have been contrary to the Eighth Amendment to the Constitution guaranteeing the right to life of the unborn child. The Supreme Court overturned the injunction and concluded that a woman or girl had a right to an abortion if her life was at risk because of the pregnancy, including from the risk of suicide.

The government elected to put three decisions before the people in referenda to clarify matters, namely, to guarantee citizens the right to information on abortion, the right to travel for one, or to remove the threat of suicide as a ground for allowing an abortion. Around six in ten people supported the right to information and to travel but rejected the proposal to remove the grounds of suicide. The government had another go at rescinding suicide as a ground for abortion in a referendum in 2002 but this was also defeated, albeit by a much tighter margin.

While only one-third of the public had supported liberal positions on abortion and divorce in the early 1980s, by the mid-90s the country was roughly evenly split but with a slight majority for greater liberalisation – and that was where the momentum lay.

The first opinion poll I can find that asks explicitly about same-sex marriage dates from 2004. Forty-four percent of those who expressed an opinion were in favour of it. That was a mere eleven years after homosexuality was decriminalised. Just over a decade later, in 2015, more than 60 per cent of the population supported its legalisation in a public ballot. The love for Ireland on social media that day, from all over the globe, exceeded anything that I had ever seen before or since.

Three years later, in 2018, two-thirds of voters opted to repeal the Eighth Amendment in the full knowledge that a liberal abortion regime would be introduced for the first twelve weeks of pregnancy. The year after that, more than eight in ten voters opted to further liberalise our divorce laws by removing the requirement for a four-year separation beforehand.

The referenda outcomes of the 2010s clearly demonstrate how our society has transformed into a much more inclusive one. More than three-quarters of us still tick the 'Catholic' box on the census form, but how we practise that and the extent to which we let our morals limit the lives of others has fundamentally shifted.

'It is down to something like a third of the population saying that they practise their Catholic religion in the ways required by the Church. It is mainly about births, marriages and deaths for very many,' says Smyth. 'Those votes would not have been possible without that moving of religion to a different place in Irish social and political life. People were saying, "Okay, religion's ovetr there and it's a personal matter for me, it is not the business of the state."'

The American NGO Freedom House has published an annual review of political rights and civil liberties around the world for the past fifty years. Its most recent report ranks Ireland sixth best in the provision of civil liberties and personal freedoms.[18] It is an astonishingly high ranking given our recent history.

Yet there is the opportunity to go further. Freedom House points out the need for hate crime legislation and stronger laws against bribery and garda corruption. Smyth highlights the need to address homelessness, dismantle direct provision for asylum seekers, and enable dying with dignity. Whenever the public have been asked for their view, they have proved to be generous in their empathy and support for those who need our help.

We Are the Most Generous People in Europe

Countries ranked by their population's acts of generosity, 2009–18

SOURCE: CHARITIES AID FOUNDATION

We Irish like to believe we are more generous than other people. Well, it turns out to be substantively true.

The Charities Aid Foundation has compiled a list of the most generous nations using survey data from 126 countries gathered over the course of a decade. It places Ireland as the fifth most generous on the planet and the most generous people in Europe. Nearly seven in ten of us say we have donated money to charity in the past month, over six in ten say we have helped a stranger, and nearly four in ten have volunteered their time to an organisation.[19]

Interestingly, we sustained our position right through the deep economic difficulties of the Great Recession. In fact, the Central Statistics Office surveys show that households significantly *increased* the money they donated to charity during the crisis.[20] By their most recent estimate, households donate an average of €195 a year to charitable causes.

Volunteers, furthermore, give an average of 19 hours a month of their time to helping their chosen sporting, religious, political or charity organisations.[21] And they get back as much as they give. Those who volunteer are more likely to rate their level of life satisfaction and wellbeing as 'high' or 'very high' than those who do not. They know they are playing their part in building our social fabric, strengthening our society and making this a great place to live.

The beautiful thing about generosity is that it spreads health, wealth and happiness. Acts of generosity build a sense of trust and cooperation. We feel closer to others, and they to us. That greater connection boosts our mutual sense of wellbeing and our sense of community. In a self-reinforcing 'cascade of generosity', your generosity in turn inspires others to be more generous, which makes our communities work better together and increases our national generosity quotient for the betterment of all.[22] That strengthens our society and helps make this a great place to live. Keep it up.

Better Lives for Women

EVERYTHING THAT I HAVE EXPLORED SO FAR HAS BENEFITTED BOTH WOMEN AND MEN, ALBEIT SOMETIMES TO DIFFERENT DEGREES. BUT THE POSITION OF WOMEN IN IRISH SOCIETY HAS BEEN DRAMATICALLY TRANSFORMED AND THAT IS WORTH CELEBRATING IN ITS OWN RIGHT.

THE RIGHTS OF women were curtailed for a long time in independent Ireland. As recently as the 1970s, most were unable to drink a pint in a pub (half-pints only – *if* you were permitted entry), to sit on juries, to collect their children's allowance (the legislation specified that it had to be paid to the father), to get a barring order against a violent partner or to refuse to have sex with her husband.[1]

Thankfully, all that has changed. Indeed, so much progress has been made in recent decades that the country is now ranked as the seventh best in the world in which to be a woman.[2] Now, that's truly remarkable. Only four Scandinavian countries, New Zealand and Nicaragua are considered to have greater gender parity.

Let me illustrate the extent of some of this change and how it has benefitted our society at large.

75 Irish Women Are Having Fewer Children

Average number of children born to women during their reproductive
years, 1960–2019

SOURCE: THE WORLD BANK

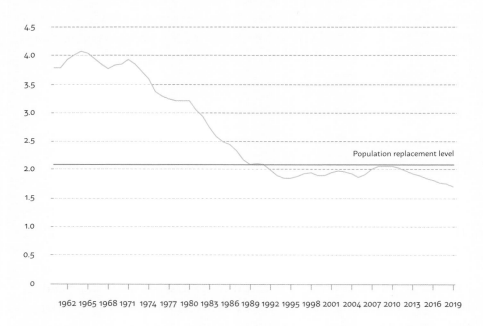

For the past 30 years Irish women have not been bearing enough babies
to keep the indigenous population of the country from shrinking.

Each procreating couple obviously needs to have a pair of children to
replace them in the next generation. But allowing for the fact that some kids
unfortunately do not live through to adulthood, each woman in fact needs
to bear an average of 2.1 children to ensure the population is maintained.
Irish women last produced that many children back in 1990. Most recently,
they are only bearing 1.7. We have never had so few children.

Is this an achievement? I believe a lot of women would think so. In the

1960s and early 70s the average was four children per women. There wasn't much time available outside of family life for pursuing self-fulfilment or for making your own contribution to society.

How then is the Irish population still growing? Two of the achievements that I highlighted earlier have more than compensated. Firstly, the fact that we have added years to our lifespans in recent decades means that we are living significantly longer than our parents did, swelling the numbers of those aged over 50 at the same time that the number of newborns is shrinking. Secondly, we have had a huge wave of immigration since the start of the Celtic Tiger that has augmented the indigenously born population.

The growth in the years that we are adding to our lives will eventually peter out, however. Although we can continue to welcome new immigrants to maintain population growth, our lower birth rate means that the recent rapid rise in Ireland's population will not be matched again in the decades ahead. In fact, forecasters reckon that we will never reach a population of 6 million people. The latest estimates are that we will top out at 5·8 million in 2057, after which the country will start shrinking.[3]

This is where the 'demographic time bomb' comes into play. Without a steady influx of immigrants to offset our lower birth rate, there will be fewer and fewer people of working age to sustain economic growth and to pay for the healthcare and pension needs of the growing number of retired elders. (That's one for my next book.)

Hang on, doesn't Ireland have one of the highest birth rates in Europe? Yes, it does. Ireland sits alongside France and Sweden at the top of the European childbearing charts.[4] But there isn't a single country in Europe where women are bearing enough children to sustain the national population.

So what explains our sharp drop? Why did women halve the number of children they bore in just 20 years? Blame contraception! Or, rather, thank contraception.

Contraception was illegal in Ireland until 1980. Yes, illegal. Banned. Entirely prohibited.

Senator Mary Robinson attempted to introduce the first bill to liberalise the law into the Seanad in 1971 but the major political parties did not allow it a reading. In response, feminists travelled by rail to Belfast and returned to Dublin laden with contraceptive devices to highlight the illogicality of the law. Predictably, the Catholic Church hierarchy was outraged. The Bishop of Clonfert claimed that 'not since penal times was the Catholic heritage of Ireland subjected to so many insidious onslaughts on the pretext of conscience, civil rights and women's liberation'.[5]

A landmark case before the Supreme Court in 1973 began the process of change. In *McGee v. The Attorney General* in 1973, the court ruled that there was a constitutional right to marital privacy, which allowed for the use of contraceptives. It took six years for our legislators to take action but, finally, in 1979 the Minister for Health, Charles Haughey, secured support for a bill enabling pharmacies to dispense contraceptives to those who had a prescription from their GP for 'bona fide family planning' purposes. It came into force the following year, enabling women to have a degree of control over their own fertility for the first time.

New laws in 1985 removed the need for a prescription for those aged over 18, despite opposition from the Archbishop of Dublin, who claimed the legislation would send Ireland down a 'slippery slope of moral degradation'.[6]

The slope it helped send us down was one of declining fertility, although the Church's past influence is still playing a role in keeping us at the top of Europe's birth rate league. 'We have a history of Catholic norms, we have a history of being a pro-natalist society, and children have been valued,' explains Dr Margret Fine-Davis, Senior Research Fellow at Trinity College Dublin's Department of Sociology.

Fine-Davis has been tracking the attitudes of the Irish public over the past five decades. In the mid-1970s, women's ideal family size was four children. Today it is between two and three. 'They also are conscious of the economic factors that mean that they can't afford to have as many children as they would like. They're sometimes choosing now between one and two children, rather than two and three children, because of the cost of childcare. They have to adjust their ideal to what is feasible.'

Women's control over their own fertility has enabled them to make a greater contribution to the nation's development, and has played a part in altering the shape of Irish families.

76   Our Families Are Becoming More Diverse

Figures for marriages, births and families showing that marriage is less common, births outside marriage increased, and brides and first-time mothers are older, 1970–2019

SOURCE: CENTRAL STATISTICS OFFICE[7]

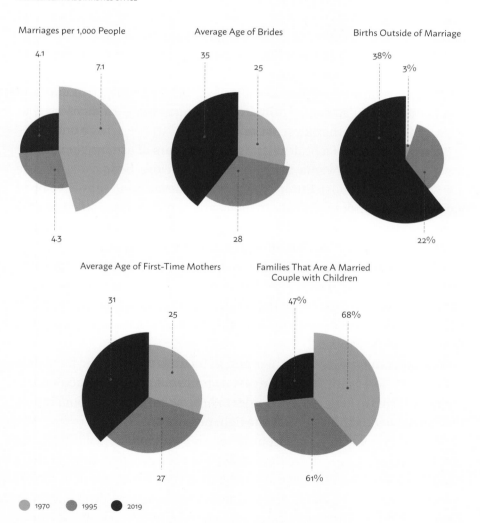

Marriages per 1,000 People

4.1
7.1
4.3

Average Age of Brides

35
25
28

Births Outside of Marriage

38%
3%
22%

Average Age of First-Time Mothers

31
25
27

Families That Are A Married Couple with Children

47%
68%
61%

1970   1995   2019

Our families have never been more diverse. For a start, we are far less likely to get married than our parents were. There was a marriage boom from the early 1970s. Only one in ten women aged 35–44 was not, or had never been, married by the mid-1980s. Nowadays, three in ten women in that age bracket are single, and marriage rates are the lowest they have ever been.

The difference is partly accounted for by the rise of cohabitation. More than eight in ten of us agree that it is better to live with someone before you marry them, and seven in ten agree that cohabitating provides a solid family basis too.[8] 'People are putting a higher value on the decision to have a child together and lesser value on marriage per se as an indicator of commitment,' says Fine-Davis.

The increasing value that women place on autonomy, freedom and independence is also contributing to later marriages – so much so that Irish brides are now the oldest in the world!

The average age of a bride in Ireland is 35 years of age, or 34 years for first-time brides. Slovenia and Estonia come close behind us, but we are well ahead of most European countries, never mind less developed nations, where brides tend to be in their early or mid-twenties (just as they were here back in the 1970s).[9] Our average bride today is, on average, a whole ten years older than her mother was when she married.

'Women want to make a go of their career and not settle down so quickly,' explains Fine-Davis. 'They know that, once they get married, they will have children and have to look after the children and that it will be very difficult to keep working because there is not enough childcare and there's not enough flexible working.'

'The other thing is that both men and women are trying to find their ideal mate. Because sexual mores have eased up and cohabitation is acceptable, they don't have to get married in order to have an intimate relationship, so they are taking their time to find the right person.'

Given that cohabitating is considered to be a suitably solid basis for family creation, it is unsurprising that the average age of first-time mothers – at 31 years – is now three years younger than the average age of first-time brides. This has contributed to an explosion in births outside of marriage. Back in 1970, just 3 per cent of all children were born 'out of wedlock'. Today that figure verges on four in ten.

The number of cohabiting families with children has grown six-fold in the past two decades. The number of single mothers has also increased by 75 per cent. Combined with strong growth in cohabiting and married couples *without* children, this has resulted in the 'traditional' family of a married couple with children now constituting a minority of Irish families. They remain the largest family type by far at just under half (47 per cent), but both unmarried families with children (whether cohabiting or one-parent families) and married couples without children each constitute nearly a quarter of our families today.[10]

Are these changes for the better? Insofar as they result from – and contribute to – the empowerment of women to develop themselves and to contribute even more to Irish society, they unquestionably are. In allowing women more time to gain a complete education and to establish themselves in their careers, the benefits that flow are many, and for many.

The Majority of Women Now Have a Third-Level Education

Never have so many of us been in possession of certificates, diplomas, degrees and doctorates. But it is women who have embraced this opportunity most of all. We achieved something remarkable in 2018 when the majority of working-age women could point to having completed some form of further education.

The graph tells a story of extraordinary growth in qualifications for both genders. However, more women have held third-level qualifications than men since the turn of this century. And the majority of men have yet to pass the achievement milestone that women have.

The removal of barriers to women's entry to the workplace was an incentive for more to pursue higher education. As Professor Áine Hyland, former Head of Education in University College Cork, explains it, 'in the 1950s, only about 3 or 4 per cent of the population went on to universities and only a quarter were female. The explanation is very simple: why would you go to university when, as soon as you got married, you weren't allowed to work anymore?' Within a generation of the removal of this law, by 1992, women constituted the majority of university students.

Percentage of women and men aged 25–64 with a third-level education, 1989–2019

SOURCE: OECD[11]

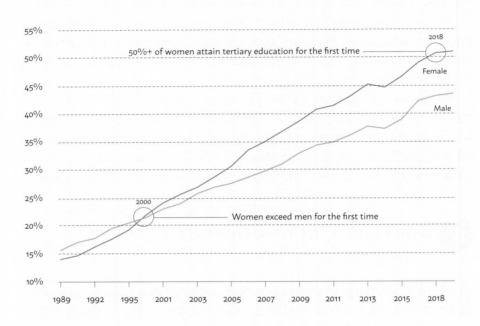

With greater and greater numbers of women progressing to higher education as the sector expanded, society and the workplace was bound to change in turn. The additional years spent in education, combined with the burgeoning careers they spawned, played their part in pushing out marriage and childbirth. The change also meant that the best available talent was increasingly female, prompting companies to hire proportionally more women and to transform the workplace.

78 Women Have Entered the Workforce in Huge Numbers

Percentage of women aged 20+ looking after home/family or in the labour force, 1971–2016

SOURCE: CENTRAL STATISTICS OFFICE

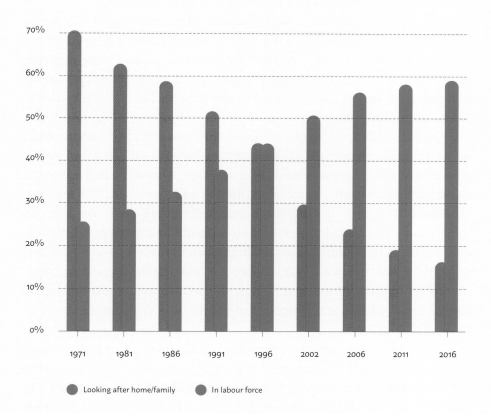

● Looking after home/family   ● In labour force

This graph highlights the transformation of opportunity for Irish women like no other. It beautifully illustrates the 'Big Crossover' – that is, the shift that Ireland underwent from containing women in their homes to unleashing their economic and social potential.

X marks the spot. 1996. The point when the number of women in the workforce exceeded the number solely looking after their home or family for the first time.

In the early 1970s the overwhelming majority of women aged 20 or over engaged in home duties. Just a quarter were employed or seeking employment, most of whom were single. Just 7.5 per cent of married women were working.[12] That degree of labour-force participation places us somewhere between where Libya and Saudi Arabia are today.[13]

'Ireland is unique among developed Western societies in relation to the constraints on women's roles, which continued well into the 1970s and '80s,' explains Fine-Davis. 'Because married women were expected to make their lives in the home, it probably did not seem unreasonable to create a social order which actually provided obstacles to their participation in employment.'

There were plenty of obstacles to overcome in the 1970s. 'It was normal to see job advertisements in the newspapers with different pay scales which favoured men, particularly married men, who were seen as having to support families and hence be entitled to a higher wage. The tax laws also were designed to discourage married women from working, as their income was added to that of their husband and taxed at his highest marginal rate. In the early 1970s the highest marginal rate was 70 per cent and there was at times a 10 per cent surtax, bringing the highest marginal rate to as much as 77 per cent. Thus married women whose husbands earned salaries taxed at the highest rate could expect to take home just 23 per cent of their salary.'

If that were not enough, there was also the 'marriage bar', which required women to give up their jobs upon marriage if they were employed in the public service, in non-primary school teaching and in some other sectors such as banking. There was a widespread view that men and school-leavers had a greater right to a job. In Fine-Davis' research, more than 70 per cent of people agreed that 'when there is high unemployment, married women should be discouraged from working' in 1978.[14] Workplace discrimination was blatant. Childcare centres were nearly non-existent.

It was a determined woman indeed who would face all of these obstacles and yet manage to go out to work! But change was coming. The arrival of the women's movement challenged these practices, and the government abolished the marriage bar in 1973 on foot of a recommendation of the Commission on the Status of Women.

Ireland's membership of the EEC opened our eyes to the attitudes and practices of other countries, which were more advanced on women's issues and gender equality. More tangibly, in 1975 Europe mandated that Ireland introduce laws to ensure equal pay and in 1977 to eliminate gender and marriage employment discrimination, resulting in the abolition of marriage bars in the private sector.

'The attitudes and behaviours and experiences in other countries like the United States and Britain were coming flooding into Irish households through their television set,' explains Fine-Davis. 'That coincided with the opening up of international travel so people were seeing other ways of life.'

'It was a convergence of all of those factors, along with the legalisation of contraception that enabled women to control their fertility, that opened up participation in the workforce in a way that had not been possible before.'

The 'X' crossover moment of the mid-1990s coincided with the take-off of the Celtic Tiger. 'It finally became apparent that women's labour force participation, particularly that of married women, not only was *not* taking away jobs from men and school leavers, but it was in fact significantly contributing to the boom.'

Today, the majority of adult women are in employment or seeking employment. The figure is as high as eight in ten amongst those aged in their late 20s and early 30s.[15] Only 16 per cent of women are engaged full-time in home duties, which is roughly the same number that declare themselves retired from the workplace.[16]

This growth in labour-force participation has tapered off over the past decade or so. Partly this is due to the growing number of young women in further education, and partly it is due to our aging population having a greater number of older women who are now retired or unable to work. However, women have still not caught up with men's level of participation and remain behind their sisters in most other European countries too. Why does the final stage of the Big Crossover remain incomplete?

'Women still have a dual burden. They may have equality in the workplace, but then they have to come home and look after the functioning of the household and taking care of the children,' says Fine-Davis. 'If a woman is working full time, she has to get her child to the childcare centre before she gets to work, and she needs to get to work on time and struggle with the traffic and then pick up the child at the end of the day. The synchronicity issues, and the traffic issues, and the cost issues are horrendous.' Our national childcare provision leaves a lot to be desired.

'And then she has to go home and cook dinner. And she has to find time to shop for that dinner. And then she has to wash the dishes. And then she has to put the child to bed. And men still are not carrying out their fair share of housework or childcare – they are not putting in the minutes!'

The evidence is stark. One of the most comprehensive studies of how Irish women and men spend their time revealed that women spent, on average, one hour and 18 minutes a day cleaning on weekdays, whereas men spent just 12 minutes. The male contribution equates to just 15 per cent of the women's work. Women also spent an average of one hour and nine minutes per weekday cooking, compared with 16 minutes spent by men. While men spent more time on DIY, this did not come close to compensating for the long hours women put in cooking, cleaning and shopping.[17] Come on lads, this one is on us.

If women are putting in equal hours in the workplace, are they getting rewarded the same as men? The evidence is that the gender pay gap has been continuously shrinking, decade after decade, but that one remains. 'In Biblical times, women got paid 60 shekels for every hundred a man did. The gap was pretty much that until recently!' In the 1970s women's pay in Ireland was precisely that. By the 80s it had edged up to around 68 per cent that of men. In the 90s it reached 73 per cent. And by the noughties it was 86 per cent. It hasn't budged any closer to parity since.[18]

However, recent evidence suggests that the gap between university graduates has shrunk to single digits and can be explained by differences in subject choices, with more men choosing to study for higher-earning professions.[19] The elimination of the final vestiges of a century of discrimination is within our grasp.

International studies have, furthermore, found that when male and female employees were at the same job level in the same company and worked in the same function, the gap disappeared.[20] The trick to closing it, therefore, is to ensure that women reach the same seniority levels as men. 'Women still are not in senior positions in most companies. They're not on boards. There's this slow improvement, but there are still traditional attitudes and norms to overcome,' concludes Fine-Davis.

There is, at least, one important senior leadership position women have held more often than men in recent decades.

79 Ireland Has Had a Female Head of State for Longer Than Nearly Any Other Country

Female presents / prime ministers in power over the last fifty years

SOURCE: WORLD ECONOMIC FORUM[21]

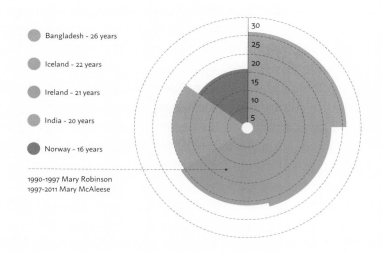

Bangladesh - 26 years

Iceland - 22 years

Ireland - 21 years

India - 20 years

Norway - 16 years

1990-1997 Mary Robinson
1997-2011 Mary McAleese

The president of Ireland is the highest political office in the land. We elected Mary Robinson as the first female president in 1990 for a seven-year term, followed by Mary McAleese for two terms. Those 21 years with a female head of state are remarkable in an international context. Only Bangladesh and Iceland can claim to have had female presidents or prime ministers for longer.

The presidency is not equivalent to the office of Taoiseach, of course. There is a chasm of political power between the two positions and we have yet to garner the courage to take that leap. Nevertheless, we can be proud of where we have got to in recent decades, even if there was little to celebrate about the early years of the State's existence.

While Irish history can boast of Countess Markievicz as the first women ever elected to the British House of Commons and the first female cabinet minister in Ireland, both of those feats predated the establishment of the Irish Free State. It was not until 1979 that independent Ireland acquired its first female cabinet minister with Máire Geoghegan-Quinn's appointment as Minister for the Gaeltacht. And it wasn't until 1981 that the number of women elected to Dáil Éireann exceeded ten for the first time.

'Up until then, pretty much every single elected female politician was related to a former male TD. Political parties could not imagine women being in political life unless the woman was a daughter or a wife of a former TD! It shows how hard it was for women to break through and it also shows how deep nepotism in Irish politics ran at the time,' points out Yvonne Galligan, Professor of Comparative Politics at Technological University Dublin.

The political culture began to change in the 1970s as Irish society did. Ireland's opening up to the world, her nascent economic development, and the return of emigrants who had different expectations all played their part. However, it was the growth of the women's movement that principally challenged the status quo.

Several feminist leaders who sought to pursue political change found a home in the socially democratic wing of Fine Gael under the leadership of Garret FitzGerald. Activists such as Monica Barnes, Gemma Hussey and Nuala Fennell succeeded in winning election as TDs for the party in 1981 and 1982. Although less successful electorally, the Labour Party too embraced the advancement of women and had a high-profile activist in the person of Senator Mary Robinson.

Robinson left the Labour Party in the early 80s and retired from the Seanad in 1989, after serving twenty years, to concentrate on her legal and academic career. The following year, however, the Labour Party nominated her to run for the presidency with the support of the Workers' Party and the Green Party.

She was not expected to win. After all, no women had ever been elected to the office before nor had anyone who was not the official Fianna Fail candidate. Their candidate on this occasion was the Tánaiste Brian Lenihan, who had over twenty years' experience as a cabinet minister. What hope had an ex-senator nominated by a small left-wing party?

'Rather than saying that she was a Labour Party candidate, she put together this very, very broad coalition of people that would have been seen as the one-third minority in Irish society. These were the people that campaigned in the 80s for divorce and campaigned against putting the Eighth Amendment into the Constitution – both of which lost by two-thirds to one-third. She wanted to appeal to the growing sense of liberalism in Irish society that was not captured by the other candidates,' explains Galligan.

But Robinson had to overcome an image problem. 'She was known as the radical feminist senator from Dublin. Certainly, she would not have been a comfortable choice for a Catholic conservative voter. She went around the country not once but twice, and in some cases visited places three times, so that people got to know her and got a chance to speak with her and to see that she was not this fearful feminist, but was actually somebody who was trying to make life better for everyone in Irish society.'

Significant missteps by the Lenihan campaign handed Robinson her win. Firstly, Lenihan denied phoning President Hillery in 1982 to ask him not to dissolve the Dáil following a no-confidence defeat for Taoiseach Garret FitzGerald so that Charlie Haughey could attempt to form a government instead. When a recording of an interview he gave to a UCD history student emerged in which he said precisely the opposite, he declared his interview quotes to be incorrect 'on mature recollection'. But his credibility was damaged, and he was removed from his ministerial role.

An outburst of sexism by Fianna Fail minister Pádraig Flynn caused further outrage when he criticised Robinson's clothes and hairdo and claimed she had a newfound interest in her family and in being a mother now that she was a candidate. 'An electorate hearing that at this stage was saying, "This is about expressing a new Ireland, expressing an Ireland where women have equal status with men, expressing an Ireland where everybody has choice and opportunity, so maybe we should go with *that* candidate on this occasion."'

Brian Lenihan won more votes, achieving 44 per cent of first preferences, while Robinson garnered 39 per cent. However, more than three-quarters of the votes from the third-placed candidate, Fine Gael's Austin Currie, transferred to Robinson and handed her victory.

She had promised to be an activist president, in contrast to her predecessors. 'She got out and about an awful lot. She was invited to the opening of every bookshop and every town hall in the country and she accepted many of them. The early 90s were still tough economic times and she wanted to give heart to local communities.' It made her wildly popular with the public – at one point her approval rating topped 92 per cent.[22]

Robinson understood well how to deploy 'soft power' and the potent value of symbolism. She placed a candle in the window of her official residence, Áras an Uachtaráin, for the Irish diaspora around the globe. She paid a personal visit to Queen Elizabeth II for the first-ever meeting of an Irish president and a British monarch, and later undertook the first-ever official visit of a president to Britain.

But perhaps her greatest symbolic act was her decision to shake hands with Sinn Fein president Gerry Adams during a visit to Belfast at a time when the IRA campaign of violence was still ongoing. 'Sinn Fein were pariahs in the electoral system and in the political culture at the time. There was a backlash against her for that, both in Northern Ireland and in political circles in the south. It was a brave thing to do, but it was the right thing to do.' Nearly eight in ten of the public agreed with her action in a subsequent opinion poll.[23]

Although Robinson only served one term before taking up the role of United Nations High Commissioner for Human Rights, her election proved pivotal for women's progress in politics. 'Political parties had to begin to take women's candidacy seriously. The electorate were expecting it. Women felt that they had a part in bringing Mary Robinson to office, had a part in her great presidency, and no longer were going to say, "Well, politics is for the boys",' explains Galligan.

The next general election, in 1992, saw the number of women elected to Dáil Éireann exceed twenty for the first time. And there were four female candidates (alongside only one male) in the presidential election to choose Robinson's successor in 1997. The winner, in a return to form, was the Fianna Fail candidate Mary McAleese.

McAleese was a Belfast-born Catholic and a legal academic. She took office just a few months after the final IRA ceasefire that would enable peace talks to conclude with a comprehensive settlement in Northern Ireland. "Mary McAleese's time in office was very commensurate with the peace process. That was *the* big agenda on the island, and she was the right President at the right time to bring that agenda south of the border."

She hosted garden parties on the Twelfth of July to welcome representatives from both communities in Northern Ireland. Her husband, Martin McAleese, worked behind the scenes with former loyalist paramilitary leaders and communities to bring them into the peace process. She jointly inaugurated the Island of Ireland Peace Park in Belgium with Queen Elizabeth II in memory of all the soldiers from the island of Ireland who served in World War I. And perhaps her greatest symbolic achievement was hosting the first-ever State visit of a UK monarch to independent Ireland when Elizabeth visited in May 2011. By the end of her 14-year period as president, McAleese had officially visited Northern Ireland on over one hundred occasions.[24]

Both women changed quite fundamentally the concept of the office of president and the role it played in representing, and engaging with, the people of Ireland. 'They left a combined legacy of an activist presidential role, endowed with heightened public visibility and renewed sense of relevance for the people and for the politics of the time. It is a measure of their success that towards the end of their terms of office, each woman was more popular with the public than they were on their presidential election day.'

The progress that women had made in securing Dáil representation, however, stalled in the late 1990s and into the noughties. The powerful contributions made by our female presidents did not convert into the election of a greater number of women to the legislature. At a time when the Celtic Tiger brought more and more women into the workforce and into leadership positions in civil society, the contrasting low number in the Dáil was becoming untenable.

'The turning point came at the economic crisis of 2008 onwards. The public, as a whole, began to reflect on who we are and are our political institutions fit for purpose? The issue of gender imbalance in political life really came to the fore and became a topic of political debate in a way that it had never been up to that point in time,' says Galligan.

'The Women's Studies Centre in Cork organised a conference on women's representation in September 2010. What was different about this was that the auditorium was full – it was packed out! So instead of a conference at which we might be speaking to 25 or 50 people, we were actually speaking to 250 people. The mood in the room was palpable, and the people there were not the usual suspects. They were from all generations, from all backgrounds. [...] I thought, this is a moment of change.'

Attendees at the meeting established the 50/50 Group to campaign for the introduction of candidate gender quotas. It proved to be the right movement at the right time. Both Fine Gael and the Labour Party incorporated the proposal into their election manifestos for the 2011 general election. With both parties then elected to form the next government, a law introducing gender quotas for parliamentary elections was in place by July 2012.

The law does not force a political party to run candidates of either gender – rather it committed to halving their State funding unless at least 30 per cent of their candidates were women at the next general election. This stick was sufficient to ensure that all parties were in compliance for the subsequent 2016 election. The result was a step change. There was a 90 per cent increase in the number of female candidates before the electorate and a 40 per cent increase in the number elected – a record 35 women were returned.[25]

Progress stalled in the 2020 election though, with only one more woman elected. As we approach our hundredth anniversary as a State, a mere 22.5 per cent of our parliamentary representatives are female. That places us 92nd in the world.[26] For all the remarkable progress that I have highlighted elsewhere, this is nothing to be proud of.

While we are well behind most of our peers, we are on our way to making fundamental change. The quota increases further at the next general election to guarantee that at least 40 per cent of candidates will be female.

As incumbent members of the Dáil retire, or are defeated, the power of the quota system will kick in, with four in ten of the options before us for their replacement being female. And the electorate are as happy to vote for a woman as they are for a man.[27] Change will eventually, but inevitably, follow.

Once women are elected, we need to keep them there. The work–life balance of our politicians can only be described as appalling. For the sake of our politicians we need to make the job more family-friendly by providing flexible working hours, maternity leave, paternity leave and carer's leave. The nation benefits from these jobs being attractive to talented people.

A beautiful milestone was achieved in 2014 when most of the leadership of our justice system became female-led: we had a female Minister for Justice, Attorney General, Director of Public Prosecutions, Chief State Solicitor, Garda Commissioner and Chief Justice. That was the same year that we became the first country in the world to have a female majority in a legal profession in our solicitors.[28]

The unleashing of women's potential has been a critical element underpinning our national success in recent times. Our experience shows that the further we travel down the road to equality, the better it will be for all of us.

Better Lives for Children

THE LIVES LED BY CHILDREN TODAY ARE NEARLY INCOMPARABLE TO THOSE OF A CENTURY AGO. THEIR IMPROVED PHYSICAL HEALTH, GREATER QUALITY OF EDUCATION, AND THE RESPECT THEY ARE SHOWN AS INDIVIDUALS, TRULY ALLOWS THEM TO REALISE THEIR POTENTIAL IN A WAY THAT NO PREVIOUS GENERATION WAS ABLE TO.

THE 'DEMOCRATIC PROGRAMME' adopted by the first Dáil in 1919, before independence was secured, made a strong pledge to the children of the nation. One of its eight paragraphs was dedicated to a commitment to improve their circumstances:

"It shall be the first duty of the Government of the Republic to make provision for the physical, mental and spiritual well-being of the children, to secure that no child shall suffer hunger or cold from lack of food, clothing, or shelter, but that all shall be provided with the means and facilities requisite for their proper education and training as Citizens of a Free and Gaelic Ireland."[1]

Unquestionably, that commitment has been substantively delivered upon. Children today are vastly better nourished, better housed and better educated than they were in 1919. The respect that we show them today, irrespective of their birth status or ability, is incomparable.

I am not saying that there are no children who go hungry or who have insufficient shelter today. I am rather saying that the improvements over the century have been astonishing and that the number of such children has reduced from the majority to a small number. While the State was unable to be of any practical assistance to most families a century ago, it now has the resources and the willingness to help, and the lives of our children have been vastly enriched as a result.

We Recognise the Discrete Rights of Children

Amendment to the Constitution of Ireland in 2015

'the State recognises and affirms the natural and imprescriptible rights of all children and shall, as far as practicable, by its laws protect and vindicate those rights'

We have afforded our children a parity of esteem in recent decades that was lacking in the State's early years. The only mention of the rights of children in the Constitution of the Irish Free State was a guarantee of attendance at schools in receipt of public money.

The later Constitution of Ireland in 1937 did no better. Although families were recognised as the 'natural primary and fundamental unit group of Society', the text placed a higher value on the parent than on the child. The rights of children, again, received only a single mention, to grant the State the ability to step in as guardian for vulnerable children 'with due regard to the natural and imprescriptible rights of the child'. But what rights was it referring to?

Our view of children as individuals, equal to adults and with their own set of rights, evolved much later. The most significant milestone on that journey was our ratification of the United Nations Convention on the Rights of the Child in 1992.

The Convention is the most widely ratified instrument in international law. Every eligible state in the world has ratified it with the sole exception of the United States of America. 'It came into force in rapid time,' explains Professor Ursula Kilkelly, former Dean of the Law School in University College Cork and author of *Children's Rights in Ireland*. 'Ireland is a good citizen of the world and we were among the early countries to do so.'

The document incontrovertibly altered the State's relationship with children. 'The Convention recognises children as individual rights holders, as individuals worthy of a voice and of exercising rights in their own right. And it sees the State as ultimately responsible: in the same way the State is responsible for vindicating *our* rights as adults, it's responsible for vindicating the rights of children.'

Ratification unleashed three decades of transformational progress for Irish children. We were one of the first nations in the world to publish a National Children's Strategy in 2000 following wide consultation with children, parents and those working with and for children. It was a ten-year plan with a blueprint to improve the lives of children by ensuring they had a voice, would be better understood and would receive high-quality supports and services.

Progress on the first two goals was impressive. Our first National Longitudinal Study of Children, Growing Up in Ireland, was initiated. The youth parliament, Dáil na nÓg, and nationwide youth councils, Comhairlí na nÓg, were founded as fora for children's voices. The Ombudsman for Children was established to promote the rights and welfare of children and to investigate complaints about services provided to them by public organisations. There was no longer a requirement for an adult to complain on your behalf or the possibility of a grievance being dismissed because it came from a person aged under 18.

However, progress on the provision of additional services was more limited as the recession curtailed the availability of resources to put in place adequate social work services for children in care and of treatment and counselling for children who had experienced abuse.[2]

A Minister of State for Children was first appointed in 1994, just after we ratified the UN Convention. This was superseded by the creation of a full Minister for Children and Youth Affairs in 2011 to give a voice to children at the cabinet table.

Finally, in 2012, the citizens of Ireland were given the opportunity to fill the gaps in the Constitution. The amendment was comfortably passed by 58 per cent of voters, although only a third of people came out to vote on the day. A legal challenge delayed its implementation until 2015, when the Constitution was finally updated to recognise the rights of children and to commit the State to the protection and vindication of those rights.

'It was a fitting response to all of the horrendous examples of how badly we had treated children – both the government and Irish society – over many, many decades,' says Kilkelly.

A Commission to Inquire into Child Abuse had been established by the Irish Government in 1999 to investigate abuse in institutions for children – the majority of which were residential reformatory and industrial schools operated by Catholic Church orders and funded and supervised by the Department of Education. It was commonly known as the Ryan Commission after its chair, Mr Justice Seán Ryan.

The Commission's report was published in 2009. It concluded that the entire system had treated children more like prison inmates and slaves than people with legal rights and human potential, that some religious officials had encouraged ritual beatings and consistently shielded their orders amid a 'culture of self-serving secrecy' and that government inspectors had failed to stop the abuses.

The report was a shocking indictment of how children had been treated by so-called 'religious orders' that disregarded the core principles of Christianity. But their actions had the tacit endorsement of the State and Irish society at large. The passing of the Constitutional amendment could be viewed as an act of societal atonement.

Has Ireland moved sufficiently from being a laggard in recognising and protecting children's rights to a leader? 'Looking internationally, I think we are doing reasonably well,' says Kilkelly. 'If I were to pick an area where we lead the way internationally, it's in participation. The children's rights approach is that children must be part of the decision-making process where it concerns them, and they must have a voice and a representation in that process. We had our first national strategy for children's participation in 2015, and that has rolled out through various organisations to put children at the centre of decision-making.'

There are, of course, further steps we need to take. 'We are much weaker on legislative implementation than on the non-legal measures. Lots of times, laws would be drafted and even enacted before anybody thinks about whether children are impacted by them.'

The health system, after education, is one of the most important places for children's well-being, yet we do not have any legislation on children in healthcare. Kilkelly cites the design of the forthcoming National Children's Hospital as an example of a missed opportunity. 'Nobody looked at that from a children's point of view. It didn't involve children and isn't designed with children in mind. Yet some other countries have really embedded child-friendly healthcare and revolve their healthcare system around children.'

Ireland came from behind most of our European peers, but now we find ourselves better than many of them. We are a progressive nation today, but we must still address the reputational issues arising from our historical mistreatment of children. We should not hesitate, therefore, to be ambitious in showing global leadership in further implementation of the UN Convention and adopting a rights-centred approach to children's issues. It will help to draw a line under past misdeeds and will serve today's generation very well indeed.

We Have Abolished Corporal Punishment

Number of states that started prohibiting corporal punishment of children in each decade and select countries that implemented this, 1970s–2010s

SOURCE: GLOBAL INITIATIVE TO END ALL CORPORAL PUNISHMENT OF CHILDREN[3]

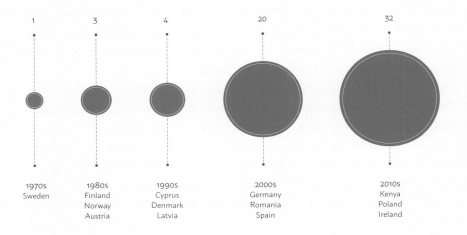

1	3	4	20	32
1970s	1980s	1990s	2000s	2010s
Sweden	Finland	Cyprus	Germany	Kenya
	Norway	Denmark	Romania	Poland
	Austria	Latvia	Spain	Ireland

Amongst our past misdeeds as a nation was the way we allowed our children to be beaten at home, in school and in institutional care settings. In fact, more than simply being allowed, it was often encouraged and rarely restrained. By today's standards, much of what was tolerated would be regarded as abuse.[4]

We can take comfort from its abolition in all settings here in 2015. But Ireland was no leader in this respect. Sweden was the first nation in the world to outlaw all corporal punishment, in the 1970s. Three more nations followed in the 80s and four more in the 90s. However the trickle became a flood in the noughties with a further 20 nations changing their laws, followed by 32 more in the 2010s, including Ireland. We were the 47th nation to do so, behind 20 of our fellow EU nations who took the positive step before we did.

Corporal punishment in the home and in national schools was accepted practice up until the 1980s. The prevailing law, the Children Act of 1908, specifically allowed for 'the right of any parent, teacher, or other person having the lawful control or charge of a child or young person to administer punishment to such child or young person'. It was widely held that 'a good beating never hurt anyone' and that some corporal punishment was necessary to maintain discipline, to instil respect for authority and to rear 'good citizens'.

Although parents' right to punish was unchallenged for a long time, extreme violence in schools began to be highlighted by parents in the 1950s in the letters page of Dublin's *Evening Mail*. The Department of Education had an extremely poor record of acting on parents' complaints against teachers and served, more often than not, to protect the wrongdoer even when they were in blatant and frequent breach of the rules. In the few instances in which parents persisted in taking teachers to court for their behaviour, judges often awarded minimal damages or merely asked the teacher to apologise. Some correspondents pointed out that the courts were imposing larger fines for cruelty to animals than they were for cruelty to children.[5]

A small group of concerned parents decided to take action. In 1955 they formed the Schoolchildren's Protection Organisation to lobby the Minister for Education to abolish corporal punishment in national schools. Seventy harrowing letters detailing teacher abuse were published as a booklet, *Punishment in Our Schools*, to highlight the issue. Successive ministers refused to consider abolition. In fact, the minister of the day (and later Taoiseach) Jack Lynch altered school rules to allow leather straps to be used alongside canes in administering punishments despite the dissenting voices.

In the late 1960s and early 70s a new group called Reform was founded to fight for the same aim. The Irish Union of School Students lent them their support and published a survey showing that 84 per cent of schools surveyed used corporal punishment in some form. More than nine in ten of them were boys' schools. The implements used for punishments included leather straps, T-squares, hurleys, sticks and tree branches! The students concluded that 'it would seem that there are some sadists and other sexual perverts in charge of classes in Irish schools'.[6] How right they proved to be.

It took until 1982 for the Department of Education to finally appreciate that the tide had turned against its approach to keeping discipline in the classroom. A simple circular to schools changed the rules and banned teachers from smacking or hitting children. Although we could take some solace from the fact that this was four years before the United Kingdom did the same, we were one of the very last countries in all of Europe to instigate a ban in schools. France had had one since World War I.[7]

It was a further two decades before there were any restrictions placed on punishment in the home, and the degree of progress was equivocal. The Children Act of 2001 repealed the 1908 law and made it an offence to assault children, but it retained a defence of 'reasonable chastisement' for parents or guardians. So excessive hitting was made illegal, but moderate slapping remained okay.

Once again, our membership of the European Union came to our aid. In May 2015 the European Committee of Social Rights ruled that Ireland was violating the European Social Charter by continuing to allow physical punishment. The Children First Bill happened to be working its way through the Oireachtas at the time and the opportunity was taken to add a prohibition of the 'reasonable chastisement' defence. The impact being that, when the final Act was signed into law by the President in November 2015, all forms of corporal punishment were belatedly outlawed.

While our children have never been more aware of their rights than they are today and parents have never been more progressive in their parenting approach, we don't know how widespread the use of corporal punishment remains in the home. There are no official measures in place. 'There was a, rightly, increased profile of domestic abuse and violence during the Covid pandemic,' points out Ursula Kilkelly. 'Children weren't particularly visible in that debate, yet they were hugely victimised by it. What you don't count, you don't see.' We should confirm that our good intentions have translated into good behaviour for the betterment of the lives of all our children.

82 All Our Children Now Get the Education They Need

Government investment in special needs education

SOURCE: DEPARTMENT OF EDUCATION, NATIONAL COUNCIL FOR SPECIAL EDUCATION⁸

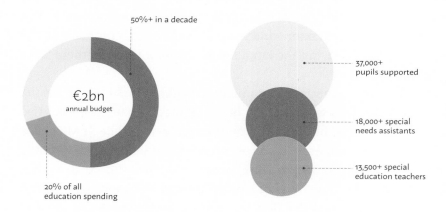

50%+ in a decade

€2bn
annual budget

20% of all
education spending

37,000+
pupils supported

18,000+ special
needs assistants

13,500+ special
education teachers

Every child now has the opportunity to get the education they need in a way that was far from the case even twenty years ago. State spending on educating those with special needs has ballooned. It now invests €2 billion a year, a figure that has grown by 50 per cent in just a decade. This employs more than 13,500 special education teachers and 18,000 special needs assistants to provide support to over 37,000 pupils.

One-fifth of all the State's spending on education is now invested in meeting special needs in primary and secondary level. This is more than the total sum spent on the third-level sector.

When the State was formed there was essentially no support for children with learning difficulties. There were three special schools in the entire country. St Mary's School for Deaf Girls in Cabra in Dublin was run by the Dominican order, St Joseph's School for Deaf Boys in Cabra was run by the Christian Brothers, and St Joseph's School for the Blind was run by the Carmelite order in Drumcondra, Dublin. Children from all over the country came to board at these schools from young ages.

Until the early 1990s practically all education and care of children with special needs was carried out by the religious orders. The Constitution commits the State to providing 'for' free primary education, but it is missing the words 'every child'. 'It took the State off the hook in terms of taking the initiative,' explains Associate Professor Joseph Travers, who heads the School of Inclusive and Special Education in Dublin City University. 'You had resources issues, of course, and you also had a heavy emphasis on the cultural aspects of reviving the language at primary level, so there were different priorities.'

It was not until the 1960s that momentum began to build to address the needs of children who were literally being ignored. 'Again, the initiative was not from the State but from voluntary organisations like St Michael's House and the National Association of Parents and Friends of the Mentally Handicapped. They started to raise issues and they started to set up special schools. The Daughters of Charity formed a school in the Navan Road in 1964, which was the first for children with a moderate general learning disability. That was a major step forward in showing these children can be included in education as well as those with mild disabilities,' explains Travers.

Other influential developments occurred in parallel. 'A diploma course in Special Education was established in St Patrick's College in Drumcondra which was ground-breaking. It took in teachers for a full year on full salary for professional development. There was a special education inspectorate set up within the Department of Education. The Irish Association of Teachers in Special Education, IATSE, was formed. So you had a cohort of teachers debating and moving things forward.'

Finally, the State began to appreciate that it must act. A landmark report from the Commission of Inquiry on Mental Handicap in 1965 recommended a separate, special school system be established to meet the need.

'Why did it not recommend a more inclusive system? You need to take into cognisance the number of really small schools in Ireland at the time, with dilapidated buildings, no special needs assistance, and no psychological services. In that context, if you're faced with asking those schools to take children with special educational needs or build a brand new school in a greenfield site with a lower pupil–teacher ratio, you could see why they would go for the separate special schools.' This led to the creation of a parallel system to cater for children with physical, mental and sensory impairments, with more than 100 such special schools established in the following few decades.

Children with severe disability remained uncatered for, however. It took one persistent mother to change that. Marie O'Donoghue's son Paul was left profoundly disabled after contracting a viral infection at eight months. He, and similar children, were deemed the responsibility of the Department of Health, yet they were not sick. When Paul was denied full-time admission to state-funded educational facilities, Marie mounted a legal challenge.

In 1993, when Paul was eight, the High Court issued a landmark ruling, which found that his constitutional right to a free primary education had been breached. The judge ruled that Paul had been discriminated against and pointed to evidence that providing education for children with severe mental disabilities could improve their lives. For the first time, the constitutional right to education was deemed to explicitly cover the needs of children with severe disabilities.

Sadly, the State vowed to appeal the decision rather than meet the needs of all such children. Four years later, the case came back before the Supreme Court. The government recognised the injustice, however, and withdrew the appeal on the day the case was due to be heard. It finally ushered in an era of education provision by the nation for *all* its children.

The case contributed to an utter rethink of the State's role in education provision for those with special needs. The report of a Special Education Review Committee in 1993 recommended that, as far as possible, we should pivot to providing education for all children in mainstream schools rather than in segregated, special facilities – ideally alongside all other students in the same classroom. Special schools were to be retained along with special classes in order to provide a continuum of provision to match a continuum of children's needs – and to provide a fallback if it didn't work out for a particular child in a mainstream class.

The pivot started in 1998. Education Minister Micheál Martin announced an automatic entitlement for mainstream schools to special education resource teachers and to special needs assistants. Autism was, furthermore, recognised as a distinct educational category that was to be provided for in mainstream schooling.

'The consequence was an absolute massive surge in appointments of resource teachers and special needs assistants,' explains Travers. 'It was a huge expansion from a low base. At that time there were about 300 care assistants in the system, around 100 resource teachers, and maybe 1,500 learning support teachers. We now have over 18,000 special needs assistants in the system and around 14,000 special education teachers.'

We are delivering extremely well on the ambition to have most students in mainstream schools: 98 per cent of students are educated this way. 'We have around 2 per cent of our student population attending special schools or special classes, which represents about 16,000 students. Internationally, this would be on the low side – some countries have four, five or six percent of students.'

So how many students need extra support? Perhaps up to a quarter. Travers says that various surveys have identified figures of between 18 and 25 per cent.

The good news is that all have access to some level of support, albeit that the quality may vary from school to school and from class to class. 'It's not mandatory that a teacher does an additional qualification to work as a special education teacher, so students have access to varying levels of support. It has been improving, however, and I'd certainly say all students would have their needs met to some degree.'

That is some achievement. From zero provision by the State to full acceptance of its responsibilities to every child. From a view that some children were ineducable to a recognition that every child can benefit from appropriate education. And from the provision of education through an entirely separate system to an inclusive approach centred on mainstream schools and underpinned by a continuum of support. We have truly embraced education for all.

83 Our Teenagers Are Physically Healthier

Percentage of 15–16-year-olds who have drunk alcohol, smoked cigarettes or used cannabis in 1995 and 2019

SOURCE: EUROPEAN SCHOOL SURVEY PROJECT ON ALCOHOL AND OTHER DRUGS[9]

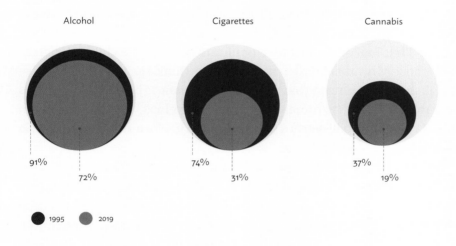

Teenagers are healthier today than their parents were at the same age. They are eating better, exercising more and consuming fewer harmful substances.

Practically every child had consumed alcohol at some point before they were 15 or 16 years of age back in 1995. Today that figure is down to seven in ten. It is still very high, but the trajectory is positive. Three-quarters of mid-teen children had tried smoking twenty-five years ago. That figure has plummeted to less than a third. Even the small proportion that has experimented with cannabis has halved.

What's going on? Well, for a start, retailers are more likely to actually follow the law and not sell alcohol or cigarettes to children. 'When I was their age, there was absolutely no problem getting access to alcohol. You could tell them that you were 13 and they'd just laugh and sell it to you. The risks of selling to somebody who's under 18 now are much greater,' says Professor Saoirse Nic Gabhainn of NUI Galway's Department of Health Promotion.

'Even if you're a drug dealer and you're selling to a student who's 22 and you're caught, the consequences are very different than if you're selling to a 14-year-old. We know, in relation to drugs and alcohol, that access is the key driver of use and access has been severely reduced.'

Significantly too, children's attitudes towards some of these behaviours have changed. 'There is a rise in "healthism" – the cult of the fit and the healthy. That has major negative implications on some children, particularly those with disabilities or those who think they aren't attractive enough, but it does mean that more children want to be healthy,' explains Nic Gabhainn. 'And, as romantic attraction develops, there is this notion that kissing somebody who's a smoker, unless you're a smoker yourself, is truly *vile*.'

The introduction of the Social, Physical and Health Education (SPHE) syllabus to the junior cycle in schools in the early 2000s has undoubtedly played a role. There is also a lot more information available for children themselves. Online resources such as SpunOut.ie are hugely influential sources of factual content for Irish youth, written by Irish youth, in the language of Irish youth. What a positive change from the entirely unreliable information we heard third-hand from friends when we were kids.

The diets of our teenagers measure up well when compared to their European peers. Irish teenagers are more likely to eat fruit and vegetables daily and are less likely to eat sweets and drink sugared soft drinks.[10] This is, however, a relative measure of success. 'The rates of eating vegetables are incredibly low. We don't rank too badly internationally because they're really bad everywhere,' explains Nic Gabhainn, who oversees the collection of the Irish figures.

Where Ireland has had success is in reducing the amount of sweets and sugared drinks consumed. Not only is that a positive health change in and of itself, but it also increases the possibility that more nutritious items will fill stomachs instead.

An increasing focus on health education has helped, but so too have improvements in nutritional standards in schools. When I was a kid everyone brought a packed lunch. Even if you had a few spare pennies to spend on a treat for yourself, you weren't allowed to leave the school grounds! As the country got a bit richer, children had more disposable income and that was most likely to be spent in fast food outlets close to the school or in buying unhealthy treats from vending machines inside the school itself.

There has been an increasing emphasis on providing meals in schools and in ensuring their menus are healthy. We are also far along the path to eliminating vending machines in schools. Work undertaken by Nic Gabhainn and her colleagues for the Irish Heart Foundation revealed that chocolate, crisps, sweets and fizzy drinks were there for the asking in almost half of post-primary schools. Thanks to the highlighting of the issue, the Oireachtas Joint Committee on Education and Skills proposed an outright ban on vending machines selling unhealthy snacks in 2018.

In the same year Ireland joined a short but growing list of nations in introducing a tax on sugar-sweetened drinks. Twenty cent per litre was added to drinks with between 5 and 8 grams of sugar per 100 millilitres and thirty cent per litre on drinks with more than that. 'Children don't have that much money so small price differentials make a much bigger difference to younger people and to poorer people who are wondering how many cans they can get in a week.'

Cutting out more bad foodstuffs is vital in the fight against obesity. Today's children are significantly heavier than they were in our grandparents' time. Between the late 1940s and the turn of this century, the average 14-year-old girl gained 50 per cent in weight (adding 19 kg to reach 59 kg), while the average boy added a stunning two-thirds (another 24 kg to reach 61 kg).[11] Insofar as this is a result of better nutrition, needless to say, that is a good thing. But when it culminates in increasing numbers of children with obesity and weight problems then the gains have swung too far. The good news is that there doesn't appear to have been much more weight gained over the past two decades. These nutritional improvements have to have helped.

Our teenagers are also more physically active nowadays and are far more active than most of their European peers, Nic Gabhainn's studies show.[12] 'There's obviously a strong community sports culture in Ireland with the GAA particularly. Also children here have a lot fewer cultural opportunities. Classical music would be massively popular in lots of areas of Europe where children would engage in dance and music activities. They're not so prevalent here.'

The increase in activity has been encouraged by greater government and local authority investment in sports facilities and parallel improvements to the school Physical Education curriculum. Parents are also more likely to enrol their kids in clubs nowadays. 'Rather than teenagers saying "I'm going out," instead it's "I'm going to the gym" or "I'm going down for a swim." There's a lot fewer hanging around street corners like the old days.'

How are children impacted by the fact that their lives are busier and more structured? 'I grew up in Galway and we used to go down to the Spanish Arch and start talking to the Americans for the craic,' says Nic Gabhainn. 'We used to sit on the bridge and go, "what part of America are you from?" [...] because we were so bored. I was mad to get going into the world and see new things and do new things, but children aren't bored like that anymore. What good came from that boredom for us as a generation is hard to quantify so there are unknown consequences for the lives of today's children.'

We should celebrate the progress we are making in improving the health of today's youth. However, it would be a loss for the nation if the next generation were less up for having the craic with tourists and maintaining the reputation for sociability that we are world famous for!

Teenage Pregnancies Have Fallen Dramatically

The number of teenage pregnancies in Ireland is low and the trend is one of steep decline. There were fewer than 870 teenaged mothers in 2019 out of 60,000 births. That's 1½ per cent. Allow for the fact that 18- and 19-year-old mothers are captured in those figures, and the actual number of births to children was a mere 170. That's closer to a ¼ of 1 per cent.

Yes, that's 170 too many, but look at how the number of teenage births has tumbled year after year since the turn of the century. In 1999, 6 per cent of all babies were born to teenagers. We have made wonderful progress in letting children be children and enabling young women to get a good start in adult life without being burdened with unplanned pregnancy.

Number of teenage births in each year, 1999–2019

SOURCE: CENTRAL STATISTICS OFFICE

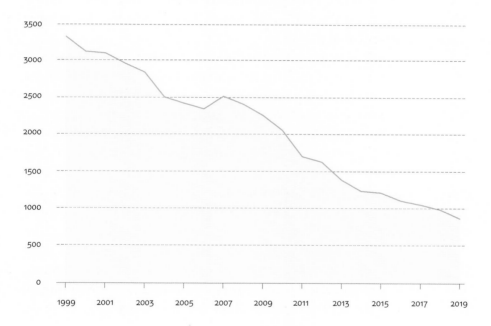

How so? For a start, girls can now manage their own fertility with contraception. Recall that it was only in 1985 that adults were given access to contraception without a prescription for the first time. Further liberalisation, spurred by a fear of the spread of AIDS in the early 1990s, led to the removal of the ban on selling condoms to children and the legalisation of condom vending machines in 1993. That didn't take long to have an impact.

There was also a growing consensus about the need for better quality sex education and for the school system to provide a consistent and comprehensive overview of the topic in the absence of that being provided at home. The government established an Expert Advisory Group on Relationships and Sexuality Education that recommended, in 1995, the development of guidelines for schools from primary right through to second level.

An interim curriculum for Relationships and Sexuality Education was developed right away as an element of the SPHE syllabus. It became a mandatory part of the primary school curriculum in 1999 and for junior cycle students in 2003. My kids smile and cringe simultaneously at the memory of receiving 'the talk' in sixth class. But at least they know more now than I did at that age.

'If you look at that by age of the pregnant girl, the under 15s have almost disappeared,' points out Professor Nic Gabhainn of NUI Galway. 'There's more understanding of what leads to pregnancy. There was a gap even in that basic knowledge amongst younger teenagers in the past.'

Is it too much to expect a similar level of education across all our schools? That is not yet happening in Nic Gabhainn's view, and some children are losing out. 'There are still some schools, and they are usually boys-only traditional secondary type schools – not the vocational schools or the community schools – that are still not going there; so girls often learn a lot more than boys.'

Sex education by smartphone is no substitute. Nic Gabhainn is an advocate for the inclusion of porn education in the curriculum to pre-empt negative impacts on sexual behaviour but also on kids' expectations of body standards and their acceptance of themselves as they are.

Great progress, so, but more to do.

 85　Youth Crime Is in Sharp Decline

Whatever kids are getting up to today, it's not criminal. The number of children who come into contact with gardaí and are referred on to the Youth Diversion Programme to divert them away from involvement in more serious crime has halved in a decade. Similarly, the number of offences coming before the Children's Court has halved too. Of course, the figures are dependent on how good gardaí are at identifying children involved in criminal activity in the first place and in building strong cases against those who have committed serious crimes, but the reduction is stark and indicative of a real drop in youth crime.

Number of children referred to Garda Diversion Programme and number of offences before the Children's Court, 2007–2017

SOURCE: IRISH YOUTH JUSTICE SERVICE, THE COURTS SERVICE[15]

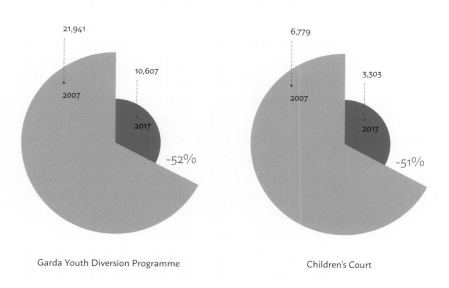

21,941

10,607

2007

2017

-52%

Garda Youth Diversion Programme

6,779

3,303

2007

2017

-51%

Children's Court

'Youth crime is not a problem. An awful lot of what we deal with is low level – it's more antisocial behaviour than it is serious criminal offending,' says Professor Ursula Kilkelly of UCC. 'There's a real appreciation that court is not the place for most children, and detention is not the place for most children. So our system is set up to divert children away from the courts and from detention, and that's been working well over the last ten years or so.'

The Garda Youth Diversion Programme was established informally, and with a good deal of foresight, in the 1960s. The current programme stems from the Children Act of 2001, which put the programme on a statutory footing. 'Since then we've had a national diversion programme where specially trained gardaí members, called Juvenile Liaison Officers, act as specialist police to work with children who come into conflict with the law.'

It is a progressive system of police caution and support. 'A Juvenile Liaison Officer makes an intervention into the life of the young person, usually with the family, and has a formal conversation about their behaviour and what needs to happen. It's a warning shot.'

For more serious cases, there can be a formal caution and a conference. 'In the main those end up as a family conference. They get everybody around the table to agree the steps that need to be taken to keep this young person out of trouble. It could be keeping them in school, keeping them away from negative peer influences, or getting them involved in suitable training.' The children are supervised for up to 12 months so there is a longer-term investment by the Gardaí in keeping them on the right track.

Ireland's Diversion Programme is cited as a world-leading example in crime prevention. 'I haven't seen anything as widespread, as mainstream as it internationally,' says Kilkelly. However, not every child is suitable for the programme. 'They have to accept responsibility for their behaviour, and they have to agree to be cautioned. Around 75 per cent of children are admitted to the programme. The quarter who aren't are mainly referred for prosecution and they are the cases we see in the Children's Court.'

The Children Court was created in parallel in 2001 to deal with most offences committed by children away from the mainstream courts system. The judges receive special training and parents are obliged to attend and participate. It is a private court so proceedings are 'in camera' (a term that means precisely the opposite of what it sounds like), that is to say, there can be no reporting that might identify the child in any way.

When the court decides a child must be detained for serious crimes, they are no longer sent to prison. The last prison accepting children, St Patrick's Institution on the grounds of Mountjoy Prison, was closed in 2017. Instead, all such children are sent to the Oberstown Children Detention Campus in north County Dublin.

Kilkelly chairs the board of management of the facility. 'The establishment of a child-focused facility for the detention of under 18s is something that we really are ahead of many other countries on. In most cases where you have youth detention, it's a penal environment staffed by prison officers. Oberstown is a *care* environment for children who are in detention. The staff there are residential social care workers.'

Residents leave the facility with their life chances considerably enhanced. 'They leave with education they didn't have, they leave in better health than when they came in, they have undertaken work on offending behaviour – building up their own resilience and empathy and understanding of the harm they have caused – and they have better family relationships.' Although the campus can hold 60 residents, the number detained has declined in recent years in line with the decreasing number coming before the courts.

Ireland's strong economic growth over the past decade and the consequent reduction in unemployment has, undoubtedly, played a role in curtailing crime. 'The things that work in youth offending are not very complicated,' points out Kilkelly. 'It's really about family support and education.' Smaller family sizes ensure each child gets more attention than they did in the past, and we are retaining more kids in school for longer. All of which points to the likelihood of further reductions in the years to come.

INCONTESTABLY, OUR CHILDREN today lead much better lives than any generation that has come before them. It is a remarkable series of achievements that has delivered so much of what the founders of the State wanted to accomplish a century ago.

I give the last word to Professor Saoirse Nic Gabhainn. 'We should be hugely proud of our children. They're bright and engaged and energetic and a huge amount of fun. And that's come from the opportunities we're providing to them, the education that they're getting, the ability to interact with others and to work towards their goals in sports or in creativity. If we open up and listen to them, we have so much to learn and we'll see the way forward to further improve their lives.'

(12)

Increasingly Environmentally Conscious

WE ARE MORE AWARE OF OUR IMPACT ON OUR ENVIRONMENT, AND ITS IMPORTANCE TO PRESERVING OUR QUALITY OF LIFE, THAN ANY GENERATION BEFORE US. IN MANY RESPECTS WE ARE DAMAGING THE LAND, THE AIR AND THE WATER WE RELY ON TO LIVE HEALTHILY AND TO PROSPER. BUT AS OUR KNOWLEDGE HAS GROWN OVER THE DECADES, SO TOO HAS THE ACTION WE HAVE TAKEN AS A NATION.

INCREASED ENVIRONMENTAL CONSCIOUSNESS has changed our behaviour for the better, even if we are not yet addressing everything that we need to.

We have dramatically increased our forested land, even if we now realise that we need greater diversity in our trees. We have dramatically reduced air pollution, even if there is further to go to prevent unnecessary premature deaths. There has been a revolution in how well we treat our waste water, yet the quality of our rivers and freshwater is declining. We

317

are reducing the amount of waste we produce and we are recycling more, but progress has stalled in recent years. We are fast growing the amount of renewable energy we produce, yet our carbon emissions are amongst the worst in Europe.

Our growing understanding of our environmental impact has made it perfectly apparent that we need to broaden our areas of action and accelerate change. We have a long way to go, but it is important to acknowledge the progress that we have already made.

86 Our Forested Land Is Increasing

Percentage of total land area under forests, 1928–2017

SOURCE: DEPARTMENT OF AGRICULTURE, FOOD AND THE MARINE[1]

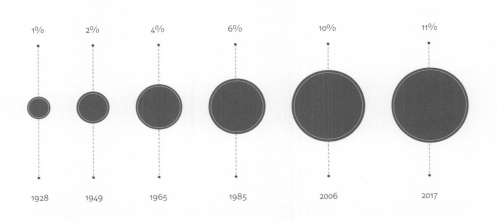

| 1% | 2% | 4% | 6% | 10% | 11% |
| 1928 | 1949 | 1965 | 1985 | 2006 | 2017 |

We have increased the amount of land under forestry more than ten-fold since the foundation of the State. Our forested area is now estimated to be 770,000 hectares or 11 per cent of our total land area. This is the highest level in over 350 years.

The progress has been substantial, but the starting point was horrendous. A mere 1 per cent of our land was planted when the Free State came into existence. Given that the island was predominantly covered in woodland when humans arrived here around 9,000 years ago, what happened to leave us in such a bad place?

'The story of deforestation goes back a very long time in Ireland,' explains Pádraic Fogarty, author of *Whittled Away: Ireland's Vanishing Nature* and campaigns officer with the Irish Wildlife Trust.[2] 'In the popular imagination it was the British that destroyed our forest to build military ships for Henry VIII, but even by the time the British got here there was very little forest left. You read stories about Ireland in the late 1800s and there's hardly a tree standing anywhere.'

The need for land for crops and grazing is the consistent factor accounting for deforestation down the ages. Wood was also the universal source of fuel and building material. Resource pressure grew hugely as the country's population tripled between 1700 and 1840 to more than 8 million people.[3] While the Famine reduced this pressure for a while, land reform in the late 1800s resulted in the transfer of holdings from landlords to their tenant farmers, and the forests declined yet further as the new owners cleared more space for agriculture.

The Irish Free State therefore inherited a denuded landscape containing no more than 89,000 hectares of forest. A modest afforestation programme began straightaway on poor quality land that was deemed unfit for agricultural purposes, given the priority of ensuring the country could produce sufficient food to feed its population.

World War II provided another economic shock and prompted a reversal of some of the gains in afforestation, given the need to source fuel and timber domestically. The government recognised the risk to the country's fuel security, as well as the opportunity to create rural employment, and announced its most ambitious long-term afforestation plan in 1948 – a 40-year programme to cover 1,000,000 acres (400,000 hectares).

This was not about replenishing the natural woodlands we had lost historically. 'The motivation was to generate income,' explains Fogarty. Monoculture crops were planted en masse. Most of the trees were Sitka spruce conifers, a native of the Pacific coast of North America. It does not produce a high-quality wood so much of it ends up as wood pulp, in pallets or fences or toilet paper.

For all intents and purposes the national target was realised on schedule in the late 1980s. However, it required a change in tack to do so. Up until that point the State has nearly exclusively led the afforestation effort. But there was less and less suitable public land available and the government persisted with its policy of avoiding planting on agricultural land.

The solution was to involve the private sector with funding provided by the EU. Grants stimulated an explosion of planting in the late 1980s and 90s. In fact, private forestry development quickly exceeded the State's efforts and peaked in 1995 when nearly 24,000 hectares were planted – the highest level ever attained in the State – three-quarters of which were on private land. The business model mirrored that of the public sector, consisting predominantly of conifers grown for commercial timber.

Coillte was established to run the commercial forestry business for the country in 1988. With little suitable land available, its focus has been to manage existing plantations on public land for the past couple of decades rather than to further expand. With continued growth in the private sector, though, the ownership of the forests that cover 11 per cent of our landmass today are split 50–50 between the public and private sectors.

There has, however, been a gradual slowdown in private sector planting over the past two decades. Given the absence of any State expansion, this has resulted in the amount of land being forested in recent years falling back to levels not seen since the 1940s – before the 1948 plan kicked in.

Whether we are planting the right type of trees or not, this loss of momentum does the country no favours. There are a range of factors contributing to it. In the same way that State land began to reach capacity, many farmers were planting trees on marginal lands that would not generate an income from other agricultural activities, but much of that is now already utilised. Some of the remaining land is recognised to have biodiversity value and is therefore no longer eligible for grant aid as it might have been in the past.

Fogarty also identifies a stigma in the farming community to planting trees instead of raising livestock or tillage. 'Forestry has a bad reputation.

In farming culture, planting trees is seen as kind of giving up on your farm. It's seen as *not* farming.' The application of higher environmental standards has further contributed. It can be time-consuming and expensive for landowners to meet the standards required for planting permits to be granted.

The slowdown means that we remain well behind practically every other European nation in forest cover. The average EU country has a third of their land mass under forest. Only Malta has less coverage than we do.[4]

We know our climate is under intense stress and carbon capture in forests is a necessary part of the solution. It has prompted the government to reverse the trend of millennia. Afforestation of agricultural land is to be encouraged at last. The government's 2019 plan to stimulate expansion contains some nice headlines: 22 million trees are to be planted every year for the next 20 years – a total of 440 million altogether. However, that only translates into 8,000 hectares of new forest annually, which is about 20 per cent less ambitious than the 1948 plan was. Nevertheless, the direction of travel is welcome.

'If we got the policies right, Ireland could be dramatically different in 50 years' time in a good way,' says Fogarty. 'We need to restore some elements of naturalness to our forests and to build up a body of native woodlands. Bord na Móna have nowhere left to go in terms of peat extraction, for example, so there's a lot of land there that is available for woodland and wetland generation just for the amenity of it and just for the wildlife value of it. If we could do that in our uplands and along our river corridors as well, I don't think we'd be very far from 30 to 40 per cent of the country under some kind of forest cover.'

Commercial forestry will need to consider a more natural approach such as 'close to nature forestry'. 'That doesn't mean you have to use only native trees, but you have to respect the soil and you have to have an element of natural regeneration and you have to be able to do forestry like we've never done it in Ireland before.'

There is a big prize. Forests can play a significant role in delivering our commitment to reduce greenhouse gases. 'You also have immense amenity and recreation value, you have immense wildlife value, they will prevent and alleviate flooding, they help to reduce the impacts of extreme weather events, they clean our water. Even in towns and cities, having more trees and better quality green spaces is good for our physical health, it's good for our mental health, and it's inspirational.'

Adding more forests will improve our lives more than any other use of the land.

 ## Air Pollution Is Decreasing Significantly

Tonnes of fine particulate matter (PM2.5) emitted, 1990–2018

SOURCE: ENVIRONMENTAL PROTECTION AGENCY

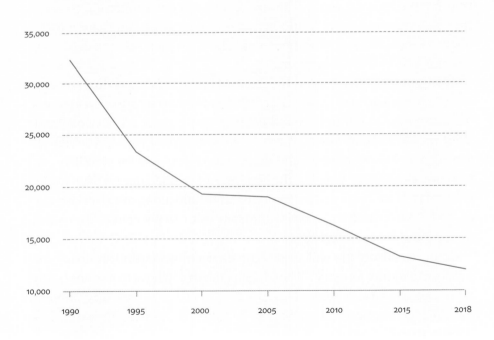

We have improved our air quality substantially over the past few decades. Despite our population and our economy growing strongly, we are pumping out far less noxious emissions into the air that we, and other plants and animals, then breathe back in.

The graph shows the number of tonnes of fine particulate matter ($PM_{2.5}$) that we pump into the atmosphere annually. These are amongst the most dangerous pollutants. $PM_{2.5}$ particles have a diameter of less than 2.5 micrometres – about 3 per cent the diameter of a human hair. As they are so small and light, they tend to stay longer in the air than heavier particles, increasing the chances that we will inhale them into our bodies. They can penetrate deep into the lungs and even the circulatory system, thereby worsening chronic diseases such as asthma and bronchitis and causing increased premature deaths from heart and lung disease.

We are doing our bit to reduce the damage. Our emissions of $PM_{2.5}$ have decreased by nearly two-thirds since 1990 – from over 32,000 tonnes to just 12,000.[5]

Similarly, we have almost obliterated our sulphur dioxide emissions as our power stations have shifted from oil and coal to gas and installed new pollution-control technologies. There has been a 93 per cent reduction in their emission – from over 180,000 tonnes in 1990 to a little over 12,000 today – with health benefits for those prone to respiratory problems.

Not all our emissions have been going in the right direction – I will highlight later our utter failure to control CO_2 and its negative contribution to climate change. However, air quality in Ireland is very good by international standards. Roughly 2 per cent of us are exposed to outdoor air pollution in excess of World Health Organization limits, while the average across most developed nations is over 60 per cent![6]

'Because we haven't been a particularly industrialised country and because the airflow direction tends to be coming from the Atlantic, we're in a very good position,' explains Laura Burke, Director General of the Environmental Protection Agency (EPA). 'In saying that, we have seen exceedances of recommended levels on occasion, and the scientific evidence is increasingly concluding that there is *no* safe level of pollution.'

The EPA was established as an independent agency in 1993. It had a strong focus on curbing industrial pollution initially, which delivered substantial reductions within a decade. That coincided with improvements in urban air quality as smoky coal bans were introduced.

I well remember, as a student in the 1980s, waiting for the bus home from UCD at Belfield on a cold winter's evening and looking towards the city centre to see the skyline shrouded in smog. You could taste the acrid smoke in the back of your throat when you breathed too deeply. We didn't appreciate how much harm it was doing us at the time.

The State was exceeding EU safety limits. The newly appointed Minister of State with responsibility for environmental protection, Mary Harney, took decisive action by banning the sale of bituminous 'smoky' coal in the Greater Dublin Area in September 1990. The ban resulted in a 70 per cent decline in air pollution in the city and saved an estimated 8,000 people from premature deaths due to heart and lung-related diseases in subsequent years.[7]

The ban was extended to Cork in 1995 and to other major urban areas by 2003. But it took until September 2020, a full 30 years after Dublin's ban was introduced, before it was extended to urban areas with a population of more than 10,000 – thereby encompassing half the residents of the State.

Anyone remember leaded petrol? Unleaded was introduced in the mid-80s after lead pollution was found to reduce children's IQ scores in cities. It was also implicated in violent – crime researchers linked the switch to unleaded fuel use in the United States to declines in urban crime rates in later years.[8] Leaded petrol was phased out here in 1999.

New technology has improved car engine efficiency and reduced emissions over the decades. However, transport remains one of our primary sources of air pollution alongside our use of solid fuels for home heating. For all the good progress we have made, an estimated 1,300 people still die prematurely in Ireland every year due to $PM_{2.5}$ air pollution from these sources.[9] It is clear what we need to do next.

We must all make the move to fully electric vehicles. It simply eliminates noxious emissions. But it is residential use of solid fuels that remains the largest problem. 'We should stop smoky fuels in *all* urban areas. It's not only smoky coal – things like peat and wet wood all have an impact.' A planned nationwide ban on these fuels is an important contribution in the short term. Beyond that, a total shift away from solid fuels towards natural gas and heat pumps – combined with improved insulation to keep heat from leaking out – will make a huge difference to your neighbour's health. That's a change you can make today with the support of existing government grants.

88 Waste Water Treatment Has Substantially Improved

Urban waste water treatment, 1997–2019

SOURCE: CSO/ENVIRONMENTAL PROTECTION AGENCY[10]

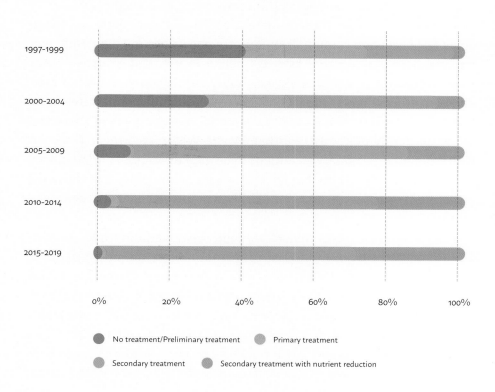

We have taken a huge leap forward in reducing the environmental damage of our waste water in recent decades. What was flushed down your toilet and poured out of your plughole was dumped straight into the environment until relatively recently. In the mid-1990s nearly half of all our waste water received no treatment at all, or merely had 'preliminary' treatment to remove bits of rags and plastics and grease, before flowing straight out to sea or into nearby rivers and lakes. Horrific.

Twenty-five years later, that figure is less than 1.5 per cent. More than 97.5 per cent of our water today receives secondary treatment whereby bacteria break down the pollutants before disposal. Over 30 per cent of it undergoes additional treatment to reduce nutrients like nitrogen and phosphorus, which can affect plant and wildlife in the receiving water bodies.

It represents a true transformation of how we deal with our waste, albeit that we were coming from a pretty poor place to begin with. The improvement was spurred by a €3 billion investment in urban waste water infrastructure between 2000 and 2010. 'There has been a huge investment,' explains Laura Burke. 'There were significant new treatment plants in areas like Dublin, Cork, Galway and Waterford – all of which was driven primarily by the EU's Urban Waste Water Treatment Directive, which required secondary treatment to be in place for most urban areas.' The EU kindly footed the bill for most of the work. 'You'll see those EU investment signs as you go around if, like me, you visit lots of waste water treatment plants!'

That work is not yet complete, though. We are still not fully meeting EU standards. Dublin's (and the country's) largest treatment plant, in Ringsend, does not have sufficient capacity to adequately treat everything it receives today, never mind help to support the city's ongoing expansion. More significantly, 35 of our towns and villages have no treatment plants whatsoever and discharge raw sewage into the environment daily. They include Arklow, Cobh and Moville, as well as popular tourist areas such as Roundstone, Spiddal, Kilkee and Castletownbere on the Wild Atlantic Way, and Ballyvaughan in the Burren Geopark.

We can't truly claim to be the Emerald Isle and yet have human waste wash up on our beaches. We must invest to eliminate that final 1.5 per cent of urban waste that is untreated.

But what of rural Ireland? Some of the group waste water schemes in villages and rural areas are connected to treatment plants. However, there are nearly half a million standalone septic tanks and domestic treatment plants installed for one-off houses and small developments. They have been identified as causing significant pressure on 11 per cent of our rivers and lakes that are classified as 'at risk' of environmental degradation.[11]

A registration and inspection regime was introduced in 2012 to protect water bodies from systems that are not working properly. 'That is starting to really have an impact,' says Burke. 'The pressure on water quality in our rivers is due to nutrients from waste. It had been agriculture and waste water that were the two main sources. Now it's mainly agriculture.'

The water quality in our rivers and lakes has improved over the years, so there are much fewer highly polluted sites today. 'Unfortunately, what we're also seeing is that areas that would have had pristine water bodies thirty years ago have significantly reduced. You've lost the best of the best and the worst of the worst, and we're kind of in the middle space.'

The reduction in the number of pristine river waters has been dramatic – from over 500 sites in 1990 to merely 20 today.[12] 'It really is linked back to agriculture. You've got a higher number of dairy cattle, for example, over the last few years and that is having an impact. So there are more nitrates in the rivers and more phosphorus as well.'

Given the country's ambition to further grow our agricultural exports, the only way to achieve this without causing further environmental damage is to find a way to break the link so that the growth in one does not result in a deterioration of the other. 'There's significant talk about efficiency in agriculture, but the environment doesn't understand efficiency. It only understands the total environmental load,' explains Burke. 'The cattle may be more efficient but, if there's more of them, they're causing a problem.'

We have come a long way, but where do we need to get to in order to finish the job with waste water treatment? 'The end goal is that we treat all of our waste water to a standard that the receiving environment can accept. You don't need nutrition reduction in all waste water treatment plants, but what you do need is a higher standard than what is currently there.' That will include bringing those small towns and villages into the fold so no more of our waste is dumped untreated in the forlorn hope that some ecosystem somewhere will simply deal with it on our behalf without any consequence.

 ## We Are Generating Less Waste Than We Did a Decade Ago

Kilograms of municipal and household waste generated per person, 1995–2018

SOURCE: ENVIRONMENTAL PROTECTION AGENCY

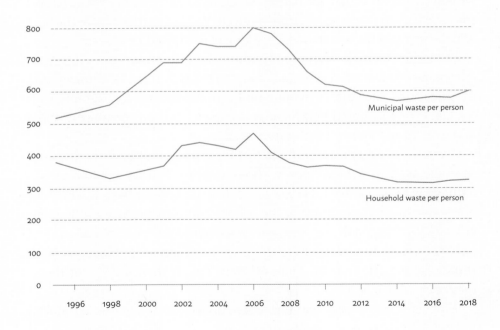

We are filling our bins with less waste per person than we did ten years ago. The amount of household waste that each of us generates has been the lowest on record in recent years. It peaked in 2006 at 470 kg per person and was most recently measured at 324 kg – a decline of nearly one-third.

When you also include commercial waste, to get the total for all municipal waste, we are still generating a quarter less waste than we did fifteen years ago despite the strong economic growth in between. It's a solid improvement.

Having said that, our population has increased by over 620,000 people since 2006. Remember, the environment doesn't understand efficiency in the use of resources – only the total environmental load. Some of the reduction in waste generation per person has therefore been offset by our larger population; nevertheless, our waste footprint as a nation is smaller now than it was in the mid-noughties.

'Look where Ireland was in the 90s, compared to where we are now. There was no focus on waste. There was no focus on recycling. There was no focus on recovery. It was very much a throw-away society,' explains Laura Burke.

That changed from the early 2000s. Partly because Europe told us to get our act together, and partly because we were simply generating more and more waste and running out of places to hide it.

The EU's first waste directive dated back to 1975 and had the aim of safely regulating waste disposal in a manner that would protect human health. Ireland essentially ignored it. You could say we didn't have the financial wherewithal to implement it. But maybe we just didn't care.

It took twenty years for Ireland to enact the directive into national legislation in the Waste Management Act of 1996. The EPA then enforced stricter standards to stop pollutants entering the soil and water, and the number of official landfill sites reduced sharply. However, that did not stop the European Commission receiving complaint after complaint from Irish citizens reporting illegal landfills and vehicle scrapyards, with no meaningful response to their appeals to local authorities. These offenders were rarely pursued and fines were paltry. The Commission's pleas to the authorities to act to protect the environment fell on deaf ears.

So the Commission took Ireland to court in 2001 in the first-ever case of a systemic breach of the Waste Framework Directive. It alleged complete and utter failure by Ireland to act in line with the law. It took four years for the case to work through the European justice system, but the Court of Justice sided unequivocally with the Commission when it passed its judgement.

The government knew the game was up. Belatedly, it began to act.

We made a bold statement in March 2002 when we introduced the first national plastic bag levy anywhere in the world. A 15 cent tax was charged for bags that shops would previously have given away for free. Consumers were encouraged to switch to heavier plastic bags or cotton 'bags for life' that could be reused. The tax resulted in an immediate decrease of over 90 per cent in the number of bags in circulation. From an incredible 328 bags per person per year when the levy was introduced, usage fell to only 21.[13]

I recall finding myself in a Dublin department store the day it was introduced. As I went to the till to pay for whatever goods I had, the person in front of me was giving out yards to the sales assistant about it. I chipped in to say I thought it was a good initiative. My fellow customer turned to say she didn't disagree, but the store no longer had *any* bag available for her to carry her purchase home in, and that was going to be a problem given that it was a fragile wooden ornament. A fair point, I had to concede. Some retailers simply hadn't thought it through.

We got our recycling act together around the same time. We moved from a single black bin for all household waste to two, with the introduction of the green bin for paper and plastic. Two then morphed into three from 2008 as brown bins for organic waste became an added feature.

'I remember going over to Germany and seeing how they had all these separate bins and I was fascinated by it, but I wondered "would it ever take on in Ireland?"' says Burke. 'As soon as people got their separate bins, they were actively putting their packaging waste in it. That idea of making it easy for people really worked, and when we raised awareness and said, "look, this is the right thing to do" then people really bought into it.'

There was the carrot of free recycling bins for households, but there was a stick too. Charges were introduced for using landfill sites in 2002, which even local authorities had to pay. Initially the charge was €15 per tonne, but the cost was increased rapidly in the late noughties and early 2010s to €75 a tonne. 'When you made landfill a lot more expensive, you then had the waste operators looking for cheaper options, which were also the recycling options, so there was a huge benefit to that.'

Our shift away from simply burying our waste problem is another success story. In the early 90s we had nearly a hundred local authority landfill sites in operation.[14] Nowadays, we have just five. 'They operate to a different standard. They are lined landfills, they're catching methane, they're engineering operations rather than a hole in the ground,' says Burke. 'You had around 90 per cent of our waste going to landfill and it's now down at around 15 per cent. So that's very positive.'

Most of our black-bin waste is now converted to energy through inciner- ation. This avoids the environmental problems of landfills such as odours, methane emissions and leakage of contaminated water, as well as the remediation costs associated with looking after the dumped waste for ever- more. It also means we can manage more of our waste at home without having to export it to another country for burial or incineration there.

However, incineration releases greenhouse gas emissions so recycling is clearly a better choice wherever feasible. We therefore need to ensure recyclable material is not diverted to incineration because it is viewed as an easier and cheaper solution.

Our Recycling Rates Are Generally High and Above Target

We are good recyclers. Our recycling rates for metals and for glass and for paper and wood are all well in excess of our national targets for 2025. We are far behind our targeted aluminium and plastic recycling rates, but there is still time to improve those. All in all, we recycle roughly two-thirds of our packaging waste. Not bad at all. However, back in 2012 we were recycling nearly three-quarters.[15] Our recycling rates are, surprisingly, on the way down.

How do we get the country back on track? Burke suggests waste operators should each be given targets to hit particular levels of recycling and should work with their customers to better segregate their waste to help achieve those. It may also be time to consider an incineration levy. Just as the landfill levy made recycling more commercially attractive than dumping waste, so the same could be achieved again by raising the cost of incineration.

Recycling rate of various materials

SOURCE: ENVIRONMENTAL PROTECTION AGENCY

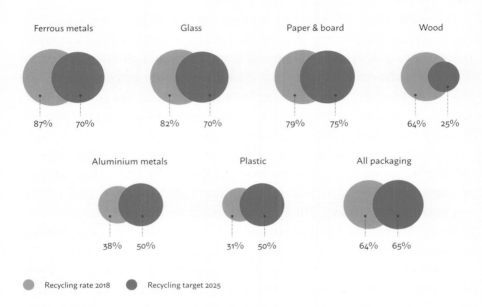

| Ferrous metals | Glass | Paper & board | Wood |
| 87%　70% | 82%　70% | 79%　75% | 64%　25% |

| Aluminium metals | Plastic | All packaging |
| 38%　50% | 31%　50% | 64%　65% |

● Recycling rate 2018　　● Recycling target 2025

The obligations on the producers of packaging waste could also be increased. If you are producing the waste and then handing it on to consumers who purchase your goods, shouldn't you be obliged to do more to take it back and recycle it yourself than simply making it someone else's problem?

Something the government is considering – and which is in place in other countries – is a deposit return scheme. It's actually not a new idea for Ireland. 'When I was a kid, you were able to bring bottles back to the bottle bank and get some money for it,' recalls Burke. 'It is not the whole solution, but it's a way of getting people to really buy into bringing material back and nudging the recycling levels up.'

Of course, accumulating less waste in the first place is the ideal solution. The kilograms of waste each of us produces has begun to edge up again since the low point of five or six years ago as our increased consumer spending results in more packaging to throw away. Yet tighter EU targets will ask us to reduce it further in the next decade as we endeavour to move towards a circular economy. That's one that aims to eliminate waste altogether through the continual use of resources by employing product reuse, sharing, repair, refurbishment, remanufacturing and recycling.

I believe dematerialisation has a role too. As we embrace digital products and services, our physical resource use decreases to practically nothing. After all, what am I supposed to do with all that old Talking Heads vinyl and all those hundreds of CDs I bought to 'upgrade' my vinyl collection? They are just rotting in my garden shed. However, my kids need never buy a piece of plastic, be it coloured either black or silver, to enjoy every piece of music ever made via their smartphone. That's a win–win for the planet too.

90 Our Use of Renewable Energy Sources Is Growing Emphatically

Switching our energy production away from fossil fuels and towards renewable sources is vital for the planet's health; by reducing our contribution to climate change through CO_2 emissions, we will also benefit our personal health by further reducing air pollution. We have made a good start over the past two decades.

The amount of energy the country consumed in 2020 was roughly the same as in 2001, yet the CO_2 emissions from it have dropped by approximately a fifth. And that same level of energy now supports an economy that is one-and-a-half times as large.[16]

The country had agreed a target with the European Union to produce 16 per cent of all our energy needs from renewable sources by 2020. We missed that, sadly, coming in close to 12 per cent. We missed the target for transport, we missed it for heat generation, and we probably missed it for electricity production.

Our ambition for electricity, however, was much greater than it was in the other two sectors – the target was to have renewables deliver 40 per cent of all our electricity needs. The final figures for 2020 are not in yet. If we missed it, the good news is that it was only by a whisker. In 2019, 36.5

per cent of our electricity was renewable, and we were growing that by around 3 percentage points each year.

Share of electricity consumption from renewable sources, 2001–19

SOURCE: SUSTAINABLE ENERGY AUTHORITY OF IRELAND

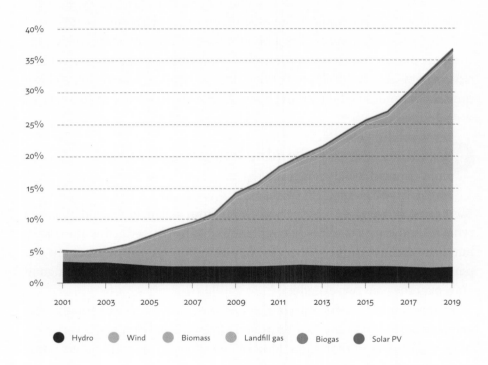

Hydro   Wind   Biomass   Landfill gas   Biogas   Solar PV

Our growth in renewable electricity generation has been truly phenomenal. Renewable sources contributed just 5 per cent in 2001 and that was practically all hydroelectric power, mainly from the Shannon Ardnacrusha hydroelectric station that was built in the 1920s.

In just two decades we have increased the contribution of renewables eight-fold. They are now our second largest source of electricity after natural gas. Practically all of the growth has been through the addition of wind power. Just 1 per cent of our electricity was wind generated in 2001, but by 2019 that figure comfortably exceeded 30 per cent and was more than three times that generated from coal, peat and oil combined.

Two per cent more came from hydro-generation and 3 per cent from the burning of biomass and gases captured at landfill sites. Collectively, our use of these renewable sources reduced our CO_2 emissions by 4.8 million tonnes and saved nearly €300 million in fossil fuel imports in 2019 alone.

It was always going to be wind that would lead Ireland's switch to renewables, given our geographical situation. We don't have a lot of high mountains that can generate large water flows for hydro stations. We don't have long hours of strong sunlight that can generate lots of solar energy. And no one has yet managed to reliably harness the waves for power generation.

Wind is an abundant natural resource in Ireland, needless to say. The government initially put auction schemes in place for suppliers to bid to provide wind-generated electricity at a fixed cost. The lowest bidder won. Semi-state companies Bord na Móna and the ESB got involved first because they had the land and relevant experience. Ireland's first commercial wind farm was commissioned by Bord na Móna at Bellacorrick in County Mayo in 1992. New commercial companies such as Airtricity followed later. Today, there are over 250 wind farms countrywide.

'There's no other country in Europe that has the same amount of wind-generated electricity,' explains Dr Lisa Ryan, Assistant Professor in Energy Economics in UCD. 'It has been an enormous success story commercially, from an environmental perspective, and also technically.' Think about the complexities of integrating wind power – providing a huge amount of electricity one windy day and then very little when it's calm – into an electricity system which has to ensure there is sufficient power for you to start your washing machine whenever you need to. Ireland has become a leader in managing these variable sources of power.

Can the persistently strong growth in renewable electricity generation continue for the next decade? Yes, says Ryan, it has to. 'Right now, we have a target of 70 per cent renewable electricity for 2030. That's considered very ambitious, especially when you take into account that our demand for electricity is forecast to increase because we will be electrifying heat and transport as well. But it's doable.'

Part of the solution is new technology that is arriving in a very timely manner: wind farms at sea. 'When I started working in this area in around 2002, offshore wind seemed like a dream scenario. But floating wind turbines have undergone a revolution in cost reduction in the last few years,' explains Ryan. 'It'll start on the east coast, but the big game-changer will be when we get it off the west coast where there's really a lot of wind. The scale could be huge.'

It opens up the possibility of us generating more electricity than we can use on windy days. What a great position to be in. We will be able to export some of that to Britain or France through interconnectors but, ideally, we will find new ways to store the energy locally so we can draw it down as we need it. Mega-batteries may have a role as their cost continues to fall. Others are looking at passing that excess electricity through water to create hydrogen and oxygen. That hydrogen can then be stored and burned for energy when the wind is low.

It's an exciting time. We have come a huge way in increasing our self-reliance in energy over the last twenty years, but the next twenty could be utterly transformative. One way that things will undoubtedly be different is that we will all be driving cars that will be powered entirely by this renewably generated electricity. The next frontier in our consumption of renewable energy is in transport.

We have had ambitious targets for the adoption of electric vehicles (EVs) for the past ten years but we missed them every year. However, it is fair to conclude that it wasn't our fault. 'The problem with Ireland setting technology targets for electric cars is that we don't research or develop or produce any of these technologies ourselves. We're technology-takers. You can provide grants all you like, but it's pointless if there is nothing to buy.'

The technology is finally coming of age and the incentives we have in place for purchasing EVs are generous by European standards. They made up 3 per cent of new private cars sold here in 2019. That's absolutely tiny, but it is triple the number that were sold the year before and it's in line with the European average. We are on the verge of take-off, at last.

The last cars fuelled solely by petrol or diesel will be sold here in 2030. The current government target is for 936,000 EVs and plug-in hybrids on Irish roads by then. That is equivalent to one-third of the 2.8 million vehicles that are currently on our roads. It is another hugely ambitious target. Is it achievable? Ryan believes we can come close. The cost of the battery can account for up to 80 per cent of an EV's price,[17] 'but battery costs are coming down and I would be optimistic that in the next five years car prices will be nearly at parity.'

If they do, and if we maintain the level of incentives we have now, Ryan estimates that we could have 450,000 pure EVs on the road by 2030, leaving aside plug-in hybrids. Any hesitancy we might feel will fade away as more of them are on the road. 'People who are risk averse don't like battery electric cars because of "range anxiety" [the fear of running out of battery charge before you have completed your journey]. But it's pretty irrational because all the new cars run for 400 or 500 kilometres, which is way more than what most people drive in a day.'

Ryan is optimistic about the benefits they offer rural residents, in particular. 'I see this huge opportunity for people in rural Ireland because they have to drive everywhere – there's never going to be a good public transport system for them – but most people don't drive more than 100 kilometres in a day and they have their own house so they can charge the car in their driveway at night. The fuel savings that they make will be phenomenal.'

91 ## Our Homes Are Exceedingly More Energy Efficient

Energy ratings of domestic buildings by their year of construction, 1700–2020

SOURCE: CENTRAL STATISTICS OFFICE

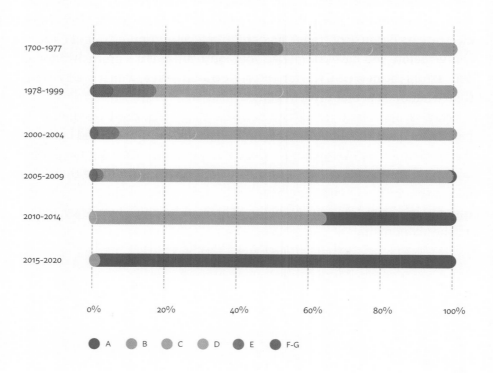

The more energy-efficient our homes are, the less energy we need to use to heat them. That clearly saves us money and reduces the CO_2 emissions from the fossil fuels we burn, but it also makes them a hell of a lot more comfortable to live in. Did your mother ever tell you to wear a jumper around the house in the winter if you wanted to keep warm (and to keep the family fuel bills down)? Modern Irish homes have no such worries.

The energy efficiency of the homes we build has improved in leaps and bounds in just the past ten years. Every house sold or rented or availing of an energy grant has had to have a Building Energy Rating (BER) since 2009. The scheme rates buildings from 'A' to 'G' based on the amount of energy used for space and hot-water heating, ventilation and lighting and the associated CO_2 emissions.

Since 2015, 97 per cent of new houses are in the most energy-efficient 'A' bracket. Just a decade before, most new houses were 'C' rated with less than 1 per cent achieving an 'A'. The critical difference is that an 'A' home takes only one-third as much energy to heat, saving householders two-thirds on their bills and reducing CO_2 emissions proportionately.[18]

The transformation of our approach to house-building has been rapid. In fact, the World Bank rates Ireland amongst a handful of leading countries in our embrace of energy-efficient building standards.[19]

Our newer houses contrast with ones built in earlier decades. We weren't a wealthy country until recently, and you can see that clearly in the standard of our historic housing stock. The first regulations governing the insulation requirements of new houses were only introduced in 1979. There were incremental improvements in these requirements that can be seen in the increase in 'B'-rated homes and the decline in the number of 'D' and poorer-rated categories. However, it was only at the end of the noughties that we really got our act together.

'It became very clear that a lot of buildings that went up during Celtic Tiger years were still very poor quality. There were a few scandals over the size of the buildings and the really thin walls and doors. That put pressure on politicians to introduce stronger building codes,' explains Dr Lisa Ryan.

We were hurried along the path by the EU, whose Energy Performance of Buildings Directive required us to introduce the BER scheme and to set energy efficiency targets for new homes. Ireland was, however, one of the first countries to put this in place. 'We were very quick to adopt the directive, and better than many countries in getting our rating scheme off the ground. In tandem, we brought in stricter building codes.' The requirements have tightened again since the end of 2020: all new homes here must now be 'nearly zero-energy buildings' – that is, built to our A2 BER standard.

That constitutes great progress – however, it is our historic housing stock that now needs to be addressed. The average Irish home emits more energy-related carbon dioxide than those in any other EU country – nearly 60 per cent more than the average elsewhere.[20] There are two reasons for this: the size of our houses and how we heat them.

The floor area of the average Irish dwelling is amongst the largest in Europe. This is partly because so few of us live in apartments. We have the lowest proportion of apartment-dwellers anywhere in Europe – fewer than one in ten of us, compared to a third of Europeans as a whole, and as high as two-thirds of Spaniards.

The bigger problem, though, is how we heat our homes. Half of us are using the high-carbon fuels of coal, peat or oil. More than a third of households use oil – the highest proportion of any EU country apart from Cyprus – and around 15 per cent rely on coal and peat – more than any other European country apart from Poland.

We need to retrofit existing houses to improve their insulation and replace their existing heating systems with electric heat pumps. 'We are quite well suited to heat pumps in Ireland because we have these standalone houses with gardens so you can put the heat pump outside,' points out Ryan. 'You will save on your energy bills and, probably more importantly, you'll have this greater comfort in your home. A lot of Irish people live in quite poor, cold homes and they don't quite realise the difference it's going to make. It'll be far cosier and warmer.'

The personal benefits of retrofitting are matched by benefits for the planet in fewer CO_2 emissions contributing to climate change. We simply must play our part in addressing that global challenge. 'Ireland was a poor country for a long time and we had that mindset that we couldn't do things,' says Ryan. 'Between our younger people and our politicians, I think that we have now reached a better understanding that this is just something we'll *have* to do.'

Our achievements in addressing our environmental challenges are more recent than many of the other topics I have explored. That progress has occurred in the last ten or twenty or, at most, thirty years. What has fundamentally changed is our understanding of our environmental impact as the science has developed.

'As a country and as citizens, we are much, much more aware of our environment and the importance of our environment than we were in the 90s,' points out Laura Burke. 'We impact on environmental quality but also the quality of our environment impacts on us as well.'

In many areas, we are well on the way to making the changes we need to make. In others, we are only at the beginning. But the courses of action we must take and the benefits that will accrue to us for taking them have never been clearer. As a nation, we now have resources at our disposal to invest in those transformations, as we must. The next few decades will be exciting indeed.

EIRE

22

First Irish UN Peace-keeping Force, The Congo 1960

Helping the World

EVEN BEFORE WE WERE A WEALTHY COUNTRY, WE HAD A
WELL-ESTABLISHED TRADITION OF GLOBAL SOLIDARITY AND
PRACTICAL ASSISTANCE FOR THE WORLD'S POOREST. AS OUR
WEALTH HAS INCREASED, SO TOO HAS WHAT WE HAVE BEEN
ABLE TO DO FOR THE WORLD. BY ANY COMPARISON, IT IS A
RECORD TO BE PROUD OF.

92 The Irish Government Is Amongst the World's Top Spenders on Overseas Development Aid

WE ARE AMONGST the top spending nations in the world on foreign development aid. Government funds spent to promote the economic development and welfare of developing countries are called 'official development assistance' (ODA). We invested €870 million in ODA in 2019, still a little shy of the peak of €920 million we spent in 2008 before the crash.

Bigger countries spend more than us, of course, but we are the 19th largest spender on ODA in the world. When you take account of the relative size of our economy, we are the 12th highest investor in terms of the share of our Gross National Income (GNI). And when you take account of our population size, we are the 10th largest investor in ODA per capita.[1]

Government expenditure on official development assistance, 1974–2019

SOURCE: IRISH AID

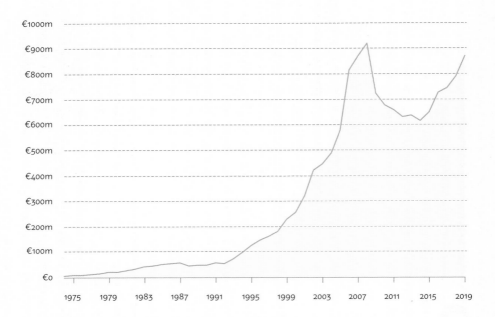

We can be very proud of any one of those figures. From not spending a single penny on foreign aid fifty years ago, we have come a long way in helping to improve the lives of the world's poorest and most vulnerable people. Our first contribution was in 1974 when the government established Irish Aid within the Department of Foreign Affairs and committed the grand sum of £1.5 million punts (€1.9 million) towards its first set of projects.

Three factors converged to kick the government into action. One was the establishment of two of our biggest development charities: Concern in 1968 and Trócaire in 1973. Concern was founded by John and Kay O'Loughlin-Kennedy in response to famine in the breakaway province of Biafra in Nigeria. Biafra's attempt to secede caused the displacement of millions and a blockade of food and medicine by the Nigerian authorities. At the height of the crisis, it was estimated that 6,000 children were dying every week. Concern raised enough funds to send a ship full of supplies to the region.

'The Biafra crisis was very visible – it was the first televised humanitarian crisis,' points out Caoimhe de Barra, CEO of development charity Trócaire. Trócaire was established in response to subsequent emergencies, notably flooding in Bangladesh. There was growing public pressure for Ireland to be doing something to help.

The second key factor was the fact that Garret FitzGerald was the Minister for Foreign Affairs at the time. 'This was always a central passion of his – he really strongly believed in social justice generally, but in global social justice as well.' Fitzgerald established the Irish Aid programme in his department.

Finally, we had little choice. Having acceded to the EEC in 1973, we were obligated to contribute to European development funds.

Irish Aid programmes were initially centred on what we thought we could offer the world. 'It involved looking at what we had done that had been useful to us in transitioning from an inward-looking and fragile economy in the 1950s to a more modern, outward-oriented and industrialised state by the 1970s and the 1980s. What big projects really helped that are unique to Ireland and that we can bring?'

Answers included horses and bogs. Our first official programme of assistance began in 1975 to Lesotho, the enclave country within South Africa. We sent them Connemara ponies to improve the bloodline of their native Basotho pony that farmers relied on for transport. Then we sent Bord na Móna engineers to Burundi to advise on using their peat bogs as an indigenous fuel source.

Our aid budget increased slowly but steadily, by three or four million each year, up until 1987. Economic belt-tightening resulted in a cut of a quarter and a five-year wait until expenditure was restored to previous levels. Our aid contributions started to take off properly in the Celtic Tiger era when the financial constraints diminished. The first government White Paper on Foreign Policy was produced in 1996. 'It put human rights and development at the heart of our foreign policy,' says de Barra. 'There was a feelgood sense – "we can do this" – and there was an international obligation.'

The UK was the real development pioneer at the time. Prime Minister Tony Blair and Chancellor for the Exchequer Gordon Brown had a strong belief in global justice and foreign aid and established a new Department for International Development under a cabinet minister in 1998. 'They set the tone in terms of the quantum of aid and invested in a lot of research and knowledge generation. That pulled Ireland's standards up a bit [...] and made it easier for us to do the right thing.'

And, boy, did we do the right thing. Our annual aid budget went from €142 million in 1996 to over €920 million in 2008! That was greater than a six-fold increase in a little over a decade. We were able to do a lot of good.

And then the country went broke. We cut our aid budget by a third. You could argue about the relative degrees of poverty at home and abroad and the respective moral claims for support. The more relevant point, perhaps, is that the economy subsequently fully recovered but our ODA contribution has not yet. It was, at least, heading in the right direction pre-Covid.

So how is our money spent? Irish Aid's stated ambition is to reach those furthest behind first. It mainly focuses its resources on the least developed and most fragile countries in sub-Saharan Africa such as Ethiopia, Uganda, Tanzania, Malawi and Mozambique. Close to 60 per cent of our aid is spent on bilateral programmes to assist specific countries and the balance is contributed to the work of multinational organisations such as those operated by the EU, the United Nations and the World Bank.[2] A very significant share of our programmes target gender equality as well as mitigating the impacts of climate change and providing humanitarian assistance.

'The Irish government always excelled in making sure that the focus was on basic services that benefited the poorest: health, education, social protection, as well as having a strong human rights focus,' says de Barra.

It's no longer a case of sharing what worked for us in our own development. Rather, it's about identifying what the country reckons it needs and putting their government, their institutions and their civil society in the driving seat to design the solutions to their problems. 'The Irish government sees itself as a partner with the national governments that it works with and it coordinates and collaborates in its assistance with other institutions and other governments.'

What Ireland is extremely good at is giving without asking for anything in return. Our aid is 100 per cent 'untied'.[3] There is no quid pro quo. 'Ireland focuses on the most poor and the most vulnerable and is very genuine about that. For other governments, there can be a strong focus on mutual benefit – on creating environments which are conducive to trade relations or are conducive to people not migrating.'

The Overseas Development Institute publishes a *Principled Aid Index*, which highlights the degree to which donor countries use ODA to advance their own long-term national interests. Ireland has ranked as the number one most principled aid-giving country in the world every year that they have produced their report.[4]

'It's partly because of our culture and the tradition and values we hold as a society: it's about solidarity, it's about global justice, it's about ending poverty,' says de Barra. 'Then, over the years, there have been powerful figures whose presence and achievements we are proud of and whose influence generates pressure to put human rights first. This includes people like Mary Robinson and Mary Lawlor [the United Nations Special Rapporteur for human rights defenders]. And, of course, there are the NGOs who are vocal and active in ensuring that the Irish Government is true to its word and principles.'

The global community has long aspired to an ambition for every developed country to invest 0.7 per cent of the value of its GNI in foreign aid. Only five countries delivered on that ambition in 2019: Luxembourg, Norway, Sweden, Denmark and the UK. Ireland came closest in 2008 when it reached 0.59 per cent. Although our level of expenditure is nearly back to where it was then, the fact that our economy has grown even more strongly since means that we only invested 0.31 per cent of our GNI in 2019. That's quite a gap in ambition.

Our previous government committed to finally reaching the 0.7 per cent level by 2030, by which time it was estimated our aid budget would have grown to €2.5 billion.[5] It remains to be seen if the pandemic has thrown us off course, even though it has undoubtedly increased the need for more aid to offset its impact on the world's poorest.

'Covid-19 has created critical health issues for the citizens of poor countries whose healthcare systems and capacity are weak, but there are secondary economic and social effects too. Take remittances. Migrant workers who typically would have sent remittances home – and which were the mainstay of not just families but whole communities – that has seen a huge downturn. And there's been a downturn in trading and production, whether it's the manufacturing of finished products or the production of raw material and commodities. So reduced government revenues, fewer jobs and a lack of that informal income from remittances has caused really huge damage.'

Curtailing aid budgets in the face of such suffering would be morally unjust when we have come out of this so much better. We should furthermore recognise that those in developing countries are going to need even more support to manage the increasing challenges of climate change and ongoing population increases.

Investing in educating as many children as possible, for as many years as possible, is one way that we can truly change the world. 'Investment in girls' and women's education is particularly important because you have a very short cycle between a girl being born and the point at which she starts having a family, potentially as a result of being a victim of sexual violence, and repeating that cycle,' explains de Barra. 'I lived in Malawi for three years and saw the devastating impact of early pregnancy – girls aged 13–14 starting families that were financially unsustainable – and the transformational effect of keeping girls in particular, but also boys, in school.'

Irish Aid invests approximately 80 per cent of its bilateral aid towards gender equality and female empowerment initiatives, much of that in education. That is twice the proportion of most other donor countries.

We know what needs to be done. We know that Ireland will act first and foremost in the interests of those who need our help most. We simply need to continue on the trajectory to which we have committed and support them to an even greater extent than we have done so up until now.

93 Our Citizens Donate More for Overseas Aid Than Those in Any Other Country

Average annual private donation for overseas aid per citizen, 2017–19

SOURCE: OECD[6]

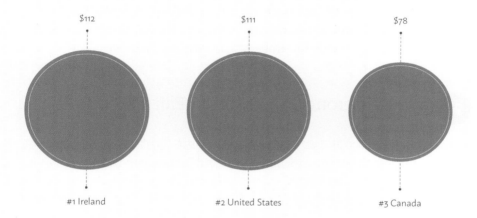

| $112 | $111 | $78 |
| #1 Ireland | #2 United States | #3 Canada |

I have already shown how the Irish are one of the most generous people in the world. But how good are we as citizens in aiding the world's neediest? There isn't much data available to compare countries on this, but what there is shows us top of the pile.

The amount of private monies that are channelled through NGOs and foundations for development assistance and relief are tracked by the OECD. Per head of population, they show that the people of Ireland contribute more than any other country. We just pip the Americans, and there is clear water between both of us and the Canadians.

The tradition of donating for overseas assistance, in particular, is well embedded at a young age. Didn't we all get handed Trócaire cardboard collection boxes every Lent throughout our school years? I always loved solving the origami puzzle of working out which flap went where to construct the box. Some years I just couldn't get it right and the coins would edge out of the sides at the bottom as more were fed in at the top. At least you could plonk them back in again in an endless cycle that gave you multiple gratification for the same donation over and over!

'Ireland is quite an extraordinary society. I think it's true that Irish people are, per head of population, more generous with their private donations,' says Caoimhe de Barra. 'Fundraising in Ireland is so alive and it's so community driven.'

If we all recognise the importance of continuing our assistance and make the same – or a greater – contribution, then we can continue to be proud of what we are doing directly for those who need our help most.

94 We Are Strong Supporters of Fair Trade

Average sales of Fairtrade-labelled products per person in 2017

SOURCE: FAIRTRADE[7]

#1 Switzerland €74

#2 Ireland €70

#3 Finland €42

#4 Sweden €39

#5 Austria €34

There's aid and then there's trade. Most people in poverty in developing countries will never receive a financial handout from a foreign government or a development agency. They do what they can to earn a living and struggle on.

What they produce may, however, be worth a multiple of what they are paid to produce it by the time it reaches our hands. Think of the beans in that €4 cup of coffee or the cocoa in that €3 slab of chocolate. The price we are paying is roughly double the daily wage of the farmers who grew them.

The idea of fair trade is to pay producers a higher, fairer price for their goods as a more efficient way of promoting sustainable development for a greater number of people than traditional charity and aid.

We are strong supporters of fair trade in Ireland. We purchased more than €380 million worth of goods certified as fair trade by Fairtrade Ireland in 2018 – a figure that has increased four-fold in just a decade.[8] Their sales in Ireland, on a per capita basis, are second only to those in Switzerland.

Such success had humble beginnings. 'Individuals who had been overseas volunteers came back and wanted to continue the work,' explains Peter Gaynor, Executive Director of Fairtrade Ireland. In the 1980s they founded Traideireann to sell craft goods from developing countries through mail order, charity shops and market stalls. The Irish Fair Trade Network (IFTN) was subsequently established to coordinate the various initiatives, with the financial support of Christian Aid and Oxfam Ireland. The network became a registered charity in 1995 and introduced the Fairtrade certification mark.

Bewley's was the first company to commit to buying Fairtrade certified coffee. 'We started talking to Patrick Bewley and it took maybe a year or two for them to realise this was something they could do. After much conversation, they found a cooperative they could buy from in Costa Rica and made a decision to import two tonnes of Fairtrade Certified coffee in November 1996.'

Bewley's needed the coffee to sell well. IFTN activated its network to help create demand. 'All the NGOs, the church groups, the volunteers, they got in touch with people they knew and got their workplaces to convert to fair trade. As awareness grew in the public and through the media, it created a momentum that brought Bewley's further along and brought other companies in behind them.' Coffee suppliers like Robert Roberts and

Java Republic followed and, later, the Insomnia Coffee chain.

It took a while longer to get Fairtrade-certified products onto the supermarket shelves, though. Retailer Fergal Quinn was a convert and ensured that Superquinn was the first Irish retailer to stock Fairtrade product. The supermarket chain even went so far as to forgo all the profits they made on Fairtrade products in order to enhance their affordability.

Once Fairtrade goods were available in shops, it became possible to extend the available range. 'We moved from coffee to tea and then coffee, tea, chocolate and bananas,' explains Gaynor. 'About 13 per cent of the Irish banana market now is Fairtrade, and it's still growing.'

The growth in Fairtrade sales here has been extraordinary. Year after year, even throughout the depths of the Great Recession, sales grew strongly. The first setback was experienced in 2020 as Covid closures of cafes and restaurants dented coffee sales. But demand will bounce back. 'Businesses have realised that it is a commercial proposition. Companies see other companies doing things, some of the retailers see other retailers doing something, and that helps to motivate them. So it's not just lectures from us about the need to do good – people feel they can make money out of it and also look after other people.'

In an era of increased public expectation of sustainable behaviour by corporates, Fairtrade is the perfect way for many to contribute and to be seen to do so by carrying the label on their goods.

So how exactly does your purchase help others? Fairtrade offer farmers a guaranteed minimum price for their goods that provides them with a fair return and sufficient income to raise their family. If the market price is higher, great, the producer sells for that. But if prices are low, then they are guaranteed to earn enough to sustain themselves. Furthermore, they are paid a premium on top of this that is made available for investment in community projects. 'They decide themselves how they want to use it,' says Gaynor, 'it's their money.'

The goods we purchased in Ireland generated €2.4 million in premiums in 2019. How was it spent? 'Most of them are still thinking about hunger: how can they provide affordable food to their members? So they put shops into their communities so they can manage the pricing better. Or business development: they put in new seedlings for cocoa or coffee. Very, very simple things like buses and bicycles – if you're walking 5 or 10 kilometres to work and you get a bicycle, it's a significant improvement.'

I view our high spend on Fairtrade products as representative of the desire of Irish people to help those less fortunate than themselves. It is true of Irish consumers and it is true of Irish companies. In recent years Bewley's has moved to 100 per cent Fairtrade coffee. That's every single bean they sell under the Bewley's brand. The fact that we generate more Fairtrade sales per person than nearly anywhere else has a lot to do with the fact that we consume a great amount of restaurant and café coffee. Ask if it's Fairtrade the next time you purchase a cuppa and a chocolate bite.

There remains a lot to be done, though. Only 7 per cent of the world's cocoa is fairly traded today. 'The majority of cocoa farmers in Ghana and the Ivory Coast are living on *half* the World Bank's extreme poverty level. Even though they sell cocoa that ends up in wealthy countries like Ireland, the producers are experiencing biblical levels of poverty.'

Fair trade has an important role to play, even if it's not Fairtrade. Other sustainability certification schemes exist and big brands are even creating their own. If they achieve the same end for the producer, it doesn't matter which consumers buy. 'Realistically, Fairtrade will never grow to such an extent that we will take over the cocoa market. But we don't have to,' agrees Gaynor. 'If we nudge things in a particular direction then we can make an impact even if it doesn't come out branded as Fairtrade at the end.'

Fairtrade Ireland has a network of volunteers around the country who promote the concept in their locality and in schools and who encourage consumers and businesses to make the ethical choice. 'Fairtrade in Ireland wouldn't be successful without the huge amount of Irish people out there who for decades have done huge work to promote fairer trade,' concludes Gaynor. The willingness of the Irish to volunteer their own time to help improve the lives of the world's most needy is genuinely impressive.

We Have a Strong Tradition of Volunteering for Overseas Assistance

Average number of volunteers for UN programmes per million citizens, 2017–19

SOURCE: UNITED NATIONS VOLUNTEERS[9]

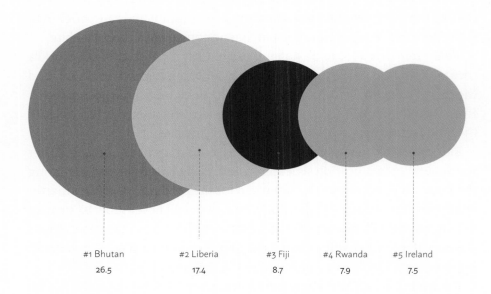

#1 Bhutan	#2 Liberia	#3 Fiji	#4 Rwanda	#5 Ireland
26.5	17.4	8.7	7.9	7.5

We are not just great volunteers at home; we have a strong tradition of volunteering for overseas assistance, from the religious mission-aries who paved the way, through ones the State later facilitated, to those who volunteer today to work with our NGOs or multinational organisations. Amongst all the countries that supply volunteers for the UN's programmes around the world, for example, the 40 or so Irish individuals who do so each year help to make us one of the top five source countries per capita.

Ireland's missionary tradition was a particularly powerful way in which we provided assistance to the world's poorest. The earliest missionary activities in the modern period were undertaken by the Protestant churches to Africa and Asia in the late-eighteenth century. The Catholic tradition started in earnest in the middle of the nineteenth century when a number of French Catholic missionary institutes, such as the Holy Ghost Fathers and the Society for African Missions, expanded into Ireland to train priests for missions to the British colonies.

Many clergy also followed in the footsteps of emigrants to care for the new communities of Irish that were building up in Britain and the United States at the end of the nineteenth and in the early twentieth century. As these became well established with their own local clergy, the focus of the Irish church turned elsewhere and a range of home-grown Irish Catholic missionary organisations were formed in the years following independence, such as the Columban Sisters, the Holy Rosary Sisters, the Medical Missionaries of Mary and the St Patrick's Missionary Society. Their activities focused on Latin America, Asia and Africa. They grew rapidly after World War II, reaching a peak of around 5,600 Irish religious personnel working across 86 countries in the early 1980s. On a per-capita basis, that placed Ireland in the top tier of Catholic nations engaging in foreign missions, alongside France, Belgium and Italy.[10]

'The role of the missionaries in the history of development assistance just can't be underestimated,' says Caoimhe de Barra, Chief Executive of Trócaire. They operated schools, health clinics and hospitals throughout developing nations. 'That experience that touched almost every family meant that there was an understanding of what was happening in other countries. A sense of generosity, solidarity and responsibility grew strongly from that.'

The desire to help was felt not only by the clergy. 'My mum, as a young person in the 1950s and 60s, wanted to go on the missions but she didn't want to be a nun, so she became a nurse. By the time I was in my teens, I wanted to work for global justice, but I had other choices beyond nursing, teaching or joining a religious missionary congregation.' Our missionary tradition declined in line with falling church vocations, but new ways of playing a positive role in the world opened up.

The government was pivotal in establishing a new avenue in the early 1970s. In parallel with the foundation of Irish Aid, it also established the Agency for Personal Service Overseas (APSO) to facilitate skilled volunteers who wanted to avail of a development assistance placement of two years or more. Over its 30-year history, the organisation sent more than 10,000 doctors, nurses, teachers, technicians and others with specialist skills to developing nations. A huge number.

'As an educator, for example, you were not going to replace a local teacher, you were going to share skills with them,' explains de Barra. 'That was all very positive at a point where many countries in Africa had been left in such an abysmal state by their colonial masters that they simply did not have the skills. Julius Nyerere famously said, when he came to power as President of Tanzania, that there were only a handful of Tanzanian university graduates in the country! So for at least one generation post their independence, that skill share was required.'

Over time, APSO's mandate became outdated. The greater availability of skilled local workers meant that we didn't have as much to teach them. Then, as our own economy boomed to full employment during the Celtic Tiger, the stream of suitably qualified volunteers dried up. APSO ceased operations in 2001.

We are, therefore, not likely to see as many volunteers committing their time overseas in the future as we did a generation ago. But that does not mean that we cannot be of assistance. 'There are much more nuanced and sophisticated models nowadays that involve people spending some of their time volunteering, but it might not necessarily be in another country, or it might be really specific skills – like the Law Society supporting the government of Ethiopia or of Malawi to develop their legal systems.'

For those of us that are drawn to help, there are just as many ways to be of service as there ever were.

96 We Have an Unrivalled Record in UN Peacekeeping

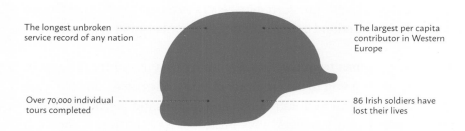

The longest unbroken service record of any nation

The largest per capita contributor in Western Europe

Over 70,000 individual tours completed

86 Irish soldiers have lost their lives

Ireland has the longest unbroken record of international peacekeeping of any nation. Irish soldiers have been deployed overseas on United Nations operations continuously since June 1958.

Given the small size of our Defence Forces, our contribution has been great: we are the largest per capita contributor of peacekeeping forces in Western Europe and North America. Ireland has participated in over 20 peacekeeping missions and completed over 70,000 individual tours.[11]

From the very foundation of the State there was an evident desire for involvement in international affairs. Only four months after it came into existence, the Free State applied to join the League of Nations. The League had been founded two years previously, in the aftermath of World War I, as the first worldwide intergovernmental organisation with a mission to maintain world peace. While joining was undoubtedly about announcing independent Ireland's entrance onto the world stage, it equally served to test the bounds of sovereignty with Britain, which was initially of the view that it would speak for the Free State and all of its dominions at the League.[12]

Ireland embraced the opportunity for multilateralism and successfully sought election to the League's governing Council in 1930. As the Minister for External Affairs and Taoiseach, Éamon de Valera became a recognised spokesperson for smaller countries at the League's gatherings. Irish diplomat Seán Lester was appointed as deputy general secretary in 1937 and served as the body's last secretary general from 1940.

The League proved sadly impotent in the face of rising tensions amongst member states in the late 1930s and the outbreak of World War II. It folded in 1946 and transferred its assets to the newly formed United Nations, although Ireland had to wait until December 1955 to be admitted as a member.

'There was a sense from the very beginning that a country the size of Ireland was never going to be a military or economic power, and we were going to have to rely on multilateralism and organisations like the United Nations to protect our interests,' says Professor Ray Murphy of the Irish Centre for Human Rights in the National University of Ireland Galway.

When the UN secretary general asked the country to contribute observers to its peacekeeping mission in Lebanon in 1958, the government and Defence Forces were more than willing. It wasn't an especially challenging assignment. The same cannot be said of the next request that came – for us to contribute troops to the Congo in 1960.

The politics of the Congo were complex. Belgium had reluctantly granted independence to the country, which is the size of Western Europe. Its newly elected government was undermined by the presence of 10,000 Belgian soldiers, tribal rivalries and white settlers who were determined to stay. On top of that, its richest province, Katanga, attempted to secede. The government sought help from the UN as well as from the Soviet Union.

Ireland dispatched an initial contingent of 250 men less than two weeks after being asked to participate. Nearly 6,000 more were to follow over the course of the four-year-long mission. 'For a country of our size, and given the strength of the Defence Forces at the time, we had a very significant number of troops in the Congo. And though their heart was in the right place, the level of training and equipment was nowhere near the standard that we have today.'

The UN was still new to peacekeeping and soldiers were tasked with a mission that looked fine on paper but had little relevance to the facts on the ground. 'Though we went out as peacekeepers, in reality Irish soldiers often ended up as peace enforcers, having to resort to the use of force to an extent and degree that was not anticipated at the outset.'

The siege of Jadotville has become the best-known incident of the Congo mission in recent years as the subject of a Netflix movie starring Jamie Dornan as Commandant Pat Quinlan. A company of 155 Irish soldiers found themselves posted to an isolated base 100 kilometres from the nearest UN compound. A five-day long siege ensued in which the Irish contingent held off successive waves of attack by more than 3,000 Belgian, French and Rhodesian-led Katanga separatists.

The Irish fought until their last bullet was spent before surrendering without incurring a single casualty. It is estimated that they killed around 300 insurgents and injured 1,000.[13] They were held hostage for a month before returning home to anything but a hero's welcome as the powers-that-be considered their surrender to be an embarrassing defeat. That record has been put right in recent decades.

That no life was lost in the siege was a testament to the leadership and professionalism of those troops. Sadly, however, 26 Irishmen were to lose their lives over the four years of participation in the Congo mission. Ireland, nevertheless, saw it through to the end despite its challenges and the casualties. 'It was of enormous benefit to the Defence Forces in terms of their national and international reputation and they were taken more seriously as a consequence.'

Ireland was again asked to provide significant manpower for the peace-keeping mission in Lebanon that began in 1978. It is the mission in which more Irish personnel have been involved than any other – over 30,000 have served to date. Unsurprisingly, therefore, it has also experienced the greatest number of causalities. Forty-six personnel have died in Lebanon, albeit some from accidents rather than combat.[14]

Ray Murphy completed two tours on this mission during his service in the army. 'There were periods of relative calm and quietness but it's one of those missions that can erupt at very short notice and we have been involved in some difficult operations. Operations like Grapes of Wrath [in 1996] where Israel shelled South Lebanon for effectively a week and most soldiers were in a bunker with any civilians that they could bring in in order to protect them. That was a bombardment the nature of which you'd find during the Second World War.'

Even when such bombardments weren't taking place, there were random acts of violence, shootings at UN personnel and improvised explosive devices to avoid. Across our various UN missions in the Congo, Lebanon, Cyprus, Ethiopia and Eritrea, Liberia, Chad and the Golan Heights over more than six decades, a total of 86 soldiers have lost their lives. 'It reflects our commitment and the level of our participation, and the dangerous missions and environments in which we have sometimes found ourselves.'

While the training and equipment of our forces have never been greater, the complexity and riskiness of UN operations have increased. 'Today you have a major military operation, but you also have a major police presence and a significant civilian component responsible for the rule of law, human rights and child protection. So the mandates are much more complex,' explains Murphy.

What is being asked of the troops on the ground is also much more dangerous. UN mandates increasingly allow peace enforcement, that is, enabling offensive military operations as well as self-defence.

So what is it that makes our soldiers so effective? 'Irish soldiers are very professional and serious about their role. When they go abroad, they want to do the best that they can, and they want to fulfil the mission and they want to be seen to be doing so. They see themselves as ambassadors for the country and for the United Nations.'

He highlights a few characteristics that make the Irish stand out. 'It's the forbearance that Irish soldiers have been able to show in the face of really serious provocation that is one of their great characteristics. We will not escalate a situation of tension; we'll tend to de-escalate.'

Murphy also highlights our natural empathy and support for the ordinary population. 'You will find soldiers of all ranks and of all ages in sympathy with the ordinary civilians in their area of operations. There may not be an official policy to support them, but they'll begin doing something to assist. Soldiers in Lebanon began to support a local orphanage, for example, or you would be giving food to people that you knew were hungry.'

Our continued participation in UN missions brings benefits for our Defence Forces as well as for the populations we are helping to protect. 'There's a huge practical value for soldiers to have the opportunity to work with other armies in the world and practise their soldiering skills.' It also helps to retain that expertise in our Defence Forces as the prospect of overseas service keeps good soldiers interested in continuing to serve.

We have shared our expertise with the world too. A UN Training School for peacekeeping operations was established in 1993 in the Curragh camp in County Kildare. It has trained a modest 2,100 international personnel to date. It is government policy, however, to create a more substantive Institute for Peace Support and Leadership Training there.

Murphy believes the Institute to be an ideal fit for us. 'Our history of involvement in peacekeeping and our history of engagement with the United Nations and multilateralism makes us a good host country to have such a place. We have a lot to offer, given the experience of the Defence Forces and An Garda Síochána, and there are a lot of academics in international relations and human rights in various institutions.' It represents another substantial opportunity for us to deepen our contribution to the UN and to broaden our assistance to the world.

 ## Ireland Is Considered One of the Leading Contributors to the Common Good of Humanity

Every nation likes to think that the world should be thankful for its existence and for what it has contributed. But if you set out to objectively measure the contribution of the nations of the world to the common good of humanity today, what would that show? Astonishingly, the first attempt to do this concluded that Ireland was the 'goodest' country in the world at the time.

The Good Country Index was developed by independent policy advisor Simon Anholt in 2014. 'It tries to measure exactly how much each country on Earth contributes, not to its own population, but to the rest of humanity,' he explains. 'According to the data, no country on Earth, per head of population or per dollar of GDP, contributed more to the world than Ireland. This is not about money. This is about a government and a people that care about the rest of the world and have the imagination and the courage to think outwards.'

We all know that perceptions influence how we act towards others. Before he developed the Good Country Index, Anholt had been tracking perceptions of countries through annual surveys of thousands of citizens in twenty different countries since 2005.[15] 'Countries depend enormously on their reputations in order to survive and prosper. If a country has a great positive image like Germany or Sweden or Switzerland, everything is easy and everything is cheap. You get more tourists. You get more investors. You sell your products more expensively. If, on the other hand, a country has a very weak or a negative image, everything is difficult and everything is expensive.'

Leading countries in Good Country Index

SOURCE: THE GOOD COUNTRY[16]

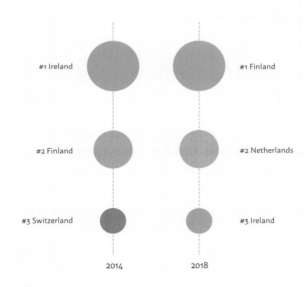

#1 Ireland
#1 Finland

#2 Finland
#2 Netherlands

#3 Switzerland
#3 Ireland

2014
2018

Having accumulated a database of over a billion data points, he crunched the numbers to find the answer to the question that every government wanted to know: how can we improve our image? The answer turned out to be about doing good outside countries' own borders. 'The questions in the survey which are about commitment to climate change, commitment to poverty reduction, commitment to human rights, all of the questions that tend towards the external impact of a country for good or for bad – as distinct from its domestic performance – are the ones that drive the overall rating.'

'It turns out that we don't admire countries primarily because they're rich, because they're powerful, because they're successful, because they're modern, because they're technologically advanced. We primarily admire countries that are *good*: countries that seem to contribute something to the world in which we live, that make the world safer or better or richer or fairer. Those are the countries we like.' Generosity towards others pays off as much at the national level as it does at a personal level. The more we contribute and collaborate, the more competitive we become.

Anholt constructed the Good Country Index to measure the actuality that informs people's perceptions. He identified thirty-five global indicators that were sufficiently robust to incorporate into the index. They include some of the things I have written about elsewhere, such as the number of peacekeeping troops, the extent of charity giving, FDI outflows and the number of Nobel Prize laureates. It also includes many things I have not touched on, such as arms exports, the amount of hazardous waste exported, and the number of refugees and foreign students hosted. It was across this wide set of collective measures that Ireland performed, on average, better than anywhere else when the results were calibrated for the size of our population and our economy.

The index is updated every year or two. Ireland has not claimed the top spot since its initiation. We placed third in 2018 but fell to fifteenth place in 2020. However, 'looking at Ireland's rankings in the subsequent years, it turns out that Ireland does well *every* year. This is a list of 150 countries so the difference between first and fifteenth is not hugely significant: Ireland is still in the top 10 per cent,' explains Anholt. Our strong economic growth over the past decade has not helped our ranking, given that the measures are adjusted each time to account for a country's GDP.

So why does Anholt believe we do so well? Our open disposition, for one thing. 'If you're a relatively small and relatively geographically isolated nation, you're forced to look outwards and you're forced to trust your fortunes to cooperation and collaboration because that's your only means of avoiding abject poverty. Through that experience, you learn the value of cooperation and collaboration. It is why EU membership is a natural for Ireland.'

The empathy and authenticity of our people, furthermore, engenders trust and facilitates that cooperation. 'The world knows that the Irish are authentically gregarious and good-humoured and warm-hearted and that, in combination with Ireland's deeds on the international stage, make them trust it.'

Now that Ireland has attained the status of being a 'good' and trusted country, Anholt believes that a responsibility follows suit. 'The gold standard of good governance in the twenty-first century is harmonising your domestic and your international responsibilities. Broadly speaking, Ireland does a better job than most at balancing those two things. And that brings a responsibility, because the only way that humanity and the planet are going to survive is if *all* countries figure out how to balance their domestic and their international responsibilities.

'Ireland understands part of the recipe for that and, therefore, it's Ireland's responsibility to share that with as many other countries as it possibly can.' To help the world in the next phase of its development, in other words.

A Happier People

IS IT NOT THE PROMISE OF HAPPINESS FOR ITS CITIZENS THAT
CONSTITUTES THE VERY RAISON D'ÊTRE OF NATION STATES?
IF SO, IRELAND IS CURRENTLY DELIVERING THAT VERY WELL
INDEED.

 Our Quality of Life Is the Second-Highest
in the World

Ireland's rank in the UN Human Development Index, 1990–2019

SOURCE: UNITED NATIONS DEVELOPMENT PROGRAMME

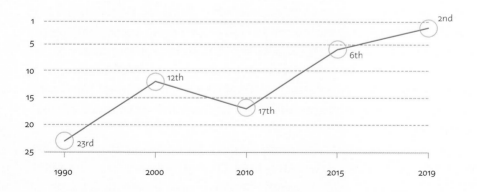

The quality of life for those of us lucky enough to live in Ireland is second to none. Sorry, let me correct that. It's second to one: Norway. According to the United Nations' annual assessment of human development across every country on the planet, we are the second best country to live in today alongside Switzerland.

Thirty years ago, we were outside of the top twenty. The economic wealth generated by the Celtic Tiger enabled a rise up the table as our standard of living increased. The subsequent crash undid some of that progress and sent us tumbling back down the ranking. It was not that the UN's assessment of our human development notably decreased in these years. Rather, our progress stalled at a time when others in the world continued to make advances.

Our subsequent rise over the last decade has been stellar in contrast. We climbed fifteen places, rising from seventeenth in the world to second. No other leading nation has seen their degree of development improve as much as ours has.

The elements that the UN include in their measure are three-fold: have citizens achieved a long and healthy life, a high level of education and a decent standard of living? As I have shown, our life expectancy, our level of education and our standard of living have all increased markedly over recent decades, and continue to do so.

The UN assesses standard of living by measuring Gross National Income (GNI) per capita. It is a reasonable measure of the resources available to each citizen to provide shelter, freedom from hunger and mobility. In Ireland's case, although GNI is a far more appropriate metric than GDP due to the inclusion of multinational activity in the latter, the Central Bank has developed the more refined GNI* measure to further reduce distortions, such as those from international companies that relocate their headquarters here or from the movement of intellectual property.

If we substitute GNI* per capita for GNI, then Ireland drops down the UN rankings to eighth place.[1] An extraordinarily positive place to be, nevertheless. It is not our economic growth that has contributed most to our rise over the decades, in fact, but the increase in the amount of education that each of us now receives.[2]

It may be fairly argued that the Human Development Index is narrowly defined and excludes measures of poverty, human rights, governance, security and social cohesion, for example. But I have demonstrated that the trends in Ireland in all of these areas are consistently in the right direction.

Ireland hasn't any place left to go in the UN rankings. We are now unequivocally in the top tier of the world's most developed peoples. It is a fantastic achievement of the entire population, its civic leaders, business people, public servants, elected officials, local communities, non-profit organisations, charities and many others. Ireland has been changed utterly through our collective effort. It is undoubtedly something that those who secured our independence would celebrate and be enormously proud of. They might also be excused a degree of schadenfreude to see the UK ranked below us in 13th place.

We have pulled apart from the Anglocentric world (Canada and the US are placed 16th and 17th) and placed ourselves in the company of the world's most renowned progressively democratic nations such as Norway, Iceland and Sweden as well as the world's wealthiest like Switzerland, Hong Kong and Germany.

The future challenge facing us will be to maintain the position that we have gained. To do so will necessitate continual increases in our human development as others will benefit too from growing economic wealth, extending lifespans and improvements in education levels.

We must continue to develop simply to stand still.

 ## 99 We Have Never Had Greater Equality of Opportunity

The opportunities that economic growth, greater education and extended lifespans are providing us with have never been greater. And those opportunities have mostly been made available to all. We have never had greater equality of opportunity in Ireland than we do today.

Most of us recognise that we have spread our wealth reasonably fairly. Our society has not been driven further apart by our increasing national wealth; it has been driven together. Recall that, unlike some other countries, our wealth inequality has declined over the past thirty years. The middle class has grown and the percentage of both high earners and low earners has shrunk.

Unsurprisingly, then, when asked to compare Ireland today to Ireland of thirty years ago, 74 per cent of us say that opportunities for getting ahead in life have become *more* equal. That's a greater number than in any other Europe country. The improvements that we have experienced are tangible.

Attitudes to fairness and equal opportunities

SOURCE: EUROPEAN COMMISSION[3]

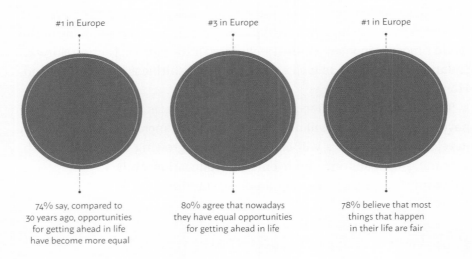

#1 in Europe

#3 in Europe

#1 in Europe

74% say, compared to 30 years ago, opportunities for getting ahead in life have become more equal

80% agree that nowadays they have equal opportunities for getting ahead in life

78% believe that most things that happen in their life are fair

You could conceivably believe that things have improved but that they remain pretty unequal. But that is not what most of us think. The vast majority, eight in ten, say that we have equal opportunities to get ahead in life today. It puts us in the very top tier of EU nations once again in terms of perceived equality. And a pervasive sense of equality bestows the benefit of social capital, thereby building mutual trust and a sense of shared values that enables us to flourish in a positively reinforcing virtuous circle.

Equality is a multifaceted thing. It pervades all aspects of our lives from our ability to educate ourselves to our fullest potential, through our ability to advance in the workplace, to our ability to fairly access the services and goods that we need. I showed earlier how joining the EEC had immediate benefits for gender equality in the workplace. Our employment equality protections were significantly expanded in 1998 when new legislation prohibited discrimination and harassment on nine grounds altogether: gender, marital status, family status, sexual orientation, religious belief, age, race, disability, or membership of the Traveller community.

A new EU directive in 2000 resulted in the introduction of additional laws to prevent discrimination in the provision of goods, services, accommodation and education on these same grounds. We have attained a high level of protection of equality in our society. Of course, an enshrinement of rights does not of itself guarantee equality in practice in every facet of society. But it provides the basis for rooting out the laggards and enforcing change.

And our society has changed pervasively as a result. Do most of us believe life in Ireland to be fair nowadays? Yes, we do. Roughly eight in ten, again, believe that most things that happen in our lives are fair. It is also the highest proportion of any population in Europe.

There is no arbitrary or prejudiced force of the State acting against our interests. We have created a country which, on the whole, applies its resources and its laws fairly and in our interests. The fact that the vast majority of us believe that to be the case is positive for our mental and physical health, and it encourages innovation and entrepreneurship, which pays society further dividends.[4]

Of course, the results are not universal. Two in ten people do not feel those equal opportunities are available to them or that life is fair. They tend to be those with the lowest levels of education, those on the lowest incomes, those who are widowed or divorced or those in poor health.[5] Needless to say, it behoves us to understand what support can be made available to them and how their personal circumstances might be changed to reduce the barriers they face to fulfilling their potential.

Retaining a widespread perception of fairness in society is essential if we are to distribute our limited public resources to support those who need them most. Research shows that if we do not believe that fairness is prevalent then we are far more likely to fight for our share of whatever is available and to feel that others do not deserve theirs.[6] A political narrative of striving for even greater fairness in our society is therefore important to state and restate.

We also need to ensure we embrace everyone, including our newest citizens and immigrants, if we are to continue to uphold fairness and high levels of opportunity for all. There can be no 'equality hypocrisy' by which we espouse equal rights for all but then differentially favour those groups most like us over others who are more different. Prejudice must be challenged. The nation's happiness hinges on retaining what we have achieved.

We Lead Happy Lives

The people of Ireland have never been more satisfied with their lives. Given all the progress I have highlighted, is it really any surprise?

Well, the extent of it might be. Five in ten of us say we are 'fairly' satisfied with the lives we lead today, and four in ten say we are 'very' satisfied. That totals nine in ten. In fact, the number of satisfied people reached a record high of 96.6 per cent in 2018. That's pretty remarkable.

You'd be wrong to think that although you're satisfied with your own life, others aren't with theirs. There are things we all want to improve about our situation, of course, but in the round practically all of us are content with where we find ourselves today.

Ireland's initial nascent economic success in the early 1970s, which saw emigrants returning to Ireland in strong numbers for the first time, was a period of very high life satisfaction. The economic tribulations of the 80s led to a decline, although it is worth noting that even in the very worst of times, in 1988, three-quarters of people were still content with the lives they were able to lead.

The Celtic Tiger era brought increased happiness for a lot more people and more than nine in ten of us were satisfied in most years. The crash, needless to say, undid some of the progress – but perhaps to a much lesser extent than you might have envisaged. Even at its lowest point, in 2013, more than 82 per cent were satisfied with their lot.

Percentage of people satisfied with their life, 1973–2019

SOURCE: EUROPEAN COMMISSION[7]

The subsequent rebound brought us to new heights – breaking through the 95 per cent satisfaction level for the first time on record. So if you believe that there was some magical time in the past when things were better than they are today then the evidence is entirely against you. As I will explain later, nostalgia is a psychological artefact that slips on the rose-tinted glasses we all have in our back pocket, but it is not reality.

Is life satisfaction a true measure of happiness, though? Might we not be satisfied with our job and our home and hobbies but still be unhappy about our intimate relationships or our family situation? Psychologists assess happiness across three dimensions. One is life satisfaction, and the other two are the frequency with which we feel positive or negative emotions.[8] The best way they have found to assess these is to simply ask people.

The most recent survey of the happiness of the people of the EU, undertaken in 2017, found that the Irish were the happiest of all.[9] A whopping 97 per cent of us agreed or strongly agreed that we were generally happy people. Two percent said they were neither happy nor unhappy. A mere 1 per cent said they were definitively unhappy.

The scientific study of happiness has flourished over the past couple of decades. There is now plenty of evidence as to what makes people happy as individuals and what makes the population at large content. I have distilled the results of hundreds of studies into one table for you.

Factors that contribute to happiness at a national and
a personal level

SOURCE: MULTIPLE RESEARCH STUDIES[10]

What makes a population happy	What makes a person happy
Economic development	Higher income
Globalisation	Greater education
Level of democracy	Being married /cohabiting
Rule of law & absence of corruption	Social support
Good governance	In employment
Political stability	Occupational prestige
A progressive tax regime	Work–life balance
Adequate income security	Good health
A good healthcare system	Physical activity
Healthy natural environment	Leisure pursuits
Urbanisation	Holidays
High level of trust & community	Generosity
Personal & political freedom	Sense of meaningfulness
A flourishing society	

Common to both individuals and the population as a whole is income. The more resources we have at our disposal the more we can ensure we can adequately feed, clothe and house ourselves and our families. Similarly, the more resources the State has at its disposal, the more it is able to provide for its citizens.

Greater globalisation is linked to greater national happiness, most likely through the increased economic growth it stimulates. Nations that seek to retreat from the world or adopt protectionist policies are pursuing a course of action that will reduce their citizens' well-being, not increase it.

The more democratic a country, the stronger the rule of law, the lower the amount of corruption, the better the quality of governance and the greater the degree of political stability, the happier the population. Citizens are reassured when their voice matters and they know they will be treated as equally as anyone else. They can take the risk of starting a business or investing or saving if the country is a stable one and they have confidence that the law will protect their interests.

A progressive tax system, in which those who earn more pay proportionally more, provides the State with greater resources to provide adequate income supports for those that need them and a good quality healthcare system. A healthy natural environment, with low levels of pollution and more green spaces, contributes to happiness as does – perhaps paradoxically – greater degrees of urbanisation. However, urban centres offer more varied job opportunities and greater levels of income that lead to greater personal life satisfaction.

Societies that have higher levels of interpersonal trust and high levels of political and personal freedoms are ones that bring the greatest amount of happiness to the greatest possible number of citizens. And the research shows that we are happiest when our society as a whole is doing well. It is not just about us feeling good as individuals; we feel best when those around us are doing well too and our country is flourishing.

Look at that list of factors again and reflect on Ireland's performance on each of them. We are fortunate to live in a country that has delivered improvements on every one of these in recent decades. Guided by the intuition and insight of its citizens, and what we could glean from the rest of the world, Ireland has landed on the magic formula for a happy nation.

The secret to personal happiness is, of course, closely related to what works for the population as a whole. Money does buy happiness because it ensures you can provide sufficiently well for yourself and your loved ones. But there is a limit. Once you have enough to live well, additional income makes you a little bit less happy with every thousand euro you earn. In Western European countries, the optimal income level appears to be a little over €40,000 for maximising your emotional well-being and just over €80,000 for maximising your life satisfaction.[11] Your happiness won't plummet if you earn more, but the additional work time and stress involved in realising greater levels of earnings will take their toll on your overall well-being.

Higher education levels make you happier – partly because that can help you realise greater income. Those who are married or cohabiting are that bit happier than those who are single or divorced or widowed, and those with a network of friends or relatives who offer them social support are happier than those without. Having a job, and ideally a prestigious one, provides people with a positive sense of purpose and a forum for enjoyable social engagement. Work–life balance is important, however, as good health is central to well-being and having time for leisure pursuits and sports and other physical activity, as well as taking holidays, all increase our happiness levels.

It is not just about what you have for yourself: the more generosity you show to others the greater your own happiness becomes. We get great self-satisfaction from helping others. And a sense that there is meaning in our lives, and a value that we can contribute, makes us happier still.

I have shown how we have made progress in every one of these areas over the past fifty years. The fact that we are living longer than before also provides us with more opportunities for happiness in our lives than our grandparents had. It enables us to invest in lifelong learning and development, to enjoy more leisure time and time with family post-retirement and to savour our personal achievements and experiences to a greater extent.

Surely 2020 and 2021 were different, though? The impact of the Covid-19 pandemic was to turn our world upside down and so many of the things that we counted on as a source of happiness were taken from us:

our friendships, our socialising, our work, our leisure activities, our holidays, perhaps no less than our means of making a contribution to society for some. How was our happiness impacted?

In short, severely. In the middle of the third national lockdown, in February 2021, more than four in ten of us rated our overall life satisfaction as 'low'. Pre-Covid, in 2018, the equivalent figure was less than one in ten. Almost six in ten reported that their mental health or well-being has been negatively affected by the pandemic, with one in five of those aged 18 to 34 saying that they were downhearted or depressed most or all of the time.[12] Difficult days indeed.

The key concern is whether this downturn was merely temporary, whilst we lived through various degrees of lockdowns and enforced physical isolation, or whether there will be any long-term reduction in our happiness as a result. The available evidence suggests that we will bounce back strongly. The factors that make us happy animals won't change. If we can get as many people as possible back to work quickly then our high levels of life satisfaction will return in short order.

National happiness is a target worth aiming for. It is not some ephemeral fluffy thing that should be of no concern to governments. Greater happiness causes better mental and physical health, thereby achieving significant healthcare savings.[13]

Similarly, it has been shown to lead to better social relationships, greater generosity and increased participation in voluntary organisations, thereby increasing the country's social capital and sense of community. It delivers strong economic benefits too through greater creativity and better work performance.[14] There is a virtuous circle at play here whereby the delivery of greater national well-being increases the very factors that make more members of our society happier still.

15

How We Achieved This

IRELAND'S DEVELOPMENT HAS EXCEEDED THAT OF MOST OTHER NATIONS. CHANCE PLAYED ITS PART, OF COURSE, BUT THERE ARE FOUR FACTORS THAT SUPERCHARGED OUR SUCCESS. THE INVESTMENT IN EDUCATING OUR PEOPLE, THE STRENGTH OF OUR COMMUNITY BONDS, THE STABILITY OF OUR GOVERNMENT AND STATE INSTITUTIONS, AND OUR OPENING-UP TO THE WORLD, PROVED TO BE THE FORMULA NEEDED TO FLOURISH.

GLOBAL ADVANCES IN medicine, science and technology have benefited Ireland enormously. A country our size can only be a technology-taker, rather than a substantive leader, aside from in niche areas or as part of an international collaboration. Yet we have taken these innovations and applied them, alongside our own indigenous resources, to excellent effect.

We have realised the ambition of our nationalist forebears – our country has taken its place amongst the nations of the world. But it has done better than that. It has taken its place amongst the *leading* nations of the world.

Why have we been more successful than others? If the primary role of the State is to protect and provide for the needs of its citizens then it is fair to say that the Irish State has, by and large, diligently fulfilled its mission over the past century.

We had no grandiose ambitions to distract us from our primary purpose. We have no realistic basis on which to achieve world dominance, no arguable claim over the resources of another place, no desire or reason to subjugate others, nor any colonist legacy that we need to pay moral or financial reparations for. We were a nation born at the right time into a modern era of governance without the shackles of a toxic history to weight us down. This was the vision of the nation's founders after all: the betterment of the people, not the aggrandisement of the State.

The initial plan was one of self-sufficiency and cultural isolation in order to break with Britain, find our feet and build a new state for a Catholic people with a Celtic culture. But it was self-evident by the late 1950s that this was doing little to improve the lives of the ordinary citizens. A new path was chosen that opened the country up to the world, most particularly to our European neighbours. That exposed the need to educate our people better to play their part on the global stage and investment in education began in earnest.

We never had much of an indigenous 'elite' in this country. There was no class system in the way that there was in some of our neighbours. Some people did better than others, of course, but we are a small enough country in which everybody has a cousin doing better or worse than them. Social distance is small and family bonds are valued. As the country rose, we rose together. We did not increase inequality: we worked to decrease it.

We had the benefit of a political and civic system that stayed the course without venturing off to the extremes of the far left or the far right. There were plenty of wrong turns and cul-de-sacs along the way, but the ambition to deliver the betterment of the people was not lost on our political leaders, whatever you may think of their ideology or their competence.

Our national success is far from that of government alone, though. Very many have played a part. Every employer who took a risk to expand their business, every civic leader who campaigned for greater openness, every residents' association member who volunteered to better their community, every teacher who shared their knowledge, every civil servant who ensured the country functioned smoothly. The list is practically endless, of course.

But over the last few decades it has been evident that what we were doing was working. Yes, not for everybody, everywhere, every time. But for most people, most places, most of the time. Together, we have found the blueprint for national well-being. Through a focus on fulfilling the needs of our population, we have crafted for ourselves a high standard of living and a happy place in which to live.

Our Blueprint for National Well-being

The blueprint for national well-being: a hierarchy of public needs

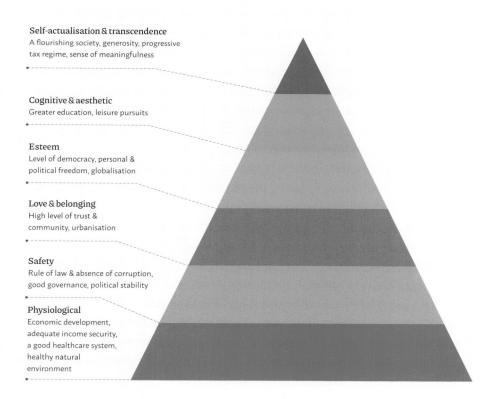

Self-actualisation & transcendence
A flourishing society, generosity, progressive
tax regime, sense of meaningfulness

Cognitive & aesthetic
Greater education, leisure pursuits

Esteem
Level of democracy, personal &
political freedom, globalisation

Love & belonging
High level of trust &
community, urbanisation

Safety
Rule of law & absence of corruption,
good governance, political stability

Physiological
Economic development,
adequate income security,
a good healthcare system,
healthy natural
environment

Psychologist Abraham Maslow is best known for his work in identifying the hierarchy of human needs. Although Maslow mapped the needs of individuals, we can take the factors that have now been identified as contributing to the well-being of a country's population and merge them with his model to produce a hierarchy of national needs.[1] The result is a blueprint for national well-being. It confirms that the progress that Ireland has made over the past 50 years has contributed directly to its citizen's welfare.

At the bottom of the hierarchy are the **physiological needs** – the most basic ones needed for human survival. Of the factors that have been identified as contributing to national happiness, here is where economic development provides the financial means for citizens to look after themselves and where the state steps in to provide adequate income security if they cannot. A good healthcare system and a healthy natural environment help us to live healthier and longer-lasting lives. In Ireland, our real incomes have risen markedly over the decades, poverty has declined and the middle-class has grown, our spending on health has mushroomed, pollution has decreased, and we are living far longer lives as a consequence.

Next up are the **safety needs**, which, in a national context, are ensuring that there is a solid rule of law, an absence of corruption, good quality governance and political stability. Crime in Ireland is at a low level and decreasing, people have demonstrably high levels of satisfaction with our institutions of state, and corruption is very low by international standards.

Then come the needs for **love and belonging**. I include urban living here as, although it serves to meet several different needs, it reduces isolation and makes it easier for people to find companionship. Ireland has transformed from a rural to an urban country over the past fifty years while successfully maintaining high levels of community and inter-personal trust.

Esteem needs comprise the desire to be recognised by others and to feel respected. Personal and political freedoms enable individuals to express themselves and to be respected for who they are. A high level of democracy ensures that their views count in deciding how the country is run. I believe globalisation fits here too. While free trade delivers financial benefits that help people to meet physiological needs, an open and internationally engaged society offers its citizens opportunities to contribute and be recognised on the world stage. Ireland has become one of the world's most democratic and globalised countries, and the personal freedoms it affords its citizens have increased in leaps and bounds in recent years.

Maslow's later work then identified **cognitive and aesthetic needs** – that is, the need for knowledge, understanding and beauty. This is where I believe two of the factors identified as contributing to individual happiness have a role at the population level. Greater education brings personal benefit, but a highly educated population also contributes to national well-being by enabling the country to better benefit from globalisation and by fostering greater levels of freedom and higher standards of governance. I include leisure pursuits here too as they often involve people using their talents in ways that are of benefit to their communities, e.g. in creating art or music, in coaching sports, or simply by attending cultural events and dining out. The Irish people are now extremely well educated, have more leisure time and make world-leading contributions to literature, acting and music.

Finally, top of the pile, Maslow identified the need for **self-actualisation and transcendence**, or the realisation of one's full potential and the need to reach out beyond oneself to help others. A flourishing society and a widespread sense of meaning is evidence of this. So too are greater levels of generosity and the acceptance of a progressive tax regime in which those who can give the most willingly do so to assist those who have the least. We are a generous nation – both as individuals and in terms of our development aid – and our tax and social support regimes are amongst the world's most equalising. We find ourselves better positioned than any previous generation to contribute to the betterment of ourselves, our communities, our country and the world. The evidence I have presented throughout is that Irish society is flourishing.

This is why our happiness and our well-being are at all-time highs. We have deployed the resources at our disposal to address the full set of needs that our population has. Not every individual's needs are yet fully met – and in an imperfect human society they may never be – but we have done the best job of any generation yet at fulfilling as many of them for as many people as possible. Inequality in our national happiness levels has indisputably declined considerably as a result.

We have uncovered the blueprint for a flourishing nation and we are building out our society accordingly and successfully. There will inevitably be changes to this over time as new research identifies other 'must haves' and as the next generation add their wishes to the plan, but the route to further success is now evident.[2]

Economic growth proved essential in providing the resources to achieve our success. That gave us the financial capital to invest in our well-being. But there are four factors, in particular, that I believe have been critical to Ireland's success story by helping to generate those economic resources that have enabled the self-actualisation of the nation.

Education

Ireland transformed the availability of education for its population in the late 1960s and 70s, firstly, with the introduction of free secondary level education and then with the creation of the technical college system. Within a decade, children who had only had the prospect of completing primary education were provided the opportunity to take the education escalator right through to third level.

Ireland had been an extreme laggard in educational provision up until then. The UK had introduced free secondary education in the 1940s and France had it in place since the 20s. However, its enthusiastic adoption was transformative for the life prospects of subsequent generations of Irish people and it transformed the country too. The investment in developing our 'human capital' enabled us to attract more financial capital. By the 1980s the IDA was promoting Ireland as the home of the highly educated 'Young Europeans'.

Third-level education has changed from being something for a tiny percentage of school leavers to being the norm for most. Nearly half of all working-age adults have now completed some form of tertiary education – the highest in any European nation after Luxembourg.[3]

The quality of our second-level education is very strong too. Our teenagers are amongst the best in the world in reading literacy and perform significantly better than most countries in mathematics and science.[4] Our system is also relatively equitable, with notably fewer differences between our schools than are found in other countries.

The benefits of such a large amount of high-quality education have been exceptional for both individuals and the country. Better qualified persons have greater employability, realise higher earnings, have higher levels of productivity and show greater innovation. They also take greater care of their own health and that of their children.[5]

The fact that the population was better qualified benefited the country in its search for international investment. It kicked off a virtuous circle in which a greater number of higher qualified people were employed by international firms and their suppliers, resulting in greater tax revenue for government and reduced expenditure on income supports, which enabled greater investment in expanding education, further increasing the amount of productive and creative talent available, thereby attracting yet more international investment in job creation.

More jobs resulted in new career opportunities for women, which in turn contributed to reductions in family size and brought about greater equality in the workplace and in society at large. Retaining children and youth in education for longer contributed to lowering crime rates. All of this helped to build greater social cohesion – the more educated we are, the more likely we are to donate to charity, for example – and our improved health behaviours helped increase our longevity.

Studies of regional growth across Europe have identified education as the leading determinant of economic development.[6] The higher the share of tertiary-educated workers in the labour force, and the more internationally ranked third-level universities present in a region, the greater the area's economic growth. This was the path Ireland took long before science provided the evidence for its worth.

Community

We trust each other highly. Three-quarters of the population agree that, generally speaking, most people in Ireland can be trusted. One in eight of us aren't sure. But that leaves only one in eight who don't believe that is the case.[7] Within the European Union, our high trust level is on a par with that of Sweden and is behind only Finland and Denmark.

Those mutual bonds of respect power a strong sense of community. It is evident in the nationwide strength of the GAA and our other community sports. It is evident in our high levels of volunteerism and financial donations to help others.

Our tightness of community might have felt repressing and depressing in the 1950s, but it proved to be a strength as we developed economically. Economic opportunities arose in a reasonably egalitarian manner (albeit unquestionably for men before women). Through hard work and with the right education, very many were able to raise their living standards and to join the expanding middle class. Parents were able to help their children attain a greater standard of living than they had enjoyed themselves.

Our deep community and family bonds encouraged mutual support for mutual benefit. It wasn't about getting ahead of others; in the main we sought to bring others with us and to raise all boats as the tide came in. That is why 80 per cent of us agree that they have equal opportunities for getting ahead in life today, just like everyone else. Income inequality has fallen over recent years, not increased.

Greater economic opportunity and our ever-increasing openness as a society changed the nature of Ireland's community relations. Negative aspects, such as restrictions on individual freedom and the suspicion of outsiders, reduced and the positives were enhanced. Our predominant disposition changed from exclusionary to inclusive.

Some media commentators still refer to us as a nation of begrudgers from time to time – a people who do not like to see others do well. Petty jealousy exists in human beings everywhere, but there is simply no evidence that we are more begrudging of each other's success than those in any other nation. In fact, the evidence suggests that the opposite is true. Only one in ten say that they do not have equal opportunities to get ahead in life – so what is there to be envious of, exactly?

What we have in abundance is 'social capital'. That's the networks in society, together with the shared norms, values and understandings, that facilitate cooperation between individuals and groups. It is impossible for society to function without it. Its foundation is trust.

The policies that consecutive Irish governments have pursued have been precisely the right ones to build greater levels of trust in society.[8] Increasing the nation's level of education played an important role by rising people's levels of income and improving the quality of our public services.

Reducing income inequality, particularly through redistributive measures to support the less well-off, was important in endeavouring to leave no one behind. Growing levels of personal freedom and maintaining press freedom had a powerful effect on trust by expanding the inclusiveness of Irish society, holding institutions and individuals to account and growing a sense of fairness.

The benefits to Irish society of the greater social capital that these policies engendered were both economic and social. Greater interpersonal trust helps grow national income.[9] It reduces barriers to trade and it gives people greater confidence to make investments. It is a fallacy to believe that as economic wealth increases so social bonds weaken. Both reinforce the other.

The wealthier we are, the *more* likely we are to help those in need. In a recent study, researchers dropped stamped addressed letters on the streets of a dozen cities and a dozen towns and villages throughout the UK and waited to see if they were posted.[10] In another experiment, the same researcher dropped a series of cards on the ground in front of strangers and measured how many times people came to help her pick them up. In yet another test, she deliberately made to cross the road in front of slow-moving cars to see if they would stop to let her cross.

The researchers expected to find that people would be less willing to help in more urban areas. They found no difference whatsoever – living in an urban environment does not make you any less likely to be helpful to others. What they found instead was that the wealthier the neighbourhood was, the more likely people would come to their aid. Greater trust helps build better communities, which helps improve its economic wealth, which helps build greater trust, which helps build better communities.

Trust also increases our willingness to cooperate with and to assist those much further afield. Populations of countries with higher levels of interpersonal trust have more favourable views of international institutions such as the EU and UN and are more in favour of their governments compromising with other nations in international affairs.[11] Ireland has, of course, been a steadfast supporter of UN peacekeeping efforts for many decades and currently has the most favourable view of the EU of any member state.[12] Our generous investment in development aid is also noteworthy. Our high trust levels have reinforced popular support for openness and engagement with the world, which has obvious benefits for a small nation.

Our sense of community was apparent for all to see during the Covid crisis: the volunteer services to assist the elderly and others at risk; the street gatherings to applaud frontline healthcare workers; our support for our local business people; the reaching out to our neighbours. We came together in a time of great peril to support each other through it. Our unity in following official health guidance resulted in an infection and mortality rate below that of most other European countries.

Greater social capital improves our mental health and helps us to manage stress better, but it also improves physical health in protecting against cardiovascular disease, diabetes and some cancers by encouraging people to make healthier life choices. Countries with higher levels of trust therefore experience greater longevity, just as Ireland has.[13]

Our policymakers are equally members of our community and are close to their problems. The solidarity that flows from greater social capital motivates choices for fairer policies that reduce social and health inequalities. Our proportional representation electoral system, furthermore, requires government to bring as many people on board as they possibly can with key decisions. The diverse coalition governments that result have been a strength, not a weakness. It should not be surprising that the level of trust in our public institutions is so high.

Openness

Ireland is one of the most globalised countries on the planet. We slug it out with the Netherlands annually to see which of us will top the ranking of the world's most globally interdependent nation – economically, socially, and politically.[14]

We were always bound to have an external orientation as a small nation. However, the continuous flow of Irish emigrants undoubtedly super-boosted this. There was a regular return of letters communicating the realities of life overseas, and Irish newspapers took a corresponding interest in the current affairs of destination nations. Remittances from relatives were a boost for local communities and served as a promise of the economic well-being available abroad. Right since we chose to open our economy to foreign companies in the late 1950s, our diaspora has played a hugely important role in sending foreign investment our way.

Our openness to foreign trade took a further step with our membership of the EEC in the early 1970s, and then it took a gargantuan leap with the arrival of the EU's single market in the early 90s. We were to the forefront in availing of the opportunities offered by both.

Our economic success saw the return of some of our emigrants in the 70s and again from the 90s. They brought back with them different standards and expectations of social openness, in particular regarding the role of women in society, which helped to embolden the nascent women's movement. It laid the seeds for the commencement of our social openness. The decline of the doctrinal power of the Catholic Church over its parishioners empowered a freedom of thought that led to the adoption of even greater liberalism – epitomised by the overwhelming support for same-sex marriage and abortion at the ballot box.

Our increasing education levels and our ever-expanding window on the world through television facilitated a cultural openness too. By virtue of being a small country, our indigenous cultural output was unavoidably limited in scale. We are native English-speakers, however, so the world has been our oyster and our consumption of global content constituted a far greater share of our cultural consumption than in larger countries.

That opened our minds and it altered our identity. It helped us to think differently about who we are and our place in the world. It expanded our sense of 'us'. No longer did our self-concept stretch only from our local community as far as our national borders. Increasingly it encompassed the multifaceted global communities to which we felt we also belonged.

We can now engage with our passions and join tribes of like-minded souls in a way that was simply impossible before the invention of mass media, the internet and globalisation. Cross-border communications and trade widen our horizons, break down our old tribal barriers and consequently make us less nationalistic. More than half of Irish people today describe themselves as both 'Irish and European'. Fewer than one in four say they are 'Irish only'.[15] And as we expand our sense of 'us', we expand our empathy for others and our learning from them.

Our openness has even extended to our borders. As EU members we have guaranteed freedom of movement to fellow Europeans, but we have been generous in our welcome for immigrants from further afield too. Our recent population shift dramatically illustrates our transition as a nation from one of homogeneous white Catholics to one that is among Europe's most ethnically diverse. And that will bring us further benefits in the decades ahead.

Some folks give globalisation a bad rap. Don't believe the hype. It has done more for poverty reduction and improving the lives of people on the planet than any other economic development in history. Not only has it spurred economic growth, it has promoted gender equality and improved human rights.[16] Of course, there have been instances of exploitation and abuses in poorer nations, but don't let the exception curse the whole. To throw up trade barriers would hurt the populations of developing nations hard. Job losses would ensue, children would be removed from school to help earn enough for the family's subsistence, thereby reducing the prospects of the next generation, and it would make people more vulnerable to exploitation and to illness.

Hang on, though. Even if it has raised the living standards of developing nations, hasn't it lowered those of developed nations and cost us jobs? Absolutely not.

Globalisation has boosted output in developed economies.[17] It has enabled firms to increase their investment in R&D and innovation, it has made it easier for new companies to start competing with old incumbents, and it has increased employment through both exports and imports. It has spurred the spread of new technology, helping to make economies greener and more productive, and it has improved the quality of management in firms and employees' working conditions. Furthermore, it has raised household income by helping to reduce inflation and increasing real wages by lowering the cost of goods that previously were affordable to only the few.

And it has sparked massive innovation. Think of the Pfizer/BioNTech Covid-19 vaccine that was developed by a Turkish immigrant to Germany, clinically trialled by Irish company ICON across four continents, manufactured in Belgium and Germany and the United States, and then exported around the world to save lives everywhere. That was globalisation working at its best.

Finally, it is worth saying that globalisation does not turn us all into greedy capitalists. It actually makes us more empathetic and increases our fairness and generosity. When you are trading regularly with others, you are far more open to striking a bargain from which you both benefit.[18] That, of course, is in your long-term interest if you expect to continue to trade and exchange goods into the future.

Ireland, therefore, chose the right path in the 1950s. By opening up to let in the sun, we were empowered to fulfil our natural potential. It enabled our highly educated population to deploy their skills and competencies in a fulfilling and impactful manner, and our social skills won us new friends and influenced people.

Global competition proved good for us. There were job losses in some sectors that found they could not compete with goods produced elsewhere – we lost our textiles industry, our car assembly, our sugar and coal sectors, for example. But the gains more than made up for the losses. We had more people in employment in recent years than ever before, at higher wages, and enjoying a much higher standard of living.

Openness has furthermore made us a more tolerant people. Globalisation encouraged the growth of social capital; it did not undermine it. We have learned the lesson that other nations sometimes struggle to accept: the more you embrace openness and globalisation and tolerance and diversity and cooperation, the more you benefit. This is not a zero-sum game where someone loses if someone else wins. International cooperation benefits everyone involved. Our experience testifies clearly to that.

Stability

Ireland is now one of the world's longest continuous democracies – a member of a club of only 12 nations on the planet that have an unbroken democratic record of 100 years or more. Our island status, our avowed neutrality and the military success of the Allied powers saved us from the calamity of World War II. We also defended our democracy against the internal threat posed by the Provisional IRA and other armed groups that sought to overthrow our elected government and replace it with their own socialist state.

That continuity permitted stability; and that stability facilitated our success. Most fundamentally, it ensured an uninterrupted century of the rule of law and security of property rights – both of which are essential incentives for individuals to innovate and contribute economically, as well as for the attraction of foreign investment. There is little point in taking financial risks if you can't obtain personal benefit from doing so and if you don't have a recourse to law to settle any disputes that might arise.

We experienced stability likewise in our politics and policies. Every government in the State's first century was led by Fianna Fáil and Fine Gael or their predecessors. The two parties had a common origin in the nationalist movement and differed primarily on their view of Northern Ireland. Their vision for the development of the nation and its people was not wildly different. While other politicians railed against the electorate's overwhelming support for the big two, their electoral dominance resulted in a political moderation that benefited the nation. The extreme left-wing and extreme right-wing parties that have caused divisions in other parts of Europe did not find the space to breathe in Ireland.

While the economic mismanagement of various governments in the late 1970s and again in the noughties did the country nothing but damage, their achievements over the past 50 years or so speak positively for our governance as a whole. Respective governments' persistence in educational development, in attracting foreign investment, in pro-employment policies, in progressive taxation, in growing income security, in providing public healthcare, in increasing our social freedoms, in reducing corruption and in upholding democracy were all the right choices to have made.

Maybe you feel that many of these developments should have happened long before they did, or to a much greater extent, but we can see that where we have got to in recent times has benefited us well. In fact, our satisfaction with our democracy is outstanding on an international level. At a time when dissatisfaction has grown in many countries, Ireland constitutes one of only seven nations that can unequivocally be described as 'content' with their democracy and where levels of support have grown over recent decades.[19]

This institutional, political and policy stability has gifted us high levels of 'institutional capital'. Good-quality, inclusive institutions that uphold the rule of law, regulate markets and support effective government drive economic prosperity and position countries to benefit from globalisation.[20] Democracies are best at delivering positive social and economic outcomes for their populations, but the greatest rates of improvement in these occur during periods of political stability.[21]

EVERY HUMAN BEING is born with innate potential that can be maximised if their environment allows. Countries are a means of pooling resources in an effort to support every citizen to live a good life and to fulfil their potential. The blueprint that countries need to follow to deliver national well-being is now apparent. The good news is that Ireland is a leader in its implementation.

Like most plans, it requires resources to deliver. Ireland has had great success earning the financial capital required to fund it. We did so by investing in developing our human capital through accessible, high-quality education. We grew our reservoir of social capital through the support of our strong communities. We banked institutional capital through stable democratic governance and strong public institutions.

These capital resources positioned us strongly to compete on the global stage as we opened up to the world. Our initial success in doing so provided us with the financial resources to further invest in the blueprint and to continue to develop ourselves, making Ireland an ever more competitive country in a virtuously reinforcing manner.

There were, of course, many other factors that helped us on the journey that I have detailed throughout the book. The EU's investment of billions of euros in physical capital was important in improving our roads and airports and water quality and telecommunications infrastructure. And we unwittingly borrowed heavily from the environment's natural capital.

The course we took was not direct – we took many wrong turns – but we have arrived at a remarkable place. Ireland is one of the very best countries in the world in which to live today. We are a progressive, liberal democracy which is committed to bettering the lives of one and all, and we are having greater and greater success in doing so. The leaders of 1916 can be at peace in their graves – it worked out just fine. Mainly.

Why It's Hard to Believe

WAIT A MINUTE. SURELY ALL THIS STUFF CAN'T BE TRUE?
AREN'T THERE A HUNDRED WAYS THAT LIFE IN IRELAND HAS
GOT FAR WORSE OVER THE PAST CENTURY?

IF YOU FIND all this change for the better hard to believe, you are not alone. A survey of the populations of 17 of the world's most developed countries found that more than six in ten people thought the world was getting worse. Three in ten said it was staying the same or they didn't know, leaving a mere one in ten who said it was getting better.[1]

By practically any measure that matters, the tiny number of optimists have it right. In 1990 36 per cent of the world's population lived in extreme poverty. Today that figure is less than 8 per cent.[2] The improvements we have made in medicine have helped to add nearly ten years to the average human being's life expectancy in the same time.[3] The number of adults in the world with second- or third-level education has more than doubled in those three decades and now hugely exceeds the numbers with only primary education or none.[4] Everywhere, in nearly every single country, the lives of ordinary people have been meaningfully improved within their own lifetimes.[5]

And as I have shown, this is more true in Ireland than almost anywhere else.

Yet it takes time to change the world appreciably and, as we make progress on each problem, new challenges inevitably emerge. Covid-19 is one example. Poverty increased, education was suspended for many, and life expectancy took a hit. But the speed with which we developed vaccines for it was unparalleled in human history. That itself is evidence of the incredible progress that is taking place.

So why on earth are so many of us prone to seeing the glass as half empty? Or, frankly, nearly drunk dry? It's our psychology. Call it human nature. Evolution has endowed us with a series of inbuilt biases that twist how we see the world. Here are the five biggest biases that give you a blind spot for progress and deceive you into believing that things are going to hell in a handbasket.

#1 You Are Programmed to Hear Bad News

Bad news cascades out of our smartphones and TV sets and bleeds all over our newspapers. Mostly everything reported there is bad news or perhaps neutral. Little of it is positive. The negative tone of the Irish media increased with the arrival of British tabloid newspapers in the 1990s and 2000s, and the subsequent pervasiveness of 24-hour news channels meant we could indulge in constant exposure.[6]

Then along came smartphones and social media to take the negativity and accessibility to a new extreme. Bad news on the doorstep. And on the bus. And in the coffee queue. And in the bathroom. It can be relentless.

It is human nature to pay more attention to bad news than to good news. That's partly why we see so much of it: we are being served up what we want to hear.

Humans suffer from a 'negativity bias'. We are programmed for bad stuff to impact a lot more than the good. Bad information is processed more thoroughly. Bad emotions and bad feedback have more impact on us. Bad impressions and bad stereotypes are quicker to form and more resistant to change. And we are more motivated to avoid bad self-perceptions than to pursue good ones.[7]

In evolutionary terms, this is unsurprising. Our ancient ancestor who surmised the moving bushes represented a stalking lion lived to tell the tale to a suitably impressed mate who gifted us their genes. Paying more attention to bad news facilitated human survival. The instinct does not serve us well in the twenty-first century, however, as we waste time and mental energy looking for lions all around us when life-or-death situations are so few and far between. But it's a tough instinct to beat.

Political science researchers Marc Trussler and Stuart Soroka at Montreal's McGill University invited students to come to their lab to participate in an eye-tracking study. The volunteers were first asked to select some stories about politics to read from a news website so that a camera could establish some baseline eye-tracking measures. They then watched a short video during which their eye movements were to be tracked and they finally completed a questionnaire on the kind of political news that they like to read.[8]

The experiment was, however, a ruse. There was no eye-tracking camera. The researchers were merely interested to find out which news articles the participants would choose to read from amongst their carefully balanced set of positive, neutral and negative stories.

You guessed it. Participants more often chose to read the negative stories. In fact, those who were most interested in current affairs and politics were most likely to opt for the bad news! And yet, when asked, these people said they preferred good news and that the media was too focused on negative stories.

Not only are we, therefore, predisposed to see more of the problems around us and less of the positives, but a further psychology bias doubles down on our prejudice. The very concept of psychological bias was first identified by psychologists Amos Tversky and Daniel Kahneman in the early 1970s when they established the existence of what they labelled 'availability bias'.[9] They found that we estimate the probability of an event or the frequency of a kind of thing by the ease with which instances come to mind.

That results in us judging the likelihood of a flood, an earthquake, an airplane crash or a terrorist attack on how easily we can imagine or recall such a thing happening. And if that is what we are seeing frequently in our news consumption then we are prone to thinking that those things occur a lot more frequently than they do in reality. We come to believe that there are more negative than positive things happening in the world because it's harder to think of as many examples of the latter.

None of this is good news for your mental health. The more bad news you look at, the more likely you are to feel anxious and sad.[10]

Incredible as it seems, those who extensively followed media reports of the terrorist attack on the Boston Marathon suffered *more* acute stress than did people who were directly exposed to the bombings themselves or through a close relationship.[11] The content and quantum of news today amplifies and spreads distress far beyond the communities directly affected.

When Covid-19 first began to rage in Europe I became addicted to the live streams on news websites. For a whole week I had the BBC live news feed in one window, Sky News open behind that, and RTÉ and the *Irish Times* too for good measure. I felt compelled to cycle through each of them every five minutes and, if there was no update, I kept refreshing the browser window in case it had stalled and I might have missed something important.

All I got was a cascade of worrying news on repeat, as the same thing inevitably appeared four times across each news site. After a week of this, I had enough. It was too depressing, evidently never-ending, and I honestly couldn't give enough attention to my work with the constant gnawing need to have another gawk.

Reducing the number of negative stories in mainstream media, and putting the information they contain into context, would help us see the world in a more balanced way. Nevertheless, the news will always be somewhat more negatively biased given the valuable role it has in democratic societies of holding government and corporates and civic leaders to account. That's part of the job description.

#2 Good Stuff Takes Time but Bad Stuff Happens Quickly

We have all heard the one about boiling the frog. Supposedly, if you put a frog in a pot of cold water and very gradually increase the temperature, the frog doesn't notice the increase and will remain there until it boils to death.

You hear it used a lot as a metaphor: change in our own environment can sometimes happen so slowly that we fail to notice it.

Well, let me clear up the facts – it's a myth. The frog never boils in real life. Its survival instinct kicks in and it will jump out of the pot every time.

However, it is true that humans are bad judges of slow change. We pay disproportional attention to things that happen quickly. And that leads us to our second misleading factor: there is a speed differential in human progress. Good progress tends to happen incrementally over decades, while bad stuff tends to happen quickly, so long-term progress is harder to spot.

It can take a hundred years for a forest to mature but only a weekend to burn it to the ground. It can take a decade to design and build a new commercial airline but only a few minutes to crash it. It can take years to develop and roll a vaccine out across the world, but a pandemic can take hold in just weeks.

Environmental scientists have labelled this phenomenon the 'shifting baseline syndrome'. The French/Canadian marine biologist Daniel Pauly originated the term in the 1990s to explain the collapse of fish stocks. He argued that each generation of fisheries scientist accepts as a baseline the stock size and species composition that occurred at the beginning of their careers and uses this to evaluate changes. When the next generation of scientist starts their career, the stocks have further declined, but it is the stocks at that time that they consider a new baseline. Over a few generations, the baseline shifts significantly for the worse and the stock decline is catastrophic but underappreciated.

The application of the syndrome has since been widened out across the environmental sciences to reflect the fact that each new human generation accepts as natural or normal the situation in which it was raised. Knowledge is not passed on from generation to generation and, even within our own lifetimes, we forget what was 'normal' just ten or twenty years before.

Dr Sarah Papworth and her colleagues at Imperial College London tested the memories of Yorkshire villagers about the most common birds in their area twenty years before and compared their answers to available records.[12] They found that older people were more correct – demonstrative of a generational difference in understanding how the bird fauna had changed over time.

About fifteen years ago I was a guest speaker at a tourism conference in Norway. It took place in early spring in a regional location that required a long drive from the airport up and over the mountains. My driver was a retired local tourism official. As we climbed up higher and higher, the remnants of winter snow could be seen around us. My companion proudly pointed out his family's winter cabin as we passed it but, sadly, he remarked that the snow fell much less frequently nowadays and remained for a much shorter time than when he visited as a child. He was the first person I ever met who could point to the impact of climate change within his own lifetime.

A recent study shows just how shockingly short our personal memories are and how quickly most of us acclimatise to change in the weather. Dr Frances Moore of the University of California in Davis led a team that studied weather commentary amongst two billion geo-located Twitter posts by American users over two-and-a-half years.[13] They identified 60 million weather-related tweets and cross-referenced them with local temperatures at the time and historical weather data.

Unsurprisingly, people were more likely to tweet about the weather if it was unusual for the season where they lived – warm conditions in winter, for example, or cool temperatures in summer. It was what people considered 'unusual' that was so shocking. The researchers found that people's reference points only extended about five years back. Temperature changes that would have been remarkable if compared to earlier years had rapidly become a new 'normal' through repeated exposure.

In a world that is slowly getting hotter all the time, we are prone to noticing extreme weather less. The implications for climate change are alarming. If our psychology deceives us into ignoring weather and climate events that happened more than five years ago, even the changes we notice will seem small. We can be easily deluded into thinking that our climate is not changing much at all.

While scientists are rightly worried about our blindness to long-term environmental degradation, the very same psychological processes are at work in blinding us to long-term positive change. It is what I call 'PADing':

that is, suffering from 'progress attention deficit'. It's our inability to recognise slowly occurring positive change in our natural, socio-cultural, political and economic environment. We have an inbuilt inability to see the big picture when it stretches out over a decade or more.

Perhaps it can be explained by the fact that the average lifespan of humankind averaged around 35 years for practically all of our existence. And the lifestyle of one generation did not differ in any meaningful way from that of their grandparents or great-great-grandparents before them. There wasn't any time frame that our ancestors needed to worry about beyond the present, nor any gradual changes in their environment that were worth noticing. It is only the dramatic progress that we have made over the past couple of centuries that has revealed the shortcomings of our short attention span.

#3 Everything Seemed Better When You Were Younger

For my older readers, particularly those aged 60 and older, there can be a sense that things were better when they were in the prime of their youth. Our brains romanticise the past as we age and can, therefore, cause us to errantly conclude that things are getting worse. As Ireland's population ages in the decades ahead this stands to become an increasingly prominent distorting factor with implications for how we view ourselves as a society and what might motivate our choice at the ballot box.

It was in the 1980s that psychologists first identified the tendency for us to best remember events that happened to us in our teens and twenties. They found that we are less good at remembering what occurs in later decades of our life, up until we reach our sixties and seventies when we can more easily recall recent events. The effect was labelled the 'reminiscence bump' by Professor David Rubin of Duke University in North Carolina.[14] It may be due to the fact that we experience so much for the first time in our adolescence and early adulthood that the novelty factor lays down powerful memories for us.

It is not just that we remember more of what happened in our earlier years: we remember those years much more positively than the later years of our life. Dr Anja Leist of the University of Luxembourg and her colleagues asked hundreds of Germans, aged from their 40s through to their 80s, about the critical events in their lives – both positive and negative.[15] She confirmed the existence of the reminiscence bump but found it only occurred for positive life events. People report more frequent negative events in middle age and these increase in frequency with growing age. That can result in a sense of nostalgia and a perception of personal decline.

Rubin himself led an insightful study which found that Americans' general knowledge about current affairs, sports and the Academy Awards mirrored the reminiscence bump.[16] We are likely to be more knowledgeable about what happened in the world when we were in our teens and twenties than we are in any subsequent decade of our lives! Our world image is partially frozen in time.

Given the tendency to look at our past through rose-tinted glasses, it is easy to see how this can give rise to 'declinism' – i.e. the belief that a society or a country or the world is declining and its best days are behind it. This, as I have endeavoured to show, is a psychological fallacy and incongruent with the facts.

#4 An Improving World Makes You More of a Critic

Recent research by Harvard psychologists David Levari and Daniel Gilbert has uncovered a previously unknown psychological bias that they have labelled 'prevalence-induced concept change'.[17] The pair found that as a problem becomes less common, we widen our definition of it to include more things. That is to say, when problems become rarer, we count more things as problems. So as the world improves, we expand our definition of bad news to find more things wrong with it! We do so even to the extent of findings problems when there are none there at all.

The team proved the bias in some intriguing ways. In one experiment, they invited volunteers to their lab and gave them a simple task: take a look at a series of computer-generated faces and decide which ones seem threatening. The faces were carefully designed to range from very intimidating through to very harmless. As the experiment progressed, they began to show people fewer and fewer threatening faces. Participants responded by labelling a wider range of faces as threatening. When they ran out of threatening faces altogether, people started identifying faces as threatening that they had previously called harmless.

In another experiment, they asked volunteers to play the part of reviewers of proposals for scientific research studies. The spectrum of proposals before them varied from very ethical to very unethical and they had to decide whether to accept or reject each of them. Once again, when the researchers lowered the prevalence of unethical studies mid-way through the experiment, participants started to label innocuous studies as unethical. In other words, as the prevalence of unethical research proposals decreased, participants' concept of what was unethical expanded to include proposals that it had previously excluded.

This bias is a deep-rooted one. Even when participants were explicitly told that the prevalence of instances would change, and even when they were instructed and *paid* to ignore these changes, they still couldn't help themselves!

What is going on inside our brains? The answer lies in how we process information. We are constantly comparing what is in front of us to its recent context. Instead of carefully deciding how threatening a face is compared to all other faces, the brain can only store how threatening it is compared to other faces it has seen recently. When threatening faces are rare, therefore, new faces are judged relative to mostly harmless faces and so even slightly threatening ones appear scary. Our brain prefers to work in relativities, it turns out, than in absolutes.

The challenge for progress is that the more of it there is, the more likely we are to notice the exceptions. Journalists are as susceptible to this bias as any of us – but that can have an amplification effect. Media researchers have found that when immigration or violence decline in society, they attract *increased* newspaper coverage.[18] Similarly, as airplane crashes have decreased in frequency, the media coverage each one gets has been found to *increase*.[19] Unsurprisingly, people grew more fearful of flying as a result despite the fact that it was markedly safer to do so.

#5 If You're Misled Often Enough, You'll Come to Believe It

Donald Trump was judged a master of mistruth: he has been assessed as the American President who told the greatest number of lies by some significant margin.[20] But when he claimed that the 2020 presidential election was 'stolen', despite all the evidence to the contrary, a lot of people believed him. Surveys after that election showed that more than 70 per cent of voters for the Republican Party believed that the result was fraudulent.[21]

Trump's repeated claims play into the fifth bias in our brains, which holds us back from recognising positive progress: if a false statement is repeated often enough, we will start to believe it. Similarly, if some Irish commentators and politicians repeatedly tell you that we live in a 'failed state' or one that is in a perpetual state of crisis, then part of you will come to believe that it is true regardless of the evidence before your eyes.

This is the 'illusory truth effect', first identified by university researchers in Pennsylvania in the late 1970s. When asked to assess the truth of something, we check whether it is in line with our existing understanding or if it feels familiar. Repetition makes statements more familiar. When we hear something for a second or third time, the brain responds to it faster and misinterprets that fluency as a signal for truth.

It's partly how advertising works. By hearing a claim again and again we come to accept that it *must* be true and that the product is indeed worth paying more for 'because you're worth it'. At least truth in advertising is regulated, unlike in politics.

Researchers at Yale University decided to test the extent to which fake news is considered more believable as a result of repetition.[22] They sourced fake stories from a fact-checking website, mixed them with genuine news headlines and designed them all to look like Facebook posts. Nearly 1,000 research participants were shown a selection of the stories and were asked if they would share them on social media. Later in the study, they were asked to rate a selection of stories for accuracy, some of which had been included in the earlier question about sharing. The findings were crystal clear: even after just one repetition, participants were more likely to rate articles they had seen before as true. A single exposure to fake news on Facebook makes you more likely to believe it.

In fact, this brain hack continues to work even when we know what we are being told is false. You would think that if people knew that the Pacific Ocean was the largest ocean on Earth then telling them that the Atlantic Ocean was the largest would have no effect. Well, a study to test this very supposition demonstrated that the deception still worked![23] It is not that people completely changed their minds, but it caused them to begin to doubt themselves and moved them from a view that the statement was 'definitely false' to 'probably false'. Every time a lie is repeated, it appears slightly more plausible.

Sadly, the creation of social media has enabled lies to be repeated many times over at the click of a 'share' button. An astonishing study by researchers at the Massachusetts Institute of Technology investigated the diffusion of verified true and false news stories shared on Twitter from 2006 to 2017.[24] They examined more than 125,000 stories tweeted by about 3 million people more than 4.5 million times. They found that fake news diffused significantly farther and faster than the truth in all categories of information, and this was particularly true of false political news. And they found the amount of false news to be demonstrably increasing.

The more I have examined the research, the more I have shifted from being a vocal supporter of the benefits of social media to being wary of the damage it is doing to democracy. There is a significant social cost to enabling such a free flow of fake news. It damages people's trust in the good intentions of others, in particular those of our political and civic leaders, who are subject to incredible hatred and misrepresentation online. That fosters hostility, creates division and ultimately makes democracy unworkable if it leaves no potential coalition partners willing to trust each other enough to work together for the common good of the people.

It demonstrates that we need to beware of those who always tell us that nothing is going right and that the country is in a scandalous state. The continual repetition of the claim that there are multiple 'crises' in virtually every area of Irish life hacks your brain into accepting that they are there. And the outcome can only be disillusionment.

If the electorate become convinced that things are bad and getting worse then it encourages disengagement – why bother voting if no one can get us out of the sorry state we appear to be in? It contributes to the rating of politicians and political parties as amongst the least trusted institutions of state.

Although this is a particularly intractable bias that has an effect even when you know the claim to be false, there is hope. Recent studies provide evidence that fake news can be combatted by asking people to reflect on the factual accuracy of statements before they are exposed to it.[25] Hopefully this book has provided you with plenty of reason to reflect on what you read and hear about our progress.

LIFE IN IRELAND has improved massively and is continuing to do so. At the same time, there remains much injustice and inequality. There are very many amongst us who would benefit from wholesale improvements in their lives. Both things are true simultaneously: our continued improvement and the difficulties facing many.

Our psychology has evolved to direct our attention towards the latter without giving due cognisance to the former. But a balanced perspective has never been more important given the rapid pace of change today. We need a good sense of where we stand in order to decide where we should head to next.

Room to Improve

I HAVE DISCUSSED SOME OF THE INCREDIBLE ACHIEVEMENTS OF OUR FOREBEARS AND PEERS THAT HAVE TRULY SET IRELAND APART FROM MOST OTHER NATIONS ON THE PLANET. BUT THERE IS MUCH WORK STILL TO BE DONE. LET ME HIGHLIGHT JUST TEN PRIORITY AREAS THAT WE NEED TO TACKLE SUCCESSFULLY IN ORDER TO CONTINUE TO PROGRESS POSITIVELY INTO THE CENTURY AHEAD.

 ## We Are One of the World's Worst Contributors to Climate Change

THE EMISSION OF greenhouse gases, particularly carbon dioxide (CO_2), into our atmosphere is blanketing the planet, leading to global warming and causing increasing global temperatures, changes in precipitation, rising sea levels and more extreme weather. Every country must play a part in addressing this existential challenge. Right now, we are failing to do ours. Our CO_2 emissions per person are amongst the highest in Europe.

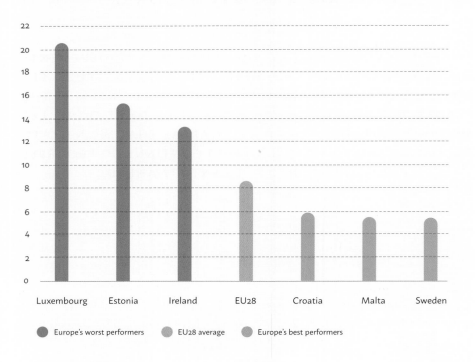

Tonnes of CO_2 equivalent emitted per person, 2018

SOURCE: EUROSTAT/CENTRAL STATISTICS OFFICE[1]

Ireland emits more than 13 tonnes of CO_2 (or equivalent gases) per inhabitant per year. Thirteen tonnes each! Only Estonia and Luxembourg do worse. The EU average is 8.5 tonnes with the top-performing nations clocking in at under 6 tonnes – less than half our total.

We had agreed a target with the EU to reduce our emissions by 2020 to 20 per cent less than they had been in 2005. But we didn't even come close. We achieved a reduction of only a few per cent.[2] Miserable. And unfair.

It can be argued that it was easier for other European countries to reduce their emissions as they had a history of heavy industry that could be modernised or shut down. Ireland's largest-emitting sector is agriculture, which has undergone growth over the past decade, pushing those emissions higher when they needed to be reduced. Transport and energy generation are our next biggest sources of emissions.

Energy is where we have had the greatest success in reducing our emissions. They are more than 40 per cent below what they were back in 2005 even though we are consuming more electricity as our population has grown. The continuing decrease reflects the benefit of modern gas-fired power plants replacing older peat- and oil-fired plants as well as the increasing share of renewable sources.

But there is more to do. 'We're still burning coal in Moneypoint power station. There's no way of justifying that, it just shouldn't be happening,' says Laura Burke, Director General of the Environmental Protection Agency (EPA). 'In fact, Moneypoint was offline for most of 2019 and we saw a reduction of *one million* tonnes of emissions.' Our total exit from coal and peat burning, when it comes, will have knock-on benefits in reduced air pollution and in greater decarbonisation of the residential and transport sectors in turn as the electricity they consume will be cleaner.

Transport emissions are slightly lower than they were in 2005, but that followed a mammoth increase in the 1990s and early noughties as the Celtic Tiger increased the number of people commuting, the distances they were travelling and the numbers of cars in each household. The subsequent recession helped bring those figures down somewhat, but the step-change that we now need to make is the electrification of everything that moves – from our cars and our buses right now to our vans and trucks in the future. Strong incentives will be required to encourage people to make the switch.

And then there is agriculture. It accounts for 35 per cent of all our greenhouse gas emissions – the same as the energy and transport sectors combined. It is the only sector that has seen an increase in emissions over the past 15 years despite the national mandate to reduce them. Why? Once the EU milk quota was removed, the number of dairy cows shot up by more than a third. That's not reconcilable with reducing our emissions and it's not reconcilable with protecting our environment.

'We can't portray Ireland as clean and green if our greenhouse gas emissions are going up, our water quality is going down, and our ammonia emissions are going up,' says Burke. 'One of the arguments that is often made is that you need to treat methane emissions from cows differently to other emissions because they're short-lived rather than long-lived. There's an argument for that, but in Ireland they're still going up and that's the issue.'

It is time for a mature discussion on where the agricultural industry is going in the future. If the country needs our farmers to reduce their carbon footprint then isn't that precisely what we should be incentivising them to do? 'You could move to paying farmers for ecosystem services. At the moment, you won't get some payments if you're not utilising land. It would be the opposite: your payment would be for you *not* to utilise the land in order that it could store carbon.' That could mean rewetting drained lands, planting more forest and rehabilitating peatlands, for example. It would be a very different type of agriculture from what we have been used to.

A radical and rapid rethink is required if we are to make up for lost time and to hit our 2030 target. The 2021 Climate Action Act commits us to a 51 per cent reduction (over 2018 levels) by 2030. That means reducing our CO_2 emissions by between 4 and 5 per cent every year this decade.

The aim is to accelerate the pace of reduction thereafter and to become carbon neutral by 2050. We would store as much carbon as we would use each year thereafter. It's massively ambitious and entirely necessary.

Change will bring opportunities and benefits ranging from new, high-quality employment opportunities in our local communities to improved air quality, reduced traffic congestion, warmer homes and better health. We need government and industry to work together to realise those, but we can each act today to upgrade our homes, change our source of heating and electricity, and switch to electric vehicles and public transportation.

Ireland must play its part if it is to remain a credible contributor to helping the world as it faces into its biggest challenge. There is no plan(et) B, as the Climate Strike poster says.

2 Our Biodiversity Is in Decline

Condition of protected habitats and their trends %

SOURCE: NATIONAL PARKS & WILDLIFE SERVICE[3]

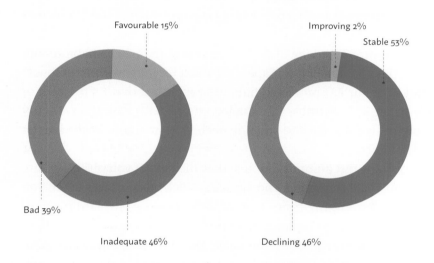

Favourable 15%

Improving 2%

Stable 53%

Bad 39%

Inadequate 46%

Declining 46%

Forget about our contribution to the entire planet for a moment; we are not even close to looking after our patch of it well. We are destroying wildlife habitats all over the country.

The EU Habitats Directive of 1992 forced us to designate important wildlife conservation areas as Special Areas of Conservation (SACs). The areas we have identified as SACs cover approximately 17,000 square kilometres – roughly half of which are on land and half are marine or large lakes. They might be bogs, sand dunes, heaths, lakes, rivers, woodlands, estuaries or sea inlets. The directive also protects 25 specific species, including salmon, otters, bottlenose dolphins, freshwater pearl mussels and Killarney ferns.

Special Protection Areas (SPAs) are also designated in places to protect rare and vulnerable species of birds or those that use Ireland for migration. Our SPA network encompasses nearly 6,000 square kilometres of terrestrial and marine habitats, some of which are also in SAC areas.

Ireland is poor enough at designating sites under the directive. Only 13 per cent of our land mass is designated as Special Areas of Conservation or Special Protection Areas. That puts us near the very bottom of the EU league with only Denmark doing appreciably worse. The EU average is 18 per cent, with many countries protecting twice as much of their land area as we are.[4]

But what we are *appalling* at is then ensuring that these habitats are protected in practice, not just on paper. The most recent government report on the status of our EU-protected habitats concluded that 85 per cent of them are in an unfavourable (i.e. inadequate or bad) condition. Nearly half (46 per cent) demonstrate ongoing decline. Remember, these are the protected habitats!

When you wipe out animals' homes, they die out. 'If you're in your late 40s like I am, you'll remember the air being thick with insects when you were a child in the summertime. The car windscreen was splattered with insects, moths would gather at night time around street lights or, if you were camping, there would just be insects everywhere. And now there aren't,' points out Pádraic Fogarty, author of *Whittled Away: Ireland's Vanishing Nature*.[5] 'They've just gone.'

Needless to say, that has an impact up the food chain. 'Most of our bird life depends on insects, and though we've not seen a total collapse in our bird population, we've seen many birds effectively disappear. If a bird goes from being common in every county in Ireland down to less than 100 pairs in one or two counties, that's effectively extinct. Whatever job it did in the countryside is not being done anymore. The corncrake, for instance, is extinct from every county except for a handful of spots in the north-west. That has happened to many, many species.'

'Many of our fish that we used to eat for dinner are in that category. We don't eat whiting for dinner anymore – they're just not there. Herring populations have collapsed all over the place. So have salmon. So have eels. The abundance of life that existed, even in the 70s, has just gone off a cliff.'

The 1970s was the decade when the world began to wake up to environmentalism and Ireland was no exception. Éamon de Buitléar was making TV programmes about Irish wildlife on a par with David Attenborough. Our first environmental agency, An Foras Forbartha, got up and running. We passed the first piece of legislation to protect wildlife, the Wildlife Act, in 1976. Politicians made commitments to create national parks and nature reserves around the country. We were off to a good start.

But the enthusiasm didn't last. Fogarty, ironically, sees the introduction of the Habitats Directive as a contributory reason because it disempowered local politicians, who came to view protection as a European project. I suspect our early idealism also crashed into realpolitik. Everyone salutes the idea of a nature reserve as long as it is not going to restrict what I can do with *my* land. 'A lot of those protected areas are on private lands so that is where the problem comes in, dealing with farmers and landowners. If you mention "designated area" to a farmer today, the look on their face will tell you everything!'

Instead of something that benefits the land and therefore the landowner, protection has translated into limitation and loss. A farmer with a wet end to their field or part that is bramble-covered will have their European Common Agricultural Policy payments deducted because of it. We have a system that actively penalises farmers for having wildlife on their land!

But even where the State owns the land, we are failing. 'We have a National Parks and Wildlife Service, which was defunded after the economic crash. Its project budget was cut by 70 per cent and there was no hiring. The task of the National Parks and Wildlife Service is to manage our national parks, it's to enforce the Wildlife Act, it's to implement the Habitats Directive and the Birds Directive, and we give them less money than we give the greyhound industry!'

While the government took steps to increase funding for the service in 2021, remember that the vast majority of our countryside is not designated as a special protection area so the harm that is happening there is unobserved and unrestricted. We are simply not encouraging sufficient consideration of nature in the uses we incentivise.

Transforming so-called 'unproductive' natural land into farmland for food production or forestry for timber or stripping peatlands for fuel is economically rewarded, but our wildlife pays for it with their lives. 'In order to continue to grow the volume of milk powder from a dairy farm, you have to pollute your river,' claims Fogarty. 'You have to release greenhouse gases, and you have to use chemical sprays to eradicate anything that isn't grass in your field, and that means you're not going to have bees and you're not going to have butterflies.' Industrialised fishing has similarly depleted and destroyed our fish stocks, emptying out our seas.

We have laws that are designed to ensure we get the balance right, but they are not being acted on. 'We have been drawing up plans for biodiversity protection now since the 1990s. We have a law that was supposed to have ended all overfishing by 2020. Yet these things don't get implemented. And why is that? I think partly it's because politicians don't tend to win elections based on saving the curlew from going extinct!'

Ireland became only the second country in the world to declare a climate and biodiversity emergency, on 10 May 2019, just a week after the UK had been the first. There was no immediate legislative response, however. A nice headlining statement of intent with little substance behind it.

'There are about 36 cases outstanding before the European Court of Justice charging Ireland with environmental infringement. Why are we not implementing environmental law? I think that fundamentally comes down to our societal relationship with nature, that we see nature as an obstacle to economic development.'

That is how the battle to save nature is often framed in the media. 'Whether it's climate action, or ending turf cutting on bogs to save protected areas, these things are portrayed as negative, as being an attack on our culture and an attack on our livelihoods and an attack on our way of life.'

I believe that there is an awakening, though. The success of David Attenborough's recent TV programmes and his activism on climate change and biodiversity has made us question our previous assumptions. The searching questions asked by our kids today are beginning to stir our guilty conscience.

What do we need to do to stop the rot and aid nature's restoration? 'In the short term, we need to invest in the National Parks and Wildlife Service, we need to invest in nature-friendly farming and fishing and forestry and in nature-friendly towns,' says Fogarty. We need to build our collective understanding of how to live and work in a way that is mutually beneficial to the flora and fauna we live amongst. To appreciate that we are *of* nature, not *apart* from it.

We acknowledged that the rights of children were undervalued in the past by making a change to our Constitution and placing them there indelibly. We should now do the same for the natural environment. It would help to reset the priorities of our legislators and to guide our judiciary.

As Fogarty says, 'We have a wonderful opportunity now if we grasp it, if we really pulled together at every level from our community right the way up through local authorities through to the office of the Taoiseach. [...] What a wonderful country we would have in 50 years' time if we embraced it.'

Ireland Is the Second-Most Expensive Place to Live in Europe

Price levels in Europe's most expensive countries relative to the EU average in 2019

SOURCE: EUROSTAT⁶

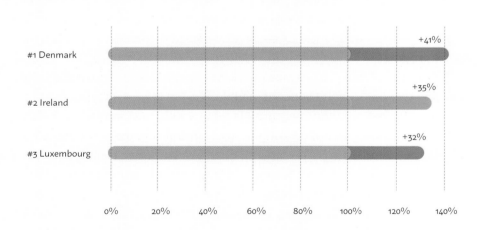

It may be a joy to live in Ireland, but you pay a price for the privilege. The prices of consumer goods and services are way above the rest of the European Union. A typical basket of items costs 35 per cent more than the European average, making us the second-most expensive EU country to live in after Denmark.

Our prices are most out of line for alcoholic and tobacco products. We are the most expensive country in the EU for these, with our prices 90 per cent above average. Having said that, we have made a deliberate decision to tax these products highly for health reasons which, as I showed earlier, has paid positive dividends in reducing consumption.

Less positive is the fact that we are amongst the most expensive countries for communications services such as mobile phones, landlines and broadband. Our restaurant and hotel prices are well above the norm, while the cost of food and energy and transport are all above average too.

Our cost of furniture is, however, well below average and household appliances, consumer electronics, clothing and footwear are generally as cheap here as anywhere else in Europe. The analysis, though, does not include important day-to-day costs such as housing and childcare.

The problem with being an expensive country to live in is that talented people will move away or will never locate here in the first place. We can't just choose to be a high-wage, low-cost country, but we certainly need to strive towards being a high-wage, lower-cost economy if we are to continue to attract the talent and the investment we need to sustain the country's future progress.

'Thirty years ago, the typical project the IDA was attracting was probably two-and-a-half thousand people in a big manufacturing facility. Half the cost base in manufacturing is what you import in raw materials so the labour costs are important but, in the grand scheme of things, it's a third of the overall thing. IDA projects now are one or two hundred people in services or R&D and 70 or 80 or sometimes 90 per cent of the cost base of those firms is wages. So the cost of labour and the cost of living is hugely important now,' explains Ronan Lyons, Assistant Professor of Economics at Trinity College Dublin. 'It's *how many* projects have we lost, rather than have we lost *any* projects.'

Our geography is part of the challenge. 'It is tougher because we're a smaller country and we're quite spread out. Sprawl contributes to the high cost of living because it makes healthcare more expensive, it makes broadband more expensive, it even makes retail more expensive if you've to spread goods out over a bigger number of stores.'

Most impactful of all, however, will be increasing competition, which can be partly achieved by further opening up to attract lower-cost providers from elsewhere in Europe. Think about the impact that Aldi and Lidl's arrival had on the food sector, for example. We need to seek to replicate that in communications and energy and transport provision, for example.

Lyons also highlights the need to tackle the high cost of insurance and legal services. Doing so would have knock-on benefits to other areas. Reducing the price of insurance would help reduce costs in the childcare sector, for example. Reducing legal costs would reduce the cost of purchasing and developing housing. Our childcare and accommodation costs are completely out of line with those in other countries and we need to find solutions to both if we are to continue to progress as a nation.

4 Our Childcare Is Amongst the Most Expensive in the World

We are a country that values children and we like to have more of them than nearly any of our European neighbours. We also aim to provide equality of opportunity in the workplace. But we are failing to put in place sufficient supports for parents of young children to be able to reconcile these competing objectives. The cost of childcare in Ireland is amongst the highest to be found anywhere in the world.

For two parents on the average wage with two pre-school children, childcare will absorb around 18 per cent of their take-home pay. That is the fifth-highest in the world, behind Switzerland, the United Kingdom, New Zealand and Japan. The comparable figure in Norway is just 5 per cent. In Spain it is 4 per cent. In Italy it is zero – the state provides fully funded childcare for all.

'Think of a woman at this stage in her career when she's in her 20s or early 30s and having her first and second child. One or two thousand euro a month for a young couple who have a mortgage and are at the early stages of a career when it's important to really work hard and make a good impression and really focus on your job. How can you also have children and pay for all that private childcare?' asks Dr Margret Fine-Davis of Trinity College Dublin. 'It's just an impossible situation.'

Percentage of net household income required for childcare

SOURCE: OECD[7]

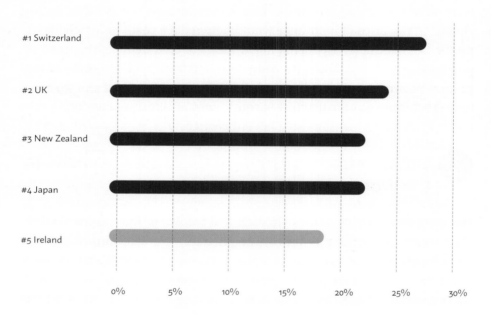

The difference with many other European nations is that they have put in place public provision. Irish policy developed differently. 'Because so few married women were in the workforce until the early 1970s, childcare was not on the policy agenda.' Despite a plethora of reports over the decades, no meaningful government initiatives were forthcoming. It took until 1998, when married women were flooding into the workforce to energise the Celtic Tiger, before European and national funding was made available to increase the supply and quality of childcare. A billion euro was spent up until the Great Recession establishing and upgrading childcare facilities and supporting the salaries of childcare workers.

The State's approach was to subsidise childcare services in the community and to only directly provide services to the disadvantaged. The Child Benefit Allowance was increased substantially over several budgets to assist with childcare costs, and a €1,000 annual childcare payment for children under six was introduced in 2006. However, the sums went nowhere near covering the actual costs involved.

A notable change took place in 2010 with the introduction of a free pre-school year for three-year-olds. It was the first time the State took some direct responsibility for care provision for pre-schoolers. The programme offers up to three hours of care per day in a centre of the parents' choice, with a focus on the child's educational development. The take-up of the programme has been high, with over 90 per cent of eligible children availing of it, and it was subsequently extended to provide a second year.

However, this provision falls far short of providing a complete childcare solution for working parents. 'It involves two-and-a-half hours or three hours a day for children that's free for five days. So that comes to about 15 hours a week,' explains Fine-Davis. 'But if a woman is working full time, that's a 35-hour week. So if she wants to cover her childcare for the full day, she has to pay for the rest of it. That's a problem. And they still don't provide care for children under three.'

An absence of affordable care is a block on further increasing female participation in the workforce. It limits women's ability to fully utilise the education that they, and the State, have invested so much in acquiring. And it limits women's potential to contribute to Irish society and to the development of the nation.

This is especially so for single mothers, a high proportion of whom are not in employment. 'Lone parents have particular constraints because they have less time available due to a lack of support from a partner. They are also at relatively high risk of poverty because of lower educational levels together with low employment rates. Unless such women are helped out of this poverty trap, the cycle of poverty is likely to be perpetuated into the next generation.' Childcare is an essential component of the support they need.

This will require a pivot from government. It takes responsibility for primary and secondary and tertiary education; why not for preschool education for all ages? It would significantly expand the role of the State, but for the clear benefit of its citizens and for society at large. It would enable staff-to-child ratios to be brought up to international best practice standards and lead to quality improvements in the education that our youngest children receive.

'It's a question of government priority,' points out Fine-Davis. 'We spend the lowest amount of GDP on early childhood education of nearly any other country. We are way at the bottom of the league, alongside Turkey and the Czech Republic.' Ireland is now in the fortunate position where it can afford to support the development of its youngest citizens, as so many other countries do, as well as the talents and aspirations of working parents.

5 We Are Not Building Enough New Homes

Number of house completions in select years, 1993–2020

SOURCE: THE HOUSING AGENCY

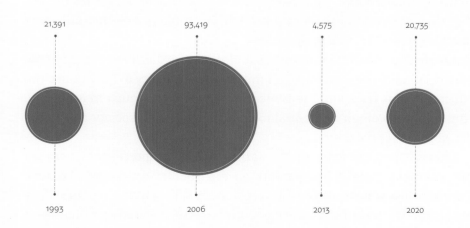

| 21,391 | 93,419 | 4,575 | 20,735 |

| 1993 | 2006 | 2013 | 2020 |

We can all agree that there is a housing crisis. We are simply not building enough homes for those who need them.

Throughout the 1970s, 80s and early 90s we built an average of 22,000 homes a year. The explosion of growth during the Celtic Tiger years reached a peak of over 93,000 dwellings built in 2006. The subsequent market collapse was absolute. Fewer than 5,000 homes were built in 2012 and 2013. Those were figures last seen during World War II when building supplies were simply unavailable.

We have experienced a nascent recovery in recent years with 2019 witnessing a return to the pre-Celtic Tiger levels. Nevertheless, a decade of insufficient supply to meet ongoing demographic growth has left a legacy of frustrated young adults unable to buy a home and facing exorbitant rents.

So how many new homes should we be building each year? Central Bank economists says we need 34,000 annually for the next decade to keep pace with the natural population increase and the expected influx of immigrants.[8] However, if you further allow for the fact that our average household size is falling – and, therefore, you need more homes to house the same number of people in the future – then that figure rises to 47,000 a year.[9] That's a huge gap to fill.

Although we had built an excess of homes before the crash, the vast majority of them were not in the major cities where we needed them. 'Dublin and Cork did not build too much housing in the noughties; they built just about the right amount or maybe a little bit less. When you go into a big unemployment crisis, it will look like you have too much housing for a short period and that was true in Dublin's case – for a year and a half it looked like it had too much. But by 2011 Dublin and Cork had already bottomed out in terms of rents and it was clear then that those cities needed new homes built, and new *rental* homes built in particular.'

With so few new homes built in Dublin, rental costs in the city practically doubled over the following decade.[10] They have now reached a level in excess of that in any other EU capital city, including Paris and Berlin.[11]

So why are we not building forty or fifty thousand new homes a year if the demand is there for them? The short answer is that the cost of building homes where they are most needed puts them outside the price range affordable for many people. And if a developer does not believe that he or she can sell them at a profit then the land will be used for something else or perhaps not at all.

A variety of factors are at play. Land prices have risen, particularly in the urban areas where people most want to live. As more land is developed, there are fewer and fewer sites available for large-scale developments that can deliver cost-effective housing – in turn increasing the demand for, and the price of, the remaining development land.

Demographic change is a contributory factor. As our household sizes decrease, the cost of housing each of us increases. 'Whether you're a household of one or a household of five, you need wiring and plumbing and core space and the permission to build – all of which costs money. So it's not that the cost of a home for one person is a fifth of the cost of building a home for five people,' says Lyons.

Direct construction costs account for between 40 and 60 per cent of the cost of a residential development so it is the increases in these that have arguably played the biggest role in putting new homes beyond the reach of many.[12] Construction costs have risen as our building regulations have required higher and higher standards of construction.

Increasing standards were a response to the poor quality of some of what was built during the Celtic Tiger years. 'Regulations were brought in between 2006 and 2016 about minimum sizes, about lifts and basement car parking spaces, and ceiling heights, and balcony depth, and energy efficiency, and all kinds of stuff. These things bring benefits to the people who do get to enjoy them, but they all add to the cost.'

Increasing the cost of building a home inevitably reduces the number that can be built and sold profitably. And it is, of course, those in the lowest income brackets who lose out. Lyons is not suggesting that introducing the regulations was not the right thing to do. Rather, we need to be aware of the cost as well as the benefit of each of them and to consider bringing in countervailing grants or other financial supports to cover the additional costs if we want to keep house prices down.

We can also act to reduce land costs. A tax on vacant sites and derelict sites in urban areas was introduced in 2018 to discourage landowners from hording land and waiting for its value to increase rather than using it now for housing. The taxes have, however, been implemented haphazardly in different local authority areas and have yet to prove to be of any notable value in stimulating development.

Lyons is an advocate of a more comprehensive property tax, whereby tax would be paid on the true value of the site if it were to be put to the best possible use for society. 'Suppose you're a golf club in Dublin 4 and you're using up maybe 100 acres of the most expensive residential land in the country. I'm not saying we should ban golf clubs! What I'm saying is that you should pay society for the fact that you're underusing those acres. And the same if you're Dublin Bus and you've a bus depot in Dublin 4 or Clontarf. You should pay based on the best permissible use of that site – that is, if the site were empty tomorrow, what would it be used for? And if it would be used to put 200 apartments on, then you should be paying tax as if it were 200 apartments.'

Existing family homes and farms would be exempted, but Lyons' approach would capture everything else in an egalitarian manner. It would hugely improve the availability of land for development and bring down the cost of whatever we built. Denmark and Estonia have this in place so there is no reason we could not do it here.

As we become an increasingly urban society with shrinking household sizes, where we build our future homes, and the types of homes that they need to be, will evolve. Urban homes for one or two people will dominate. They will be apartments and townhouses rather than the detached or semi-detached suburban houses we have focused on building up until now. Those already lucky enough to be in their own houses need to be open to neighbouring infill housing and new developments if we are to address the crisis and meet our future housing needs as a nation.

We, furthermore, need to get used to the fact that more of us will be renting our homes too. 'You typically end up with housing for smaller households being rented because the upfront costs are so great that one organisation will build a block of these things and they'll just rent them out. And there's nothing wrong with that.' It's a common model in most other European countries that needs to become part of our housing solution too.

However we choose to do it, we need to rapidly ramp up construction of affordable new homes. This is to avoid excluding an entire generation from the possibility of owning one and also to restore the country's competitiveness in being able to attract skilled labour and avoid excessive demands for higher wages to cover inflated rents and mortgages. Failure to do so will exacerbate the painful growth in homelessness that we have experienced in recent years.

6 Homelessness Has Hugely Increased

Number of homeless adults and children, 2014–21

SOURCE: FOCUS IRELAND/DEPARTMENT OF HOUSING, LOCAL GOVERNMENT AND HERITAGE

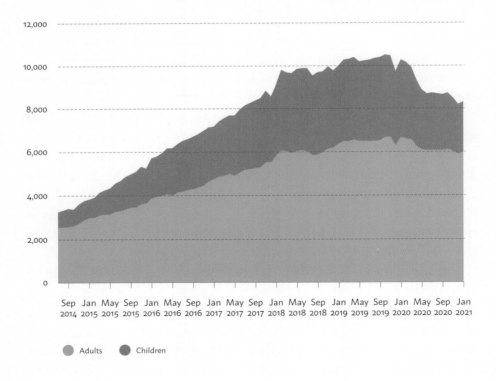

Homelessness has become a serious problem in recent years. Reliable measurement of the number of people who are homeless only started in 2014. Over the following five years, the number more than tripled. Sadly, the increase was proportionally greater amongst children, where the number grew more than five-fold, to leave nearly 4,000 children without a home in 2019.

It is important to acknowledge that most people are homeless for a relatively short time. 'When you're trying to understand homelessness, think of a river and not a lake,' says Mike Allen, Director of Advocacy for Focus Ireland. 'Some people get stuck, but actually there's a huge number of people going through and the vast majority move out of it very quickly.' The flipside of that is that the official figures only give us a snapshot in time – the number of adults and children who found themselves homeless *at some point* in the past decade is a multiple of this.

There are two primary causes of homelessness. There are structural factors such as the lack of affordable housing and unemployment or poverty resulting in an inability to afford a home; and there are personal factors such as addictions, mental health issues or family breakdown. 'The people who tend to be stuck in homelessness the longest tend to have mental health issues or addiction issues. That's why they get stuck, but it's not why they become homeless.'

The recent rise in homelessness is driven by the fact that we are just not building enough homes. If there are not enough to go around, then it is those most vulnerable amongst us, or those on the lowest incomes, who are most likely to lose out in the hunt for one.

Before the Great Recession Ireland was doing really well in tackling homelessness. 'In the 1970s and 80s, the homeless were seen as a single, probably an older, man with drink problems on the street. But you began to get the emergence of more women's homelessness and family homelessness, so the Irish State identified this as an issue that they could deal with.'

The government established a Cross-Departmental Team on Homelessness, which published the State's first strategy for reducing homelessness in 2000. The health services and the local authorities and NGOs worked together to provide all the dimensions of support that each individual needed. Local authorities maintained rough sleeping teams to support people moving off the streets and into shelters. Those who were housed were provided with social supports to help them to hold onto their tenancy rather than just being left to fend for themselves.

Such excellent progress was made that the follow-on strategy in 2008 aimed to entirely eliminate rough sleeping and long-term homelessness by 2010. We came very close to doing so. 'We probably reached the lowest level of homelessness that we had achieved in the post-war period,' says Allen. 'There was no rough sleeping outside of Dublin of any significance. Nobody was rough sleeping in Cork or Galway. And the numbers in homeless emergency accommodation had fallen to a considerable level so we were actually closing homeless shelters.'

The collapse of the Celtic Tiger did not stop progress, at first. 'Although the crash happened in 2008, things continued to get better in homelessness until about 2011 or 2012. Then the effects hit us like a delayed wave.'

The collapse of the construction of new homes collapsed the construction of social housing also. The era when local authorities built their own housing stock was long gone. From 2000 on, in return for granting planning permission for a private development, up to 10 per cent of the houses or apartments that were built could be reserved for social housing. A wonderful concept that delivers social integration. But when the private sector stops building altogether, there is simply no additional social housing available when it is most needed.

It wasn't just the absence of new social housing that was a problem; the private rented sector actually began to shrink. 'The rental sector had grown enormously from 10 to 20 per cent of the housing stock over the boom period. A lot of that was people buying a house as an investment. When things started to go bad for them, they tried to get out,' explains Allen.

'We have quite a high level of security for tenants in the private rented sector under Irish legislation, with one big proviso, which is you can end the tenancy if the landlord wants to sell or to move a family member back in. So that's what started to happen, and you started getting very large numbers of families becoming homeless from about 2014. People who were working ending up becoming homeless because the landlord was selling up and they couldn't find anywhere else to go.'

Other landlords identified a growing opportunity to earn more income by replacing long-term tenants with short-term holiday letting through new websites like Airbnb. 'It was a very unfortunate thing to happen in parallel to the overall shortage of housing. It didn't *cause* the shortage, but it exacerbated it.'

It was families that ended up bearing the brunt of these market forces. 'In 2013 there's probably about 200 homeless families max in the whole of Ireland. So suddenly it's 1,000 families, and suddenly it's 1,500 families, and there was really no homeless family infrastructure in the same way as there were shelters going back decades for single people.'

The State responded by increasing the amount of emergency accommodation available. A lot of it was in hotels. It is worth pausing to consider the irony of that. Some families were losing their tenancies to enable the dwelling to be rented to tourists. So the families with nowhere to go were being housed in hotels, thereby forcing more tourists into the market for rented properties. And, as tourist demand increased, so did the appeal for landlords of turfing out more long-term tenants. That constitutes the very definition of a vicious circle.

Hotels or other temporary accommodation are obviously completely unsuitable places to try to raise a family. Dedicated facilities for housing homeless families together were created. A homeless Housing Assistance Payment was made available to provide extra welfare payments to homeless families to price themselves back into the rental market. And a greater proportion of the available social housing was offered to those who were homeless. It has begun to pay some dividends with the number of homeless families dropping over the past two years. It is not that fewer people are becoming homeless but rather that there are an increasing number of places that they can go.

The success with families is not yet being replicated with single adults, where the numbers have remained fairly constant for a few years now. Rough sleeping remains an issue in Dublin even though the number of shelter beds available has more than doubled in the past six or seven years.

We need a plan to end homelessness – not only to reduce it, as the current government ambition is. It needs to be an integrated plan too. What worked well in the past was a joined-up approach across local authorities, the health services and NGOs. We are a small country. It isn't hard to provide the holistic supports that our most vulnerable neighbours need if we put our minds to it.

Fundamentally, of course, any solution to this issue is tied up with the fact that we simply need more homes built. But that needs to include a sufficient amount of social housing, and homeless people need to get priority access to those homes as they become available.

With political commitment, better social supports and increasing construction, there is no reason we cannot effectively eliminate homelessness in Ireland. It has been done elsewhere in Europe.[13] And we nearly achieved it here just a decade ago.

 ## Most of Us Have Excess Weight or Obesity

Percentage of those aged 15+ living with normal weight, overweight or obesity

SOURCE: DEPARTMENT OF HEALTH

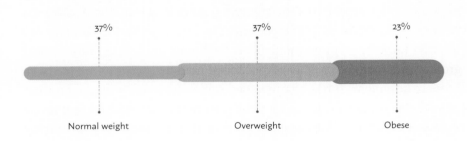

| 37% | 37% | 23% |
| Normal weight | Overweight | Obese |

Our nutrition has improved over the century. Our forebears were not getting enough calories and vitamins and minerals to fulfil their body's genetic potential. That's one of the reasons why we are taller and living longer than them.

We have, however, swung too far in the other direction. It is not famine we have to fear nowadays but feast. The Department of Health's Healthy Ireland survey finds that a minority – fewer than four in ten adults – can be classified as having normal weight. Six in ten of us live with excess weight. Nearly a quarter of the entire adult population now lives with obesity.[14]

While the growth in excess weight we are experiencing is far from an Irish phenomenon – it is being experienced in every developed nation in the world – the prognosis for Ireland is the worst in all of Europe, by some accounts. A study for the WHO predicts that we will be the most obese country on the continent by 2030 if the trends we have experienced in recent decades continue.[15] Nearly nine in ten of all adult men and women are forecast to have excess weight by the end of this decade. Half of us are expected to be living with obesity.

These are shocking figures. And they will have shocking impacts on our health, our quality of life and our very lifespans. It took a few decades of widespread smoking before science was able to definitively link it to cancers and early deaths. You had to wait for smokers to start dying prematurely in sufficient numbers before you could quantify the impact. A similar fate may await those amongst us with excess weight who are in their 40s and 50s today – it will take a full generation to see the health impacts work through.

Endocrinologist Dr Jean O'Connell, who chairs the Association for the Study of Obesity on the Island of Ireland, points out that obesity is a brain-related disease. Up to 80 per cent of obesity is determined by genetic predisposition, not by environmental factors. (In that respect, your weight is almost as genetically determined as your height.)

Despite this, the public health message puts the emphasis on eating less and exercising more. There is clearly a benefit in everyone becoming healthier, regardless of their body size, but O'Connell is clear that encouraging dieting is no solution. 'If people are finding a new way of eating is helping them to lose weight and they're feeling better, I always say, "That's great. Is it healthy and nutritious? Are you enjoying it? And do you think you can eat this way for the rest of your life?" If the answer is yes, fantastic. If the answer is no, it's no good.'

It is not just about improving what we eat. If you are not getting enough sleep, or if your sleep is regularly interrupted, your hunger hormones go up. Shift work has a similarly negative effect on your body's ability to manage energy. Chronic physical or psychological stress does the same. And so do some prescribed medications, in particular some antidepressants.

The multifaceted causes of excess weight will require multifaceted solutions. There is no silver bullet.

Altering food production and marketing has a central role to play. 'Food companies spend millions on making their product appealing, brightly coloured, and in exactly the position in the supermarket where your child is going to see it,' points out O'Connell. 'We have to address what's going into processed food and how it's being marketed heavily to children and adolescents and families. Most major social media platforms have restrictions on advertising of tobacco, alcohol and gambling to children but there are hardly any such restrictions in place around unhealthy food.'

And it goes all the way through to the laws and policies we put in place. 'The government doesn't reimburse people for medications to help manage their weight because they mistakenly think "why waste money for medication when you can just eat less and that will solve the problem". And that's why there isn't enough funding for bariatric surgery services and why we don't have education programmes for GPs and public health nurses and in schools.

'We need to change the narrative around obesity, so we all understand that obesity is a complex disease and, if you are living with this disease, it is not your fault,' concludes O'Connell. 'If we all stopped judging people because of their body size, then they might be more inclined to ask for help from a healthcare professional and we'll have more research and funding for treatments.'

We will need to make structural changes to our society to avoid the cataclysmic health impacts that we are storing up for our future. We are not alone, of course – scientific and medical advances made elsewhere will help us to manage the challenge. Urgent action is required at an individual level, yes, but more importantly at a societal level and a government level if we are to preserve the health gains that we have made in recent decades.

8 Third-Level Funding Has Halved

Reduction in funding per student

SOURCE: PARLIAMENTARY BUDGET OFFICE[16]

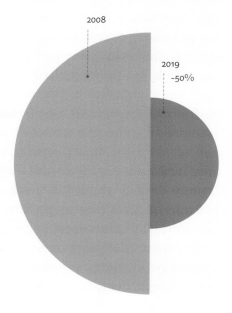

2008

2019
-50%

Increasing our level of education has been one the critical success factors that underpins Ireland's success in the world. Yet since the Great Recession, government investment in higher education has declined sharply. Student numbers have charged ahead but government investment has yet to even be restored to pre-recession levels. The result is that the level of government funding per student is half what it was back in 2008.

'The rhetoric of government ministers has escalated about how important higher education is, and how vital it is to national economic salvation, but that rhetoric is combined with a much more parsimonious approach to higher education funding,' observes Dr John Walsh of Trinity College Dublin's School of Education. 'The period between 2008 and 2015 saw the greatest decline in public resources devoted to higher education since the 1950s. At a time when student numbers were expanding rapidly, the proportion of public funding for higher education declined significantly.'

Institutions scrambled to make up the loss of income from new sources. One strategy that proved successful was to grow the number of international students from outside the EU who pay much higher fees for the privilege of attending an Irish college or university. Sadly, the Covid outbreak put paid to that approach with students unable or unwilling to leave their home countries. It left an estimated half a billion euro black hole in the sector's finances.[17]

Student registration fees have increased to a record high. And costs have had to be cut too. The student-to-staff ratio increased from 16:1 in 2007 to 20:1 a decade later, with a consequent impact on the quality of teaching.

Irish universities are now tumbling down the league table of international rankings. Trinity College Dublin, University College Dublin and the University of Limerick have each dropped by around 40 places since 2011. Dublin City University and University College Cork have both dropped around a hundred spots. Maynooth University has dropped 200. And Technological University Dublin has dropped more than 400.[18] The National University of Ireland Galway has bucked the trend and risen nearly 50 places, but overall that's a pretty depressing picture of third-level education in Ireland today.

This is not in Ireland's national interest. To renege on our policy of developing our human capital is to eliminate the country's competitive edge in the twenty-first century. It is cutting off our nose to spite our face.

Remember, we are not genetically smarter than previous generations. We simply failed to invest sufficiently in the potential of many of those who went before us. If we are to continue to improve the lives of as many of our citizens as possible then it behoves us to continue to invest in their futures. Education to the highest possible level – not just when we are young, but throughout our lives – is a critical success factor for us as individuals and together as a nation.

9 Our Government Debt Is Amongst the Highest in the World

Gross public debt per person, 1995 –2022

SOURCE: EUROPEAN COMMISSION[19]

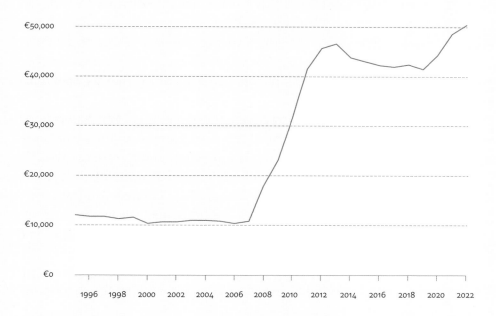

Here is Ireland's debt mountain. And it is very steep indeed.

The amount of public debt we incurred before the economic crash of 2008 was stable at around €40 billion. That is to say, the government had borrowed €10–12,000 for every man, woman and child in the country. It was far from an excessive amount and, with hindsight, it is a wonder we did not take the opportunity to pay it all off when we had the resources to do so. Government, no doubt, took consolation from the fact that as our economy accelerated rapidly, the amount we owed as a percentage of our GDP or GNI was shrinking fast.[20]

The crash reversed that in quick time. With a huge sum required to support the banking sector, our debt quadrupled in just five years. By 2012 the country owed €210 billion – nearly €46,000 for every one of us. Although that figure had barely shifted before Covid hit, our continued population growth was spreading the load and making some inroads into reducing the amount owned per person.

Needless to say, the Covid crisis undid all of that and pushed our borrowing to new record heights. It is estimated that the country will owe €250 billion by 2022. That is approximately €50,000 each. Even if the government set aside €2.5 billion a year to pay back the principal sum, it would take us 100 years to pay it all off! However, the annual interest payments alone total over €5 billion – equivalent to what we spend on capital investment each year.[21]

Sure, doesn't every country owe huge sums of money? Yes. But, believe it or not, we are amongst the most indebted nations on the planet. We share the accolade with Japan, the US, Belgium and Italy. Even though interest rates are at an historic low, countries with rising public debt suffer slower economic growth than those where it is falling.[22] And we need economic growth to provide us with the additional resources to repay the debt. There is a delicate balance to avoid entering a vicious circle of economic stagnation.

It will also become increasingly difficult for us to reduce our debt as our population ages. More public pensions to pay, more healthcare for older folk and proportionally fewer people of working age paying taxes will diminish our ability to tackle the debt mountain.[23] Action sooner rather than later is therefore important.

Post-Covid, the first priority is to restore a balanced budget. We need to ensure that we can hold on to the social and economic gains we have made; we need to endeavour to avoid the damage that austerity measures impose; and then we need to look to invest in Ireland's future.

Although some political parties promise to spend, spend, spend if they are in government, our history offers us a strong lesson in the value of fiscal restraint. The overspending in the late 1970s left us unprepared for the oil crises that followed and undid the embryonic economic growth that openness was beginning to deliver. The overspending of the Celtic Tiger era and our unpreparedness for the Great Recession similarly hurt many in the austere years that followed.

We cannot spend beyond our means. The only way that we can continue to improve our quality of life is through ongoing economic growth that provides the uplift in tax revenue we need to pay our debts and invest in our future. That is why our education levels, our community spirit, our openness and our national stability need to be protected and nourished. Together, these will spur the provision of the additional resources that we need to tackle the challenges I have identified and to continue on the journey of national well-being.

10 Fewer of Us Are Voting

Turnout in general elections, 1973–2020

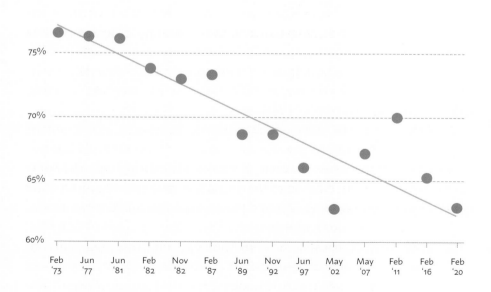

We cannot keep our nation on a positive course if we are not all invested in its success. We have a proportional representation electoral system that allows every citizen's voice to be heard. A vote cast here has more relevance and more impact than a vote cast in many other democracies. To opt not to vote is to opt out of having a meaningful say on the trajectory and speed of the changes that I have highlighted throughout.

Our continued advancement is tied to the quality of the government we have in place. The evidence I have presented suggests that politicians who are committed to nurturing the success factors that have brought us this far, and who have policy platforms to address the areas where more progress is needed, are those who require support if we are to continue to flourish.

Even if you believe that we need to go in a different direction, or perhaps to prioritise other areas where progress has been insufficient, a failure to voice that at the ballot box results in a less representative government focused on addressing the concerns expressed by others.

The right to vote was divorced from property ownership requirements and extended to the general public in Great Britain and Ireland in 1918. However, this was not true universal suffrage. While men aged over 21 could vote, women had to be aged over 30. It was the Irish Free State that introduced equality in 1922 by reducing the voting age for women in Dáil elections to 21. Just 100 years ago. And it was only 50 years ago, in 1972, that the voting age for both genders was reduced to 18. The ability of all adults to influence the course of the nation is a relatively recently won right. Yet our exercise of it is in decline.

Over three-quarters of the registered electorate voted in the general elections of the 1970s. In the 80s and 90s the figure declined but still exceeded two-thirds of us. However, in 2002 and again in 2020, the figure fell to just 63 per cent – the lowest participation rate since the State's first general election in 1923.

Why are we increasingly opting to let others decide our future? One-third of non-voters say it is because they have not registered themselves to vote, one-third identify practical issues on polling day (that they were away from home or had difficulty getting to the polling station, for example) and most of the final third say they are either not interested in politics or are disillusioned with it.[24]

I have seen research results like this many times in my career. If you did not bother to get yourself registered to vote or did not manage to overcome the practical difficulties of turning out on polling day, the truth is that you weren't sufficiently motivated. It may be a step too far to say that most of these voters are equally uninterested in or disillusioned by politics, but I believe it's fair to conclude that most of them were just insufficiently interested or enthusiastic. That smacks of complacency.

'It's certainly not unique to Ireland,' points out journalist Shane Coleman. 'It's a feature across the western world that as we become more prosperous, as we become better educated, ironically, we are less engaged with politics.' Surveys show that the less education people have, the less likely they are to vote. Yet, surprisingly, as Ireland's education levels have shot up in recent decades, our total voter participation levels have declined.

'I was in a pub in Crossmaglen last year and there were copies of the *Irish Independent* on the wall from the 1940s and 1950s. As a journalist, I found it fascinating because there'd be six or seven stories on the front pages, and they were *all* stories about global issues. Something that Eisenhower was bringing before the Houses of Congress was *page one* of the paper! Most of them wouldn't even get into the newspaper now, never mind be on page one. It just struck me that despite all our education, people were more engaged, were more interested, were more informed about what was going on in the world back then than we are now.'

It is reasonable to assume that cynicism is an increased factor, driven by the political scandals of the 1980s and '90s and the failure of politicians to avoid the economic collapse of the late noughties. I have also discussed the repeated narrative of 'crisis' that is thrown liberally into political discourse – inevitably leading to voter disillusionment with the fact that no politician seems to be able to 'solve' our urgent problems, despite their promises to the contrary. And, of course, we are prone to underestimating precisely how much positive change has been delivered by our politicians over the decades.

Perhaps voters believe that it matters less who is in power nowadays. Given our high levels of education and wealth, do we think that our destiny is far more in our own hands than in the hands of the government? Some may feel that it's irrelevant who is in power – it won't impact much on their lives one way or the other.

We cannot honestly claim that we have less time available for politics than our forebears. But perhaps there are simply more things to fill our days and to fill our minds? On-tap entertainment is omnipresent wherever we go via the smartphone in our pocket. When you have infinite digital worlds to explore, movies to stream, music to listen to and hobbies to indulge, then politics can get relegated to the back seat – or even to the boot.[25]

If there is one important lesson we can learn from looking to our Anglophone neighbours to the east and to the west, it is the danger of voter disengagement. Failure to build a shared understanding of the country's successes and comfort with its current direction can tear the country apart.

In complacency, there is jeopardy. To continue to build on what we have achieved, to deliver for the next generation that will follow us, we need everyone engaged. Let us leave no one behind. We all have a job to do.

(18)

Continuing Our Progress

THIS IS A BOOK FOR OPTIMISTS. IF YOU ARE A CYNIC ABOUT THE PRESENT OR A PESSIMIST ABOUT THE FUTURE THEN YOU MAY HAVE EXPERIENCED RAISED BLOOD PRESSURE LEVELS THROUGHOUT. YOU MAY ALSO WISH TO PUT THE BOOK DOWN AT THIS POINT, BECAUSE I CONTEND THAT IF OUR PRESENT IS EXCELLENT, OUR FUTURE WILL BE EVEN BETTER. IF WE DON'T MESS IT UP.

LET'S START BY accepting that we have done well as a nation. There is no cause to be smug; but there is good reason to stop doubting ourselves or putting ourselves down. We may be a small nation still, but we are no longer an underdog. We should take time to recognise and celebrate our successes from time to time, and a 100th birthday is as good an occasion as any.

My overview of a century of progress shows that most of the first half century resulted in very little of it at all. It was when we opened up to the world and invested in our self-development that we began the journey to a vastly better quality of life. It is the people who are alive today who changed Ireland utterly.

Generation Instigation started us out on the right path. These were the people born from the 1940s through to the 1960s who started their working lives in the 60s, 70s and 80s. Many of them availed of free second-level education and, unlike their predecessors, most were not obliged to emigrate to find work. By bringing their skills and expertise to bear at home, they were able to avail of the opportunities offered by Ireland's opening to the world, our participation in the EEC and the attraction of multinational investment. They instigated social, cultural and economic change that set the country up for success, and they were the first Irish generation to reap the benefits of those changes.

Generation Transformation were those born in the 1970s and 1980s who came of age in the 90s and the noughties. They joined forces with their predecessors to drive the transformation of the nation during the Celtic Tiger era. Unlike any prior generation, a huge number of them attained third-level qualifications. That enabled us to attract well-paying, highly skilled jobs and to massively boost the country's income and exports, supported by billions of euros of infrastructural investment from the EU. This was the generation that utterly changed the face of our workplaces as the Big Crossover saw most women proceed to take up employment with no intention of leaving it once they got married or had children. Although many were hit hard by the subsequent economic crash, this generation brought us so far forward as a country that we were never going back to the way we were before.

Generation Expectation is now taking the reins – that is, those born in the 1990s and noughties, who have come into the workforce since the 2010s. Although some caught the tail-end of the crash, the recovery was so strong, and their anticipated living standards are so high, that the expectations of this generation exceed anything that any previous cohort could have hoped for when they were the same age. While they were struggling to deal with the crash's legacy of insufficient housing before being hit with the challenge of colossal unemployment through the Covid crisis, they are destined to tackle the problems that face them and to take us even further forward.

It is a sign of our success that what so many have worked so hard to gain can now be taken for granted. We have come to expect things to be this good, and we can drive on from here in the never-ending ambition to raise every person in Irish society further up the hierarchy of national well-being.

The starting point of today's 'Generation Expectation' is so very different, but this generation is unlikely to see the rate of improvement that the previous one did simply because we have already earned promotion from Division 2 to Division 1. To achieve the same level of economic wealth and well-being as their parents would be a perfectly good outcome for many – enabling them to have a decent income, good health, a high-quality place to live and the freedom to pursue their careers and personal interests. That is not a reason not to push forward and to endeavour to fulfil everyone's reasonable expectations – rather it is a note of caution to avoid frustration if the pace of advancement proves slower.

Under all circumstances, however, we want to avoid a reversal. We know too well that continued progress is not inevitable. Look to the recent history of the United States: the election of Donald Trump was followed by four years of reversal of progress on environmental issues, in international trade, in immigration, in personal freedoms, in political ethics and in compassion. Some aspects of the economy flourished but the well-being of Americans declined and the nation's happiness level was recorded at its lowest on record.[1]

We are one of the world's leading, progressive, liberal democracies. It is time to reconceptualise ourselves as being amongst Nordic peers, not alongside our historical cousins of Britain or America. It goes without saying that we should continue to maximise mutual trade opportunities with our Anglophone neighbours, to enjoy mutual cultural exchange and to ape their successful policy initiatives for our own self-improvement. But we can learn more and benefit more from cooperation with those who share our high quality of life and who have sustained their leadership positions over many decades.

To continue going forward, we need to protect and further develop that which has got us here: inclusive politics and economic policies that are built on the four foundational blocks of our nation's success: education, openness, community and stability.

Continuing to expand participation in education, in particular increasing the numbers completing third level, is essential to drive greater national well-being. In his most recent book, renowned political scientist Robert D. Putnam shows how equality and the economy both grew significantly in America from the 1920s through to the 1970s as educational participation increased due to the expansion of public high schools and universities.[2] That growth in educational participation stalled in the mid-70s and, almost immediately, the upward trend in greater equality was reversed and began a decline that has continued to this day.

A failure to produce ever more highly qualified graduates coincided with an explosion in demand for them as high-tech jobs came to the fore. The individuals who had the right expertise saw their salaries shoot up, whilst those without the right qualifications experienced salary stagnation. The lesson is simple: more widespread education leads to more equality.

Quality of education is just as important as its prevalence in delivering benefits for both students and society. We must restore our per-student investment in higher education to its pre-economic crash level. Furthermore, we must look at supporting and incentivising lifelong learning. We will all be fit and able to work for more years than our parents were. With most jobs now in faster-changing service sectors, and with a green economy transformation underway, we will experience a need to upskill several times during our working lives. Those who cannot will fall behind, to their detriment and to that of the country as a whole. By investing more in our human capital, we can develop high-skilled centres of global excellence in sectors beyond our existing domains of manufacturing, customer support and finance.

Remaining an open, pro-globalisation economy will be central to this. Internal resistance is bound to grow as we take for granted what has got us here. Johan Norberg, author of *Open: The Story of Human Progress*, argues that every previous period of openness and innovation in history has ended due to 'Cardwell's Law': technological progress encounters resistance from groups that believe they stand to lose from innovation and they manipulate the political system to suppress it.[3] They may be political elites, businesses with old technologies, workers with outmoded skills, or old folk who feel anxious because things just aren't the way they used to be. They may endeavour to stop change with bans, regulations and monopolies to limit trade or restrict adoption. But to let them have their way would be for everyone to suffer. Instead, they need to be supported through periods of essential change.

Retaining our social openness is vital too. There is a way to go yet before women attain equality at all levels of Irish society and we reap the full benefits. And we are only beginning to embrace our immigrant communities and the 'new Irish' and what they have to offer our country culturally and economically. Their connections with people and places around the world will enable us to reach beyond the traditional diaspora and to develop new partnerships for mutual benefit.

Although it was said that Covid-19 was indiscriminate in who it infected, it was not indiscriminate in who it impacted. Sectors such as tourism and hospitality, non-essential retail and construction were closed for significant lengths of time. This impacted most on those aged under 35, those with lower levels of education, those in part-time employment and the non-Irish.[4] These groups and their communities will need our support over the next few years to get back on their feet.

Through kindness and cooperation we can preserve our social cohesiveness and build back to where we once were. 'Paying it forward' is a real thing. Numerous psychology studies have shown that generosity propagates. If we are kind to others, they really do pass on that goodwill in turn through greater acts of kindness to those in their social circle.[5] Helping others in our community builds the trust and social capital that are essential for national well-being.

We all know how Facebook was used as a platform to sow division in America and in Britain. We cannot stand by and let that happen here. Regulation of social media platforms is an important step. Hate crime legislation that encompasses online material is vital. And our police force needs to step into the twenty-first century and tackle this as a priority.

A safe and constructive political discourse is essential if we are to build on our progress. I have highlighted how underrepresented women remain in political life, never mind our ethnic minorities. Tackling toxic online abuse is a prerequisite to encouraging the contribution of all to building a better Republic. This is as much about preserving our national stability as it is about our sense of community.

Fake news has played a large role in undermining faith in political institutions elsewhere. To preserve our institutional capital reserves, we will need to control and kill it. There is much irony in the fact that Facebook and Google have pocketed the advertising spend that Irish news organisations relied on to fund professional journalism. We need to balance out the lies by financially supporting free and fair indigenous news media.

At our utmost, we must avoid political polarisation. Putnam's compilation of all the evidence he could identify for America across the twentieth and twenty-first centuries led him to conclude that economic inequality and polarisation have moved in lockstep over the entire period. That is, as polarisation decreased in the first half of the twentieth century so did inequality; and as it increased from the 1970s on, so has inequality. The evidence is that it is not inequality that drives polarisation, it is the other way around. In the long run, he concludes, polarisation can produce democratic breakdown. And, ironically, that polarisation is very often driven from the top by democratically elected politicians.

Our political centrism has proved to be a virtue. This is not an argument to vote only for Fianna Fáil or Fine Gael for evermore – surely it is only a matter of time before Sinn Féin is in government – but it is a marker that ideological politics can seed division and thereby undermine its ability to deliver the very improvement in well-being that voters wish to see.

America's inverted U-shaped trajectory offers us a wider warning too. Seventy years of positive social, cultural and political progress has been followed by sixty years of reversal. Putnam identifies the underlying cause as a shifting focus from individualism to inclusivity and back again. The world wars and Great Depression turned the focus of the American people and of policy makers towards addressing societal issues. But a perfect storm of crises in the 1960s and 70s triggered a reversal when such issues as the Vietnam War, the assassination of the Kennedys and King, Watergate and the civil rights upheaval undermined the nation's self-confidence and its faith in institutions, the rule of law and honourable leadership. People started to think only of fixing themselves.

The lesson is that decades of positive development can be reversed if individualism takes precedence over community and the pursuit of equality. And that necessitates successfully tackling mounting problems in order to give the population confidence in governance. We must ruthlessly tackle the challenges I have identified to avoid disaffection and alienation that would undermine our collective faith in the national well-being project.

We must prioritise addressing issues that directly affect the quality of life of our young adults, such as the provision of a decent supply of housing, more affordable childcare and bringing youth unemployment back to pre-pandemic levels. We must also reverse our depletion of natural capital by tackling climate change and biodiversity loss to avoid damaging our well-being and that of others on the planet. Our children have called us out on this one and, out of respect for them and their futures, the only choice is radical action.

Declining voter participation is sometimes taken as a sign that our democratic structures are not fit for purpose in the modern era. I see no fundamental problem with the manner in which we elect our public representatives. However, it is true that, in an ever more complex society, we cannot expect those representatives to be equally expert in every aspect of Irish life. We will need to find new ways to augment their knowledge and for the public to inform their decision-making. That is why I am in favour of politicians commissioning focus group research and hiring special advisors. These are exactly the sort of modern-day tools they should be utilising to carry out their jobs proficiently.

We should, furthermore, continue to explore other ways to develop our democracy and to expand its inclusivity. Ireland is already deemed a leader in 'deliberative democracy' in which we convened representative groups of citizens to come together through the Constitutional Convention and Citizens' Assembly to consider such topics as same-sex marriage, abortion and gender equality. Their balanced and deliberative consideration of the issues served to demonstrate that the minds of the people were often ahead of where our politicians believed them to be. That gave our leaders the confidence to allow the general public to have their say and to enact landmark social change.

This contemporary approach to finding solutions to complex issues offers the promise of moving our society forward in an inclusive manner that engages people on the issues and minimises polarisation. We should seek to expand it to cover other topics and other levels of government –

for example by deploying participatory budgeting in local government so communities can have a say in how money is spent in their own locality.[6]

We are not 'there' yet. Our high quality of life is not evenly distributed across everyone in Irish society. We may never be able to achieve that. But the human condition is to drive for improvement. Our last achievement quickly becomes our psychological 'set point' from which we invariably wish to drive on. It is the very psychological force that has powered human innovation and our development as a species; and it will continue to drive Ireland to an even better place, if we just let it.

We will all benefit from being crystal clear on where we want to get to. Politicians, policy makers and economists are prone to focusing on GDP or GNI or GNI* as the be-all and end-all of our success as a nation. Financial capital growth is unquestionably vital to providing the resources to do what needs to be done. But far less attention is given to measuring our human, social, institutional and natural capital, as well as individual well-being. These are what matter most to the people of Ireland. We need to put in place a set of national well-being accounts and assess government progress in delivering targeted improvements.[7]

We have good reason to be optimistic. Ireland's past is worthy of little nostalgia because there was damn all to be nostalgic about![8] Our national journey has unequivocally been towards the light; we have gained much and lost little. Is it any surprise that one global study concluded that 'the most optimistic people in the world may be young, economically secure, educated women in Ireland'?[9] We have more of those today than we have ever had before. Let's help them to further foster the well-being of our nation for the century ahead.

And let's start by all getting on the same page. We have a great story to tell of remarkable achievement. Let's spread the good news in our schools and colleges, in our workplaces, in our media and social media, so that no one fails to appreciate our progress. Buy another copy of this book and gift it to a friend or a family member for a start.

Acknowledgements

First and foremost, I must acknowledge the great work of all the data collectors, analysts, statisticians and researchers over the past century who have made this analysis possible. If nobody had thought to measure it then we would have never known. You have my utmost respect and thanks for all your good work.

In particular, I must pay tribute to the Central Statistics Office. Various teams in the CSO were more than willing to help me with my queries and to analyse or source data as required. My thanks especially to Assistant Director General Richie McMahon, who kindly gave me his copy of *That was then, This is now – Change in Ireland 1949–1999*, which marked the 50th anniversary of the creation of the CSO and tracked changes in Ireland in the second half of the twentieth century.

When my concept for this book was germinating, I met with fellow writer and the director of the Little Museum of Dublin, Trevor White, to seek his advice. I suggested I might write about ten trends that had shaped Ireland over the past century. He suggested making it a hundred. With hindsight, all I can say to that is 'thanks a lot, Trevor'. This would have been a very different book without your input!

Needless say, it is impossible for me to be an expert in every aspect of Irish life. I am, therefore, hugely grateful to all my interviewees, who were so generous in sharing their expertise and insight into their specialist areas. Unquestionably, I could not have written this without you.

Thank you also to Nicki Howard at Gill Books, who had faith that this was a book worth bringing to fruition, and all the team at Gill.

Thanks to Trevor and to Frank Humphreys for enduring draft manuscripts and giving me their honest feedback. Thanks to Djinn von Noorden for the hundreds and hundreds and hundreds of suggested edits to the final manuscript that improved it immensely.

Thanks to my sister Elaine for the occasional distractions spent researching unrelated topics.

And thanks again to my wife, Ann, and Fionn, Gráinne and Susie for the support and understanding you showed me. I promise to vacuum-clean the entire house every weekend for evermore in return.

Any errors are entirely mine.

Endnotes

INTRODUCTION

1 United Nations Development Programme (2020), 'Human Development Report 2020. The Next Frontier: Human Development and the Anthropocene', New York. Accessed online at http://hdr.undp.org/en/2020-report.

2 Franklin M. Zaromb et al. (2018), 'We Made History: Citizens of 35 Countries Overestimate Their Nation's Role in World History', *Journal of Applied Research in Memory and Cognition*, vol. 7, issue 4, December 2018, 521–28.

3 Survey undertaken by AA Car Insurance (2018): https://www.theaa.ie/blog/behaviour-roads-worsening-according-motorists.

CHAPTER 1

1 Barry O'Halloran (2019), 'Dublin house prices up almost nine times the rate incomes grew', *The Irish Times*, 31 May 2019, https://www.irishtimes.com/business/construction/dublin-house-prices-up-almost-nine-times-the-rate-incomes-grew-1.3910136.

2 However, under-reporting was a problem in those early years and some believe that the actual death rate was closer to one in 10 children in the 1920s. See Verrière, J. (1979). *La population de I'Irlande* (Mouton, Paris).

3 The Registrar General, William J. Thompson, highlighted in his 'Annual Report of the Registrar-General of Marriages, Births and Deaths in Ireland 1923' that 'the illegitimate infant mortality as derived from the records for 1923, is about 6 times the mortality among legitimate infants', is nearly three times greater than that of England and Wales and 'must be regarded as excessive' (p. xxiii).

4 Mel Cousins (1999), 'The Introduction of Children's Allowances in Ireland 1939-1944', *Irish Economic and Social History*, vol. 26, 35–53.

5 More information on the historic trends in fertility can be found in John Fitzgerald (2016), 'A Hundred and Fifty Years of Vital Statistics: Documenting Demographic Change in Ireland', *Journal of the Statistical and Social Inquiry Society of Ireland*, vol. XLV, 177–201.

6 The 1922 figure is taken from the Annual Report of the Registrar-General of Marriages, Births and Deaths in Ireland 1923.

7 P. Kennedy (2010), 'Healthcare Reform: Maternity Service Provision in Ireland', *Health Policy*, vol. 97, 145–51.

8 Wikipedia, 'List of road traffic accidents deaths in Republic of Ireland by year', https://en.wikipedia.org/wiki/List_of_road_traffic_accidents_deaths_in_Republic_of_Ireland_by_year.

9 Henry G. Tempest (1914), *The Irish Motor Directory: A directory and reference book for motorists 1914/15* (W. Tempest, Dundalgan Press, Dundalk).

10 Eurostat (2020), 'Over 23 000 victims of road accidents in the EU in 2018', accessed at https://ec.europa.eu/eurostat/en/web/products-eurostat-news/-/ddn-20200701-1.

11 Burial of Suicide Act 1823.

12 For more analysis of this see Christopher Henry Cantor, Antoon A. Leenaars & David Lester (1997), 'Under-reporting of suicide in Ireland 1960-1989', *Archives of Suicide Research*, 3:1, 5–12.

13 Brendan Walsh and Dermot Walsh (2010), 'Suicide in Ireland: The Influence of Alcohol and Unemployment', UCD Centre for Economic Research Working Paper WP10/35.

14 Brendan Walsh (2017), 'Life Expectancy in Ireland since the 1870s', *The Economic and Social Review*, vol. 48, no. 2, Summer 2017, 127–43.

15 UNDP data for 2019 in Wikipedia article 'List of countries by life expectancy' available at https://en.wikipedia.org/wiki/List_of_countries_by_life_expectancy.

CHAPTER 2

1 My thanks to the team in the Vital Statistics Unit of the CSO for identifying a comparable coding system to enable an approximate comparison to be made.

2 S.A. Plotkin and E.A. Mortimer (1988), *Vaccines* (Philadelphia: Saunders).

3 Jean Koch (1997), *Robert Guthrie – the PKU story: Crusade against mental retardation* (Pasadena, Calif.: Hope Pub. House), 65–6.

4 World Health Organization mortality database, accessed on 28 February 2021.

5   L. Andersena et al. (2002), 'Assessing a Decade of Progress in Cancer Control', *The Oncologist*, June 2002, vol. 7, no. 3, 200–4.

6   The *John Player Tops of the Town* amateur variety show aired on RTÉ TV from the mid-60s through to the mid-90s.

7   'Knot on top for Dublin's smoking bus users', *The Irish Times*, 13 February 1988, p. 1.

8   An up-to-date list can be found at the World Health Organization's website at https://www.who.int/tobacco/surveillance/en/.

9   ICF International for the Department of Health (2015), 'An assessment of the economic cost of smoking in Ireland'.

10 Z Kabir et al. (2013), 'Modelling Coronary Heart Disease Mortality declines in the Republic of Ireland, 1985-2006', *International Journal of Cardiology*, 3 Oct; 168(3): 2462–7.

11 Irish Heart Foundation (2008), 'National Audit of Stroke Care'.

12 Citing euros in real terms means that the figures are adjusted to eliminate the impact of inflation in the economy, using 2010 as the base year. Sourced at https://stats.oecd.org/viewhtml.aspx?datasetcode=SHA&lang=en#, July 2019.

13 Seán Prior (2018), 'Budget 2019 Papers: Trends in General Medical Services (GMS)', accessed at http://www.budget.gov.ie/Budgets/2019/Documents/Trends%20in%20General%20Medical%20Services%20(GMS)%20Scheme.pdf.

14 M. Starr, L. Dominiak, A. Aizcorbe (2014), 'Decomposing growth in spending finds annual cost of treatment contributed most to spending growth, 1980–2006', *Health Aff* (Millwood). 2014;33(5): 823–31.

15 The percentages are of those aged 16 and over.

CHAPTER 3

1   G.A. Holmes (1948), 'Report on the Present State and Methods of Improvement of Irish Land', Dublin.

2   Quote contained in Cormac O'Grada (1997), *Rocky Road: The Irish Economy Since the 1920s*, p. 151.

3   'Ireland really is the garden of Europe, survey finds', *The Journal*, 26 October 2013. https://www.thejournal.ie/eurostat-ireland-covered-by-the-most-grasslands-in-europe-1148673-Oct2013.

4   The data on current farm size is taken from the Central Statistic Office's 'Farm Structure Survey 2016' and the historic data is for 1915 and sourced from the CSO's 'Life in 1916 Ireland: Stories from statistics' publication.

5   The Economist Intelligence Unit (2021), 'Global Food Security Index 2020', available at https://foodsecurityindex.eiu.com.

6   The 1922 survey did not ask about some items such as alcohol, which may have resulted in an overestimate of food expenditure in that year.

7   Historical prices have been converted from pounds to euro/cent and the measures from imperial to metric. The reported cost is either for the month of May/June or is the annual monthly average.

8   Adults are defined as those aged 15 and over.

9   This assumes a bottle of vodka is 700 ml, a bottle of wine is 750 ml and a beer has an ABV of 4.3%. This analysis, and much of the subsequent data cited here, is to be found in D. Mongan and J. Long (2016), 'Overview of alcohol consumption, alcohol-related harm and alcohol policy in Ireland', HRB Overview Series 10, Health Research Board: Dublin.

10 OECD (2019), 'Health at a Glance 2019: OECD Indicators', OECD Publishing: Paris. Accessible online at https://www.oecd-ilibrary.org/social-issues-migration-health/health-at-a-glance_19991312.

11 These calculations are contained in Mongan and Long's 2016 report published by the Health Research Board, referenced above.

12 Data referenced in the NCD Risk Factor Collaboration study.

13 NCD Risk Factor Collaboration (2016), 'A century of trends in adult human height', *eLife*, vol. 5, e13410, accessed at https://elifesciences.org/articles/13410.

CHAPTER 4

1   Urban is defined as living in towns in excess of 1,500 people. Rural is defined as living in smaller communities or outside of these. Dublin refers to the full county area.

2   Brendan M. Walsh (1999), 'Urbanization and the regional distribution of population in post-Famine Ireland', UCD Centre for Economic Research Working Paper Series WP99-24, University College Dublin School of Economics.

3   Padraic Kenna (2011), *Housing Law, Rights and Policy* (Clarus Press).

4   Every town with a population greater than 10,000 in 1926 is included here. The Cork,

Limerick, Galway and Waterford figures for 1926 are for the cities only.

5   Kenna (2011) above.

6   Michelle Norris (2013), 'Varieties of home ownership: Ireland's transition from a socialised to a marketised policy regime', Geary Institute Discussion Paper WP2013/06, University College Dublin.

7   These are private households in permanent housing units.

8   Ruth McManus (2011), 'Suburban and urban housing in the twentieth century', *Proceedings of the Royal Irish Academy: Archaeology, Culture, History, Literature*, vol. 111C, Special Issue: Domestic life in Ireland, 253–86.

9   David Duffy, David Byrne, John FitzGerald (2014), 'Alternative Scenarios for New Household Formation in Ireland', *Quarterly Economic Commentary*, Spring 2014, ESRI: Dublin.

10 Ronan C. Lyons (2018), 'Ireland in 2040: Urbanization, demographics and housing', *Journal of the Statistical and Social Inquiry Society of Ireland*, vol. XLVII, Trinity College Dublin.

11 These descriptions and the following data from the 1946 census are sourced from Ruth McManus (2011), 'Suburban and urban housing in the twentieth century', *Proceedings of the Royal Irish Academy* Section C 111(-1): 7–70.

12 Cliodhna Russell (2017), 'ESB map shows when over 1,300 Irish towns, villages and parishes got electricity', *The Journal*, 24 September 2017. https://www.thejournal.ie/esb-map-electricity-came-to-ireland-3610313-Sep2017/.

13 Brian Ó Gallachóir, 'Electricity in Ireland: a brief history (1916-2015)', *Eolas Magazine*, available at https://www.eolasmagazine.ie/electricity-ireland-brief-history-1916-2015.

14 Michael Shiel (2003), *The Quiet Revolution: The electrification of rural Ireland* (O'Brien Press, Dublin).

15 Read more about the Rural Electrification Scheme online at https://esbarchives.ie/rural-electrification.

16 McManus (2011), cited earlier.

17 Lindsey P. Smith, Shu Wen Ng & Barry M. Popkin (2013), 'Trends in US home food preparation and consumption: analysis of national nutrition surveys and time use studies from 1965–1966 to 2007–2008', *Nutrition Journal*, vol. 12 (1), no. 45.

18 Suzanne M. Bianchi, Liana C. Sayer, Melissa A. Milkie, John P. Robinson (2012), 'Housework: Who Did, Does or Will Do It, and How Much Does It Matter?', *Social Forces*, vol. 91, issue 1, 55–63.

19 J. Gershuny & J.P. Robinson (1988), 'Historical changes in the household division of labor', *Demography*, vol. 25, issue 4, 537–52.

20 A.J. Litton (1961), 'The Growth and Development of the Irish Telephone System', *Journal of the Statistical and Social Inquiry Society of Ireland*, vol. XX, part V, 1961/1962, 79–115.

21 Adrian Redmond (ed.) (2000), *That was then, This is now: Change in Ireland, 1949–1999*, Central Statistics Office.

22 Techarchives, 'Ireland's first computers: 1956–1969', https://techarchives.irish/irelands-first-computers-1956-69/.

23 L. Blaney (2018), 'Accidents, Americana, and Automobility: 1950s Irish Car Culture'. *Éire-Ireland*, 53(3), 242–67.

24 Quotations from the Irish American Cultural Institute e-newsletter article 'Accidents, Automobility, and Americana: An Investigation of the History of Irish Car Culture from the Latest Issue of Éire-Ireland by Leanne Blaney' accessed at http://iaci-usa.org/images/2-19_enews.pdf.

25 Eurostat, 'Passenger cars in the EU'. https://ec.europa.eu/eurostat/statistics-explained/index.php/Passenger_cars_in_the_EU-#Overview.

26 Catherine de Courcy (2009), *Dublin Zoo: an illustrated history* (Collins, Dublin).

CHAPTER 5

1   The figures are for institutions aided by the Department of Education and Skills. The gap in the numbers attending primary and secondary level nowadays is a function of the length of time of each curriculum. Primary level typically involves eight years of education, whereas second level is typically six years in length. Currently, there are roughly 60,000–70,000 students enrolled in each year in primary and secondary-level education.

2   This, and the subsequent quotation, is cited in John Coolahan, S. Drudy, P. Hogan, Á. Hyland, S. McGuinness (2017), *Towards a Better Future: A Review of the Irish School System* (Irish Primary Principals' Network and the National Association of Principals and Deputy Principals).

3   The quotation, and some of the subsequent

figures, are cited by John Walsh in 'Creating a modern educational system? International influence, domestic elites and the transformation of the Irish educational sector, 1950–75', Brendan Walsh (ed.), *Essays in the History of Irish Education* (Palgrave Macmillan, London), 2016, pp. 235–66

4 This quote was also cited in Walsh's article above.

5 É. de Valera (1937), 'The Constitution of Ireland, Radio Broadcast 29th December 1938' in M. Moynihan (ed.), *Speeches and Statements by Eamon de Valera 1917–1973*, (Gill and Macmillan, Dublin, 1980), p. 365.

6 The figures for secondary level for 1970–90 are for full-time teachers; the figures for 2000–20 are for full-time equivalents.

7 The year refers to the year of school entry – i.e. 2010 is the cohort who entered school in 2009–10 and would have been expected to have completed their Leaving Cert five or six years later. Figures previous to 2000 are estimates calculated from the Department's Annual Statistical Reports. Thanks to James O'Brien, statistician in the Department of Education and Skills, for advising on their calculation.

8 In 2018 94.4% of our 20–24-year-olds had completed at least upper secondary education. Only Croatia had a higher rate at 96.2%. Source: Eurostat figures available at https://ec.europa.eu/eurostat/statistics-explained/index.php?title=Educational_attainment_statistics#Level_of_educational_attainment_by_age, accessed January 2020.

9 Figure cited in John Fitzgerald (2019), 'Technical change has probably meant loss of more unskilled jobs than globalisation', *The Irish Times*, 22 March 2019, https://www.irishtimes.com/business/economy/technical-change-has-probably-meant-loss-of-more-unskilled-jobs-than-globalisation-1.3834224.

10 Adults are defined here as those aged 25–64 for 2020 and 25+ for earlier years. The most recent data is from the CSO. Previous years are modelled on CSO data by BBVA in the paper: Angel de la Fuentea and Rafael Doménech (2012), 'Educational Attainment in the OECD, 1960-2010', BBVA Research Working Paper Number 12/20, BBVA: Madrid. Accessed online at https://www.bbvaresearch.com/wp-content/uploads/migrados/WP_1220_tcm348-357479.pdf.

11 John Walsh (2018), *Higher Education in Ireland, 1922–2016: Politics, Policy and Power – A History of Higher Education in the Irish State* (Palgrave Macmillan).

CHAPTER 6

1 Andy Bielenberg (1994), 'Industrial growth in Ireland; c.1790-1910', PhD thesis, London School of Economics and Political Science.

2 The census results for 1926 show 13% of those in employment working in industrial jobs: 9.7% in manufacturing and 3% in building and construction.

3 Data sourced from https://en.wikipedia.org/wiki/Great_Depression. Note that, by comparison, worldwide GDP fell by less than 1% from 2008 to 2009 during the Great Recession.

4 Kevin O'Rourke (1991), 'Burn Everything British but Their Coal: The Anglo-Irish Economic War of the 1930s', *The Journal of Economic History*, vol. 51, no. 2, 357–66.

5 See comparison in Cormac Gráda (2008), 'The Irish Economy half a Century ago'. School Of Economics, University College Dublin, Working Papers.

6 For more on Whitaker see Anne Chambers (2014), *T.K. Whitaker: Portrait of a Patriot* (Doubleday Ireland).

7 Figures are in constant dollars at 2011 prices. Maddison Project Database, version 2020. Jutta Bolt and Jan Luiten van Zanden (2020), 'Maddison style estimates of the evolution of the world economy. A new 2020 update'.

8 Principalities and overseas territories are excluded.

9 A detailed outline of the measure can be found on the Central Statistics Office website at https://www.cso.ie/en/releasesandpublications/in/nie/in-mgnicp/.

10 The figures can be found at the page in the previous note.

11 The rank of world countries by GNI, albeit not Ireland's modified GNI*, can be found at https://en.wikipedia.org/wiki/List_of_countries_by_GNI_(nominal)_per_capita, accessed June 2020.

12 These figures have been compiled by Rebecca Stuart and made available in her 2016 PhD thesis 'Quantitative studies in Irish financial and macroeconomic history' at UCD online, https://researchrepository.ucd.ie/handle/10197/8590. Figures from 1923 to

1938 are taken from the ILO's International Labour Review. For the period 1939 to 1982, data are from Mitchell (2007). For the most recent period, data are from the Central Statistics Office (CSO).

13 The numbers emigrating each decade since the Famine can be found in Paul Sweeney's 2004 paper 'The Irish Experience of Economic Lift Off' presented at a 'Colloquium Celebrating Ireland's Presidency of the European Union, Montreal' in Bishop's University. Accessed at https://www.ictu.ie/download/pdf/celtic_tiger.pdf.

14 Data from Eurostat's dispersion of regional unemployment rates by NUTS 3 region for 2018, available at https://appsso.eurostat.ec.europa.eu/nui/show.do?dataset=lfst_r_lmdur&lang=en, accessed June 2020.

15 The numbers for 1926 and 1946 have been rounded for the purposes of illustration. In 1926 54% worked in agriculture, 13% in industry and 34% in services. In 1946 the respective figures were 47%, 17% and 36%.

16 Medium-skilled jobs are defined as those that are either non-manual or skilled manual jobs. Low-skilled jobs are defined as semi-skilled or unskilled occupations.

17 The calculation of average number of hours a week assumes a 46-week working year, thereby allowing for four weeks of holiday leave and two weeks' worth of public holidays per annum.

18 These data are available in the CSO's analysis of 'Persons aged 15 years and over in Employment (Thousand) by Sex, Usual Hours Worked and Quarter' at https://statbank.cso.ie/px/pxeirestat/Statire/SelectVarVal/Define.asp?maintable=QLF20, accessed June 2020.

19 More details of commuting times per county can be found in the CSO census reports. The information for 2016 can be found at https://www.cso.ie/en/releasesandpublications/ep/p-cp6ci/p6cii/p6td/.

20 The figures are in US dollars at 2019 current prices/PPPs.

21 OECD (2021), GDP per hour worked (indicator). doi: 10.1787/1439e590-en.

22 The data can be found in the OECD's 'Compendium of Productivity Indicators 2019', figure 2.11, 'GDP and GNI per hour worked, 2017', accessible online at https://www.oecd-ilibrary.org/industry-and-services/oecd-compendium-of-productivity-indica-

tors_22252126.

23 These data are published by the CSO in 'Output and Value Added by Activity 2017', available online at https://www.cso.ie/en/releasesandpublications/ep/p-naova/outputandvalueaddedbyactivity2017/grossvalueaddedgva/.

24 The figures relate to all enterprises employing 10 or more people, excluding the financial sector, where online sales account for at least 1% of their turnover. The data can be accessed at https://ec.europa.eu/eurostat/web/digital-economy-and-society/data/database as of June 2020.

25 Data on the number of strikes from the foundation of the State can be found in T. Brannick, F. Devine & A. Kelly (2000), 'Social Statistics for Labour Historians: Strike Statistics, 1922–99', *Saothar*, 25, 114–20.

26 Union membership figures since the foundation of the State up to 1999 can be found in Tony Dobbins (2001), 'The State of Trade Unionism', https://www.eurofound.europa.eu/publications/article/2001/the-state-of-trade-unionism. Figures for subsequent years can be found at the OECD's web site at https://stats.oecd.org/Index.aspx?DataSetCode=TUD.

27 Devine is a former editor of *Saothar*, the journal of Irish labour history, and author of *Organising History: a centenary of SIPTU, 1909–2009* (2009, Dublin: Gill & Macmillan).

28 The figures are in euros in real terms at 2015 prices.

29 You can view the historical data in the CSO's *Historical Earnings 1938–2015*, available at https://www.cso.ie/en/releasesandpublications/ep/p-hes/hes2015/aiw/.

30 The historic data has been compiled by Rebecca Stuart and made available in her 2016 PhD thesis cited above.

31 The price of goods at the end of 1996 are compared with their price at the end of 2020. Figures are rounded to the nearest 5 per cent.

32 These figures are calculated on the basis of the national median equivalised disposable income figure of €24,920 in 2018. The weightings for various household sizes can be found at https://ec.europa.eu/eurostat/statistics-explained/index.php/Glossary:Equivalised_income.

33 My thanks to statistician Eva O'Regan in the CSO for calculating the latest data.

34 Rakesh Kochhar (2017), 'Middle Class Fortunes in Western Europe', Pew Research Centre, accessible at https://www.pewresearch.org/global/2017/04/24/middle-class-fortunes-in-western-europe/.

35 A comparative analysis of our minimum wage can be found in Patrick Malone and Philip O'Connell's 2019 paper entitled 'The National Minimum Wage' and published by the UCD Geary Institute for Public Policy. Accessible online at http://publicpolicy.ie/papers/the-national-minimum-wage/.

36 The Revenue Commissioners' study of income changes during the recession evidences this. See Seán Kennedy, David Haugh and Brian Stanley (2018), 'Income Dynamics & Mobility in Ireland: Evidence from Tax Records Microdata', available at https://igees.gov.ie/wp-content/uploads/2018/04/Income-Dynamics-Mobility-in-Ireland-Evidence-from-Tax-Records-Microdata.pdf.

37 The data is from the same study mentioned previously.

38 This is true both in nominal and in real terms.

39 The latest data can be found on the Central Bank's website at https://centralbank.ie/statistics/data-and-analysis/financial-accounts.

40 This is the conclusion of research by Dr Barra Roantree at the ESRI. More at https://www.esri.ie/news/irish-tax-system-does-most-in-europe-to-reduce-inequality.

41 Data contained in Dr Roantree's Barrington lecture address, 'Understanding income inequality in Ireland', to The Statistical and Social Inquiry Society of Ireland in 2020, available at http://www.ssisi.ie/SSISI_173_03-Roantree_paper_PDF.pdf.

42 Data is for the most recent available year, 2019 for Ireland and EU countries, 2018 for the UK and 2016 for the USA.

43 John FitzGerald (1999), 'Understanding Ireland's Economic Success', Paper WP111, Economic and Social Research Institute (ESRI).

44 European Commission (2013), 'Evaluation of the main achievements of Cohesion Policy programmes and projects over the longer term in 15 selected regions (from 1989-1993 programming period to the present). Case Study: Ireland', accessed at https://ec.europa.eu/regional_policy/en/information/publications/evaluations/2013/evaluation-of-the-main-achievements-of-cohesion-policy-programmes-and-projects-over-the-longer-term-in-15-selected-regions-from-1989-1993-programming-period-to-the-present_0.

CHAPTER 7

1 How is that possible? When you measure the value of the economy in terms of Gross National Product (GDP), the value of consumption, investment, government spending and exports are added together and then the value of imports is subtracted. In Ireland's case, the value of our exports greatly exceeds the value of all the other components.

2 According to the World Bank, this was true of only eight countries in 2018: Luxembourg, Hong Kong, Singapore, San Marino, Djibouti, Malta, Ireland and Vietnam. See https://data.worldbank.org/indicator/NE.EXP.GNFS.ZS?most_recent_value_desc=true, accessed July 2020.

3 This analysis of 2014 data by the OECD was published in 'Statistical Insights: men's employment more dependent on trade than women's', available at http://www.oecd.org/sdd/its/statistical-insights-mens-employment-more-dependent-on-trade-than-womens.htm.

4 The figures are for 1949 and cited in Adrian Redmond (Ed.) (1999), 'That was then, this is now. Change in Ireland, 1949-1999', Central Statistics Office: Dublin, page 92.

5 The data is for 2019 and sourced from http://www.worldstopexports.com/irelands-top-10-exports/, accessed July 2020.

6 Agri-food goods accounted for 11% of our merchandise exports in 2017 according to Teagasc at https://www.teagasc.ie/rural-economy/rural-economy/agri-food-business/agriculture-in-ireland/. This analysis also contains the estimate that the sector accounted for around 40% of net foreign earnings from merchandise exports in 2008.

7 The figures are based on 2016 data and sourced from Bord Bia at https://www.bordbia.ie/industry/irish-sector-profiles/irish-agriculture-food-drink-sector/.

8 These facts are sourced from Bord Bia's 'Export Performance and Prospects 2019-2020', available online at https://www.bordbiaperformanceandprospects.com/annual-reports, and Sustainable Food Systems Ireland webpage at http://www.sfsi.ie/agriculture-food-ireland.

9 Christine Kinealy (1997), *A Death-Dealing*

Famine: The Great Hunger in Ireland (Pluto Press).

10 Michael Turner (1996), *After the Famine: Irish Agriculture 1850–1914*, Cambridge University Press.

11 See Bord Bia's 'Export Performance and Prospects 2019-2020', available online at https://www.bordbiaperformanceandprospects.com/annual-reports.

12 'Whiskey rush as distillery numbers hit 120-year high', *Irish Independent*, 5 January 2020. The full list is accessible at https://www.independent.ie/business/irish/whiskey-rush-as-distillery-numbers-hit-120-year-high-38834515.html.

13 Figures sourced from the Irish Farmers' Association at https://www.ifa.ie/brexit/brexit-ireland/, accessed July 2020.

14 OECD (2020), 'Exports of services, as a percentage of total goods and services exports: Seasonally adjusted', in *OECD Quarterly International Trade Statistics*, vol. 2019, issue 3 (OECD Publishing, Paris). https://doi.org/10.1787/fd90eed1-en.

15 The 2019 edition of the 'Global Location Trends' report can be found online at https://www.ibm.com/thought-leadership/institute-business-value/report/gltr2019. Thank you to Jacob Dencik of the IBM Institute for providing me with the aggregated data for 2009–18.

16 Sourced from IDA Ireland's 'Facts about Ireland, September 2019' available at https://www.idaireland.com/newsroom/publications/ida_facts_about_ireland_2019.

17 See the CSO's report 'Foreign Direct Investment in Ireland 2018', available online at https://www.cso.ie/en/releasesandpublications/ep/p-fdi/foreigndirectinvestmentinireland2018/awe/.

18 Kerry Group website https://www.kerrygroup.com/careers/search-jobs, accessed July 2020.

19 Smurfit Kappa website https://www.smurfitkappa.com/ie/about/our-history.

20 CRH website https://www.crh.com/about-crh/at-a-glance.

21 As with the previous table, Jacob Dencik of the IBM Institute has provided the aggregated data shown here for 2009–18.

22 The facts are sourced from https://en.wikipedia.org/wiki/Accenture and relate to 2020.

23 Data from https://en.wikipedia.org/wiki/Medtronic.

24 E. Delaney (2002), 'Irish emigration since 1921', *Studies in Irish Economic and Social History*, no. 8, Economic and Social History Society of Ireland.

25 Tony Fahey, John D. FitzGerald and Bertrand Maitre, 'The economic and social implications of demographic change', *Journal of the Statistical and Social Inquiry Society of Ireland*, vol. XXVII, part V, 1997/1998, 185–222.

26 The figure shown is for net migration – that is, the number of people emigrating less the number of people immigrating in any one year.

27 Enda Delaney (2002), *Irish Emigration since 1921* (Economic & Social History Society of Ireland).

28 Delaney (2002) above.

29 These figures, and others that follow, are also sourced from Delaney (2002).

30 Department of Foreign Affairs, Irish Abroad Unit (2017), 'Irish Emigration Patterns and Citizens Abroad', briefing note available at https://www.dfa.ie/media/dfa/alldfawebsitemedia/newspress/publications/ministersbrief-june2017/1--Global-Irish-in-Numbers.pdf.

31 The figures are from census results. When two censuses were completed in the one decade then it is the average figure across both.

32 The figures represent the number from each country captured in the 2016 census and excludes those born on the island of Ireland.

33 Ireland ranks in the top quartile of European Union states, based on 2019 figures. Figures sourced from 'Migrant population and immigration statistics in EU Member States' at https://emn.ie/useful-statistics/migration-and-migrant-population-statistics-in-eu-28/.

34 Around 40% of migrants here have a third-level qualification. See the 2020 report from the Department of Justice and Equality, 'Origin and Integration: A Study of Migrants in the 2016 Irish Census', ESRI, accessed at https://www.esri.ie/system/files/publications/BKMNEXT392_2.pdf.

35 Ultan Cowley (2001), *The Men Who Built Britain: A History of the Irish Navvy* (Wolfhound Press, Dublin), p. 29.

36 Enda Delaney (2007), *The Irish in Post-War Britain* (Oxford University Press) p. 42.

37 The headline figure is for 2018 and the leading country estimates are for 2017.

38 Eurostat 'Personal remittances statistics', available at https://ec.europa.eu/eurostat/statistics-explained/index.php/Personal_remittances_statistics, accessed August 2020.

39 Ainhoa Osés Arranz (2019), 'When gravity hits: projecting Ireland's migration', Irish Fiscal Advisory Council, available online at https://www.fiscalcouncil.ie/when-gravity-hits-projecting-irelands-migration/.

40 A tourist is defined as anyone who visits a country for more than one night (so day-trippers are excluded) but less than one year. Most people visit Ireland either for leisure purposes or to visit friends and relatives. Business visits are the next most frequent reason, followed by those who are here for other purposes such as attending weddings or baptisms or coming here to study.

41 The quoted sales figures, and more about the book, can be found at https://en.wikipedia.org/wiki/Irish_Journal. You can apply for an artist's residency at his cottage at http://heinrichboellcottage.com/.

42 The passenger numbers for every year of their operation can be found on Ryanair's website at https://corporate.ryanair.com/about-us/history-of-ryanair/.

43 The results are for 2007 and taken from Fáilte Ireland's Visitor Attitudes Survey. A news report citing the figures and subsequent improvements can be found at https://www.irishtimes.com/news/consumer/ireland-shedding-rip-off-republic-image-among-visitors-1.2173353.

44 The figures are taken from 'The Gathering Ireland 2013: Final Report', available at https://www.failteireland.ie/failteireland/media/websitestructure/documents/ezine/thegathering_finalreport_jimmiley_december2013.pdf, accessed July 2020.

45 The viewing figures are for season 7 and sourced from https://en.wikipedia.org/wiki/Game_of_Thrones#Viewership. The Chief Executive of Tourism Northern Ireland has claimed that one in every six out-of-state visitors that came to NI in 2018 was influenced by Game of Thrones, bringing an economic benefit of £50 million (€58 million) in that year alone (cited in https://www.irishtimes.com/business/transport-and-tourism/game-of-thrones-tourists-spent-58m-in-north-last-year-1.3867605).

46 See the list of top 10 grossing movies of all time at https://www.businessinsider.com/highest-grossing-movies-all-time-worldwide-box-office-2018-4?r=US&IR=T.

47 The World Economic Forum's biennial reports placed Ireland as third best in the world in both their 2017 and 2019 reports. In 2017 Ireland was placed behind the United Arab Emirates and New Zealand. In 2019 it was behind Lesotho and New Zealand. The 2019 report can be viewed at https://www.weforum.org/reports/the-travel-tourism-competitiveness-report-2019.

48 See the RTÉ report 'Dublin hotels have highest rates of occupancy in Europe', 6 March 2017, at https://www.rte.ie/news/business/2017/0306/857472-dublin-hotels/.

49 See the United Nations World Tourism Organization forecast in Daniel Scott & Stefan Gössling (2015), 'What could the next 40 years hold for global tourism?' Tourism Recreation Research, 40:3, 269–85. Some forecasts are even more bullish than this. Pre-Covid, IATA were forecasting a doubling of air travel passenger numbers in just 20 years. See https://www.iata.org/en/pressroom/pr/2018-10-24-02/.

50 The data is for 2019 and was accessed at https://en.wikipedia.org/wiki/Largest_airlines_in_the_world, July 2020. Four US airlines carry more passengers: American Airlines, Delta, Southwest and United. If not for the coronavirus, Ryanair would reasonably have overtaken the last two of these in 2020 or 2021, although China Southern Airlines is also going toe to toe in matching Ryanair's recent growth. The fare for 1980 is sourced from Seán Barrett's book Deregulation and the Airline Business in Europe: Selected Readings (2011), Routledge.

51 The fare for 2000 is an average of the prices quoted by Erica Roseingrave in 'Ryanair: The Growth Airline of Europe' as published in Trinity College's Student Economic Review (2000). The 2019 fare was cited as the average price for this flight on www.farecompare.com, accessed March 2020. Prices have been converted to real terms using the Central Statistic Office's CPI inflation calculator.

52 There is a good timeline of the Ryanair story to be found on their website at https://corporate.ryanair.com/about-us/history-of-ryanair/.

53 Sourced from https://en.wikipedia.org/wiki/Ryanair, accessed July 2020.

54 These statistics are sourced from an article by Trevor Buckley of Acumen Aviation entitled 'Ireland – the nexus of the global aircraft leasing industry', accessed at https://www.capital-markets-intelligence.com/feature/ireland-the-nexus-of-the-global-aircraft-leasing-industry/ in July 2020.

55 Read more about the GPA story at https://en.wikipedia.org/wiki/Guinness_Peat_Aviation and about Tony Ryan at https://www.ria.ie/news/tony-ryan-wizard-skies.

56 This is if you count the number of aircraft each are leasing. If you count the value of the aircraft then the two switch rank. This data is sourced from KPMG's 'Aviation Industry Leaders Report 2019: Tackling Headwinds', available at https://assets.kpmg/content/dam/kpmg/ie/pdf/2019/01/ie-aviation-industry-leaders-report-2019.pdf.

57 On average every Irish adult spent 13.1 nights abroad in 2018 compared to an EU average of just 6.8 nights. That is roughly the same level as the Dutch and we are only beaten by the Luxembourgers, the Swedes, and the Cypriots. Online at https://ec.europa.eu/eurostat/statistics-explained/index.php?title=Tourism_statistics#Nights_spent_abroad_by_EU-27_residents:_Luxembourg_leads_in_nights_per_inhabitant, accessed July 2020.

58 The ranking is compiled by Henley & Partner, specialists in residence and citizenship planning, as at April 2021. The index examines 199 different passports and their ability to access 227 different travel destinations. A destination is counted as requiring no prior visa if no visa is required at all for entry, if it can be obtained on arrival, if a visitor's permit is automatically granted, or if there is an electronic travel authority (ETA) given when entering the destination. These visa types require no pre-departure government approval because of the specific visa-waiver programs in place. The latest ranking is available at https://www.henleypassportindex.com/

CHAPTER 8

1 GAA is rated as Ireland's favourite sport in the 2020 Teneo Sports & Sponsorship Index with 24% of people choosing GAA, ten percentage points above soccer. The other figures are sourced from the 'Irish Sports Monitor 2019 Mid-Year Report', published by Sport Ireland. Gaelic football is the leading sport for attendance (8%) followed by hurling (5%). Gaelic football is the leading sport for which people volunteer (8%) and GAA club membership (at 11%) is second only to gym membership (at 15%).

2 Paul Rouse (2017), *Sport and Ireland: A History* (Oxford University Press).

3 Sourced from https://en.wikipedia.org/wiki/Ladies%27_Gaelic_football.

4 According to https://www.gaa.ie/, accessed October 2020.

5 These facts are sourced from Horse Racing Ireland's report 'Economic Impact Of Irish Breeding And Racing 2017' prepared by Deloitte and available online at https://www.hri.ie/press-office/economic-impact/. The figures typically refer to the year 2016.

6 All these data are sourced from the report cited above.

7 'Racing's all-time favourite', BBC News, 14 February 2003, accessed at http://news.bbc.co.uk/sport2/hi/other_sports/horse_racing/2759213.stm.

8 The accolades are noted in his biography on Wikipedia at https://en.wikipedia.org/wiki/Vincent_O%27Brien.

9 Ruby Walsh (2019), 'Unlike other sports, Irish racing really is a true worldwide success story', *Irish Examiner*, 26 October 2019. Accessed at https://www.irishexaminer.com/sport/othersport/arid-30959859.html.

10 Irish authors have won four Nobel Prizes for literature, making Ireland the country with the greatest number of winners per capita amongst countries with a population of over 1 million people. Saint Lucia, with a population of 180,000, and Iceland, with a population of 360,000, also have one winner each. There have been 55 Booker Prize winners over the period 1969–2019 of which four have been from Ireland. This is the largest number after those from England (23) and Australia (5) and the greatest number per capita.

11 Mark Henry (2021), 'Ireland' in João Freire (ed.), *Nation Branding in Europe*, Routledge. See also John Fanning (2011), 'Branding and Begorrah: The Importance of Ireland's Nation Brand Image', *Irish Marketing Review*, 21 (1&2), 23–31.

12 Donal O'Drisceoil (2017), 'The Irish writers banned in their own land', *Irish Examiner*, 20 July 2017, accessed at https://www.irishexaminer.com/lifestyle/arid-20455179.html.

13 The figures are based on all competitions up until 2021. There was no contest in 2020.

The list of all Eurovision winners is available at https://eurovision.tv/winners.

14 An analysis of the impact of some of these changes on Ireland's Eurovision performance can be found in Adrian Kavanagh's paper 'Politics, Ireland and the Eurovision Song Contest' presented at the Political Studies Association of Ireland Conference, Dublin Institute of Technology, October 2010, available online at https://www.academia.edu/347959/Politics_Ireland_and_the_Eurovision_Song_Contest.

15 Ruth Barton (2019), *Irish Cinema in the Twenty-first Century* (Manchester University Press).

16 The analysis of the home countries of the winners of the awards for best actor/actress and best supporting actor/actress from 1929–2018 was completed by Tyler Moss and can be found at https://www.wanderu.com/blog/states-and-countries-with-most-oscar-winning-actors/.

17 Day-Lewis' subsequent two Academy Awards were playing American characters in *There Will Be Blood* in 2007 and *Lincoln* in 2012. He is the first ever three-time recipient of the Best Actor Oscar.

18 Figures sourced from the Wikipedia article at https://en.wikipedia.org/wiki/Once_(film).

19 The numbers are the number of Irish pubs in each location that are members of Irish Hospitality Global, formerly known as Irish Pubs Global, in 2019. They had 5,284 member pubs outside of the island of Ireland. This figure is likely to significantly underestimate the total number of Irish pubs abroad as their USA membership, for example, is less than 1,400.

CHAPTER 9

1 Historian Samuel Huntington identifies only eleven countries as democratic in 1942 in his book *The Third Wave: Democratization in the Late Twentieth Century* (1993). They were Finland, Iceland, Ireland, Sweden, Switzerland, United Kingdom, Australia, Canada, New Zealand, the United States and Chile.

2 The Economist Intelligence Unit ranks Ireland as the sixth most democratic state in the world in their 'Democracy Index 2019'. Norway tops the list followed by Iceland, Sweden, New Zealand and Finland.

3 The data is the average scores from the Eurobarometer surveys undertaken in each year. Those who did not give an opinion are excluded.

4 R.S. Foa et al. (2020), *The Global Satisfaction with Democracy Report 2020*, Cambridge, United Kingdom: Centre for the Future of Democracy. The citizens of Switzerland have the greatest level of satisfaction, followed by Denmark, Luxembourg, Norway and then Ireland.

5 The data is the average scores from the Eurobarometer surveys across the two waves of research undertaken in 2019. Those who did not give an opinion are excluded.

6 *Meitheal* is the Irish word for a work party. Stemming originally from the system whereby groups of neighbours helped each other in turn with farming work, it is an expression of the universal appliance of cooperation to social need.

7 Transparency International (2019), *Corruptions Perceptions Index 2019*, accessible at https://www.transparency.org/files/content/pages/2019_CPI_Report_EN.pdf.

8 Michael Clifford and Shane Coleman (2010), *Scandal Nation: Key Events that Shook and Shaped Ireland* (Hachette Ireland).

9 Jack Power, 'Final bill for Mahon Tribunal to come in under €150m', *The Irish Times*, 8 March 2018, https://www.irishtimes.com/news/politics/final-bill-for-mahon-tribunal-to-come-in-under-150m-1.3420236.

10 National Consortium for the Study of Terrorism and Responses to Terrorism (START), University of Maryland (2021). The Global Terrorism Database (GTD) [Data file]. Retrieved from https://www.start.umd.edu/gtd. The figures for the 2010s are for 2010–18.

11 'List of Gardaí killed in the line of duty' on Wikipedia.com, accessed at https://en.wikipedia.org/wiki/List_of_Garda%C3%AD_killed_in_the_line_of_duty.

12 Institute for Economics & Peace (2021), 'Global Peace Index 2021', available at https://www.visionofhumanity.org/wp-content/uploads/2021/06/GPI-2021-web-1.pdf.

13 Ian O'Donnell (2005), 'Violence and social change in the Republic of Ireland', *International Journal of the Sociology of Law*, 33, 101–17.

14 I. O'Donnell & E. O'Sullivan (2003). 'The Politics of Intolerance – Irish Style', *The British Journal of Criminology*, 43(1), 41–62.

15 Binhadab, Breen and Gillanders (2018), 'The Role of a Free Press in Combating Business Corruption', Munich Personal RePEc

Archive, accessed at https://mpra.ub.uni-muenchen.de/88954/.

16 The figures for divorce and abortion and the 2010s figure for same-sex marriage are the results of referenda and sourced from the Wikipedia page 'Amendments to the Constitution of Ireland' at https://en.wiki-pedia.org/wiki/Amendments_to_the_Constitution_of_Ireland. The 1980s figure for same-sex marriage is from a 1981 opinion poll which asked respondents if homosexuality 'can always be justified; never be justified; or something in between' and allowed an answer from 1-10. Ten per cent of respondents answered positively with a score of 7 or higher. The survey was part of the European Values Study on which more information can be found at https://europeanvaluesstudy.eu/. The 2000s same-sex marriage figure is a 2004 opinion poll which asked specifically about gay marriage and was conducted by Millward Brown IMS with the results reported at https://www.irishexaminer.com/news/arid-30176905.html. The cited figure of 44% excludes 'don't knows'.

17 BBC News, 'Profile of Father Brendan Smyth', 15 March 2010, http://news.bbc.co.uk/2/hi/uk_news/northern_ireland/8567868.stm.

18 The 'Freedom in the World 2020' report is online at https://freedomhouse.org/countries/freedom-world/scores?sort=-desc&order=Civil%20Liberties, accessed May 2021.

19 Charities Aid Foundation (2019), *World Giving Index 10th Edition*, accessible at https://www.cafonline.org/about-us/publications/2019-publications/caf-world-giving-index-10th-edition.

20 The CSO's Household Budget Survey shows households' weekly average charitable donations were €2.59 in 2005, €4.40 in 2010 (a 70% increase) and then fell back to €3.75 in 2015.

21 Quarterly National Household Survey on Volunteering and Wellbeing Q3 2013.

22 Read more about the power of generosity in Jill Suttie and Jason Marsh's article '5 Ways Giving Is Good for You' in *Greater Good Magazine*, https://greatergood.berkeley.edu/article/item/5_ways_giving_is_good_for_you.

CHAPTER 10

1 'Ten things an Irish woman could not do in 1970', *Galway Advertiser*, 13 December 2012, accessible online at https://www.advertiser.ie/galway/article/57301/ten-things-an-irish-woman-could-not-do-in-1970.

2 World Economic Forum (2019), 'Global Gender Gap Report 2020', accessible at https://www.weforum.org/reports/gender-gap-2020-report-100-years-pay-equality.

3 Stein Emil Vollset et al. (2020), 'Fertility, mortality, migration, and population scenarios for 195 countries and territories from 2017 to 2100: a forecasting analysis for the Global Burden of Disease Study', *The Lancet*, vol. 396, issue 10258.

4 Department of Health (2019), 'Health in Ireland: Key Trends 2019'.

5 Quotation cited in 'Contraception in the Republic of Ireland', https://en.wikipedia.org/wiki/Contraception_in_the_Republic_of_Ireland, accessed October 2020.

6 History.com, 'This Day in History: February 20, Ireland allows sale of contraceptives', https://www.history.com/this-day-in-history/ireland-allows-sale-of-contraceptives.

7 The figures for married couple families are taken from the census reports of 1979, 1996 and 2016, respectively.

8 Margret Fine-Davis (2016), *Changing Gender Roles and Attitudes to Family Formation in Ireland* (Manchester University Press). The data is from 2010.

9 The global dataset is the United Nations 'World Marriage Data 2019', available online at https://population.un.org/MarriageData/Index.html#/home, accessed October 2020.

10 This data is taken from the respective censuses, with the most recent being from 2016.

11 OECD (2021), Adult education level (indicator). doi: 10.1787/36bce3fe-en, accessed at https://data.oecd.org/eduatt/adult-education-level.htm, May 2021.

12 Fine-Davis (2016), above.

13 World Bank, 'Labor force participation rate, female (% of female population ages 15+) (modeled ILO estimate)'. Accessible at https://data.worldbank.org/indicator/SL.TLF.CACT.FE.ZS?most_recent_value_desc=false&view=chart, accessed October 2020.

14 Margret Fine-Davis (2015), *Gender Roles in Ireland: Three Decades of Attitude Change* (Routledge).

15 According to the CSO data on labour force participation for 2019, available at

https://statbank.cso.ie/px/pxeirestat/
Statire/SelectVarVal/Define.asp?maint-
able=QLF18&PLanguage=0, accessed
October 2020.

16 According to the 2016 census.

17 Frances McGinnity & Helen Russell (2008),
'Gender Inequalities in Time: Use The Distribution of Caring, Housework and Employment Among Women and Men in Ireland',
The Equality Authority and The Economic
and Social Research Institute, Dublin.

18 The historical figures are cited in Margret
Fine-Davis (2015), *Gender Roles in Ireland:
Three Decades of Attitude Change*. The most
recent data is for 2017 from the CSO's 'Wom-
en and Men in Ireland 2019' publication,
available at https://www.cso.ie/en/releas-
esandpublications/ep/p-wamii/womenand-
meninireland2019/work/.

19 Brian Stanley et al. (2019), 'An Analysis
of Labour Market Earnings for Higher
Education Graduates in their Early Careers:
Graduation Cohorts: 2010 – 2017', Higher
Education Authority.

20 Korn Ferry (2018), 'Korn Ferry Global Gender
Pay Index Analyses Reasons Behind Inequalities In Male And Female Pay', 26 April
2018, https://www.kornferry.com/about-us/
press/korn-ferry-global-gender-pay-index-an-
alyzes-reasons-behind-inequalities-in-male-
and-female-pay.

21 The World Economic Forum calculations are
based on the period 11 July 1970–1 July 2019.
They count the number of years in the past
50-year period for which a woman has held a
post equivalent to an elected head of state or
head of government in the country, be that a
prime minister and/or president. The precise
figures for each cited country are Bangladesh
25.6 years, Iceland 21.9 years, Ireland 20.8
years, India 19.5 years and Norway 15.8
years. The 'Global Gender Gap Report 2020'
report is available at https://www.weforum.
org/reports/gender-gap-2020-report-100-
years-pay-equality.

22 M. Marsh (1999), 'The making of the eighth
President', in M. Marsh and P. Mitchell (eds),
How Ireland Voted 1997 (Westview Press and
PSAI Press), pp. 215–42.

23 Yvonne Galligan (2012), 'Transforming the
Irish Presidency: Activist Presidents and
Gender Politics, 1990–2011', *Irish Political
Studies*, 27:4, 596–614.

24 Sourced from Galligan's article above.

25 Fiona Buckley (2016), 'The 2016 Irish
election demonstrated how gender quotas
can shift the balance on female representation', London School of Economics blog post,
accessible at https://blogs.lse.ac.uk/europ-
pblog/2016/03/16/the-2016-irish-election-
demonstrated-how-gender-quotas-can-shift-
the-balance-on-female-representation/.

26 The data is the Intra-Parliamentary Union
rankings, accessed at https://data.ipu.org/
women-ranking?month=10&year=2020,
December 2020.

27 Gail McElroy (2018), 'The Impact of Gender
Quotas on Voting Behaviour in 2016', in
David Farrell, Michael Marsh and Theresa
Reidy, *The Irish Voter 2016* (Manchester
University Press), accessed at http://www.
tara.tcd.ie/handle/2262/81769. The analysis
shows that only Fianna Fáil voters have a
preference for male candidates, which does
not bode well for the party's prospects as the
gender quota increases.

28 Terri Kelly (2015), 'Profession's Perfect
Parity', *Law Society Gazette*, Jan/Feb 2015,
20–21. Accessible at https://www.lawsociety.
ie/globalassets/documents/gazette/equality.
pdf.

CHAPTER 11

1   Dáil Éireann debate, 21 Jan 1919, vol. F, no.
1, https://www.oireachtas.ie/en/debates/
debate/dail/1919-01-21/15/.

2   For a detailed review of the first strategy's
achievements see 'Ten Years On: Did the
National Children's Strategy Deliver on
its Promises?' published by the Children's
Rights Alliance in 2011.

3   Data available at https://endcorporalpun-
ishment.org/countdown/, accessed October
2020.

4   A comprehensive overview of the experience
of corporal punishment, how it was endorsed
by the authorities and the attempts to ban
it, can be found in Moira Maguire & Séamus
O'Cinnéide (2005). 'A Good Beating Never
Hurt Anyone: The Punishment and Abuse
of Children in Twentieth-Century Ireland',
Journal of Social History, 38, 635–52.

5   Letters titled 'Punishment in Irish Schools'
in *The Catholic Herald*, 3 August 1956.

6   Quoted in Maguire and O'Cinnéide's article.

7   'On this day: 25 February 1982: Parents can
stop school beatings', BBC News article,
accessed at http://news.bbc.co.uk/onthis-

day/hi/dates/stories/february/25/news-id_2516000/2516621.stm.

8   The budget figures and number of Special Needs Assistants are for 2021 as published in the Department of Education and Skills' 'Main Features of Budget 2021: Education' briefing paper. The number of teachers and pupils supported is from the National Council for Special Education's 'Annual Report 2019'. The budget increase is sourced from 'Spending Review 2019: Monitoring Inputs, Outputs and Outcomes in Special Education Needs Provision' report published by the Department of Public Expenditure and Reform and the Department of Education and Skills.

9   The survey results can be viewed at http://espad.org/report/trends-1995-2015/country-specific-trends and http://www.espad.org/espad-report-2019.

10 J. Inchley et al. (2020), 'Spotlight on adolescent health and well-being. Findings from the 2017/2018 Health Behaviour in School-aged Children (HBSC) survey in Europe and Canada. International report. Volume 1. Key findings.', WHO Regional Office for Europe. The study is of 11-, 13- and 15-year-olds.

11 I.J. Perry et al. (2009), 'The heights and weights of Irish children from the postwar era to the Celtic tiger', *J Epidemiol Community Health*, March 1, 2009; 63(3): 262–4.

12 J. Inchley et al. (eds.) (2020) *Spotlight on adolescent health and well-being. Findings from the 2017/2018 Health Behaviour in School-aged Children (HBSC) survey in Europe and Canada. International report. Volume 1. Key findings.* (Copenhagen: WHO Regional Office for Europe).

13 The number of garda programme referrals can be found on the Irish Youth Justice Service website at http://www.iyjs.ie/en/iyjs/pages/publications. The Children Court figures can be found in the Courts Service annual reports at https://www.courts.ie/annual-report.

CHAPTER 12

1   The figures in the graph and the accompanying text are contained in the publication 'Forest Statistics, Ireland 2020', published by the Department of Agriculture, Food and the Marine.

2   Pádraic Fogarty (2017) *Whittled Away: Ireland's Vanishing Nature* (Collins Press).

3   Cormac O'Grada (1979), 'The population

of Ireland 1700-1900: a survey', *Annales de Démographie Historique*, 1979, 281–99.

4   Central Statistics Office (2020), 'Environmental Indicators Ireland 2020', https://www.cso.ie/en/releasesandpublications/ep/p-eii/environmentalindicatorsireland2020/landuse/.

5   These and subsequent figures are taken from the CSO's 'Environmental Indicators Ireland 2020' report.

6   The figures refer to the share of the population exposed to $PM_{2.5}$ levels above the WHO threshold of 10 micrograms/m^3 as published by the OECD (2020), 'How's Life? 2020: Measuring Well-being', OECD Publishing, Paris.

7   Kevin O'Sullivan (2020), 'Dogged by smog: how the smoky coal ban changed us', *The Irish Times*, 31 August 2020.

8   This is the work of Jessica Wolpaw Reyes. Read about the 'Lead–crime hypothesis' on Wikipedia, https://en.wikipedia.org/wiki/Lead%E2%80%93crime_hypothesis.

9   EPA (2020), 'Air Quality in Ireland 2019', accessible at https://www.epa.ie/pubs/reports/air/quality/.

10 The figures in the graph and the text are published by the CSO in 'Environmental Indicators Ireland 2020' and sourced from the EPA.

11 In interview with Laura Burke, EPA Director General.

12 Brendan Wall et al. (ed.) (2020), 'Ireland's Environment – An Integrated Assessment 2020', Environmental Protection Agency.

13 The figures are cited in 'Recycling in the Republic of Ireland' at https://en.wikipedia.org/wiki/Recycling_in_the_Republic_of_Ireland, accessed December 2020.

14 Alan Barrett and John Lawlor (1995), 'The Economics of Solid Waste Management in Ireland', ESRI.

15 'Waste Packaging Statistics for Ireland', EPA Waste Data Release, 30 July 2020. Accessed at https://www.epa.ie/nationalwastestatistics/packaging/.

16 These figures, and those contained later in the text, are sourced from the Sustainable Energy Authority of Ireland (2020), 'Energy in Ireland: 2020 Report', available at https://www.seai.ie/data-and-insights/seai-statistics/key-publications/energy-in-ireland/. The figures for 2020 are extrapolated.

17 Michael McAleer (2020), 'Why you should –

or should not – buy an electric car now', *The Irish Times*, 7 March 2020.

18 Sustainable Energy Authority of Ireland (2014), 'A Guide to Building Energy Rating for Homeowners'.

19 Ireland has achieved the maximum possible rating by the World Bank for the 'Building energy codes' indicator set in Energy Efficiency since 2014. Only Romania, the United Kingdom and South Korea receive a similarly high score. The entire Regulatory Indicators for Sustainable Energy dataset can be viewed at https://rise.worldbank.org/scores, accessed December 2020.

20 Sourced from the above report, as are the statistics quoted later.

CHAPTER 13

1 The comparative data on ODA performance is sourced from the OECD Development Assistance Committee dataset available at https://www.oecd.org/dac/financing-sustainable-development/development-finance-data/. The most recent available data is for 2019.

2 A comprehensive overview of our ODA programme can be found in the OECD's Development Cooperation Profile for Ireland at https://doi.org/10.1787/2dcf1367-en.

3 As evaluated by the OECD in the above analysis.

4 ODI (2020), 'Principled Aid Index 2020', available at https://www.odi.org/opinion/10502-principled-aid-index.

5 Dáil Éireann Debate on Overseas Development Aid Expenditure, 21 May 2019, https://www.oireachtas.ie/en/debates/question/2019-05-21/131/.

6 The OECD dataset is 'Total flows by donor (ODA+OOF+Private) [DAC1]' and the values are 'Gross outflow from private sources', accessed at https://stats.oecd.org/Index.aspx?DataSetCode=TABLE1, and calculated in March 2021. This counts funding by national NGOs, foundations and other private bodies made to or for developing countries, multilateral organisations, special appeals (e.g. disaster relief) or international non-governmental organisations.

7 Calculated by the author from Fairtrade International's Annual Report 2017–18.

8 The 2018 sales figure is taken from Fairtrade Ireland's press release 'Another Bounce In Irish Fairtrade Spending to €382 Million –

Up 11%', 25 February 2019.

9 Calculated by the author from the figures in the United Nations Volunteers' Annual Reports 2017–19.

10 Colm Cooke (1980), 'The Modern Irish Missionary Movement', *Archivium Hibernicum*, vol. 35, 234–46. Denis Linehan (2014), 'Irish Empire: assembling the geographical imagination of Irish missionaries in Africa', *Cultural Geographies*, vol. 21, no. 3 (July 2014), 429–47.

11 'A Future of Peace: 60 Years of an Unbroken Tradition of Irish UN Peacekeeping', This is Ireland, https://www.ireland.ie/peacekeeping/.

12 Patrick Keatinge (1970), 'Ireland and the League of Nations', *Studies: An Irish Quarterly Review*, vol. 59, no. 234, 133–47.

13 'Siege of Jadotville', Wikipedia, https://en.wikipedia.org/wiki/Siege_of_Jadotville.

14 'List of Irish military casualties overseas', https://en.wikipedia.org/wiki/List_of_Irish_military_casualties_overseas, accessed December 2020.

15 This survey is known as the Anholt Ipsos Nation Brands Index and is published by Ipsos.

16 The Good Country Index can be found at https://www.goodcountry.org/index/results.

CHAPTER 14

1 Patrick Honohan (2010), 'Is Ireland really the most prosperous country in Europe?' *Economic Letter*, vol. 2021 (no. 1), Central Bank of Ireland.

2 Naomi O'Leary (2020), 'Ireland ranked second in the world for quality of life, beating Sweden, Germany and UK', *The Irish Times*, 17 December 2020, https://www.irishtimes.com/news/ireland/irish-news/ireland-ranked-second-in-the-world-for-quality-of-life-beating-sweden-germany-and-uk-1.4440009.

3 European Commission (2018), *Special Eurobarometer 471 Report: Fairness, inequality and inter-generational mobility*.

4 Constanze Eib et al. (2016), 'Fairness in the workplace relates to health over time', *HR Magazine*, 19 October 2016, accessed at https://www.hrmagazine.co.uk/article-details/fairness-in-the-workplace-relates-to-health-over-time.

5 The detailed results for Eurobarometer 471 are available on the EU Open Data Portal at https://data.europa.eu/euodp/en/data/dataset/S2166_88_4_471_ENG, accessed

January 2021.

6   Leo Ahrens (2019), 'Theorizing the impact of fairness perceptions on the demand for redistribution', *Political Research Exchange*, 1:1, 1–17.

7   The data is compiled from the Eurobarometer survey series. The figures are the average number of people each year who say they are 'fairly' or 'very' satisfied with the life they lead, with 'don't know' responses (typically <1%) excluded.

8   Together these constitute the construct of 'subjective well-being' as it is labelled in psychological research.

9   The survey is Eurobarometer 471. A report of the main findings is at https://ec.europa.eu/ireland/news/almost-8-in-10-irish-people-agree-that-most-things-that-happen-in-life-are-fair-eu-survey_en

10 For overviews of research in the area see E. Diener, S. Oishi & R. E. Lucas (2015), 'National accounts of subjective well-being', *American Psychologist*, 70(3), 234–42. L. Tay & E. Diener (2011). 'Needs and subjective well-being around the world', *Journal of Personality and Social Psychology*, 101(2), 354–65. Kayonda Hubert Ngamaba (2017), 'Determinants of subjective well-being in representative samples of nations', *European Journal of Public Health*, vol. 27, issue 2, April 2017, 377–82. John F. Helliwell et al. (eds) (2020), 'World Happiness Report 2020', New York: Sustainable Development Solutions Network. Ruut Veenhoven (2015), 'Informed Pursuit of Happiness: What we should know, do know and can get to know', *Journal of Happiness Studies* ,vol. 16(4), 1035–71. R. Layard et al. (2012), 'The causes of happiness and misery' in J.F. Helliwell et al. (eds.), *World Happiness Report*, 58-89, New York: United Nations.

11 Andrew T. Jebb et al. (2018), 'Happiness, income satiation and turning points around the world', *Nature Human Behaviour*, vol. 2, 33–8. The figures cited are for equivalised household income. They are appropriate for a one-person household, although the income needed a household with four members would only be twice these amounts.

12 CSO (2021), 'Social Impact of COVID-19 Survey February 2021: Well-being'.

13 C.W. Wiese et al. (2019), 'The Role of Affect on Physical Health Over Time: A Cross-Lagged Panel Analysis Over 20 Years', *Appl.* *Psychol. Health Well-Being*, 11: 202–22.

14 E. Diener, S. Oishi & L. Tay (2018), 'Advances in subjective well-being research', *Nat. Hum. Behav.* 2, 253–60.

CHAPTER 15

1   Although you may be familiar with Maslow's five-staged hierarchy, in subsequent work he suggested additional strata: A.H. Maslow (1970), *Motivation and personality* (2nd ed.) (New York: Harper & Row).

2   For further evidence that addressing individual and societal needs contributes to well-being see Tay and Diener's study of 123 nations. L. Tay & E. Diener (2011), 'Needs and subjective well-being around the world', *Journal of Personality and Social Psychology*, 101(2), 354–65.

3   OECD (2021), 'Adult education level (indicator)', https://data.oecd.org/eduatt/adult-education-level.htm#indicator-chart, accessed February 2021.

4   'Major international study finds Ireland's students among top performers in reading literacy', Department of Education, 3 December 2019, https://www.gov.ie/en/press-release/f6e114-major-international-study-finds-irelands-students-among-top-performe/.

5   George Psacharopoulos (2006), 'The Value of Investment in Education: Theory, Evidence, and Policy', *Journal of Education Finance*, 32(2), p113–136.

6   Jesús Crespo Cuaresma et al. (2014), 'The Determinants of Economic Growth in European Regions', *Regional Studies*, 48(1), 44–67. Aleksejs Srebnijs et al. (2019), 'Determinants of Economic Growth in the EU NUTS2 Regions', *Journal of Economics and Management Research*, 8, 6–35.

7   Eurostat (2018), 'Special Eurobarometer 471: Fairness, inequality and inter-generational mobility', European Commission.

8   Paul Zak (2009), 'The Neuroeconomics of Trust', in Roger Frantz (ed.), *Renaissance in Behavioral Economics, Essays in Honour of Harvey Leibenstein* (Routledge).

9   S. Knack, P. Keefer (1997), 'Does Social Capital Have an Economic Payoff? A Cross-Country Investigation', *Quarterly Journal of Economics*, 112 (4): 1251–88.

10 Elena Zwirner and Nichola Raihani (2020), 'Neighbourhood wealth, not urbanicity, predicts prosociality towards strangers',

Proceedings of the Royal Society B, 287: 20201359.

11 Aidan Connaughton and J.J. Moncus (2020), 'Around the world, people who trust others are more supportive of international cooperation', Pew Research Center, https://www.pewresearch.org/fact-tank/2020/12/15/around-the-world-people-who-trust-others-are-more-supportive-of-international-co-operation/.

12 European Commission (2020), 'New poll finds Irish have most positive attitude to EU', https://ec.europa.eu/ireland/news/new-poll-finds-Irish-have-most-positive-attitude-to-EU_en.

13 M.T. Majeed and T. Ajaz (2018), 'Social capital as a determinant of population health outcomes: A global perspective', *Pakistan Journal of Commerce and Social Sciences*, 12(1), 52–77.

14 Bertelsmann Stiftung and Prognos AG (2020), 'Globalization Report 2020 – Who benefits most from globalization?' (Gütersloh 2020).

15 Results from periodic Eurobarometer surveys, available at https://ec.europa.eu/commfrontoffice/publicopinion/index.cfm/Chart/getChart/themeKy/41/groupKy/206.

16 Niklas Potrafke (2014), 'The Evidence on Globalization', CESifo Working Paper, No. 4708, Center for Economic Studies and ifo Institute (CESifo), Munich.

17 Fredrik Erixon (2018), 'The Economic Benefits of Globalization for Business and Consumers', European Centre for International Political Economy.

18 Joseph Henrich et al. (2001), 'Economic Man in Cross-Cultural Perspective: Behavioral Experiments in Fifteen Small-Scale Societies', *Behavioral and Brain Sciences*, 28(6), 73–8.

19 The other content nations are identified as Switzerland, Denmark, Luxembourg, Norway, the Netherlands and Austria. R.S. Foa et al. (2020), *The Global Satisfaction with Democracy Report 2020*, Cambridge, United Kingdom: Centre for the Future of Democracy.

20 D. Acemoglu & J. A. Robinson (2012), *Why Nations Fail: The origins of power, prosperity and poverty* (New York: Crown Publishers). M. Cheng & R. Mittelhammer (2008), 'Globalization and Economic Development: Impact of Social Capital and Institutional Building', *The American Journal of Economics*

and Sociology, 67(5), 859–88.

21 Jason Luo (2020), 'State of the World: Democracy's Impact on Social and Economic Development', University of Gothenburg, Varieties of Democracy Institute: Users' Working Paper No. 36.

CHAPTER 16

1 Will Dahlgreen (2016), 'Chinese people are most likely to feel the world is getting better', YouGov.co.uk, accessible at https://yougov.co.uk/topics/lifestyle/articles-reports/2016/01/05/chinese-people-are-most-optimistic-world.

2 Sourced from the United Nation's at https://www.un.org/en/sections/issues-depth/poverty/, accessed January 2021.

3 From 'Life expectancy, 1770 to 2019' at https://ourworldindata.org/life-expectancy, accessed January 2021.

4 Sourced from 'Projected world population by level of education' at Our World in Data, https://ourworldindata.org/global-education, accessed January 2021.

5 For some inspirational reading on this topic I recommend Steven Pinker (2018), *Enlightenment Now: The Case for Reason, Science, Humanism, and Progress* (Penguin Books/Viking Press); Hans Rosling et al. (2018), *Factfulness: Ten Reasons We're Wrong About The World – And Why Things Are Better Than You Think* (Sceptre); Matt Ridley (2010), *The Rational Optimist: How Prosperity Evolves* (Harper); and Deirdre Nansen McCloskey and Art Carden (2020), *Leave Me Alone and I'll Make You Rich: How the Bourgeois Deal Enriched the World* (University of Chicago Press).

6 Gavan Reilly (2012), 'Tabloids have up to twice as many negative headlines as positive – study', TheJournal.ie, 4 April 2012, https://www.thejournal.ie/tabloids-have-up-to-twice-as-many-negative-headlines-as-positive-study-405597-Apr2012/.

7 R.F Baumeister et al. (2001), 'Bad is Stronger than Good', *Review of General Psychology*, 5(4), 323–70.

8 M. Trussler & S. Soroka (2014), 'Consumer Demand for Cynical and Negative News Frames', *The International Journal of Press/Politics*, 19(3), 360–79.

9 A. Tversky & D. Kahneman (1974). 'Judgment under uncertainty: Heuristics and biases', *Science*, 185(4157), 1124–31.

10 W.M. Johnston & G.C.L. Davey (1997), 'The psychological impact of negative TV news bulletins: The catastrophizing of personal worries', *British Journal of Psychology*, 88: 85–91.

11 E.A. Holman et al. (2014), 'Media's role in broadcasting acute stress following the Boston Marathon bombings', *Proceedings of the National Academy of Sciences of the United States of America*, 111(1), 93–8.

12 S. Papworth et al. (2009), 'Evidence for shifting baseline syndrome in conservation', *Conservation Letters*, 2: 93–100.

13 Frances C. Moore et al. (2019), 'Rapidly declining remarkability of temperature anomalies may obscure public perception of climate change', *Proceedings of the National Academy of Sciences*, March 2019, 116 (11), 4905–10.

14 D. Rubin et al. (1986), 'Autobiographical memory across the lifespan'. In D. Rubin (ed.), *Autobiographical Memory* (Cambridge University Press).

15 Anja K. Leist et al. (2010), 'Remembering Positive and Negative Life Events: Associations with Future Time Perspective and Functions of Autobiographical Memory', *GeroPsych*, 23, 137–47.

16 D.C. Rubin et al. (1998), 'Things learned in early adulthood are remembered best', *Memory & Cognition*, 26, 3–19.

17 David Levari & Daniel Gilbert et al. (2018), 'Prevalence-induced concept change in human judgment', *Science*, 360, 1465–7.

18 Laura Jacobs et al. (2018), 'Back to Reality: The Complex Relationship Between Patterns in Immigration News Coverage and Real-World Developments in Dutch and Flemish Newspapers (1999–2015)', *Mass Communication and Society*, 21(4), 473–97.

19 Toni van der Meer et al. (2019), 'Mediatization and the Disproportionate Attention to Negative News: The case of airplane crashes', *Journalism Studies*, 20:6, 783–803.

20 Wikipedia (2021), 'Veracity of statements by Donald Trump' at https://en.wikipedia.org/wiki/Veracity_of_statements_by_Donald_Trump.

21 Jan Zilinsky et al. (2021), 'Which Republicans are most likely to think the election was stolen? Those who dislike Democrats and don't mind white nationalists', *Washington Post*, 19 January 2021, https://www.washingtonpost.com/politics/2021/01/19/which-republicans-think-election-was-stolen-those-who-hate-democrats-dont-mind-white-nationalists.

22 G. Pennycook et al. (2018), 'Prior exposure increases perceived accuracy of fake news', *Journal of Experimental Psychology: General*, 147(12), 1865–80.

23 L.K. Fazio et al. (2015), 'Knowledge does not protect against illusory truth', *Journal of Experimental Psychology, General* 144(5), 993–1002.

24 S. Vosoughi et al. (2018), 'The spread of true and false news online', *Science*, 9 March 2018: 1146–51.

25 Nadia M. Brashier et al. (2020), 'An initial accuracy focus prevents illusory truth', *Cognition*, vol. 194, 104054. G. Pennycook et al. (2020), 'Fighting COVID-19 Misinformation on Social Media: Experimental Evidence for a Scalable Accuracy-Nudge Intervention', *Psychol Sci*. 2020 Jul; 31(7): 770–80.

CHAPTER 17

1   The figures are for 2018 and contained in the CSO's 'Environmental Indicators Ireland 2020' and available at https://www.cso.ie/en/releasesandpublications/ep/p-eii/environmentalindicatorsireland2020/greenhousegasesandclimatechange/.

2   Check Ireland's progress on achieving our greenhouse gas emission targets on https://www.epa.ie/ghg/indicatorsprogresstotargets/, accessed December 2020.

3   National Parks and Wildlife Service (2019). 'The Status of EU Protected Habitats and Species in Ireland. Volume 1: Summary Overview'.

4   Natura 2000 barometer statistics for 2019, available at https://www.eea.europa.eu/themes/biodiversity/document-library/natura-2000/natura-2000-network-statistics/natura-2000-barometer-statistics/statistics/barometer-statistics, accessed December 2020.

5   Pádraic Fogarty (2017), *Whittled Away: Ireland's Vanishing Nature* (Collins Press).

6   The data is from Eurostat's 'Price level index for final household consumption expenditure (HFCE) 2019', available at https://ec.europa.eu/eurostat/statistics-explained/index.php/Comparative_price_levels_of_consumer_goods_and_services, accessed January 2021.

7   The figures assume both parents are on the average wage and have two pre-school

children. The dataset is 'Net childcare cost for parents using childcare' for the year 2019, assuming both parents are on the average wage and have two children aged 2 and 3 years, accessible at https://stats.oecd.org/viewhtml.aspx?datasetcode=NCC&lang=en, accessed October 2020.

8 Thomas Conefrey and David Staunton (2019), 'Population Change and Housing Demand in Ireland', Economic Letter, vol. 2019, no. 14, Central Bank of Ireland.

9 Ronan Lyons (2020), 'Ireland's Housing Need & Policy Options: An Overview', Report prepared for Irish Institutional Property, August 2020, available at https://irp-cdn.multiscreensite.com/4065c16c/files/uploaded/Identify%20Consulting%20Full%20Report%20FINAL.pdf.

10 Trends in rental prices throughout the country can be found in the quarterly reports issued by DAFT at https://ww1.daft.ie/report.

11 Data from ECA International contained in press release entitled 'London rental market yet to feel full effect of Covid-19' at https://www.eca-international.com/news/april-2021/london-rental-market-yet-to-feel-effect-of-covid. Across the continent as a whole, Dublin is only ranked behind London, Zurich, Geneva and Moscow.

12 Gerard Kennedy and Samantha Myers (2019), 'An overview of the Irish housing market', Financial Stability Notes vol. 2019, no. 16, Central Bank of Ireland.

13 Mike Allen et al. (2020), Ending Homelessness? The Contrasting Experiences of Denmark, Finland and Ireland (Bristol University Press).

14 Department of Health (2019), Healthy Ireland Survey, Summary Report 2019. Two per cent of people were identified as underweight.

15 J. Breda et al. (2015), 'WHO projections in adults to 2030', presented at European Congress on Obesity, May 2015, Prague.

16 Parliamentary Budget Office (2019), 'An Overview of Tertiary Education funding in Ireland'. The figures relate to undergraduate students (fulltime, part time, remote and FETAC).

17 Peter McGuire (2020), 'Colleges face crisis as funding in freefall', The Irish Times, 9 June 2020, accessed at https://www.irishtimes.com/news/education/colleges-face-crisis-as-funding-in-freefall-1.4269546.

18 The rankings are the QS World University Rankings, comparing colleges' '2021 rank' to their '2012 rank' (published in 2020 and 2011 respectively). Available at https://www.topuniversities.com/universities/country/ireland, accessed October 2020. The QS rankings are based on a basket of indicators including academic and employer reputation, staff–student ratios, citations per faculty and the international nature of faculty and staff.

19 The figures are sourced from the AMECO annual macro-economic database of the European Commission's Directorate General for Economic and Financial Affairs, accessible at https://ec.europa.eu/info/business-economy-euro/indicators-statistics/economic-databases/macro-economic-database-ameco/ameco-database_en. The figures are taken from the November 2020 update and are therefore forecasts for 2020–2022.

20 Our debt-to-GNI* ratio fell from 108% in 1988 to just 28% in 2007. The data is sourced from Irish Fiscal Advisory Council (2020), 'Long-term Sustainability Report: Fiscal challenges and risks 2025-2050', accessible at https://www.fiscalcouncil.ie/long-term-sustainability-report.

21 For a comprehensive overview of our national debt situation see Department of Finance (2019), Annual Report on Public Debt in Ireland 2019.

22 The Economist (2020), 'The pandemic has sent public debt rocketing across the world', 5 May 2020, accessible at https://www.economist.com/graphic-detail/2020/05/05/the-pandemic-has-sent-public-debt-rocketing-across-the-world.

23 For a thorough analysis of the impact of our aging population, read the Irish Fiscal Advisory Council's 'Long-term Sustainability Report: Fiscal challenges and risks 2025–2050' mentioned above.

24 Central Statistics Office (2011), 'Quarterly National Household Survey: Voter Participation, Quarter 2 2011', accessed at https://www.cso.ie/en/media/csoie/releasespublications/documents/labourmarket/2011/voterq22011.pdf.

25 Increasing TV consumption was identified by Robert D. Putnam as the cause of declining voter participation in the United States from the 1960s ('Tuning In, Tuning Out: The Strange Disappearance of Social Capital in

America', PS: Political Science and Politics, vol. 28, no. 4 (Dec. 1995), 664–83). Smartphones have now given us that on steroids!

CHAPTER 18

1   Justin McCarthy (2020), 'Happiness Not Quite as Widespread as Usual in the U.S.', Gallup.com, https://news.gallup.com/poll/276503/happiness-not-quite-widespread-usual.aspx.

2   Robert D. Putnam and Shaylyn Romney Garrett (2020), *The Upswing: How America Came Together a Century Ago and How We Can Do It Again* (Swift Press), p. 47.

3   Johan Norberg (2020), *Open: The Story of Human Progress* (Atlantic Books: London), p. 10.

4   Stephen Byrne et al. (2020), 'The Initial Labour Market Impact of COVID-19', *Economic Letters* 04/EL/20, Central Bank of Ireland.

5   Alex Fradera (2017), 'Small acts of kindness at work benefit the giver, the receiver and the whole organisation', *The British Psychological Society Research Digest*, 4 July 2017, https://digest.bps.org.uk/2017/07/04/small-acts-of-kindness-at-work-benefit-the-giver-the-receiver-and-the-whole-organisation/.

6   See Rutger Bregman (2020), *Humankind: A Hopeful History* (Bloomsbury), p. 298–306.

7   As a result of a commitment in the Programme for Government, the Department of the Taoiseach and the Department of Public Expenditure and Reform started the development of a set of national well-being indicators in 2021.

8   With the exception of the wonderful, reflective work of The Boomtown Rats' 'Banana Republic' and The Radiators' 'Song of the Faithful Departed'. Check them out.

9   Matthew Gallagher et al. (2013), 'Optimism Is Universal: Exploring the Presence and Benefits of Optimism in a Representative Sample of the World', *Journal of Personality*, 81(5), 429–40.

Source data is available on request from mark@markhenry.ie
The cited website links were validated in March 2021, unless otherwise stated.

Index

50/50 Group, 292

Abbey Theatre, 238
abortion, 267, 268–9, 270, 271, 389, 449
Accenture, 193–4
accidents, 11, 16, 22
     see also road traffic accidents
Achill Island, 206
actors, 237–8
Adams, Gerry, 290
Aer Lingus, 209, 211, 212, 213, 214, 216
AerCap, 215
age, 54, 285
Agency for Personal Service Overseas (APSO), 356
agriculture, 4, 22, 59–64, 118, 119, 122, 133, 135–7, 139, 140, 163–4, 165, 172–3, 174, 179, 181, 197, 319, 321, 327, 410–12
Ahern, Bertie, 96–7, 258
AIDs, 311
air pollution, 317, 322–5, 411
Air Siam, 214
air travel, 210–15, 216–17
Airbnb, 429
airports, 174
Airtricity, 335
alcohol
     beverages, 2, 181, 183
     consumption, 48, 71–3, 262, 307–8
     prices, 157, 418
     suicide, 29
     teenagers, 307–8
Allen, Mike, 427, 428–9
An Foras Forbartha, 415
An Foras Pátrúnachta, 107
An Foras Talúntais, 60
An Garda Síochána *see* Gardaí

Anglo-Irish Trade War, 119, 133
Anholt, Simon, 361–4
ante-natal care, 18
antibiotics, 16, 20, 37
Áras an Uachtaráin, 96, 290
Archbishop of Dublin, 278
Arts Council, 232
asylum seekers, 271
     see also refugees
Attenborough, David, 415, 416
austerity, 125–6, 436, 437
autism, 38, 306
automation, 136, 139, 157, 197
availability bias, 397–8

Baileys, 183
Ballydoyle stables, 228
Ban Rules, 223, 224
Banville, John, 232
Barnes, Monica, 288
Barry, Professor Frank, 178–9, 181–2, 188, 191–2
Barton, Dr Ruth, 237, 238, 239, 241–2
bathrooms, 84, 86, 87, 163
baths, 84–5, 86, 87
BCG vaccine, 38
Beckett, Samuel, 231, 232
beef, 47, 62–4, 66, 68, 118, 181, 182–3, 184, 186, 206
     see also cows
Bewley's, 351, 353
Biafra, 344–5
biases *see* cognitive biases
biodiversity, 413–17, 449
biomass, 334, 335
Birds Directive (EU), 415
Bishop of Clonfert, 278
Blair, Tony, 346
Blaney, Leanne, 92
blood transfusions, 20
Bloody Sunday, 240

Blythe, Ernest, 95
Böll, Heinrich, 206
Bono, 236
Book of Kells, 209
Booker Prize, 229, 230, 232
Bord na Móna, 120, 321, 335, 345
Braveheart, 240
bread, 66, 70, 71
Brearton, Fran, 230, 231, 232–3
breast screening, 41, 42
breath testing, 26
Brexit, 126, 186
Britain *see* United Kingdom
British Airways, 211, 212
British Film Institute, 239
broadband, 90–1, 157, 419
Brown, Gordon, 346
Browne, Noël, 18
Building Energy Rating (BER), 338, 339–40
Burke, Laura, 323, 326, 327, 329, 330, 331, 332, 341, 411–12
Burke, Ray, 258
Burns, Anna, 232
Burundi, 345
butter, 70–1, 182

cancers, 36, 37–8, 39–42, 52, 56, 431
cannabis, 307
carbon emissions, 8, 93, 184, 318, 321, 323, 331, 333, 335, 338, 339, 340, 409–12
     see also climate change
cardiovascular disease, 48–9, 50, 388
     see also coronary heart disease; heart disease
cardiovascular health strategy, 48–9
Cardwell's Law, 446

cars, 91–3, 411
Casey, Eamonn (Bishop of Galway), 269
Catholic church
    abortion, 268–9
    cars, 93
    census data, 271
    clerical child sexual abuse, 269, 298
    contraception, 278
    decline in power, 389
    divorce, 268–9
    education, 101–2, 103, 104, 110, 164
    entertainment, 235
    film, 239
    fish on Fridays, 68
    healthcare, 50–1, 81, 164
    missionaries, 355
    Mother and Child Scheme, 18
    suicide, 29
céilís, 235
Celtic Tiger, 45, 72, 109, 115, 123–4, 128, 131, 149, 155, 167, 179, 198, 202, 251, 262, 285, 291–2, 339, 356, 368, 372, 411, 423, 428, 436–7, 444
censorship, 231–2
census data, 271
Central Bank, 368
Central Statistics Office, 70, 156, 261, 273
Channel Four, 239
Charities Aid Foundation, 272
charity-giving, 272–3, 363
    see also donations, charitable
cheese, 70, 71, 186
chicken, 62, 67, 68
Child Benefit Allowance, 421
childbirth, 11, 19–21, 73, 280, 282
childcare, 278, 280, 284, 286, 418, 419–22, 449
children
    clerical sexual abuse, 269, 298

corporal punishment, 300–2
education, 4
homelessness, 427
improved lives of, 295–6, 315
physical health of teenagers, 307–10
rights of, 296–9
size of family, 276–7
special needs education, 303–6
teenage pregnancies, 310–12
youth crime, 312–15
Children Act (1908), 301, 302
Children Act (2001), 302, 314
Children First Act (2015), 302
children's allowance, 18, 165
Children's Court, 313, 314
Children's Rights in Ireland, 297
China, 183, 184
Christian Aid, 351
Church of Ireland, 101–2
cinema, 237–42
Citizens' Assembly, 449
civil liberties, 251, 268, 271
Civil War, 252
clerical child sexual abuse, 269, 298
Cliffs of Moher, 209
Climate Action Act (2021), 412
climate change, 64, 147, 214, 321, 323, 333, 340, 346, 348, 363, 400, 409–12, 416, 449
    see also carbon emissions
Clough-Gorr, Professor Kerri, 39, 41
clover, 61
coal, 84, 119, 120, 323–4, 335, 340, 388, 391, 411
coalition governments, 252–3
cognitive biases, 7, 396–406
cohabitation, 280–1

Coillte, 320
Coleman, Shane, 251, 252, 253–4, 255, 256, 257–9, 265, 266, 439
Collins, Michael, 227
Columban Sisters, 355
Comhairlí na nÓg, 297
Commission of Inquiry on Mental Handicap, 304
Commission on the Status of Women, 268, 285
Commission to Inquire into Child Abuse (Ryan Commission), 298
Committee on Evil Literature, 231
communications, 143, 152, 156, 157, 174, 393, 418, 419
community, 4–6, 8, 385–8, 445
community schools, 103
commuting, 141
Concern, 344–5
Congo, 358–9, 360
Congress of Trade Unions, 148–9
Connacht, 14–15
consistent poverty, 166–7
Constitution, 296–7, 298, 304
Constitutional Convention, 449
construction, 22, 179, 197, 424, 428, 430
    see also homelessness; housing
Construction Industry Federation, 23
Construction Safety Partnership, 23
contraception, 277–8, 285, 311
Convention on the Rights of the Child (UN), 297, 298, 299
Cooley Distillery, 183
Coolmore Stud, 228
Corcoran, Dr Paul, 29, 30

coronary heart disease, 31–2, 36, 47, 48, 49
  see also cardiovascular disease; heart disease
corporal punishment, 300–2
corporation tax, 175, 178, 191
corruption, 257–9, 265, 375, 382, 392
Corry, Eoghan, 212, 213, 214, 215, 216–17, 219
Council of Education report, 101–2
Covid-19, 2, 8, 35, 91, 126, 130, 132, 135, 141, 145–6, 171–2, 207, 210, 213, 214, 237, 255–6, 302, 347–8, 352, 376–7, 388, 390–1, 396, 398, 434, 436, 444, 447
cows, 59, 61, 62, 63, 64, 411–12
  see also beef
CRH, 193
cricket, 223
crime, 259–64, 271, 382, 385
Criminal Assets Bureau, 263
Croke Park Agreement, 150
crop breeding, 60–1
Cross-Departmental Team on Homelessness, 427–8
The Crying Game, 240
Cumann na nGaedheal, 119
Currie, Austin, 290
cystic fibrosis, 39

Dáil na nÓg, 297
dairy, 61, 62, 64, 118, 172, 180, 182, 183, 184, 327, 411, 416
dance, 2
Darby, Tom, 44
Daughters of Charity, 304
Dawn Meats, 172
Day-Lewis, Daniel, 237, 238, 240
de Barra, Caoimhe, 345, 346–7, 348, 350, 355, 356
de Buitléar, Éamon, 415
de Courcy, Catherine, 95, 96, 97

de Gaulle, Charles, 121
de Valera, Éamon, 106, 119, 357–8
death rate see mortality rate
debt, 434–7
declinism, 402
Defence Forces, 357, 358, 359, 360–1
Delaney, Enda, 196, 197, 198, 202–3
democracy, 249–54, 265, 375, 382–3, 391, 393, 449–50
  see also political system
Dencik, Jacob, 189–90, 191, 192
Department for International Development, 346
Department of Education, 301, 302, 304, 305
Department of Foreign Affairs, 199, 344, 345
Department of Health, 18, 39, 48, 49, 51, 73, 305, 431
Department of the Environment, Northern Ireland, 26
deposit return scheme, 332
Desmond, Barry, 48
development aid, 343–50, 383, 387–8
Devine, Francis, 148–9, 150
diabetes, 36, 37, 50, 388
diarrhoea, 36, 37
diet, 16, 47–8, 49, 64, 65–8, 308, 431
Dillon, James, 59
diphtheria, 36, 37, 38
disabled people, 169–70, 175
discrimination, 175, 268, 284, 285, 286, 371
diseases, 3, 16, 18, 35–9
diversity, 6, 175, 200–3, 264, 390
divorce, 267, 268–70, 271, 289
donations, charitable, 349–50, 386

Dornan, Jamie, 359
dot-com bubble, 134
Doyle, Roddy, 232
drink-driving, 26, 27, 72
drinks, 2, 180, 181, 182, 183, 184, 192, 308, 309
driving licences, 26–7
driving tests, 25
drug use, 262
Dublin
  housing, 83, 86
  population growth, 14, 78–9
  poverty, 67
  telephones, 89
  terrorist attacks, 259–60
  waste water treatment, 326
Dublin Bus, 44
Dublin Corporation, 81, 83
Dublin County Council, 258
Dublin Opinion, 197
Dublin Zoo, 94, 95–7

earnings, 151–2, 164
  see also income; wages
Eaton Corporation, 194
ebeon, 134
e-commerce, 145–6
Economic and Social Research Institute, 166
economy, 102, 117–30, 135–7, 384, 385, 386, 387, 389, 390, 392, 444, 445
education
  Catholic church, 101–2, 103, 104, 110, 164
  employment in, 137, 157
  higher education, 113–15, 139, 376, 384, 433–4, 445–6
  importance of, 4–5, 8
  inclusive education, 304–6
  increased opportunities for, 99–100, 369, 380, 383, 384–5, 392, 393, 395

investment in, 6, 157, 191
Irish language teaching,
    105–7
lifelong learning, 139–40,
    376, 446
and poverty, 165–6
primary-level, 100–2, 103–
    4, 107, 108, 109, 110
pupil-to-teacher ratios,
    108–10
second-level, 100–3, 104,
    108, 109, 111–13, 197,
    232, 384
special needs, 303–6
universal and Christian
    principles, 171
women, 281–2, 285, 348,
    385
eggs, 70
Eighth Amendment to the
    Constitution (1983), 268,
    270, 271, 289
    see also Constitution
eircom, 134
electric vehicles, 336–7
electricity, 84, 85, 86, 87,
    333–6, 411
Electricity Supply Board
    (ESB), 86, 335
Elizabeth, Queen, 290, 291
emigration, 4, 6, 11, 13, 102,
    120, 122, 125, 131, 133, 135,
    152, 194–9, 200, 203, 261,
    262, 355, 388
employment
    from agriculture to
        services, 135–7, 140
    discrimination and
        harassment, 371
    earnings, 151–2
    e-commerce, 145–6
    in education, 137, 157
    globalisation, 391
    growth in, 122, 130–2
    high-skilled jobs, 137–40
    impact of urbanisation, 15
    jobs created overseas,
        192–4

productivity, 142–4
strikes, 146–50
tourism, 208
women, 4, 68, 283–7, 444
working hours, 140–2
    see also unemployment
energy, 318, 333–7, 411, 418, 419
Energy Performance of
    Buildings Directive, 339
energy-efficiency, 338–41
Enright, Anne, 232
entertainment, 235
environment, 175, 316–17,
    327, 329, 341, 375, 382, 445
Environmental Protection
    Agency, 323, 329, 411
Enya, 234
equal pay, 285
equality of opportunity, 175,
    369, 386, 446, 448
Euro, 123, 131, 155
European Central Bank, 125
European Commission,
    329–30
European Committee of
    Social Rights, 302
European Common
    Agricultural Policy, 415
European Convention on
    Human Rights, 269
European Economic
    Community, 121–3, 179, 181,
    202, 268, 285, 389
    see also European Union
European Exchange Rate
    Mechanism (ERM), 155
European Social Charter, 302
European Transport Safety
    Council, 27
European Union, 69–70, 123,
    125, 166, 172–5, 218, 254,
    255, 269, 320, 326, 346,
    364, 387, 390
    Birds Directive, 415
    discrimination legislation,
        371
    Habitats Directive (1992),
        413, 415

migration to and from
    Ireland, 13
Single European Market,
    122–3, 131, 175, 389
Structural Funds, 122, 131,
    173–4, 393, 444
    see also European
        Economic Community
Eurovision Song Contest,
    207, 208, 233–4
Evening Mail, 301
exercise, 48, 431
Expert Advisory Group on
    Relationships and Sexuality
    Education, 312
exports, 177–89, 197, 206

Facebook, 447, 448
Fair Trade, 350–3
fairness, 370, 371–2, 387,
    391
Fairtrade Ireland, 351, 353
fake news, 404–6, 447–8
Famine see potato famine
farming see agriculture
Farrell, Brian, 26, 27
The Favourite, 241
feminism see women,
    women's movement
Fennell, Nuala, 288
Fianna Fáil, 79, 119, 121, 122,
    165, 171, 239, 252, 289, 392,
    448
film, 237–42
financial crisis (2008) see
    global financial crisis (2008)
Fine Gael, 239, 252, 288,
    292, 392, 448
Fine-Davis, Dr Margret,
    278, 280, 284, 285–6, 287,
    419–20, 421–2
fish, 65, 66, 68, 87, 399, 414,
    416
    see also seafood
Fitzgerald, Barry, 237, 238
FitzGerald, Garret, 288, 289,
    345
Flynn, Pádraig, 289

Fogarty, Pádraic, 319, 320–1, 414, 415, 416, 417
foods
    competition, 419
    consumption, 65–8, 71–3
    diets, 65–8
    expenditure on, 69–71
    exports, 180–5, 186
    nutritional standards, 18
    prices, 152, 418, 419
    production, 59–64, 192
foot and mouth disease, 207–8
Ford, Henry, 91
foreign aid, 343–50, 353–6
foreign direct investment (FDI), 189–92, 363
forests, 317, 318–22
Fox, Billy, 260
France, 206–7
free press, 265–6, 387
Freedom House, 271
Fricker, Brenda, 237, 238, 240
fridges, 87, 88
fruit, 47, 65, 66, 67, 308

Gabhainn, Professor Saoirse Nic, 308, 309, 310, 312, 315
Gaelic Athletic Association (GAA), 221–5, 310
Gaelic football, 222, 225
Gaelic games, 221–5, 385–6
Gaelic League, 223
Gaelscoileanna, 107
Galligan, Yvonne, 288, 289–90, 292
Game of Thrones, 209
Garda Traffic Corps, 27
Garda Youth Diversion Programme, 312, 313, 314
Gardaí, 254, 255, 256, 260, 261, 263–4, 271, 361
The Gathering, 208–9
gay see homosexuality; same-sex marriage
Gaynor, Peter, 351, 352–3
GDP see Gross Domestic Product (GDP)

GE Capital Aviation Services (GECAS), 215
gender equality, 198, 285, 290, 291–3, 346, 371, 390, 447, 449
    see also women
General Medical Services Scheme, 52
generosity, 272–3
    see also donations, charitable; foreign aid
Geoghegan-Quinn, Máire, 288
Germany, 206
Gilbert, Daniel, 402–3
Gill, Professor Denis, 38–9
Gini coefficient, 168, 169
global financial crisis (2008), 124–5, 131, 150, 155, 167, 208, 254, 292, 346, 435, 436, 444
    see also Great Recession
globalisation, 8, 67, 118, 121, 122, 157, 375, 382–3, 388, 390–1, 446
GNI see Gross National Income (GNI)
GNI*, 129, 368, 450
Going My Way, 238
Good Country Index, 361–4
Goodman, Larry, 172
Google, 448
GPs, 52, 54, 56, 278, 432
grass farming, 62, 63
grass-breeding programmes, 61
Great Britain see United Kingdom
Great Depression, 118, 119, 133, 196, 448
Great Recession, 128, 135, 159–60, 174, 192, 208, 254, 273, 352, 372–3, 421, 427, 433, 437
    see also global financial crisis (2008)
Green Party, 289
Gross Domestic Product (GDP), 127, 128, 129–30,

142–3, 174, 363, 368, 450
Gross National Income (GNI), 143, 343, 347, 368, 450
Gross Value Added (GVA), 143, 144
Growing Up in Ireland, 297
The Guard, 241
Guerin, Veronica, 263
Guinness, 183, 243–4, 245
Guinness Peat Aviation, 214–15

Habitats Directive (EU), 413, 415
Haddington Road Agreement, 150
Halappanavar, Savita, 21
happiness, 1, 4, 367, 372–7, 380, 445
harassment, 371
Harney, Mary, 323
Haughey, Charles, 239, 258, 259, 278, 289
Health Act (1947), 18
Health Act (1970), 51
health and safety, 21–3
Health and Safety Authority, 22, 23
Health and Safety Executive, 43, 55–6
health boards, 50–1
health education, 49, 308–9
health promotion, 48, 49
healthcare, 18, 50–4, 81, 157, 164, 382, 392, 419
Healthy Ireland survey, 431
Heaney, Seamus, 230, 232–3
heart disease, 36, 37, 46–50, 52, 56, 73
    see also coronary heart disease
heat pumps, 340
heating, 84, 85, 86, 87, 340
height, 73–4
Henry, John, 47
Henry, Paul, 2
hierarchy of needs, 381–3

Higgins, Michael D., 240
higher education, 4, 6, 113–15, 139, 376, 384, 433–4, 445–6
Hill 16, 223–4
Hillery, President, 289
hockey, 223
Hogan, Patrick, 95
holidays, 215–17
Holy Ghost Fathers, 355
Holy Rosary Sisters, 355
home computers, 88, 90
home ownership, 81
Home School Community Liaison, 109
homelessness, 8, 149, 271, 426–30
　　see also housing
homes, 338–41
　　see also homelessness; housing
home-working, 141–2, 146
homosexuality, 3, 231, 269, 270–1
　　see also same-sex marriage
horse racing, 226–8
horticulture, 64, 180–1
hospitals, 18, 20, 41, 49–50, 53–4, 355
household appliances, 87–91
household wealth, 161–3
housework, 89
housing, 18, 19, 79, 81–7, 123, 149, 161–3, 164, 271, 338–41, 418, 419, 422–6, 444, 449
　　see also homelessness
Housing Assistance Payment, 429
Human Development Index, 367–8
human rights, 275, 296–9, 345, 347, 361, 363, 369, 390
hurling, 222, 224, 227
Hussey, Gemma, 288
Hyde, Douglas, 223
hydroelectric, 86, 334
hydrogen power, 336
hydrogeneration, 334, 335
Hyland, Professor Áine, 101,

102–3, 106–7, 109–10, 112, 281–2

IBM Institute for Business Value, 189, 190, 192
Iceland, 194–5
IDA Ireland, 189, 384, 418
illusory truth effect, 404–6
immigration, 4, 6, 13, 135, 195, 197–9, 200–3, 204–5, 277, 372, 390, 423, 445, 447
incinerators, 331
inclusive education, 304–6
income, 157–61, 375, 376, 382, 386, 390, 392
　　see also earnings
income inequality, 167–72, 386, 387
Independent News and Media, 266
individualism, 448
industry, 135–7, 148, 151, 152, 163–4, 165, 197
infant milk formula, 181, 184
infant mortality, 3, 6, 13, 16–19, 31
inflation, 70–1, 122, 123, 128, 131, 151, 152–7, 390
INLA, 260
Insomnia Coffee, 352
Institute for Economics & Peace, 261
Institute for Peace Support and Leadership Training, 361
insurance, 419
interest rates, 120
International Monetary Fund, 125
internet, 88, 90–1, 131, 134, 137, 188–9, 389
Investment in Education report, 102, 103–4
IRA, 207, 227, 251, 260, 263, 290, 291, 391
Irisches Tagebuch, 206
Irish Aid, 344, 345, 346, 348, 356

Irish Army Reserves, 240
Irish Association of Teachers in Special Education, 304
Irish Centre for Human Rights, 358
Irish Cinema in the Twenty-first Century, 237
Irish Congress of Trade Unions, 23
Irish Distillers, 183
Irish Fair Trade Network (IFTN), 351
Irish Film Board, 239, 240, 241
Irish Free State, 1, 86, 95, 106, 118, 196, 227, 231–2, 251, 319, 357, 438
Irish Heart Foundation, 47, 48, 49, 50, 309
Irish Hospitality Global, 242
Irish language, 105–7
Irish Literary Society, 230
Irish Pub Company, 242, 243–4, 245
Irish Sugar Company, 90
Irish Travel Agents Association, 213
Irish Union of School Students, 301–2
Irish Wildlife Trust, 319
Island of Ireland Peace Park, 291
IT industry, 192

Jameson, 183
Java Republic, 352
Jockey Clubs, 227
Johnson Controls, 194
Jordan, Neil, 240
justice system, 254, 255, 256
Juvenile Liaison Officers, 314

Kahneman, Daniel, 397
Katanga, 358
Kavanagh, Dr Ella, 123, 154, 155
Kavanagh, Dr Paul, 43–4, 45, 46, 126

Kelly, Luke, 236
Kerry Group, 192
Kiely, Gerard, 172, 174, 175
Kilkelly, Professor Ursula, 297, 298, 299, 302, 313, 314, 315
Kilkenny Health Project, 48
King, Helen, 181, 182, 183, 184, 186
King, Philip, 234, 235–6, 237
Labour Party, 149, 288–9
Ladies' Gaelic Football Association, 225
landfill
    gas, 335
    sites, 329, 330–1
land-loan liability, 119
Lansdowne Road Agreement, 150
law, 375, 382, 392
Law Society, 356
Lawlor, Mary, 347
leaded petrol, 324
League of Nations, 118, 357–8
learning disabilities, 304
Leaving Certificate Applied programme, 112
Leaving Certificates, 111–12
Lebanon, 358, 359–60
legal costs, 419
Lehman Brothers, 124
Leinster, 14
Leist, Anja, 401–2
leisure, 94–7, 376, 377, 383
Lemass, Seán, 81, 102, 103, 121
Lenihan, Brian, 289, 290
Les Lacs du Connemara, 206–7
Lesotho, 345
Lester, Seán, 358
Levari, David, 402–3
libel, 265
life expectancy, 1, 3, 7, 11, 30–2, 47, 68, 277, 368, 369, 376, 382, 385, 388, 395, 396, 401
lifelong learning, 139–40, 376, 446

lighting, 84
literature, 229–33
Logan, Johnny, 234
Lourdes, 216
lung cancer, 40, 42
Lynch, Jack, 301
Lyons, Ronan, 118, 119, 120, 122–4, 137, 418, 419, 424, 425
Maastricht, 122
Mahon Tribunal, 258–9
maintenance workers' strike, 148–9
Malawi, 348
mandatory alcohol testing, 26
manufacturing, 418
Markievicz, Countess, 288
marriage, 279, 280, 282, 285, 376
marriage bar, 268, 284, 285
Marriage Equality, 268
Martin, Micheál, 44, 306
Maslow, Abraham, 382, 383
McAleese, Martin, 291
McAleese, Mary, 97, 287, 291
McCabe, Jerry, 263
McCabe, Maurice, 256
McEvoy, Karen, 21
McGee v. The Attorney General, 278
McGuinness, Dr Sharon, 22, 23
McNally, Mel, 242, 243–5
measles, 3, 36, 37, 38
meat, 47, 62–4, 65, 66, 67–8, 172, 180, 181, 183
media see free press; press
Medical Missionaries of Mary, 355
medical treatment, 16, 49
Medtronic, 194
mental health, 29, 30, 295, 371, 377, 388, 398, 427
Michael Collins, 240
microwaves, 87–8
middle classes, 157–61
milk, 61, 62, 64, 66, 70, 141, 182, 184, 411, 416

Milkman, 232
minimum wage, 125, 159
Minister for Children and Youth Affairs, 298
Minister of State for Children, 298
missionaries, 219, 269, 354, 355
MMR vaccine, 38
mobile phones, 88, 90
Modified Gross National Income (GNI*), 129, 368, 450
Monaghan, 259–60
Moneypoint power station, 411
Moore, Dr Frances, 400
mortality rate, 15–16
Mother and Child Scheme, 18
motorways, 27
Mountbatten, Lord, 260
Mulcahy, Dr Risteárd, 48
multiculturalism, 200–3
multinationals, 122, 123, 144, 146, 177–8, 179, 180, 193–4
Munster, 14
Murphy, Professor Ray, 358, 359, 360–1
music, 2, 233–7
My Left Foot, 240

National Association of Parents and Friends of the Mentally Handicapped, 304
National Busworkers' Union, 44
National Cancer Registry, 39
National Car Test, 25, 26
National Children's Hospital, 299
National Children's Strategy, 297, 299
National Health Service (UK), 198
National Immunisation Advisory Committee, 38
National Longitudinal Study of Children, 297

national minimum wage, 125, 159
National Parks and Wildlife Service, 415, 416
National Roads Authority, 26
National Safety Council, 26
National Suicide Research Foundation, 29
National Union of Journalists, 103
National Wage Agreements, 154
negativity bias, 396–7
Netherlands, 74
Newstalk, 251
Nobel Prize, 229–30, 232, 363
Nolan, Brian, 166, 167
Norberg, Johan, 446
Northern Ireland
    as birthplace, 202
    Department of the Environment, 26
    economy, 118
    Fianna Fáil and Fine Gael, 392
    GAA games, 222
    Mary McAleese visit, 291
    the Troubles, 5, 259
Norway, 1, 27
nutrition, 16, 18, 430
Nyerere, Julius, 356

Oberstown Children Detention Campus, 314–15
obesity, 8, 50, 309, 430–2
O'Brien, Vincent, 228
O'Connell, Dr Jean, 431, 432
O'Connor, Frank, 232
Odd Man Out, 239
O'Donnell, Ian, 261, 262
O'Donoghue, Marie, 305
O'Faoláin, Seán, 232
official development assistance (ODA), 343–4
oil, 154, 340, 411, 436
Oireachtas Joint Committee on Education and Skills, 309

Old Age Pension, 164
O'Leary, Michael, 212, 213
O'Loughlin-Kennedy, John and Kay, 344–5
O'Malley, Donogh, 103, 114
O'Mara, Professor Frank, 60–1, 62, 64
Ombudsman for Children, 297
Once, 241
Open: The Story of Human Progress, 446
openness, 4–5, 6, 8, 386, 388–91, 445, 447
optimism, 450
Organisation for Economic Cooperation and Development (OECD), 142, 143, 349
Origin Green, 181, 184
Oscars, 237, 238, 240, 241, 242
overseas aid/assistance, 343–50, 353–6
Overseas Development Institute, 347
Oxfam, 351

packaging, 45, 330, 331, 332, 333
Papworth, Dr Sarah, 399–400
particulate matter (PM2.5), 322, 323, 324
passports, 218–19
Pauly, Daniel, 399
peace process, 291
peacekeeping, 357–61, 363, 387
peat, 120, 321, 335, 340, 345, 411, 412
penalty points system, 26
pensions, 124, 125, 163, 164, 169, 204, 277, 436
Pernod Ricard, 183
petrol, 324
pharmaceuticals, 180, 191
phenylketonuria, 39

Physical Education, 310
physical health, 307–10
picketing, 148–9
pigs, 62–3, 64, 207
P.J. Carroll & Co, 43
planning, 258, 259
plastic bag levy, 330
polio, 38
political system, 249–54, 255, 256–7, 259, 375, 380, 382, 388, 391–3, 448, 449
    see also democracy
pollution, 317, 322–5, 375, 382
population, 11–15, 78–9, 277, 285, 348
pornography, 312
ports, 174
potato famine, 12, 65–6, 78, 319
potatoes, 61, 65–6, 70, 71
poverty, 18, 67, 159, 163–7, 171, 346, 347, 351, 353, 363, 369, 382, 390, 396, 421–2
pregnancy, 310–12, 348
press, 254, 255, 265–6, 387
prevalence-induced concept change, 402–3
preventative medicine, 18, 39
prices, 152, 153–7, 417–19
primary-level education, 100–2, 103–4, 107, 108, 109, 110
Principled Aid Index, 347
private donations, 349–50
productivity, 142–4
Programme for Economic Expansion, 121, 197
progress attention deficit, 400–1
property, 123, 161–3
property tax, 425
proportional representation, 252, 438
protectionism, 118–20, 121, 123, 136, 151, 375
public debt, 434–7
public health, 16, 18, 50, 54–6
    see also healthcare

public sector, 124
pubs, 242–6
Punishment in Our Schools, 301
Putnam, Robert D., 446, 448

quality of life, 1, 3, 367–9, 450
The Quiet Man, 239
Quinn, Fergal, 352

Racing Post, 228
railways, 174
Reagan, Ronald, 170
recycling, 318, 329, 330–2
Reform, 301
refugees, 363
    see also asylum seekers
Regional Technical Colleges, 114
Relationships and Sexuality Education, 312
reminiscence bump, 401–2
remittances, 203–5, 348, 388–9
renewable energy, 318, 333–7, 411
Reporters Without Borders, 265, 266
Revenue Commissioners, 160
Riverdance, 207
Road Safety Authority, 26
road traffic accidents, 6–7, 24–7
Robert Roberts, 351
Robinson, Mary, 277, 287, 288–90, 347
Room, 241
Rouse, Professor Paul, 222–3, 224, 225, 227, 228
Rowlette, Sally, 21
Rowley, Dr Ellen, 79, 81, 85, 86
Royal College of Physicians of Ireland, 47
Royal Zoological Society of Dublin, 95, 96
RTÉ, 202, 224, 266, 398
Rubin, David, 401, 402

rugby, 223
Rural Electrification Scheme, 86
Ryan, Dr Lisa, 335–6, 337, 339, 340
Ryan, Mr Justice Seán, 298
Ryan, Tony, 212, 214
Ryan Commission (Commission to Inquire into Child Abuse), 298
Ryanair, 207, 209, 211, 212–15

Sabena, 213
Safe Pass, 23
safety, 1, 19, 21, 22, 23, 259, 261, 264, 381, 382, 403
Saint Vincent's Hospital, 48
same-sex marriage, 267–8, 270–1, 389, 449
sanitation, 16, 174
Sardou, Michel, 206–7
Scandal Nation, 257, 258
Schoolchildren's Protection Organisation, 301
schools, 101–4, 107, 109–10
screening, medical, 39
seafood, 65, 68, 180–1
seatbelts, 25, 26
Second World War *see* World War II
second-level education, 100–3, 104, 108, 109, 111–13, 197, 232, 384
September 11th 2001 terrorist attacks, 208, 213
services sector, 135–7, 140, 152, 187–9
sex education, 312
Sexton, Regina, 66–8, 69–70, 72
sexual abuse, 269, 298
Shannon hydroelectric scheme, 86, 334
Shaw, George Bernard, 230, 231
Shelley, Professor Emer, 47–8, 49, 50

Sheridan, Jim, 240
Shields, William Joseph (Barry Fitzgerald), 237, 238
shifting baseline syndrome, 398–401
shopping centres, 93
Single European Market, 122–3, 131, 175, 389
single mothers, 281, 421–2
single parents, 170
Single Transferable Vote (PR-STV), 252, 253
Sinn Féin, 290, 448
smartphones, 90
Smith, Alan, 52, 54, 56
smoking, 37, 40, 41, 42–6, 47, 48, 56, 157, 431
Smurfit Kappa, 192–3
Smyth, Ailbhe, 267–9
Smyth, Father Brendan, 269, 270, 271
soccer, 221–2, 223, 225
Social, Physical and Health Education (SPHE) syllabus, 308, 312
social capital, 6, 370, 377, 386, 387, 388, 391, 393, 447, 450
social class, 157–61, 171, 380, 382, 386
social exclusion, 166, 386
social housing, 428, 429, 430
social media, 405, 432, 447–8
social mobility, 165
Social Partnership, 122, 131, 149–50, 171
Society for African Missions, 355
software companies, 191
soil, 60
solar power, 335
solid fuels, 324–5
Soroka, Stuart, 397
Special Areas of Conservation (SACs), 413, 414
Special Education Review Committee, 305
special needs education, 303–6

Special Protection Areas (SPAs), 413–14, 415, 416
speeding, 26
    see also road traffic accidents
Sport and Ireland: A History, 222–3
sports, 221–5, 310, 385–6
Spotify, 188–9
SpunOut.ie, 308
St Joseph's School for Deaf Boys, 303–4
St Joseph's School for the Blind, 304
St Mary's School for Deaf Girls, 303
St Michael's House, 304
St Patrick's College, 304
St Patrick's Institution, 314
St Patrick's Missionary Society, 355
stability, 4–5, 8, 391–3, 445
Staines, Michael, 264
Star Wars: The Force Awakens, 209
Steering Committee on Technical Education, 114
strikes, 146–50
stroke, 49–50, 73
Structural Funds (EU), 122, 131, 173–4, 393, 444
subprime mortgages, 124
suburbs, 79, 81, 83, 93
sugar, 70–1, 90, 119, 308, 309
suicide, 28–30, 270
sulphur dioxide emissions, 323
Summerfield, Frederick Maurice, 92
Superquinn, 352
sustainability, 181, 184, 210, 353
Sutherland, Peter, 123
Swissair, 213

Tanzania, 356
taxation, 169, 375, 383, 392, 418, 424–5

teachers, 110
Teagasc, 60, 61, 184
teenagers
    alcohol, 307–8
    physical health, 307–10
    pregnancies, 310–12
Telecom Éireann, 157
telephones, 88, 89–90
Temple Street Children's Hospital, 38, 39
terrorism, 208, 213, 259–60
textile industry, 120
Thatcher, Margaret, 122, 170
theatre, 237, 238
thyroid disorder, 39
tillage, 61–2, 119
Tin Pan Alley, 236
tobacco, 41–5, 56, 156, 157, 418, 432
    see also smoking
Tobacco Free Ireland Programme, 43
Together for Yes, 267–8
toilets, 84, 85, 86, 87
tourism, 174, 186, 205–10, 242, 245–6, 362
trade unions, 148, 152
Traideireann, 351
transport, 91–3, 324, 333, 336, 337, 411, 418, 419
Travers, Joseph, 304–5, 306
Trinity College, 209
Trócaire, 344, 345, 349–50, 355
the Troubles, 5, 259, 260–1, 263, 290
Trump, Donald, 3, 254, 403–4, 445
Trussler, Marc, 397
trust, 5, 385, 386, 387, 388, 447
tuberculosis, 3, 18, 36, 37, 38, 47, 48
tumble dryers, 88–9
Tversky, Amos, 397

U2, 234
Ulster, 14–15

unemployment, 29, 118, 120, 121, 125, 126, 131, 132–5, 164, 165, 166, 171, 262, 421–2, 449
    see also employment
United Kingdom
    emigration to, 196, 199
    exports to, 186
    foreign aid, 346
    immigration from, 202
    National Health Service, 198
    political system, 251, 252
United Nations
    aid programmes, 346, 353
    Convention of the Rights of the Child, 297, 298, 299
    Human Development Index, 367–8
    peacekeeping, 357–61, 387
United States
    Donald Trump, 3, 254, 403–4, 445
    emigration to, 196
    exports to, 185, 186
    immigration from, 202
    income inequality, 170
    political system, 251, 252
Universal Social Charge, 125, 169
universities, 434
Urban Waste Water Treatment Directive (EU), 326
urbanisation, 14, 15, 78–81, 375, 382

vaccination, 19, 37, 38–9, 52, 56, 396
vegetables, 47, 64, 65, 66, 67, 308
violence, 262, 263
    see also terrorism
Volkswagen Beetle, 92, 93
volunteering, 272, 273, 353–6, 386
voting, 437–40, 449

wages, 151–2, 164, 192
   see also earnings; income
Walsh, Dr John, 114–15,
   433–4
Walsh, Michael, 216
Walsh, Ruby, 228
Walsh, Willie, 213
washing machines, 88
waste, 318, 328–33, 363
   see also waste water
Waste Framework Directive,
   330
Waste Management Act
   (1996), 329
waste water, 317, 325–8
water, 16, 38, 84, 85, 86, 174,
   327
wave power, 335
wealth, 161–3
wealth inequality, 369–70
Webfactory, 134
welfare support, 164–5, 166,
   169, 171
well-being *see* happiness
Whelan, Professor
   Christopher, 159–60, 162,
   163, 165, 166, 167, 170, 171
whiskey, 183
Whitaker, T.K., 103, 121
White Paper on Foreign Policy
   (1996), 345
*Whittled Away: Ireland's
   Vanishing Nature*, 319, 414
whooping cough, 3, 36, 37, 38
wildlife, 413–17
Wildlife Act (1976), 415
windpower, 334, 335, 336
women
   abortion, 267, 268–9, 270,
    271, 389, 449
   education, 281–2, 285,
    348, 385
   emigration, 196
   employment, 4, 68, 283–7,
    444
   equal pay, 285
   Gaelic football, 225
   height, 73, 74

   homelessness, 427
   marriage, 279, 280, 282,
    285
   number of children, 276–7
   optimism, 450
   in politics, 287–93
   rights, 275
   women's movement, 198,
    278–9, 288, 289, 389
   see also contraception;
    gender equality
Women's Studies Centre, 292
Workers' Party, 289
working hours, 140–2
Working Time Directive (EU),
   141
workplace fatalities, 21–3
World Bank, 339, 346, 353
World Economic Forum, 209
World Health Organization,
   45, 431
World War I, 79, 118, 133, 227,
   291, 302, 357
World War II, 5, 25, 79, 95–6,
   119, 120, 154, 196, 249, 251,
   319, 358, 391, 423
Wyatt, 184

Yeats, W.B., 2, 230–1
youth crime, 312–15
Youthreach, 112